MODERN IRISH

MODERN IRISH

*Grammatical structure
and dialectal variation*

MÍCHEÁL Ó SIADHAIL

CAMBRIDGE UNIVERSITY PRESS
Cambridge
New York   Port Chester
Melbourne   Sydney

Published by the Press Syndicate of the University of Cambridge
The Pitt Building, Trumpington Street, Cambridge CB2 1RP
40 West 20th Street, New York, NY 10011-4211, USA
10 Stamford Road, Oakleigh, Melbourne 3166, Australia

© Cambridge University Press 1989

First published 1989 in Cambridge Studies in Linguistics
First paperback edition 1991

A cataloguing in publication record for this book is available from the British Library

Library of Congress cataloguing in publication data
Ó Siadhail, Mícheál.
Modern Irish: grammatical structure and dialectal variation/Mícheál Ó Siadhail.
    p.   cm.
"Cambridge studies in linguistics. Supplementary volume" – Ser. t.p.
Includes indexes.
ISBN 0 521 37147 3
I. Irish language – Grammar – 1950–   I. Title.
PB1221.016   1989
491.6'25 – dc20   89-7347   CIP

ISBN 0 521 37147 3 hardback
ISBN 0 521 42519 0 paperback

Transferred to digital printing 1999

Contents

	List of tables	page	xiii
	List of figures		xiv
	Preface		xv
	List of abbreviations		xvii

0	**General introduction**	1
0.1	Broad aims	1
0.2	Historical background	1
0.3	Dialects of Irish	2
0.4	Sources	5
0.5	Labelling of examples	7
0.6	The approach	8
0.7	Adaptation of I.P.A. for Irish	8
0.8	Broad and slender consonants and the Irish spelling system	9
0.9	Concluding remarks	11

Part I Phonology

1	**Introduction to Phonology**	15
1.1	The approach	15
1.2	Common underlying forms	17
1.3	Major and minor rules	18

2	**The syllabic system**	19
2.1	Basic form of syllable	19
2.2	Epenthetic vowel	20
2.3	Syllabic adjustment	22
2.4	The secondary epenthetic vowel	22
2.5	Pretonic elision	23
2.6	Vowel coalescence	24
2.7	Lengthening in place of /h/	25
2.8	Stress	26
	2.8.1 Distribution of stress	26
	2.8.2 Stress-shift 1	27
	2.8.3 Stress-shift 2	29

3	**The vowels**	35
3.1	The vocalic system	35

vi *Contents*

3.2	Vowel separation	36
3.3	Raising and lowering of vowels	37
	3.3.1 Raising of low vowels to mid-vowels	37
	3.3.2 Raising of low vowels to high vowels	39
	3.3.3 Raising/lowering between low and mid-vowels	39
	3.3.4 Raising of mid-vowels to high vowels 1	42
	3.3.5 Raising of mid-vowels to high vowels 2	44
	3.3.6 Lowering of high vowels to mid-vowels	46
3.4	Syllable lengthening before tense consonants	48
	3.4.1 Syllable lengthening 1	49
	3.4.2 Syllable lengthening 2	50
	3.4.3 Syllable lengthening 3	53
3.5	Diphthongization	56
	3.5.1 Optional diphthongization before *ch*/*th* /h/	56
	3.5.2 Diphthongization of /iː/ before the stress	56
	3.5.3 Sporadic diphthongization of *é* /eː/	57
3.6	The vowel /ɯː/	57
	3.6.1 The vowel *ao* /ɯː/ changed to /iː/	57
	3.6.2 The vowel *ao* /ɯː/ changed to /eː/	58
	3.6.3 The vowel *ao* /ɯː/ changed to /uː/ or /oː/	58
3.7	Low vowels	59
	3.7.1 Treatment of low vowels in Connemara	59
	3.7.2 Treatment of long *a* /aː/ in Donegal	60
	3.7.3 Shortening of long *a* /aː/ before *mh* /w̃/ in Kerry	60
3.8	Falling diphthongs	61
	3.8.1 Elision of second element before a nasal	61
	3.8.2 Change of diphthong *ia* /iə/ to *é* /eː/	62
	3.8.3 Change of *é* /eː/ to /iːa/	62
	3.8.4 Elision of second element after removal of *dh*/*gh* /ɣ/	62
	3.8.5 Change of *ua* /uːə/ to /ɯːə/ or /iːə/	63
	3.8.6 Insertion of semi-vowel /w/	63
	3.8.7 Variation between *ua* /uːə/ and *ó* /oː/	63
	3.8.8 Variation between *ia* /iːə/ and *ea* /a/	64
3.9	Prevocalic glide	64
4	**The semi-vowel and consonant systems**	67
4.1	Semi-vowels	67
	4.1.1 Slender fricatives	67
	4.1.2 The voiced velar fricative	70
	4.1.3 Merger of semi-vowels with neighbouring vowels	72
	4.1.4 Removal of final semi-vowel	76
	4.1.5 Treatment of semi-vowel broad *mh* /w̃/ as a consonant	77
	4.1.6 Defricatization of the semi-vowels broad *mh*/*bh* /w̃/ and slender *mh*/*bh* /ṽʲ/	78
	4.1.7 Treatment of /h/	79
4.2	Consonants	82
	4.2.1 Overview of system	82

	4.2.2	Slender quality	83
	4.2.3	Devoicing	89
	4.2.4	Voicing	92
	4.2.5	Liquids and nasals	92
	4.2.6	Metathesis	101
	4.2.7	Expressive clusters	104

Part II Morphology

5	**Introduction to morphology**	107
5.1	The approach	107
5.2	The concept of extension	108
5.3	Regularity	109

6		**General morphological rules**	111
6.1		General discussion	111
6.2		Initial mutations	111
	6.2.1	General description	111
	6.2.2	Grammatical functions of lenition	114
	6.2.3	The insertion of *h* and hiatus	122
	6.2.4	Grammatical functions of eclipsis	125
	6.2.5	Non-reversion of initial mutations	131
6.3		Final mutations	134
	6.3.1	Slendering and broadening	135
	6.3.2	Vowel addition	139

7		**The noun**	143
7.1		Gender	143
	7.1.1	Single gender	143
	7.1.2	Double gender	145
	7.1.3	Gender agreement of anaphorical pronouns	147
7.2		Inflection	148
	7.2.1	Inflectional patterns	148
	7.2.2	Variations in inflection	154
7.3		Formation of the plural	159
	7.3.1	Long and short plurals	159
	7.3.2	Vowel addition	160
	7.3.3	Consonant extension and vowel addition combined	160
	7.3.4	Other long plurals	164
	7.3.5	Marked plural forms	165

8		**The verb**	169
8.1		Phonetic shape	169
	8.1.1	General discussion	169
	8.1.2	Verb categorized by the shape of the root	170
	8.1.3	Effect of phonological rules on the inflection	171
	8.1.4	Use of *-óidh*/*eoidh* /oːj/ and *-(a)igh* /əj/ in Category 2 verbs	172

viii Contents

	8.1.5	Variation in the use of -(*a*)*igh* /əj/ and -*óidh*/*eoidh* /oːj/ or /ahəj/ (D)	173
8.2	Grammatical categories		175
	8.2.1	Tense	175
	8.2.2	Combination of tenses and aspect	177
	8.2.3	Mood	178
	8.2.4	Personal/impersonal endings	179
8.3	Root variation and irregular verbs		185
	8.3.1	General discussion	185
	8.3.2	The irregular verbs	185
	8.3.3	Other features of irregular verbs	193
8.4	Nominal and adjectival forms		195
	8.4.1	Introductory remarks	195
	8.4.2	Verbal nouns	195
	8.4.3	The verbal adjective	198

Part III Syntax

9	**Introduction to Syntax**		205
9.1	Basic word order		205
9.2	Major variations in basic order		207
	9.2.1	Movement of pronouns to sentence-final position	207
	9.2.2	Narrative fronting	210
	9.2.3	Deletion following finite verbal forms	211
	9.2.4	Repetition of the topic	212
	9.2.5	Avoidance of finite complementation	213
	9.2.6	Sentence-initial adverbial phrases	214
	9.2.7	Omission of the substantive verb in fronting	215
	9.2.8	Use of *agus*/*is* 'and' or *ná* 'nor' in responsives	216
	9.2.9	Three further dislocations	217

10	**The copula**		219
10.1	Two verbs 'to be'		219
10.2	Forms of the copula		219
	10.2.1	Distinction between present/future and past/conditional blurred	219
	10.2.2	Distinction between preconsonant and prevowel forms blurred	221
	10.2.3	Use of preverbal particles and complementizers with the copula	221
	10.2.4	Prevention of elision of vowel in *ba* 'was'	222
	10.2.5	Use of generalized forms *is é*, *ab é*, *nab é*, *gob é*	223
10.3	Overview of syntax of copula		223
	10.3.1	Linking of nouns and pronouns	224
	10.3.2	Linking of nouns/pronouns and adjectives	229
	10.3.3	Use in prepositional phrases	231

	10.3.4	Use with *seo*, *sin*, *siúd* etc.	234
	10.3.5	Use in fronting	236
10.4	Deletion of copula	244
10.5	Responsive system	245
10.6	General discussion of copula system	249
10.7	Summary of dialectal differences	251
11	**Complementation and modal and auxiliary verbs**	**253**
11.1	Complementation	253
	11.1.1	Types of complementation	253
	11.1.2	Syntactic functions of the complement	260
	11.1.3	Extraposition	270
	11.1.4	Verbal noun complement as a unit	275
	11.1.5	Avoidance of possessive adjective in verbal noun complement	277
	11.1.6	Other types of verbal noun complement	278
	11.1.7	Verbal noun complements identified by *do* 'to'	281
	11.1.8	Complements subordinated by *agus* 'and'	284
	11.1.9	Attributive use of verbal noun complements	286
11.2	Modal verbs	287
	11.2.1	Construction of modal verbs	287
	11.2.2	Distinctive features of modal verbs	288
	11.2.3	Dialectal variation	291
11.3	Auxiliary verbs	293
	11.3.1	The substantive verb in periphrastic aspectual phrases	294
	11.3.2	The auxiliary verb *déan* 'make, do'	302
	11.3.3	Other auxiliaries	306
11.4	Summary of dialectal differences	308
12	**Non-complemental subordination and marginal syntactic features**	**311**
12.1	Non-complemental subordination	311
	12.1.1	Relatives	311
	12.1.2	Conditionals	319
	12.1.3	Questions	321
	12.1.4	Adverbial subordination	322
12.2	*Diabhal* 'Devil' etc. as a syntactic device	326
	12.2.1	The assertive usage	326
	12.2.2	The conditional usage	326
	12.2.3	The negative usage	326
	12.2.4	Conclusion	311
12.3	Questions expecting negative answers	311
12.4	Compounding of neutral coordinators with subordinators	332
	12.4.1	*Agus/is* 'and'	332
	12.4.2	*Nó* 'or'	334
12.5	Proportional correlations	335
12.6	Suspensive *ná*	336

12.7 Variant order in perfectives with *chomh* 'so' 337

Glossary 339
References 341
Index of Irish words 347

I dedicate this book to the memory of three teachers, friends and colleagues: David Greene (1915-81), Máirtín Ó Cadhain (1906-70) and E. Gordon Quin (1910-86).

Tables

0.1	Spelling of long vowels and short *a*	*page*	10
1.1	Derivations of *páighe* 'pay'		16
2.1	The epenthetic vowel		21
2.2	Development of short vowel before /h/		25
2.3	Stress-shift 1 and pretonic elision		28
2.4	Stress-shift 2: attraction of stress to a long vowel		29
2.5	Stress-shift 2 in compounds		30
3.1	The underlying vocalic system		35
3.2	Two stages of raising of low vowels		38
3.3	Examples of mid-vowel/low vowel variation		40
3.4	Variation between /e/ and /i/ in Connacht		45
4.1	Treatment of slender *ch* /xʹ/ and slender *dh*/*gh* /j/ in major dialects		68
4.2	Treatment of slender *bh*/*mh* /ṽʹ/ in major dialects		69
4.3	Outline of consonantal system		82
4.4	Munster and Connemara derivations of *boird* 'tables'		86
4.5	Derivations of *oirde*, comparative of *ard* 'high'		86
4.6	Realization of adjacent vibrant and sibilant in major dialects		100
5.1	Inflectional patterns of *margadh* 'market'		107
5.2	Examples of syllabic adjustment		109
6.1	Initial mutations		112
6.2	Initial changes due to reinterpretation of mutation 1		131
6.3	Initial changes due to reinterpretation of mutation 2		132
6.4	Initial changes due to reinterpretation of mutation 3		132
6.5	Initial changes due to reinterpretation of mutation 4		133
6.6	Development of *oscl-*, *labhr-*, *féach*		137
6.7	Slendering in third person of Connemara prepositional pronouns		139
6.8	Addition of slender ending to third singular of Connemara personal pronouns		139
7.1	Examples of double gender 1		145
7.2	Examples of double gender 2		146
8.1	Category 1 verbs		170
8.2	Category 2 verbs		170
8.3	Impersonal form endings		180
8.4	Personal endings in habitual combined with past		180
8.5	Personal endings in past		181
8.6	Personal endings in future		181
8.7	Personal endings in unmarked tense		182

10.1	Forms of copula	220
10.2	Preverbal particles with *ba*	221
10.3	Generalized forms of copula	222
10.4	Verb focusing in major dialects	240
11.1	Some idioms involving substantive verb with preposition *ar* 'on'	264
11.2	Donegal verbs of motion in aspectual function	280
11.3	Types of modal verbs	287
11.4	Verbs and verbal phrases with verbal noun and preceding object	288
11.5	The active progressive aspect	294
11.6	Stative verbs requiring preposition *i* 'in'	295
12.1	Fronted questions with direct relative	318
12.2	Fronted questions with indirect relative	318

Figures

0.1	Relationship between Celtic languages	*page*	2
0.2	Geographic location of dialects		3
0.3	Relationship between northern dialects		4
0.4	Relationship between western dialects		5
0.5	Relationship between southern dialects		5
2.1	Voice obstruction		20
4.1	Changes required for broad *dh/gh* /ɣ/		71
9.1	Sentence order in Irish		205
9.2	Possible positionings of normal grade pronouns		207
11.1	Finite and verbal noun complementation		253
11.2	Two types of subject complements		260
11.3	Extraposition of complement object		270
11.4	Possessive adjectives/pronouns in verbal noun complement		277

Preface

My thanks are due first and foremost to my wife Bríd, whose help and support was, as always, immeasurable. I owe a debt of gratitude to three friends and colleagues, Dr. Pádraig de Brún, on whose advice and assistance I so often relied, to Dr. James McCloskey for his detailed comments on the text and his unstinting support and to Dr. Arndt Wigger with whom I co-authored *Córas Fuaimeanna na Gaeilge*, which underpins Parts I and II of the present work which he also kindly read and commented on.

My gratitude is also due to the readers for the Cambridge University Press for their many useful comments and recommendations, to Penny Carter for her editorial assistance and help, to her successors Marion Smith and then Judith Ayling, and to Catherine Max.

I should also like to thank Paul O'Loughlin Kennedy and Sharon Slowey of Dublin Online Typographic Services Ltd. for their skill and efficiency in typesetting.

Abbreviations

Ar	Aran	Ih	Inisheer
		Im	Inishmaan
Bk	Blasket Island	ind.	independent
Bm	Ballymacoda		
		Ky	Kerry
C	Connacht		
Ca	Carna	lit.	literally
Cf	Cois Fhairrge	Lm	Lettermore
		Ln	Leenane
Ci	Clear Island		
Cl	Clare	M	Munster
Cn	Connacht	masc.	masculine
comp.	comparative	Mk	West Muskerry
cond.	conditional		
		Ml	Menlough
D	Donegal		
dat.	dative	Mn	Meenawania
dep.	dependent	Mo	Mayo
Dn	Dunquin		
		pl.	plural
Er	Erris	pres.	present
fem.	feminine	Rf	Rannafast
fut.	future	Rg	Ring
		Rl	Rosguill
gen.	genitive	Rm	Rosmuck
Gd	Gweedore		
		sing.	singular
Gk	Glencolumbkille		
		Tm	Tourmakeady
hab.	habitual	Tn	Teelin
		Tr	Torr
imper.	imperative		
impers.	impersonal	voc.	vocative

xvii

General introduction

0.1 Broad aims

This book is an attempt to provide a reasonably comprehensive overview of modern Irish dialects outlining both their shared linguistic structure and their diversity. It is hoped that it may prove useful both to those whose main field of concern is the study of the Irish language and to those whose primary interest is linguistic. In order to ensure a balance between the interests of both students of Irish and those of general linguistics an excess of terminology has been avoided, a number of basic concepts are explained and some background information on the Irish language is provided.

0.2 Historical background

Irish, which belongs to the Celtic branch of the Indo-European family, is thought to have been introduced to Ireland by the invading Gaels – about 300 B.C. according to some scholars. Subsequently this Gaelic language extended to Scotland and the Isle of Man. Scottish Gaelic and Manx became distinct from Irish in the seventeenth century and more gradually from each other. Gaelic may be used as a cover-term for all three languages.

The continuum of the written development of Irish is generally divided by scholars into four periods: Old Irish (*c.* A.D.600-900); Middle Irish (*c.* 900-1200), Early Modern Irish (*c.* 1200-1600) and Modern Irish. During the development Irish borrowed vocabulary from languages which impinged on it, including Latin, Norse, Spanish, Anglo-Norman (a dialect of French) and English.

In the sixteenth century Irish was the language of the vast majority of people living in Ireland. However, in the seventeenth century the Gaelic aristocracy, together with their social and literary world, were suppressed or dispersed and English, the language of the new colonists, began to dominate. The Great Famine (1846-48), which decimated the poorer rural classes, dealt a fatal blow to Irish, which now survives as a community

2 Modern Irish: grammatical structure and dialectal variation

language only in outlying and diminishing rural districts generally referred to as the Gaeltacht. The population of the Gaeltacht may now be considerably less than 25,000 with hardly any monoglots remaining.

Figure 0.1 Relationship between Celtic languages

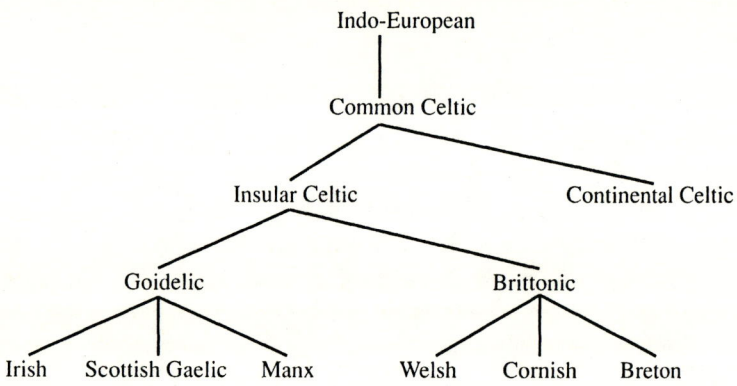

0.3 Dialects of Irish

The Modern Irish of the title refers to those dialects which have had a considerable body of native speakers during the first seventy years or so of this century. The work primarily concerns itself with what have been intuitively and traditionally regarded as the major dialects of modern Irish: Donegal, Connacht and Munster. Naturally, the dialects cannot remain in watertight categories but rather merge imperceptibly, isogloss by isogloss, into each other. A few centuries ago the Irish speaker might have travelled from Kerry to Antrim (and on to Scotland) and only noticed dialectal changes gradually shading into each other. A glance at linguistic maps of Irish (see Wagner 1958) with examples gleaned from eighty-six points in sixteen of thirty-two counties reflects, albeit palely, the historical situation. However, given the focus of this book on the communities with a reasonable number of speakers in contemporary times, the traditional division into Donegal, Connacht and Munster makes intuitive sense.

Clearly one can for convenience divide up a spectrum in different ways. It is possible, for instance, to think of a split between Northern and Southern dialects (see O'Rahilly 1932:17). For the purpose of this study it may be useful to think of Donegal and Munster as two ends of a spectrum with Galway

Figure 0.2 Geographic location of dialects

4   *Modern Irish: grammatical structure and dialectal variation*

and South Connacht as a central point. Then in very broad terms, the northern Connacht dialects of Mayo, while obviously having their own characteristics, are a halfway house between Donegal and Galway. On the other hand, Clare, which is northern Munster, is in many ways a patchwork of isoglosses with, as one might geographically expect, South Clare showing a bias towards Munster features and North Clare towards Galway. Once again clearly Clare has its own characteristics (one important one which it shares with Ring). However, in this book Clare, which does not have a sizable community of speakers, is not treated in detail and for the purposes of this account is excluded from the cover-terms Connacht and Munster.

The division of the spectrum can be further refined. Donegal can be thought of in terms of North Donegal, e.g. Gweedore, Mid-Donegal, e.g. Glenfin and South Donegal dialects, e.g. Teelin, Meenawania. Mayo can be roughly divided into North Mayo, e.g. Erris, and South Mayo, e.g. Tourmakeady. Galway can be roughly divided into East Galway, which is marginal to this account, and West Galway or Connemara, which can be further subdivided into Cois Fhairrge and West Connemara. In very broad terms it can be said of the Aran Islands that Inishmore and Inishmaan are very similar to Cois Fhairrge while Inisheer shares some features with Clare. Munster can be subdivided very roughly into Kerry, e.g. Dunquin, West Cork, e.g. Muskerry, and Ring, County Waterford.

Figure 0.3 Relationship between northern dialects

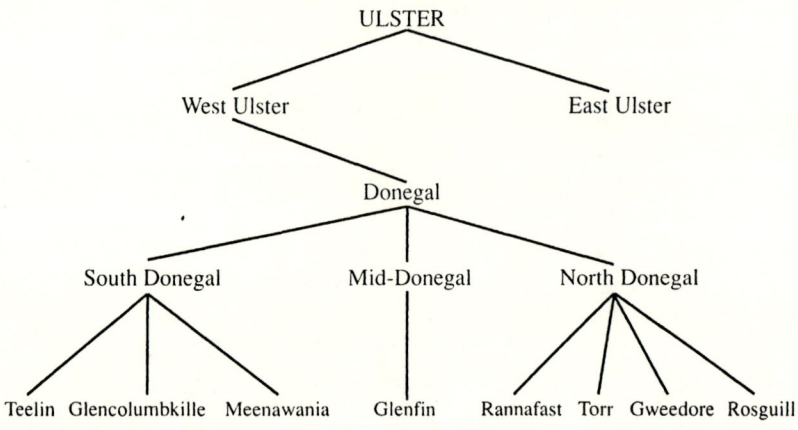

Figure 0.4 Relationship between western dialects

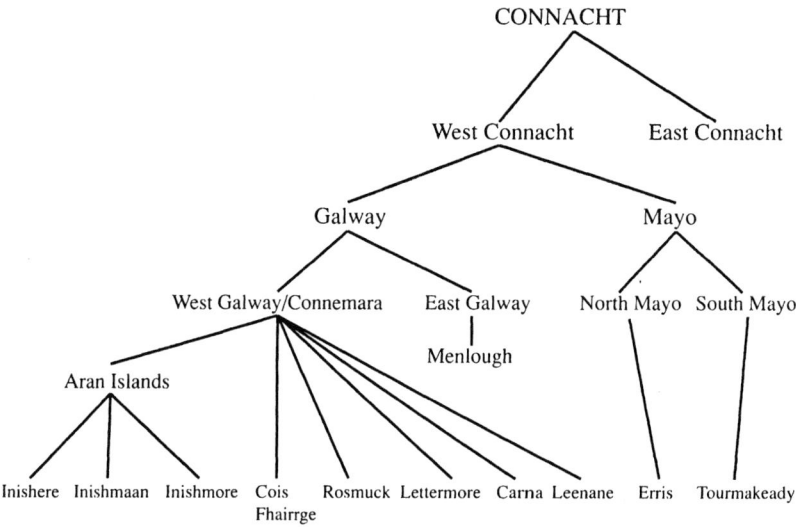

Figure 0.5 Relationship between southern dialects

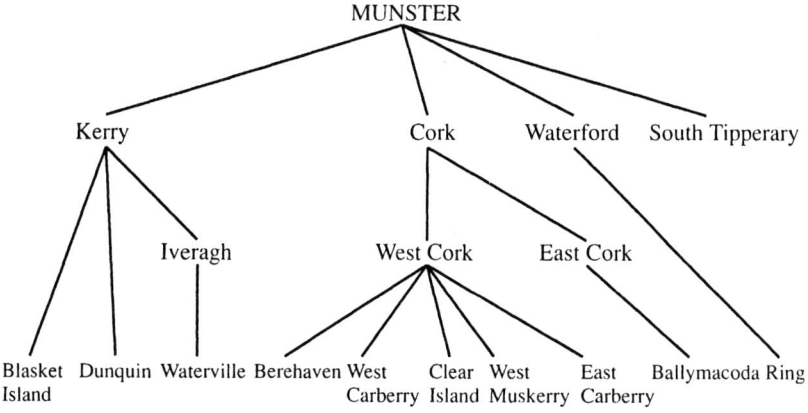

0.4 Sources

Within the major dialects of Donegal, Connacht and Munster certain areas are focussed on: Gweedore in the case of Donegal, Cois Fhairrge and Erris in the case of Connacht and Dunquin in the case of Munster. The availability of information both from native speakers of these dialects and from the literature dictated this choice. As regards Gweedore, my wife Bríd is a native speaker from the district and she and her family have provided a constant source of information on that dialect. The phonology and morphology of Erris is well served by Mhac an Fhailligh (1968), that of Cois Fhairrge by the works of de Bhaldraithe (1945 and 1953) and that of the Dunquin area by Ó Sé (1983) and earlier by Sjoestedt-Jonval (1931 and 1938). Beside the concentration on those points, the focus is often widened in Donegal to include information from Teelin, in Connacht from Tourmakeady, and in Munster from Muskerry and occasionally Ring. There are excellent sources for these secondary points in monographs by Wagner (1959), de Búrca (1958), Ó Cuív (1951), Ó Briain (1947) and Breatnach (1947) respectively. Occasionally, especially in the account of the phonology (Part I), where matters of particular interest arose, other points are mentioned in passing; the Aran Islands, Co. Galway, based on Finck (1899) and in particular Inishmaan, where I made a personal collection of examples, some of which have been published (Ó Siadhail 1978); Rosmuck, Co. Galway, based on the work of Ó Máille (1973); Torr and Meenawania in Donegal, based on the work of Sommerfelt (1922) and Quiggin (1906), Clare on that of Holmer (1962 and 1965) and Berehaven, East and West Carbery and Ballymacoda on that of Ó Cuív (1951).

Furthermore, much supplementary and valuable information regarding the primary points of focus and concerning the general range and distribution of dialectal features was obtained from Wagner's *Linguistic Atlas and Survey of Irish Dialects* (1958-69). Finally, I must make mention of *Córas Fuaimeanna na Gaeilge* (Ó Siadhail and Wigger 1975) which underpins Parts I and II of this book.

Undoubtedly, the field of syntax is not as well reported as that of morphology and phonology. Extensive use was made of the outstanding and pioneering work of Wigger (1970 and 1972a) and McCloskey (1979 and 1985) and Stenson (1981). Occasional use was also made of Ó Searcaigh (1939) and Ó Muirí (1982). Some of the material covered in the section on syntax was drawn from articles previously published and these are acknowledged in the references. The more extensive morphological studies, such as those of de Bhaldraithe and Ó Sé, were an invaluable source of examples. Several further Munster examples are drawn from literary or folkloristic works: in the case of Kerry mainly from Ó Criomhthain (1928 and 1929) and Jackson (1968), in the case of Muskerry mainly from Ó Cróinín (1980) and the occasional remarks on South Tipperary are based on Ó Maolchathaigh (1963). Further Connacht examples are taken mainly from Mac Giollarnáth (1939), Breathnach (1906, 1910, 1924), Ó Neachtain (1936), Ó Cadhain (1948), de Bhaldraithe (1977). In the case of Donegal Ó Domhnaill (1940) and Máire (1961, 1962) were useful sources. All the sentences quoted are authentic examples, the only exceptions being where examples are tabularized, and even there they are modelled on genuine examples.

0.5 Labelling of examples

If an example is specific to a dialect then the appropriate abbreviation for that dialect is given in brackets, e.g. (D) for Donegal, (Gd) for Gweedore. For an alphabetical list of abbreviations see page (xvii). On the other hand, where the example is not dialectally specific, it is left unmarked.

It should however be noted that even in the account of the syntax (Part III) there are few examples available which do not exhibit some, however minor, dialectally specific features. To illustrate the point we may take two Irish sentences meaning 'This chair is red' and 'This book is nice'. The first can be left unmarked but the second would require marking for Donegal, Connacht and Munster:

Tá an chathaoir seo dearg
'This chair is red'
Tá an leabhar seo deas (D)
'This book is nice'
Tá an leabhar seo go deas (C)
'This book is nice'
Tá an leabhar so go deas (M)
'This book is nice'

Therefore even though most of the examples in the book are taken from specific dialects and are cited as excerpted, this is not to say that they are presented to demonstrate dialectal particularities unless this is specifically stated.

In the case of the phonology (Part I) and to a somewhat lesser extent in the morphology (Part II) the examples are, of their nature, more dialectally specific. Where examples are marked broadly as Donegal, Connacht or Munster, every effort has been made to ensure that, excluding Clare, no outlying or linguistically marginal dialect contradicts the wide geographic

8   *Modern Irish: grammatical structure and dialectal variation*

labelling. However, it must be borne in mind that the aim of the work is not to delimit meticulously from all available evidence the precise range of a given rule, a task better suited to feature-by-feature maps, but rather to provide a general interpretive framework.

0.6 The approach

In Parts I and II the methodological approach is, broadly speaking, based on the model of generative phonology described by Chomsky and Halle (1968). The viewpoint is basically synchronic, but it is one which lets the grammar operate on several levels and thereby provides deeper insights into the system and, in particular, facilitates a unified comparison of the major dialects. This method is further explained in Chapters 1 and 5. The discussion has been kept relatively informal in order to avoid both the potential rigidity of an over-analytical approach and the temptation to stray into excessive theoretical debate. It is hoped that this multi-level synchronic view both describes the present and allows for the possible reflection of history in the phonology and morphology. In Part III the approach to the syntax, while it is both synchronic and dynamic in perspective, is of a more traditional nature.

It is also important to note that the objective in this book is to study the speech of speakers of Irish whose language is largely unaffected by literary influences. As the social network in the remaining Irish-speaking areas grows more complex, without a doubt different social registers evolve and include such features as literary pronunciations, neologisms, dialect mixing, use of English vocabulary, etc. Furthermore, where there are still younger speakers, there is often an accelerated pace of change, particularly in syntax and morphology. While such social features and the rate of change are worthy objects of study, they are not, with the exception of a few passing remarks in Part III, within the compass of this work.

0.7 Adaptation of I.P.A. for Irish

There are some conventional adaptations of I.P.A. for Irish which must be noted here.

Firstly, the established convention is to use /ʹ/ following a consonant to mark it as 'slender' (palatalized) as opposed to 'broad' (non-palatalized), e.g. slender *p* /pʹ/, slender *m* /mʹ/ as opposed to broad *p* /p/, broad *m* /m/. There are also some variations within the established form of I.P.A. which are generally employed to transcribe Irish. The signs for broad *ch* /χ/ and slender *ch* /ç/ are often replaced by /x/ and /x′/ respectively and this convention is followed. Rather than the international sign /ʃ/ for slender (palatalized) *s*, the sign /s′/ is sometimes preferred and the usage has also been adopted here. Furthermore, in the case of *bh/mh* the convention among Irish scholars has been, particularly in the case of Munster dialects, to transcribe the broad *bh/mh* as /v/ and the slender *bh/mh* as /v′/, while for other dialects the opposition is often transcribed as broad *bh/mh* /w/ and slender *bh/mh* /v′/. The latter procedure has been adopted in this description. It may be mentioned that the custom of transcribing broad *dh/gh* as /ɣ/ and slender *dh/gh* as /j/ (which reflects the actual realization better than /ɣ/ and /ɣ′/) has been adhered to.

The established practice among Irish scholars of transcribing a tense *l*, *n* and *r* (often written medially and finally as *ll*, *nn* and *rr*) is to use /L/, /N/ and /R/. A slender (palatalized) tense *l*, *n* or *r* is represented by /L′/, /N′/, /R′/.

Finally the customary way of transcribing a broad (non-palatalized) dental *d* and *t* is to use /d/ and /t/. Correspondingly, the slender (palatalized) *d* and *t* are transcribed as /d′/ and /t′/. Post-alveolar *d* and *t*, which are needed mainly in sandhi or for loan-words, are represented by /ḍ/ and /ṭ/ respectively.

0.8 Broad and slender consonants and the Irish spelling system

Some general remarks on the relationship between spelling and pronunciation may be useful for those with no background in Irish. (For an introductory course in Irish see Ó Siadhail 1988.)

A feature of Irish (and Scottish Gaelic and Manx) is the existence of two sets of consonants traditionally called 'broad' and 'slender' consonants. This distinction very roughly corresponds to the 'hard' and 'soft' of Russian consonants. Many linguists prefer to use the terms 'non-palatalized' and 'palatalized'. However, the actual realization in Irish of 'broad' and 'slender' is intricately linked with the phonetic context, e.g. the heavy velarization or labialization found on broad consonants before front vowels. On these grounds the traditional terms are adhered to in this book.

Basically it can be said that slender quality in a consonant is expressed in spelling by accompanying it with either *i* or *e*. Conversely, broad quality is shown by accompanying the consonant with either *a*, *o* or *u*. The choice of vowels is determined by orthographical convention. If we take a word such as *baistim* 'I baptize' the *b* before the *a* is broad, the *st* is flanked by *i* and *i* and is slender and the *m* which is after *í* is slender. A medial consonant or cluster must normally be flanked by vowels appropriate to its quality. As will emerge in Part I, the relationship between the pronunciation and the spelling of short vowels is complex, particularly the mid-vowels and high vowels. The situation with long vowels (marked with an acute accent as in, e.g., *á*) and the short low vowel is somewhat less intricate and these are exemplified in Table 0.1. The symbol V stands for a vowel, C for a broad consonant and C´ for a slender consonant. Although English glosses are provided throughout the rest of the book, they are avoided in the remainder of this section.

It may be observed that, where a consonant is in word final position slender quality is always shown by a preceding *i*, e.g. *áil* /aːlʹ/, *óil* /oːlʹ/, *úil* /uːlʹ/. When a consonant is in initial position in the case of (the high vowel) *u*, slender quality is also shown by means of *i*, e.g. *siúl* /sʹuːl/, *siúil* /sʹuːlʹ/. On the other hand before (the mid-vowel) *o* and (the low vowel) *a* slender quality is shown for an initial consonant by means of *e*, e.g. *méad* /mʹeːd/, *seol* /sʹoːl/, *Seán* /sʹaːn/, *deas* /dʹas/. (Also by convention *eo* is written without length mark, i.e. not *eó*.) Lastly, in the case of a final consonant broad quality is shown by *o* after an *i*, e.g. *síol* /sʹiːl/ and by *a* after *é*, e.g. *éad* /eːd/, *méad* /mʹeːd/, *deas* /dʹas/.

Table 0.1 *Spelling of long vowels and short* a

V	*í* /iː/	*ú* /uː/	*é* /eː/
VC	*íoc* /iːk/	*úr* /uːr/	*éad* /eːd/
CV	------	*tú* /tuː/	*lae* /Leː/
CVC	------	*súl* /suːl/	*pael* /peːl/
VC´	*íd-* /iːdʹ/	*úir* /uːrʹ/	*éid* /eːdʹ/
CVC´	------	*súil* /suːlʹ/	-----
C´VC	*síol* /sʹiːl/	*siúl* /sʹuːl/	*méad* /mʹeːd/
C´VC´	*síl* /sʹiːlʹ/	*siúil* /sʹuːlʹ/	*méid* /mʹeːdʹ/

V	*ó* /oː/	*á* /aː/	*a* /a/
VC	*ól* /oːl/	*ál* /aːl/	*as* /as/
CV	*ló* /Loː/	*lá* /Laː/	*ba* /ba/
CVC	*Pól* /poːl/	*fál* /faːl/	*bas* /bas/
VC´	*óil* /oːlʹ/	*áil* /aːlʹ/	*ais* /asʹ/
CVC´	*Póil* /poːlʹ/	*fáil* /faːlʹ/	*tais* /tasʹ/
C´VC	*seol* /sʹoːl/	*Seán* /sʹaːn/	*deas* /dʹas/
C´VC´	*seoil* /sʹoːlʹ/	*Seáin* /sʹaːnʹ/	*peain* /pʹanʹ/

0.9 Concluding remarks

The most striking result of a study of the dialects is the nuances and the subtle complexity of the relationship between the dialects. No simple statement that one dialect is more conservative than another can reflect this relationship; each feature must be considered separately. To take just one example: in some respects the copular system in Gweedore is extremely conservative, e.g. the non-use of the *é, í, iad-* insertion rule [see 10.3.1(i)]; on the other hand it is uniquely innovative in the generalization of *is é, ní hé, ab é, nab é* for both genders and numbers (see 10.2.5). It is hoped that by giving an overall picture of the system, this wide description will illustrate the variation between the dialects against the unified background of the language. In the end, despite all the variation, and given the fact that Scottish Gaelic must be regarded on sociological grounds as a separate language, one is inevitably left with the sense that Irish is a single language.

PART 1

PHONOLOGY

1 *Introduction to phonology*

There are four chapters in Part I. This chapter sketches the approach to the phonology and explains some terms such as 'underlying form', 'derivation', 'surface form' and the distinction between 'major' and 'minor' rules. In Chapter 2 there is a brief general account of the syllable, how it may be arranged and how the accent is distributed. Chapter 3 deals with vowels and their development in certain circumstances and Chapter 4 discusses the treatment of semi-vowels and consonants.

1.1 The approach

While Part I deals with the sounds of Irish and how they change and are affected by their environment, there are inevitably innumerable minor differences from locality to locality in the actual phonetic realization of particular sounds. The account, however, is concerned with a more abstract level in order to attempt to describe the relationship within the underlying sound system and in doing so to specify the outstanding differences between the major dialects. (For a distinctive feature analysis of the Irish sound system see Ó Siadhail and Wigger 1975:14.)

The approach to the various phonological rules is a dynamic one and hence naturally the order in which they apply can be of importance. This means that the ordering of these rules is often adverted to in the course of the discussion. The distribution or the order in which a particular rule applies is often what constitutes a difference between the major dialects.

The best way to illustrate this approach is with an example. If we take the noun *páighe* 'pay', we can see how it is possible to derive by ordered rules the forms that actually appear in the major dialects.

In Donegal and Mayo no rules are required: the actual realization is in fact *páighe* /**paːjə**/. A slender *gh* (or *dh*) /j/ is retained following a long stressed vowel in these dialects; another example is *léigheann* /**LˊeːjəN**/ 'reads'.

16 *Modern Irish: grammatical structure and dialectal variation*

In Connemara, the actual pronunciation is *páí* so we need a rule converting *-ighe* /əjə/ into *í* /iː/. This, in fact, is the regular development of *-ighe* /əjə/ in this situation; other examples are *truaighe* → *truaí* 'pity', *nuaidheacht* → *nuaíocht* 'news' (see 4.1). In Munster the actual pronunciation is *pá* so we need to be rid of *-ighe* /əjə/. As the rule described for Connemara is also allowed to apply in Munster, the first stage of the removal of *-ighe* is the conversion of *-ighe* /əjə/ into *í* /iː/. At this stage, we have *páí*. Then a further rule is required which deletes *í* /iː/ following a long vowel, so that *páí* becomes *pá*. There is, in fact, such a rule in Munster [see 4.1.4(ii)] and this gives the pronunciation of *truaighe* as *trua* 'pity'; *nuaidheacht* as *nuacht* 'news'. These rules are illustrated in Table 1.1.

Table 1.1 *Derivations of* páighe *'pay'*

	Donegal/Mayo	Connemara	Munster
underlying form	*páighe* /paːjə/	*páighe* /paːjə/	*paighe* /paːjə/
ighe /əjə/ → *í* /iː/		*páí* /paːiː/	*páí* /paːiː/
following long vowel *í* is deleted			*pá* /paː/
result	*páighe* /paːjə/	*páí* /paːiː/	*pá* /paː/

It should be clear from Table 1.1 that the distribution of the two rules (*-ighe* → *í* and the deletion of *í* following a long vowel) produces the differences between the dialects. It should also be evident that in order to derive the Munster form *pá* 'pay' the two rules must apply in the order (1) *-aighe* → *í*, (2) following a long vowel *í* is deleted. The rules could not be applied in the reverse order.

The form which is chosen to start out from, in this case *páighe*, is the form which most economically, that is with a minimum of generally applicable rules, allows us to derive the required forms for the various dialects. That initiating form is called the 'underlying form' as it underlies the actual pronunciation in the dialects. (The process of the application of the rules is called the 'derivation' and the actual pronunciation in the dialects may be referred to as the 'surface form'.)

It is important to point out that, while the underlying form and the historical form, as in the case of *páighe*, a borrowing from Middle English *paye*, may sometimes coincide with historical development, and indeed while the rules applied to derive the various forms may sometimes do so, this is not necessarily so. The criterion for choosing the underlying form and the derivation is one of rule economy and not a matter of historical consideration. It must be stressed that there is no implication in this account that the processes described are in any way intended to be historical. Nevertheless, it is not surprising that history is sometimes still reflected in and coincides with the present.

The notation in this book of the rules for Munster *pá* would be /paːjə/ → /paːiː/ → /paː/. It must be observed that the final form at this stage may not be the actual ('surface') pronunciation. If the Connemara *páighe* 'pay' were under discussion, the rule would be notated /paːjə/ → /paːiː/. Ultimately, in a later and more local development /aː/ appears as /ɑː/ in Connemara (see 3.7.1). Often this later rule is bracketed so that the Connemara rule can be given as /paːjə/ → /paːiː/ (→ /pɑːiː/). Similarly, if only the second stage of the Munster development is being discussed, the earlier stage may be bracketed: (/paːjə/ →) /paːiː/ → /paː/.

1.2 Common underlying forms

The phonological description aims at a level of abstraction which allows differences between the dialects to be set aside by providing shared underlying forms from which, by a set of ordered rules, the dialect variants can be derived. In general, this account of the phonology presumes that it is possible in the majority of cases to provide an underlying form from which the variants will be derived.

Naturally, there is a degree of divergence which cannot be handled by such a framework. An extreme example is where there are basic dissimilarities in the vocabulary, e.g. *srón* 'nose' beside *gaothsán* (Gd) 'nose'. There are also instances where, although the pattern of a sporadic divergence can be observed, the geographic distribution is so random that there does not seem to be much purpose in positing a common underlying form. A case in point is the variation *o/e* and *a* (see 3.3.3) in, for instance, *call* (D) beside *coll* 'hazel' or *tathant* (M) beside *tothaint* (→ *túint*) (Cf) 'exhorting'. The choice of *o/e* or *a* in such examples seems best left to the lexicon. While no common underlying form is proposed, nevertheless the discussion of the phenomenon should help to make the relationship between, for example, *tathant* and what is normally written *túint* less opaque. Furthermore, there are some cases where the underlying forms for the major dialects are too much at variance; for example *deamhan* 'demon' where *mh* is required in the underlying form, except in Donegal where *deabhan* with *bh* is needed [see 4.1.3(iii)] or *sneachta* 'snow' where an underlying *sneachtadh* is required to give a genitive *sneachtaidh* in Dunquin but not in the other major

18 *Modern Irish: grammatical structure and dialectal variation*

dialects (see 5.1). Again it was felt that little purpose was served in reconciling these variant underlying forms and it was considered better in such cases to relegate the differences to the lexicon.

1.3 Major and minor rules

An important concept is the distinction between major and minor rules (see Lakoff 1970). In describing the development of *páighe* 'pay' above, mention was made of rules being 'generally applicable'. Major rules are those applied generally to all words of a particular phonetic shape in a given context (i.e. *-ighe* /əjə/ → *í* /iː/ in Munster or Connemara in all such words). There may, of course, be a very few marked exceptions, but the vast majority of examples behave according to the rule. A minor rule is where a minority of examples behave similarly, e.g. the *é* in *féire/péire* 'pair', *féileacán/peileacán* 'butterfly', *déileáil* 'dealing' is pronounced as a diphthong /ai/ in Munster (see 3.5.3) although, in the vast majority of cases, *é* is pronounced as /eː/. The fact that there is, so to speak, a group of exceptions confers on them the status of a minor rule. Nevertheless, as a minor rule does not apply to all words of a particular shape, the cases where it is applicable must be marked in the lexicon.

2 *The syllabic system*

Many phonological rules discussed in Part I in effect alter the form of a syllable by increasing or decreasing it or by altering it in other ways, e.g.

(1)   *gorm* 'blue' /gorm/ → /gorəm/
        bóthar 'road' /boːhər/ → /boːr/ (Cf)
        am 'time' /am/ → /aːm/ (→ /ɑːm/) (Cn)

It will be necessary to distinguish here between those phonological rules which are relatively superficial, applying often only in particular dialects, and those which are more fundamental and which affect the basic system.

2.1 Basic form of syllable

It is possible to predict certain relationships between particular vowels and their surrounding consonants and to note their distribution in disyllabic words (see Ó Siadhail and Wigger 1975:68-71); some such information will emerge in the discussion of the phonological rules concerning vowels.

A further contribution to the so-called 'canonical form' of the syllable is made by describing the permitted initial and final consonant clusters. The first consonant cluster in a word such as *spleách* 'dependent' gives us an example of the longest possible cluster in Irish. There is a maximum of three consonants in initial position (i.e. /s(ʹ)/, /p(ʹ)/, /l(ʹ)/). The group at the end of a word such as *bocht* 'poor', which contains two consonants /x/ and /t/, illustrates the maximal cluster permitted in final positions. In essence, it can be said that the vowel is the lowest point of voice obstruction and that the consonants on either side (excepting initial /s/) show in mirror image a step-like progression as illustrated in Figure 2.1.

Interestingly there is, in fact, a tendency for /s/ to be used as a sort of reinforcement in word-initial position [see 4.2.7(i)].

20 *Modern Irish: grammatical structure and dialectal variation*

Figure 2.1 Voice obstruction

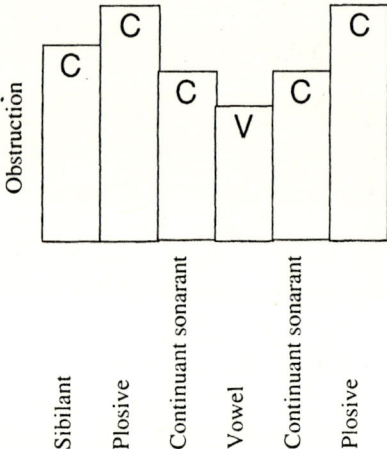

It is also possible to go further and to list the permitted combinations for an initial or final consonant cluster as a series of ordered rules (see Ó Siadhail and Wigger 1975:69).

So far, we have only mentioned initial and final clusters. There is, however, little difficulty in dealing with medial clusters, particularly as the division of such clusters is largely arbitrary. The medial consonants /l/ + /t/ in a word such as *Gaeltacht* 'Irish-speaking area' can either be divided (i.e. *Gael + tacht*) or taken as a cluster (i.e. *Gaelt + acht*). Neither division contravenes the permitted form. On the other hand, the group *mb*, which does not occur in an initial or final cluster, is found medially in a word such as *bambairneach* 'bothersome'. One way of handling this case is to place the syllabic boundary between *m* and *b* (i.e. *bam + bairneach*). Such an interpretation might lead one to expect a high frequency of complex intersyllabic clusters. In actual fact the number of kinds of consonant clusters which arise in compounding is relatively limited throughout the dialects (see Ó Siadhail and Wigger 1975:69).

There is one type of consonant cluster which demands special consideration and involves the phenomenon known as an epenthetic vowel.

2.2 Epenthetic vowel

Certain consonant clusters are broken up by the introduction of the neutral vowel /ə/. After a stressed short vowel, any voiced dental (*l*, *n*, *r*) is separated from any following non-dental (except *p* and *c*) by a neutral vowel known as the epenthetic vowel.

The rule is given here in its broadest form; although *d* is theoretically included as a voiced dental, the clusters *db, *dbh, *df, *dm, *dch and *dg are excluded by the rules governing the canonical form. This general rule is best illustrated by the following table:

Table 2.1 *The epenthetic vowel*

	b	*bh*	*f*
l	*Albain* /alǝbǝn´/ 'Scotland'	*seilbh* /s´el´ǝv´/ 'possession'	
n	*Banba* /banǝbǝ/ (name for Ireland)	*bainbh* /ban´ǝv´/ 'piglets'	*confadh* /konǝfǝ/ (D) 'anger'
r	*Bairbre* /bar´ǝb´r´ǝ/ (woman's name)	*seirbhís* /s´er´ǝv´i:s´/ 'service'	

	m	*ch*	*g*
l	*gairm* /ger´ǝm´/ 'call'		*bolg* /bolǝg/ 'belly'
n	*ainm* /an´ǝm´/ 'name'	*seanchaí* /s´anǝxi:/ 'storyteller'	
r	*gorm* /gorǝm/ 'blue'	*dorcha* /dorǝxǝ/ 'dark'	*dearg* /d´arǝg/ 'red'

Table 2.1 displays the broad general nature of this rule, which is found in all dialects. There is no example for *lch*. The lack of any example for *ng* is due to the fact that /ng/ becomes /ŋg/ at an earlier stage and is therefore not available for the application of the rule governing epenthesis. It must also be pointed out that there are no examples in the *lf* and *rf* slots. There are examples such as *deilbhfidh* /d´el´ǝf´ǝ/ 'will warp' or *dearbhtha* (→ *dearfa*) /d´arǝfǝ/ 'certain' which might be included but the devoicing of *bh* /w(´)/ to *f* /f(´)/ is undoubtedly a late and more surface change.

The following are counterexamples which validate the general rule and illustrate that no epenthetic vowel occurs either after a long stressed vowel or preceding *p* or *c* or a dental.

(2)   *téarma* /t´e:rmǝ/ 'term'
        corp /korp/ 'corpse'
        corc /kork/ 'cork'

Despite the fact that this rule is of such a general nature, there are some minor differences between the dialects. It would seem to be a particular feature of Munster dialects (see Wagner 1958:105) that the epenthesis rule may apply in compounds. Examples are:

(3)   seammháthair /sˊanəwahərˊ/ (M) 'grandmother'
        anmhaith /anəwah/ (M) 'very good'
        seanbhean /sˊanəvˊan/ (M) 'old woman'
        gearrchuid /gˊarəxudˊ/ (Mk) 'fair amount'

2.3 Syllabic adjustment

The approach which will be suggested in Part II (see 5.2) envisages certain clusters which ultimately must be split up by the rules which govern syllable formation. When a cluster arises which is unacceptable, the syllable is adjusted by the insertion of the (normally) unstressed neutral vowel. In other words, subsequent to the implementation of any inflection or any word formation rule, the syllable is adjusted if it contravenes the canonical form.

2.4 The secondary epenthetic vowel

Quite apart from the epenthetic vowel previously described and also distinct from syllabic adjustment, there is a phenomenon which can, for convenience' sake, be labelled the secondary epenthetic vowel. There are certain consonant clusters which, although permitted by the basic rules of syllable formation, may be separated by a neutral vowel. In this instance the cluster has a final nasal or liquid which is given the value of a syllable.

The secondary epenthetic vowel is most clearly heard following plosives, *m* /m/, *f* /f/, *th* /h/, *s* /s/:

(4)   eagla /agələ/ (M) 'fear'
        aigne /agˊənˊə/ (M) 'mind'
        madra /madərə/ (M) 'dog'
        Gobnait /gobənətˊ/ (M) (woman's name)
        simné /sˊimˊəˊnˊeː/ (M) 'chimney'
        seamróg /sˊaməˈroːg/ (M) 'shamrock'
        aifreann /afˊərˊən/ (M) 'mass'
        aithne /ahənˊə/ (M) 'acquaintance'
        gasra /gasərə/ (M) 'a group'

In contrast to the epenthetic vowel already discussed, the secondary one can occur after a long syllable, e.g. *cúpla* /kuːpələ/ (M) 'couple' as opposed to *dualgas* /duːəlgəs/ 'duty'. There are also examples in word-initial position, e.g. *mná* /məˈnaː/ (Rg) 'women', *drúis* /dəˈnuːsʹ/ (Rg) 'lust'.

It is evidently a fairly surface phenomenon, as it can be seen to come into play after the application of syllable lengthening (see 3.4), as can be seen in *paidrín* /paːdʹəˈrʹiːnʹ/ (Mk) 'rosary', *ampla* /aumpələ/ (Mk) 'greed'. The groups *dr* and *mp* condition the lengthening of /a/ to /aː/ and /au/ respectively before the insertion of /ə/. On the other hand, the vowel is inserted before Stress-shift 2 (see 2.8.3), so that Munster *seisreach* /sʹesʹərʹəx/ (M) 'plough-team' is stressed on the first syllable rather than on the *-each* /əx/.

2.5 Pretonic elision

There are three cases of pretonic elision. Firstly, a short vowel immediately before the accented syllable may be elided, if the ensuing consonant group does not contradict the inventory of permitted clusters. An example is *bolgam* /boləgəm/ 'mouthful' which becomes *blogam* /blogəm/ (C). The derivation is:

(5)   *bolgam* (/boləgəm/ →) /bəˈlogəm/ → /blogəm/ (C) 'mouthful'

The stressed epenthetic vowel appears as a mid-vowel (see 2.8.2).

Pretonic elision applies to a limited number of words and there is a deal of local variation, e.g. *Gearóid* /gʹəˈroːdʹ/ (Mk) (a man's name) beside /groːdʹ/ (Rg).

The second case of pretonic elision is where an initial vowel is removed:

(6)   *iníon* (/inʹiːn/→) /iˈnʹiːn/ → /nʹiːn/ (D) 'daughter'
        urball (/urəbəʟ/ →) /əˈrubəʟ/ → /rubəʟ/ (D) 'tail'
        iomarca /umərkə/ → /əˈmurkə/ → /murkə/ (Rg) 'excess'
        arán (/araːn/ →) /əˈraːn/ → /raːn/ (C, Rg) 'bread'

The third case of pretonic elision is after a pause in speech, e.g. *anois* /əˈnʹisʹ/ 'now', *an bhfuil* /ə wilʹ/ 'is it?' following a pause in an utterance can be pronounced /nʹisʹ/ and /wilʹ/.

Pretonic elision takes place after the shift of the accent to the second syllable (see 2.8.3) in words such as *salach* /slax/ (M) 'dirty' and (optionally)

24 *Modern Irish: grammatical structure and dialectal variation*

in *coláiste* /kolɑːsˈtʲə/ ~ /klɑːsˈtʲə/ (→ /kʟɑːsˈtʲə/) (Cf) 'college'. In this way, we can envisage the sequence of rules as:

(7)   *salach* /salax/ → /səˈlax/ → /slax/ (M) 'dirty'
       coláiste /kolɑːsˈtʲə/ → /kəˈlɑːsˈtʲə/ → /klɑːsˈtʲə/ (→ /kʟɑːsˈtʲə/) (Cf) 'college'

2.6 Vowel coalescence

Essentially, we are dealing here with a merger of two vowels in order to avoid a hiatus. This is, for the greater part, achieved by the removal of a short vowel beside a long vowel or beside a stressed short vowel. There are plenty of examples of this coalescence, especially in Cois Fhairrge where /h/ is removed [see 4.1.7(ii)]:

(8)   *bóthar* (/boːhər/ →) /boːər/ → /boːr/ (Cf) 'road'
       bothán (/bohɑːn/ →) /boɑːn/ → /bɑːn/ (→ /bɑːɴ/) (Cf) 'hut'
       scothach (/skohəx/ →) /skoːəx/ → /skoːx/ (Cf) 'tufted hair'
       cuthach (/kuhəx/ →) /kuːəx/ → /kuːx/ (Cf) 'rage'

In all the examples a short vowel merges into a neighbouring long vowel. Obviously, the bracketed developments such as the removal of /h/ and the vowel lengthening in place of /h/ (see *scothach* and *cuthach*) are implemented before the actual coalescence. As a result of further more local or surface developments /n/ → /ɴ/ [see 4.2.5(i)] and /aː/ → /ɑː/ (see 3.7.1) so that finally *bothán* appears as /bɑːɴ/ (Cf).

There are two important exceptions to the general rules of vowel coalescence. In the first place, /a/ or /e/ must be kept before long high vowels (i.e. /iː/ or /uː/) and form diphthongs, e.g.:

(9)   *cathaoir* (/kahiːrʲ/ →) /kaiːrʲ/ → /kairʲ/ (Cf) 'chair'
       beithígh (/bʲehiːj/ → /bʲehiː/ →) /bʲeiː/ → /bʲei/ 'cows'
       breithiúnas (/bʲrʲehuːnəs/ →) /bʲrʲeuːnəs/ → /bʲrʲaunəs/ (→ /bʲrʲauɴəs/) (Cf) 'judgment'

Secondly, a neutral vowel following a long high vowel (i.e. /iː/ or /uː/) is excepted so that the diphthongs /iːə/ and /uːə/ are preserved in words such as *ciall* /kʲiːəʟ/ 'sense' and *bua* /buːə/ 'victory'. Nevertheless, in certain words the neutral vowel is subsumed in the previous long vowel if there is a neighbouring nasal, as in *scian* /sˈkʼiːN/ (Cf) 'knife' or *nua* /Nuː/ (Cf) 'new'; for a discussion of this see 3.8.

2.7 Lengthening in place of /h/

This rule means that any short vowel before a hiatus is lengthened. When the vowel has been lengthened, the new lengthened vowel can then subsume a following short vowel. This is illustrated by the sequences in the following table:

Table 2.2 *Development of short vowel before* /h/

Example	/h/ → ø	Lengthening	Coalescence
ithir /ihərʼ/ 'soil'	/iərʼ/	/iːərʼ/	/iːrʼ/
rotha /rohə/ 'wheel'	/roə/	/roːə/	/roː/
cuthach /kuhəx/ 'rage'	/kuəx/	/kuːəx/	/kuːx/
soitheach /sehəx/ 'dish'	/seəx/	/seːəx/	/seːx/

The disyllabic quality must be preserved until the neutral vowel is lost, e.g. /kuːəx/ becomes /kuːx/ in *cuthach* 'rage'. This prevents the loss of the diphthong in a word such as *cuach* /kuːəx/ 'cuckoo' under this rule. Two additional points must be made. Firstly, vowel lengthening must be implemented after a Connemara rule which turns /a/ into /aː/ (see 3.7.1) because in Cois Fhairrge *athar*, genitive of *athair* 'father', is pronounced /aːr/ not */aːr/. The fact that there is already a long vowel /aː/ prevents lengthening in place of /h/. Secondly, morpheme boundaries can play a role inasmuch as a word such as *sruth* /sru/ (Cf) 'stream' has a plural *sruthannaí* /sruNiː/ (Cf) and not */sruːNiː/ as would be the case if there was vowel lengthening. For this reason it can be said that the loss of /h/ etc. operates prior to the suffixing of the plural morpheme. Another such example of the importance of these boundaries is *d'itheas* /dʼiːs/ ~ /dʼis/ (Cf) '[Yes,] I did eat'. In the first pronunciation /h/ is dropped, the original short *i* is lengthened and the neutral vowel merged so that the derivation is:

(10)   *d'itheas* /dʼihəs/ → /dʼiəs/ → /dʼiːəs/ → /dʼiːs/ (Cf)
       'Yes, I did eat'

In the second pronunciation the ending *-(e)as* /əs/ has been added subsequent to the disappearance of /h/ so that the derivation is:

(11)   d'ith (/dʹih/ →) /dʹi/ + s /s/ → /dʹis/

The removal of /h/ followed by lengthening and/or vowel coalescence is required for Cois Fhairrge and the Aran Islands. It is found only sporadically in other dialects.

2.8 Stress

The following discussion of the stress pattern concerns itself for the most part with how individual words are stressed. The patterns of sentence stress and word stress are interrelated, so that it will be necessary to mention the sentence stress in passing.

2.8.1 Distribution of stress

Where a word receives the primary stress, it will normally be on the first syllable and in the following discussion the initial stress is taken to be the underlying stress shared by all dialects. However, certain words which do not belong to the primary syntactic categories are stressed on the second syllable, e.g. *isteach* /ə'sʹtʹax/ 'into', *anocht* /ə'Noxt/ 'tonight'. Apart from these exceptions there is a handful of words, mostly borrowings, which are not stressed on the first syllable, e.g.:

(12)   *tobac(a)* /tə'baːk/ (Cf), /tə'bakə/ (Gd) 'tobacco'
         turnapa /tər'Naːp/ (Cf), /tər'nap/ (Dn) 'turnip'
         bricfeast /bʹrʹikʹfʹast/ (Mk) 'breakfast'

These exceptions cannot be predicted and must be marked in the lexicon.

The situation in compound words is somewhat more complex. It may be said in general, and certainly in Cois Fhairrge, that in the case of intensive prefixes a following noun or adjective is equally stressed. Examples of such prefixes are:

(13)   *an-* 'very'
         ard- 'superb'
         barr- 'top-class'
         deá- 'good'
         dearg- 'extreme(ly)'
         droch- 'bad'
         dubh- 'extreme(ly)'

fíor- 'real(ly)'
rí- 'outstanding'
síor- 'eternal(ly)'

As opposed to that, prefixes which are not intensive receive the primary stress. Examples of such prefixes are:

(14) *ath-* 're-'
      bun- 'basic'
      do- 'un...able'
      so- 'easily ...able'
      mí- (negative prefix)
      mion- 'small'
      sean- 'old'

Gweedore, and Donegal in general, seem in the main to agree with Cois Fhairrge in this basic distinction between intensive and non-intensive prefixes.

There are, of course, finer points: *i(o)n-* '---able' (and *so-* 'easily --- able' in the case of Cois Fhairrge) take a secondary stress, while the second element of the compound is given the primary stress. Another exception from the general rule is that the prefixes *chomh* 'equal(ly)' and *aon* 'any' receive equal stress to the second element of the compound, thus behaving as though they were intensifiers.

While the general distinction between intensive and non-intensive prefixes holds for Connacht and Donegal, Munster appears to apply the same rules to compound as to simple words. This means, in effect, that the two shifts of stress described in 2.8.2-3 apply equally to compounds.

As was previously pointed out, it is impossible to separate fully the sentence stress from the word stress. A good example here is the equal stress on *deá-* 'good' in a sentence such as *Bhí deáchroí* /ˈdʲɑː ˈxriː/ *aige* (Cf) 'He had a kind heart' as opposed to the phrase *le teann deáchroí* /dʲɑːˈxriː/ 'out of sheer goodheartedness' where *deá* receives the primary stress.

2.8.2 Stress-shift 1

In this shift the stress is transferred from the first syllable to the second, when both are short and separated by a nasal or liquid (i.e. /l/, /n/, /r/). The second syllable typically contains an epenthetic vowel. The third syllable will also be short. The shift does not take place if the first vowel is low (i.e. *a*). Words like *bolgam* /ˈbolǝgǝm/ 'mouthful' or *tiormaigh* /tʲˈirǝmǝj/ (for development see 4.1) 'dry' are typical; conversely, *dearmad* /dˊarəməd/ (C, D) 'oversight' is excluded because the vowel in the first syllable is low. Other words with a slightly different profile are *spirid* 'spirit' and *furasta* 'easy'. Pretonic elision, which has already been discussed (see 2.5), operates after this shift. The sequence is illustrated in Table 2.3.

Table 2.3 *Stress-shift 1 and pretonic elision*

Example	Stress-shift 1	Pretonic elision
bolgam /boləgəm/ 'mouthful'	/bə'logəm/	/blogəm/ (C)
tiormaigh /tˊirəməj/ 'dry'	/tˊə'roməj/	/tˊrˊoməj/ (→ /tˊrˊuməj/ see 3.3.4)
furasta /furəstə/ 'easy'	/fə'rustə/	/frustə/ (C)
spirid /sˊpˊirˊədˊ/ 'spirit'	/sˊpˊə'ridˊ/	/sˊpˊrˊidˊ/ (C, M)

The quality of the *r* in *furasta* 'easy' varies, e.g. *fuiriste* /firˊisˊtˊə/ → /fə'risˊtˊə/ → /fˊrˊisˊtˊə/ (Dn). In Donegal where the rule does not apply it is realized as /furəst/ (Gd).

It is noteworthy that where an epenthetic vowel receives the stress it appears as a mid-vowel (e.g. /boləgəm/ → /bə'logəm/), whereas an original neutral vowel when it receives the stress reflects the first syllable (e.g. /furəstə/ → /fə'rustə/).

The application of the rule in Donegal may be confined to *tirmaigh* /tˊrˊumiː/ 'dry', *teiligean* /tˊlˊigˊən/ 'condemn, cast up' and *urball* /rubəL/ 'tail'. In the case of trisyllabic words where the second vowel is epenthetic there are exceptions which cause variation in Connacht and Munster:

(15)   *orchar* /orəxər/ (C), *urchar* /urəxər/ (Ky) 'shot': *ruchar* /ruxər/ (Mk)
       bolgam /boləgəm/ (Dn) : *blogam* /blogəm/ (C)
       teilgean /tˊelˊəgˊən/ (Mk) 'cast' : *tligean* /tˊlˊigˊən/ (C, D) 'condemn, cast up'

Apart from instances such as *furasta* 'easy', *spirid* 'spirit', *tarathar* 'auger', the examples of words in which the second syllable is not epenthetic are mostly in Munster:

(16)   *tarathar* /traːhər/ (Mk) /trahər/ (Er) (→ /traːr/) (Cf) 'auger'
       turas /trus/ (Mk, Dn, Rg) 'journey'

tirim /tʹrʹimʹ/ (Mk, Dn) 'dry'
culaith /klih/ (Mk), /kʟuh/ (Dn) 'suit of clothes'
chonac /xnok/ [→ /xnuk/ (see 3.3.4) (Dn, Mk, Rg)] '(I) saw'
innis /nʹisʹ/ (Mk, Dn see 8.3.2(xii), Rg) 'tell'
conablach /knubələx/ (see 3.3.4) (Mk) 'carcase'
oiread /rud/ (Mk) 'amount'
iomarca /morkə/ (→ /murkə/ see 3.3.4) (Rg) 'excess amount'
cuideachta /kidʹaxtə/ [→ /kəʹdʹaxtə/ (Mk, Dn) ~ /kilʹaxtə/ → /kʹlʹaxtə/ (Mk, Dn)] 'company'
salach /salax/ → (/səʹlax/ → /slax/) (M) 'dirty'

2.8.3 Stress-shift 2

2.8.3(i) *Description of shift*. Stress-shift 2 involves the transfer of the stress from the first syllable to a long vowel or to *-(e)ach(t)*. The following table of Munster examples illustrate the shift to a long vowel:

Table 2.4 *Stress-shift 2: attraction of stress to a long vowel*

Pattern	Stress-shift	No Shift
V̆ V̄	*corcán* /kərʹkaːn/ (M) 'pot'	
V̆ V̄ V̄	*cailíní* /kaʹlʹiːnʹiː/ (M) 'girls'	
V̄ V̆	*díomhaoin* /dʹiːʹwiːnʹ/ (M) 'idle'	
V̄ V̆ V̆	*óganach* /oːʹgaːnəx/ 'youth'	
V̆ V̆ V̄	*spealadóir* /spʹaləʹdoːrʹ/ (M) 'mower'	
V̄ V̆ V̄		*méaracán* /mʹeːrəkaːn/ (→ /mʹiːarəkaːn/) (M) 'thimble'

Wagner (1964) records *spealadóir* with an initial stress for Point 12 and Wagner (1958:62) records an initial stress in *méaracán* for all points in Munster except Waterville.

The rule is that the stress is attracted to a long vowel (i.e. V̄) but it does not skip over a long vowel followed by a consonant and a short vowel (i.e. V̄ C V̆) as in *méaracán* /mʹeːrəkaːn/ 'thimble' rather than /mʹeːrəʹkaːn/ or over a short vowel followed by a consonant and a long vowel (i.e. V̆ C V̄) as in *cailíní* /kaʹlʹiːnʹiː/ rather than /kalʹiːnʹiː/. It must be noted in addition that certain nouns which must be marked as borrowings, such as *baitsiléir* /batʹsʹəlʹeːrʹ/ 'bachelor', are excluded from this rule in some dialects (e.g. Muskerry).

30 *Modern Irish: grammatical structure and dialectal variation*

The same rules would seem to apply in compounds as exemplified in Table 2.5.

Table 2.5 *Stress-shift 2 in compounds*

Pattern	Example
˘ ˘ ˘	*neamh-chiontacht* /nˈaxˊuntəxt/ (Mk) 'guiltlessness'
˘ ˉ ˘ ˘	*neamh-thuairmeach* /nˈaˈhuərˊəmˊəx/ (Mk) 'unthinking'
˘ ˘ ˉ ˘	*neamh-choitianta* /nˈaxoˈtˊiəntə/ (Mk) 'unusual'
˘ ˘ ˉ	*neamh-shuimiúil* /nˈahəˈmuːlˊ/ (Mk) 'uninteresting'

However, some prefixed elements prove exceptional, e.g. the /a/ in *leath* 'half' counts in Muskerry (and exceptionally in Ring) as a long vowel. Furthermore the negative prefix *mí-* optionally counts as a long vowel in Ring. Diachronically, it might be argued that *leath* 'half' has entered into phrase stress patterns in Muskerry and that Ring represents an intermediary stage in that process:

(17) *leath-bhulóg* /lˊawəloːg/ (Mk) 'half a loaf'
      leath-sceallóg /lˊasˊkˊəloːg/ (Mk) 'half a potato cut'
      leath-bhróg /lˊaˈwroːg/ (Mk) 'one shoe of a pair'
      leath-amadán /lˊahəmədaːn/ ~ /lˊahəməˈdaːn/ (Rg) 'half-wit'
      mí-rathúil /mˊiːrahuːlˊ/ ~ /mˊiːraˈhuːlˊ/ (Rg) 'unprosperous'

The question of morpheme boundaries also plays an important role in the inflection of the verb. In forms such as *bheidís* /vˊedˊiːsˊ/ (Mk) 'they would be' or *mholfaí* /volfˊiː/ 'one would praise', the stress does not move to the long vowel. In Dunquin and Ring the stress may be moved to the impersonal endings *-t(a)í* /t(ˊ)iː/ and *-f(a)í* /f(ˊ)iː/, e.g. *cuirtí* /kurtˊiː/ ~ /kurˈtˊiː/ (Dn) 'one used to put'. The stress may also move in the case of the second singular ending *-f(e)á* /haː/, e.g. *dhéanfá* /jeːnhaː/ ~ /jeːnˈhaː/ (Rg) 'you would do'. The stress-shift depends on the pattern of stress in the sentence. On the other hand, generally in Munster a verbal ending containing /iː/, /uː/ (derived from /əj/) or indeed /oː/ in the future of Category 2 verbs (see 8.1.4), will attract the stress even when this means the stress skipping over V̄CV̆ or V̆CV̆. In practice, this addendum to the rule is rarely needed; verbal forms such as *seachnaím* (/sˊaxnəjəmˊ/ →) /sˊaxˈnˊiːmˊ/ → /sˊaxəˈnˊiːmˊ/ (M) 'I avoid' or (*gortaghadh* /gortəɣəɣ/ →) *gortú* /gorˈtuː/ (M) 'injuring' are taken care of by the general rule and behave like *corcán* /korˈkaːn/. Nevertheless, the addendum is necessary to deal with such forms as *foghlaimeod* /**foul´ə'mˊoːd**/ (M) 'I will learn' or (*soláthraigheann* /**sə'laːrəjəN**/ →) *soláthraíonn* /**solaːˈriːn**/ (→ /**slaːˈriːn**/) (M) 'supplies' due to pretonic elision.

An important part of Stress-shift 2 is the change of stress to syllables consisting of -*(e)ach(t)* /**ax(t)**/. The rule is that the stress moves to -*(e)ach(t)* /**ax(t)**/ only when preceded by a short vowel:

(18)   *coileach* /**kəˈlˊax**/ (M) 'cock'
           beannacht /**bˊ(ə)naxt**/ (M) 'blessing'
           cruithneacht /**krəŋˊˈhaxt**/ (Mk) ~ /**kirˊˈnaxt**/ (Rg, Dn) 'wheat'
           bacacha /**bəˈkaxə**/ (M), plural of *bacach* 'lame'

Examples of -*(e)ach(t)* /**əx(t)**/ not preceded by a single short vowel are:

(19)   *feargach* /**fˊarəgəx**/ (M) 'angry'
           báisteach /**baːsˊtˊəx**/ (M) 'rain'

If the second syllable has an initial -*th* /h/, in Muskerry the stress-shift is optional:

(20)   *lathach* /**lahəx**/ ~ /**ləˈhax**/ (Mk) 'mire'
           dlitheach /**dˊlˊihəx**/ ~ /**dˊlˊəˈhax**/ (Mk) 'lawful'

In Dunquin the accent will not shift:

(21)   *fathach* /**fahəx**/ (Dn) 'giant'
           ceathach /**kˊahəx**/ (Dn) 'showery'

There is no stress-shift in words like *dorcha* /**dorəxə**/ 'dark' where there is an epenthetic vowel or in the impersonal past, e.g. *casadh* /**kasəx**/ (Dn, Mk) 'one turned', where /əx/ is derived from -*adh* /əɣ/; see 4.1.2(ii). The words *Connacht* (Mk) 'Connacht' and *Connachtach* (Mk) 'Connacht man' seem to be exceptions to the stress-shift.

2.8.3(ii) *Effect of position in sentence.* In discussing Stress-shift 2, it must be remembered that it cannot be viewed in isolation from the sentence stress pattern. This is demonstrated by an example such as *cipín* 'small stick' /**kˊəˈpˊiːnˊ**/ beside *cipín dearg* /**kˊipˊiːnˊ dˊarəg**/ 'small red stick'. Although the stress transfers to the second syllable in *cipín*, the effect of a following adjective alters the sentence stress, thus blocking the stress-shift. A similar example of the interplay between sentence or phrase stress and the individual word stress is the fact that ordinal numbers in Dunquin or Ring, e.g. *tríú* /tˈrʹiːuː/ 'third', *ceathrú* /kʹarhuː/ 'fourth' etc. are constantly stressed on the first syllable. This is because there is always an accompanying noun.

2.8.3(iii) *Order of rules.* The rule-ordering here is of significance in dealing with many cases which would otherwise have to be regarded as exceptions.

Firstly, if, as proposed in this work, a derived verbal form of the sort *bailím* /baːˈlʹiːmʹ/ 'I collect' is interpreted as a development of /balʹəjəmʹ/, then the stress-shift must be said to occur after that development.

Secondly, examples such as *lámhachán* /laːkaːn/ (Mk) 'crawling on all fours' or *lámhanán* /laːnaːn/ (Mk) 'bladder' or *áibhirseoir* /aːrʹsʹoːrʹ/ 'devil' appear on the surface to be exceptions. They seem to be disyllabic and we might expect the stress to shift to the second syllable as in *díomhaoin* /dʹiːˈwiːnʹ/ (M) 'idle'. However, if the stress-shift takes place before /w/ is removed (see 4.1.4), then these examples can be regarded as behaving regularly after the fashion of *méaracán* /mʹeːrəkaːn/ (→ /mʹiːərəkaːn/) 'thimble'. In order to handle the initial stress in *lámhacán* /launkaːn/ (Dn) and *lámhanán* /launaːn/ (Dn) the stress-shift must operate before the Munster minor rule which shortens *á* before *mh* (see 3.7.3), which combination in turn will be changed into a diphthong.

Thirdly, Stress-shift 2 must precede the insertion of the secondary epenthetic vowel. In this way, examples such as Dunquin *cúplaí* /kuːpʹəˈliː/ (Dn) 'couples', *méirscrí* /mʹeːsʹgʹəˈrʹiː/ (Dn) 'fissures', *uaigní* /uːəgʹəˈnʹiː/ (Dn) 'lonelier', while they seem to contradict the model *méaracán* /mʹeːrəkaːn/ (→ /mʹiːarəkaːn/) 'thimble', are in fact behaving like *díomhaoin* /dʹiːˈwiːnʹ/ 'idle'.

Finally, such examples as the comparative forms *cóngaraí* /kuːŋgəˈriː/ (Dn) 'closer' or *dealraití* /dʹaːrhəˈtʹiː/ (Dn) 'more likely-looking' would indicate that the stress-shift must be applied before the phenomenon which we call vowel lengthening and diphthongization. In other words, the stress is transferred to the third syllable before the initial syllable has been lengthened and such comparatives may be treated like *spealadóir* /ˌspʹaləˈdoːrʹ/ 'mower'.

2.8.3(iv) *Geographical distribution.* Although Stress-shift 2 is centred in Munster an example such as the noun *iníon* /Nʹiːn/ 'daughter' occurs in Donegal and there is also a limited version of the rule required for

Connacht (for East Connacht a version similar to that of Munster might be required; see Wagner 1958:284 and Ó Sé 1984). The change happens only where the first syllable is short and precedes /l(ʹ)/ or /r(ʹ)/ followed by a long non-high vowel (i.e. /aː/):

(22) coláiste /kolaːsʹtʹə/ → /kəˈlaːsʹtʹə/ → (/klaːsʹtʹə/ → /kʟɑːsʹtʹə/) (Cf) 'college'
Muiréad /mirʹeːd/ → /məˈreːd/ (→ /mʹrʹeːd/) (Cf) (woman's name)
coróin /koroːnʹ/ → /kəˈroːnʹ/ (→ /kroːnʹ/ → /kruːnʹ/) (Cf) 'crown'
arán /araːn/ → /əˈraːn/ [→ /raːn/ (Rg) → /rɑːɴ/ (Cn)] 'bread'

Except for a limited number of words such as arán /raːn/ 'bread', foileár /fʹlʹaːr/ 'must', biorán /bʹrʹaːn/ 'knitting needle' (see also Wagner 1958:67), coróin /kruːnʹ/ 'crown', the rule is largely optional in Connacht so that coláiste /kolaːstʹə/ ~ /klaːsʹtʹə/, etc. are possible.

2.8.3(v) *Stress-related rules*. Although this transfer of stress is not needed for Donegal, there are some related rules which are of interest. In the first place, it is significant that a final *-(e)ach(t)* /ax(t)/ retains its /a/ and is not reduced to a neutral vowel, e.g. *Gaelach* /geːlax/ 'Irish'. Secondly, unstressed vowels which are long in other dialects tend to be short in Donegal. Furthermore, in Gweedore at least, and it would seem generally in Donegal, /oː/ then becomes /a/ rather than /o/ as in *bádóir* /bæːdaj/ 'boatman' or *coróin* /koranʹ/.

Another feature is that /eː/ in the second syllable before a broad consonant is realized as /a/, e.g.:

(23) buidéal /bidʹal/ 'bottle' (Gd)
páipéar /pæːpʹar/ 'paper' (Gd)

This is part of a more general historical tendency in the language as a whole for *ea* in a second syllable to become *eá*: compare *muinéal* (Rg) 'neck' with *muineál* (Mk, Ky, C, D).

On the other hand the other originally long vowels retain their quality:

(24) arán /aran/ (D) 'bread'
guilpíneacht /gilʹpʹinʹaxt/ (Gd) 'wolfing'
barúil /barulʹ/ (D) 'opinion'
cairpintéir /karʹpʹinʹtʹej/ (Gd) 'carpenter'

It seems that this rule comes into play after long vowels have been derived from semi-vowels (see 4.1.3) so that we find *bealaigh* /bˈali/ genitive of *bealach* 'way' and *moladh* /**molu**/ 'praising' alongside *báidín* /bæːdˈinˈ/ 'little boat' and *galún* /**galun**/ 'gallon'.

3 *The vowels*

3.1 The vocalic system

The following table gives an overall picture of the underlying vocalic system for all dialects:

Table 3.1 *The underlying vocalic system*

	unrounded front	unrounded back	rounded back	
/ɯ/ /i/ /u/ /ə/ /e/ /o/ /a/	/iː/ /eː/ ------	/ɯː/ ------ /aː/	/uː/ /oː/ ------	high vowel mid-vowel low vowel
short	long	long	long	

It is also possible to describe the entire system in a binary fashion with plus or minus five features namely *high, low, back, round, length*; see Ó Siadhail and Wigger 1975:80.

An argument can be made for speaking of tension rather than of length, so that we might then speak of tension spreading from certain consonant groups to vowels (see 3.4). In practice, however, tension is expressed as length and that term is used here for convenience' sake.

The inclusion of the feature rounded/unrounded is justified by the need to deal with certain developments of /ɯː/ in words such as *saor* 'free', *saoghal* 'life', etc. (see 3.6).

At a more abstract level it is possible to collapse the distinction between the high vowels /i/ and /u/ and between the mid-vowels /e/ and /o/ and use the signs /ɯ/ for high vowels and /ə/ for mid-vowels: see 3.2.

There are certain instabilities apparent in the short vowel system. In Connemara, for example, the vowel colour is not always evident; often the oppositions between 'back' and 'front' and 'high' and 'low' are indistinct in speech. Yet, if these vowels are lengthened under the rules for vowel lengthening (see 3.4), the colour is then quite distinct, e.g. *cion* /kʼɯn/ (Cn) 'affection' contrasted with (*as*) *cionn* /kʼiːN/ (Cf) 'above'. It is also remarkable that minimal pairs such as *cur* /kur/ 'put' and *cor* /kor/ 'move' or *cuileach* /kilʼəx/ (Cf) 'tousled' and *coileach* /kelʼəx/ (Cf) 'cock', which show the opposition between /u/ and /o/ or /i/ and /e/, are extremely rare.

Apart from certain adverbs and words ending in -*(e)ach(t)* (where /a/ is retained in Donegal [see 2.8.3(v)]) and in some loan-words, the height of an underlying short vowel need not be specified outside the first syllable. In other syllables, there is a neutral vowel. The level of the vowel is immaterial unless the vowel is given stress.

Most of the changes which take place in the vocalic system relate either to the height of the vowel or to its length.

There is only one type of primary diphthong, a falling diphthong in which the first element is appreciably longer than the second: /iːə/ and /uːə/ (see 3.8). Apart from these basic diphthongs, there are others which arise from the combination of a vowel and a semi-vowel. These may occur in the derivation, as for instance in *sleamhain* /sʼlʼawnʼ/ 'slippery', or may be present in the underlying form such as *fadhb* /fajb/ (C, M) 'blow, knot of timber'. Ultimately, in Connacht, for example, the distinctions between /aj/, /oj/, /əj/ are blurred, as are those between /aw/ and /ow/, all being reduced simply to /ai/ or /au/. In Muskerry, however, a contrast between /ai/ and /əi/ is recorded and between /au/ and /ou/ among older speakers.

3.2 Vowel separation

It is possible to predict from the environment where a high (i.e. /ɯ/) or middle (i.e. /ɵ/) short vowel will be a back or front vowel. The basic rule which 'separates' (that is, determines whether it will be a back or front vowel) is quite straightforward: a back vowel is allowed before a broad consonant (*liom* /lʼɯm/ 'with me' → /lʼum/, *sop* /sɵp/ 'wisp' → /sop/) and a front vowel is allowed before a slender consonant (*linn* /lʼɯNʼ/ 'with us' → /lʼiNʼ/, *soip* /sɵpʼ/, gen. of *sop* → /sepʼ/).

There are two qualifications to that general rule:

(a) A back vowel (/o/ or /u/) is needed between a broad consonant and /sʼ/ or /xʼ/, e.g. *cois* /kɵsʼ/→ /kosʼ/ 'leg', *cloich* /kloxʼ/→ /kloh/ (dat. of *cloch*) 'stone'

(b)   A front vowel (/e/ or /i/) is needed between a slender consonant (excluding /s´/, e.g. *sionnach* /s´uNəx/ 'fox') and a broad dental (excluding /L/, e.g. *giolla* /g´uLə/ 'attendant'), e.g. *bior* /b´ɯr/→ /b´ir/ 'pointed rod'.

Munster is slightly different from the other major dialects in so far as the second condition above is narrower. The general principle (i.e. /o/ or /u/ before a broad consonant and /e/ or /i/ before a slender consonant) obtains before nasals. Although following a labial /i/ and /u/, e.g. *mion* /m´in/ and /m´un/ (Rg) 'small' are recorded, *cion* /k´ɯn / 'affection' is realized as /k´un/ (M) and *piont* /p´ɯnt/ 'pint' separates as /p´unt/, which changes to /p´u:nt/ when the vowel is lengthened. In addition, /x´/ in the first condition is seemingly not needed in Muskerry where *cluiche* /klihə/ (Mk) 'shoal, game' (complying with the general principle) is recorded, as opposed to /kLuhə/ (Dn).

Apart from the predictability of the features 'back' and 'front', there is another persuasive reason for conceiving of a theoretical undistinguished short high vowel /ɯ/ and a short mid-vowel /ə/, namely, that many of the changes of height (i.e. from low to middle, middle to high etc.) affect *both* back and front vowels. In this way the various rules for the raising and lowering of short stressed vowels can be applied to /ɯ/ and /ə/, which then are ultimately back or front vowels according to the environment.

While the theoretical short mid-vowel /ɯ/ and short high vowel /ə/ are an important concept in dealing with the vocalic system, for convenience' sake, the familiar specific symbols /u/, /o/, /i/, /e/ are for the most part used in the phonemic transcript of examples throughout the rest of the discussion of the phonology.

3.3 Raising and lowering of vowels

We are concerned here mainly with rules which determine the level of short vowels. There is quite a deal of raising and lowering involved and those movements are only predictable to a limited degree.

3.3.1 Raising of low vowels to mid-vowels

In general, when an underlying low vowel /a/ occurs between two slender consonants it is raised to a mid-vowel. By a mid-vowel is meant, of course, /e/ or /o/, for which the symbol /ə/ may be used; whether it is in fact a front mid-vowel /e/ or a back mid-vowel /o/ is determined by the environment as described in 'vowel separation' (see 3.2). Some examples of this raising are:

38 *Modern Irish: grammatical structure and dialectal variation*

(1)   *speal* /sp′al/ 'scythe' : *speile* /sp′el′ə/, gen. of *speal*
        deas /d′as/ 'nice' : *deise* /d′es′ə/ (C, D), comp. of *deas*
        leac /L′ak/ 'flagstone' : *leice* /L′ek′ə/ (C, D), gen. of *leac*
        nead /N′ad/ 'nest' : *neide* /N′ed′ə/ (C), gen. of *nead*
        ceart /k′art/ 'right' : *ceirte* /k′ert′ə/ (C), comp. of *ceart*

However, in some words of this shape, there is a two-tier raising, that is low vowels must be further raised to high vowels:

(2)   *fear* /f′ar/ 'man' : *fir* /f′ir′/ 'men'
        cearc /k′ark / 'hen' : *circe* /k′ir′k′ə/, gen. of *cearc*

The raising of a low vowel /a/ to a high vowel /i/ in examples such as *fir* 'men' and *circe*, gen. of *cearc* 'hen', could be thought of as a separate rule. Yet it is possible, and perhaps preferable, to think of it as two stages. The first stage is *fear* /f′ar/ 'man' to *feir* /f′er′/ 'men', *cearc* /k′ark / 'hen' to *ceirce* /k′erk′ə/, gen. of *cearc* 'hen', which then, obligatorily, are raised a second stage to *fir*, *circe*. This arrangement is neater because, firstly, the two stages actually appear in dialectal variation in some words:

Table 3.2 *Two stages of raising of low vowels*

Basic form	Genitive/comparative Stage 1	Genitive/comparative Stage 2
leac 'flagstone'	*leice* (C)	*lice* (M, D)
nead 'nest'	*neide* (C)	*nide* (M, D)
ceart 'right'	*ceirte* (C, D)	*cirte* (M)
deas 'nice'	*deise* (C, D)	*dise* (M)
dearg 'red'	*deirge* (M, Cn, Gd)	*dirge* (Er)

The two stages are also found within one dialect in the case of *girseach* ~ *geirseach* (Cf) (based on *gearr* + *seach*) 'young girl'. (For development see 3.4.2.)

Secondly, from a theoretical point of view it is more economical to allow another rule, which is necessary anyway to raise mid-vowels to high vowels (see 3.3.4).

Morpheme boundaries can affect the operation of the rule as can be seen in *beainín*, *bean* + *ín* /b′æːn′iːn′/ 'a little woman' or in the option between *firín*, *fear* + *ín* /f′ir′iːn′/ and *feairín* /f′æːr′iːn′/ 'a little man'.

A further factor in describing this rule is that recent loan-words such as Connacht: *ceaig* 'keg' or *peain* 'pan' [beside the older loan-word *panna* (Mk)] are exempted.

3.3.2 Raising of low vowels to high vowels

This rule involves raising an underlying low vowel /a/ to a high vowel /ɯ/ (i.e. /i/ or /u/) where there is a long *a* in the second syllable and no morpheme boundary between these two syllables. The rule is seen in examples such as:

(3) *gabáiste* /gubaːsˊtˊə/ [→ /gubɑːsˊtˊə/] (Cf) 'cabbage'
 anáil /unaːlˊ/ [→ /uNɑːlˊ/] (Cf) 'breath'
 scadán /sgudaːn/ [→ /sgudɑːN/] (Cf) 'herring'
 bearrán /bˊiraːn/ [→ /bˊirɑːN/] (Cf) 'nuisance'
 leadán /Lˊidaːn/ [→ /LˊidɑːN/] (Cf) 'burr of a teazle'

There are occasional examples of this raising before a long /oː/, as in *neascóid* /Nˊisgoːdˊ/ (Cf) 'boil'. This raising does not take place in examples such as Connacht *glasáil* /glasaːlˊ/ [→ /gLaːsɑːlˊ/ (Cf)] from *glas* 'lock' + *áil* 'ing' 'locking', where the morpheme boundary blocks it.

This rule is confined to Connacht. It is not found in Donegal. In Munster and in East Connacht (see Wagner 1958:72, 284) the vowel is pretonic and neutralized in words of this shape:

(4) *cabáiste* /kəˈbaːsˊtˊə/ ~ *gabáiste* /gəˈbaːsˊtˊə/ (M) 'cabbage' (see Wagner 1958:72)
 feadóg /fˊəˈdoːg/ (M) 'whistle'
 coiscéim /kəsˊˈkˊeːmˊ/ (M) 'footstep'
 amadán /əməˈdaːn/ (M) 'fool'

That neutralization of the pretonic vowel is found before /aː/, /oː/ or /eː/, but not normally before /iː/ or /uː/:

(5) *cailín* /kalˊiːnˊ/ 'girl'
 eascú /askuː/ 'eel'

3.3.3 Raising/lowering between low and mid-vowels

There is a certain fluctuation between the low vowel /a/ and the mid-vowel /ɵ/:

40 *Modern Irish: grammatical structure and dialectal variation*

(6) call (Tn) 'hazel': *coll* /koʟ/ (→ /kauʟ/) (Cf)
  cratach /kratəx/ (Gd) 'curlew': *crotach* /krotəx/ (Cn)
  falamh /falə/ (Cf) 'empty': *folamh* /foləw/ (Dn)
  slainneadh /slaɴ´uː/ (Tn) 'surname': *sloinneadh* /slen´ə/→ /sʟiɴ´ə/ (Cn)
  tathant /tahənt/ (Mk) 'urging': *tathaint* /tohən´t´/ (→ /toːɴ´t´/ → /tuːɴ´t´/) (Cf)

The geographic distribution of /ə/ and /a/ in any given word is extremely complex (see Wagner 1958:12, 97, 122, 214, 268) so that it is difficult to make any general statement. Such is the variation among dialects that all that can be achieved in this account is to list some of the words where this variation may occur and to tabularize the underlying vowel at chosen points within the major dialects. For convenience all the examples are written with *a* in Table 3.3.

Table 3.3 *Examples of mid-vowel/low vowel variation*

Example	Gd	Er	Cf	Dn
A(i)br(e)án 'April'	/e/ (→ /i/)	/e/	/e/ (→ /ai/)	/a/
baint 'extracting'	/e/ (→ /i/)	/a/	/a/	/e/ (→ /i/)
ca(n)g-ailt/aint/nadh 'chewing'	/a/	/a/	/a/	/o/
cnaipe 'button'	/o/ (→ /i/)	/a/	/a/	/a/
craiceann 'skin'	/a/	/a/	/a/	/e/ (→ /i/)
craith 'shake'	/a/	/a/	/a/	/o/
cras 'cross'	/a/	/o/	/o/	/o/
cratach 'curlew'	/a/	/o/	/o/	
eagla 'fear'	/o/		/a/ (→ /aː/)	/a/
eaglais 'church'	/o/	/a/	/a/ (→ /aː/)	/a/
falamh 'empty'	/a/	/a/	/a/	/o/
gaimh 'sting'	/e/ (→ /i/)	/a/	/a/	/o/ (→ /i/)
glainne 'glass'	/e/ (→ /i/)	/a/	/e/ (→ /i/)	/e/ (→ /i/)
gnaithe 'business'	/e/ (→ /i/	/a/	/e/ (→ /i/) ~ /a/	/oː/
leag 'lay'	/o/	/a/	/a/	/a/
saighead 'arrow'	/e/ ~ /a/ (→ /eː/)	/e/ ~ /a/ (→ /ai/)	/e/ ~ /a/ (→ /ai/)	/e/ → /i/ (→ /iː/)
slainneadh 'surname'	/e/ (→ /i/)	/a/	/e/ (→ /i/)	/e/ (→ /i/)

Indeed variation may occur within one district such as *gairid/goirid* (Cn) 'short', *deacair/deocair* (Cn) 'difficult', *aimhreas* /av´r´əs/, *oimhreas* /ev´r´əs/ [→ /aiv´r´əs/] (Cf) (see 3.4.2) 'doubt', or in word derivatives such as *casán* (D) 'path', *caiscéim* (D) 'footstep', which are based on *cos* 'foot'. Interestingly, the variation is also used to create onomatopoeic pairs, such as *frois frais* (Cn) 'trivialities' or *ina phroiseach phraiseach* (Im) 'in a mess', or such narrative pairs in folkloristic 'runs' as *bocóideach bacóideach* (C) 'bellying (of sails)' or *go folcanta falcanta* (C) 'with great force (through water)'.

This fluctuation might be dealt with in different ways. A shared underlying form could be assumed for each word, which would then have to be marked for a minor rule to affect the change where necessary according to the dialect. On the other hand, a more straightforward solution is not to assume a common underlying form but rather to allow various underlying forms as required for individual dialects.

Furthermore, it is impossible to give 'major' rules which deal with this variation where it is morphologically significant. The rules must be 'minor', that is they must be marked in the lexicon. There are two relevant environments. Firstly, the variation takes place between a slender and a broad consonant followed by a vowel:

(7)   *greim* /g´r´em´/(→ /g´r´im´/ → /g´r´i:m´/) (Cn) 'bite' : *greamannaí* /g´r´aməNi:/ (M, C, Tn) plural of *greim*
   sioc /s´ok/ (→ /s´uk/) 'frost' : *seaca* /s´akə/ (C, M) gen. of *sioc*
   gearr /g´ar/ (→ /g´a:r/) 'short' : *giorra* /g´ərə/ (→ /g´irə/) (Dn, Mk, Er, Tn, Gd) comp. of *gearr*
   cion /k´on/ (→ /k´in/) 'affection' : *ceanúil* /k´anu:l´/ (C) [→ /k´a'nu:l´/ (M)] 'affectionate'
   fios /f´os/ (→ /f´is/) 'knowledge' : *feasa* gen. of *fios* etc.
   ciotach /k´otax/ (→ /k´itax/ → /k´ə'tax/ (M)) 'clumsy' : *ceatach* /k´a'tax/ (Mk)
   ciomach /k´omax/ (→ /k´uməx/) (C) 'rag' : *ceamach* /k´amax/ (D)

Secondly, in words with an initial broad consonant or vowel /a/ is raised to /ə/ (i.e. /e/ or /o/) before a slender consonant and /ə/ is lowered to /a/ before a broad consonant:

(8)   *lag* /Lag/ 'weak' : *loige* /Leg´ə/ (Cn) [→/Lig´ə/ (D, M)] comp. of *lag*
   slat /sLat/ 'stick' : *sloit* /sLet´/ (Cn) old dat. of *slat*
   crann /kraN/ 'tree' : *croinn* /kreN´/ (→ /kriN´/) (Mo, D) → /kri:N´/ (Cn, Ky, Mk), gen. of *crann*

salach /saləx/ 'dirty' : soilche /selʹəxʹə/ → /selʹəhə/ → /selʹiː/ (Cf) ~
(/sailʹxʹə/ → /sailʹəhə/ → /sailʹiː/) (Cf) comp. of salach
goid /gedʹ/ (Cf, Er, Tn) (→ /gidʹ/) (M, Gd) 'steal' : gadaí /gadiː/ 'thief'
drama /dramə/ (Cn), gen. of droim 'back' : droim /dremʹ/ (→ /drimʹ/ → /driːmʹ/) (Cn)
abhainn /awəNʹ/ → /auNʹ/ (C) 'river' : oibhneacha(í) /evʹNʹəxiː/ (Mo) → /aivʹNʹəxiː/ (Cf) plural of abhainn
agam 'at me' : oige /egʹə/ 'at him', oice /ekʹə/ 'at her'
ard 'high' : oirde 'higher' (see Table 4.5)

It is worth mentioning in passing that there is a somewhat parallel, if more limited, variation between long *a* and *o* in the lexicon:

(9) *paróiste* (M) 'parish' : *paráiste* (Cn, D)
próntach (→ /pruːNtəx/) (Cf) 'unfledged great black-backed gull' : *prántach* (Er)
comórtas ~ *comártas* (Cf) 'comparison'

3.3.4 Raising of mid-vowels to high vowels 1

Broadly speaking, this alteration consists of an underlying mid-vowel (/ə/) being raised to high vowel /ɯ/ before a nasal. When the mid-vowel is situated between a broad consonant and a slender nasal the raising would appear to be required for all dialects:

(10) *gloine* /glinʹə/ 'glass'
loime /Limʹə/ comp. of *lom* 'bare'
goimh /givʹ/ 'sting'

In other prenasal environments, the picture is more complex.

In Connacht and in parts of Munster, e.g. Ring, the vowel must generally be raised in all prenasal environments, e.g.:

(11) *dona* /duNə/ (C, Rg) 'bad'
gloine /glʹinʹə/ 'glass'

Otherwise in the major Munster dialects, the vowel will not be raised between a slender consonant and a slender nasal, e.g.:

(12)　　*greim* /gʲrʲemʲ/ (→ /gʲrʲaimʲ/ (M) ['bite' : /gʲrʲimʲ/ (D, Mo) (→ /gʲrʲiːmʲ/ (Cn)]
　　　　seinnt /sʲenʲtʲ/ (→ /sʲainʲtʲ/ (Mk)) 'playing music' ~ (*seinnim* → *seimin* →) *seimint* /sʲemʲənʲtʲ/ (Dn) : *seinniúint* /sʲiŋʲuːnʲtʲ/ (Rg)

The word *teinneas* 'sickness' is exceptional in that raising is required for, e.g., /tʲinʲəs/ (Dn) and /tʲiŋʲəs/ (Rg) but not for, e.g., /tʲeŋʲəs/ (Mk).

Again, in Munster, raising prior to a broad nasal must normally be limited to specific conditions, such as when another consonant follows the nasal as in *iompar* /ompər/ → /umpər/ [which is subsequently lengthened to /uːmpər/ (Dn, Mk)] 'carry'. Contrariwise, where no consonant follows the nasal, as in *trom* /trom/ (→ /traum/ when lengthened or diphthongized) 'heavy', there is no raising.

A feature of Muskerry is that there is a set of marked words in which raising is necessary, despite the fact that no consonant follows the nasal:

(13)　　*bonn* /boN/ → /buN/ (→ /buːN/ → /buːn/) (Mk) 'sole'
　　　　fonn /foN/ → /fuN/ (→ /fuːN/ → /fuːn/) (Mk) 'desire'
　　　　tonn /toN/ → /tuN/ (→ /tuːN/ → /tuːn/) 'wave'
　　　　com /kom/ → /kum/ (→ /kuːm/) 'valley'
　　　　long /loŋg/ → /luŋg/ (→ /luːŋg/) 'ship'
　　　　Conn /koN/ → /kuN/ (→ /kuːN/ → /kuːn/) (a man's name)

In this way, there is *bonn* /boN/ → /buN/ (becoming /buːN/ after vowel lengthening) etc. This is particularly interesting because *bonn* 'coin' and *fonn* 'tune' do not belong to the set, and as raising does not apply, they will develop as /bauN/ and /fauN/ when lengthened/diphthongized. This ultimately results in the required distinction between *bonn* /buːn/ 'sole' and *bonn* /baun/ 'coin' and between *fonn* /fuːn/ 'desire' and *fonn* /faun/ 'tune'.

Following a nasal, whether slender or not, mid-vowels /o/ and /e/ must, for the most part, be raised in Connemara to /u/ and /i/ as in *modh* /mu/ 'mode', *meisce* /mʲisʲkʲə/ 'intoxication'. Elsewhere, though there is frequent raising after a broad nasal, e.g. *cnoc* /knuk/ (M) 'hill', *moch* /mux/ (M) 'early', there is only sporadic raising needed following a palatalized nasal: *meisce* /mʲesʲkʲə/ (Mk, Dn, Tn) 'intoxication' : /mʲisʲkʲə/ (Er).

Parallel to the raising of short mid-vowels is the raising of a stressed long back mid-vowel /oː/ to /uː/ before or after a nasal as in examples such as *tóin* /toːnʲ/ 'bottom', *nós* /Noːs/ 'custom', which become /tuːnʲ/ and /Nuːs/. This phenomenon is required for South Connacht (Connemara, Aran,

Tourmakeady but not Erris) and Munster (Dunquin, South Clare, Ring but not Muskerry). The fact that these vowels must be raised subsequent to Stress-shift 2 is illustrated by the following examples:

(14)   *Tríonóid* /t′r′ə'nu:d′/ (Rg) 'Trinity'
        fuinneog /f′(ə)'n′u:g/ (Dn, Rg) 'window'
        onóir /ə'nu:r′/ (Rg) 'honour'

3.3.5 Raising of mid-vowels to high vowels 2
This rule involves raising of a mid-vowel /ɵ/ to the high vowel /ɯ/ where there is a neighbouring slender consonant. There are three basic contexts in which this raising happens.

Firstly, a mid-vowel is raised when between a slender consonant and a broad consonant:

(15)   *sioc* /s′ok/ → /s′uk/ 'frost'
        bior /b′er/ → /b′ir/ 'a pointed stick'

However if the broad consonant is /g/, /k/ or /x/ (e.g. *deoch* /d′ox/ 'drink') the rule does not apply. It should be noted that otherwise *eo* (rather than *éo*) is a recent spelling convention for /o:/ between a slender consonant and a broad consonant (except /g/, /k/ or /x/) or a boundary: e.g.

(16)   *ceol* /k′ol/ → /k′o:l/ 'music'
        ceo /k′o/ → /k′o:/ 'fog'
        eolas (/iolǝs/ →) /o:lǝs/ 'knowledge'
        deoch /d′ox/ 'drink'

Secondly, this rule raises a short mid-vowel to a short high vowel between a broad consonant or boundary and a slender consonant, as in:

(17)   *goid* /ged′/ → /gid′/ (M, Gd) 'steal'
        soir /ser′/ → /sir′/ (M) 'eastwards'
        oirde /er′d′ə/ → /ir′d′ə/ (→ /i:rd′ə/) (M) 'height'

Thirdly, this rule can be used to raise to the second stage (from mid-vowels to high vowels) those low vowels which were previously raised (see 3.3.1). Examples are:

(18)　*fir* (/fʹarʹ/ →) /fʹerʹ/ → /fʹirʹ/ 'men'
　　　　circe (/kʹarˠkʹə/ →) /kʹerˠkʹə/ → /kʹirˠkʹə/ gen. of *cearc* 'hen'

Furthermore, this second stage occurs in Munster, when a mid-vowel is retained in Connacht, e.g.

(19)　*leice* /Lʹekʹə/ (C) → /Lʹikʹə/ (→ /lʹikʹə/) (M) gen. of *leac* 'flagstone'
　　　　ceirte /kʹertʹə/ (C) → /kʹirtʹə/ (M) comp. of *ceart* 'right'

The second context is undoubtedly the least predictable of all rules in the phonology. The following examples give some idea of the complex situation:

(20)　*sop* /sop/ 'wisp' : gen. *soip* /sepʹ/ (C) /sipʹ/ (M)
　　　　gob /gob/ 'beak' : gen. *goib* /gebʹ/ (C, Tn) /gibʹ/ (M)
　　　　soir /serʹ/ (Cn, Tn) ~ /sˠerʹ/ (Er, D) → /sirʹ/ (M) 'eastward'
　　　　goid /gedʹ/ (Cn, Tn, Er) → /gidʹ/ (M, Mn, Gd) 'stealing'

Nevertheless, despite the fact that there are many exceptions, it appears that raising is the general rule for Munster and for Donegal. It seems that a morpheme boundary, particularly before *-ín,* prevents raising in Munster:

(21)　*crobh* /crow/ 'paw' : *croibh* /krivʹ/ (Mn), dat. of *crobh* : *croibhín* /krovʹiːnʹ/ (Mk) 'little paw'
　　　　clog /kLog/ / 'clock' : *cloig* /kLigʹ/ (Dn), gen. of *clog* : *cloigín* /kLogʹiːnʹ/ (Dn) 'small clock'

In Connacht, on the other hand, apart from the fact that a mid-vowel is invariably retained before consonants or consonant groups which condition lengthening or diphthongization, e.g. *moill* /meLʹ/ 'delay', which is eventually diphthongized to /maiLʹ/ in Connemara, there is an extraordinary amount of local variation, as can be seen in the examples in Table 3.4:

Table 3.4 *Variation between /e/ and /i/ in Connacht*

Example	Cois Fhairrge	Tourmakeady	Erris
sloigeadh 'swallowing'	/i/	/i/	/i/
reilig 'graveyard'	/i/	/e/	/e/
toil 'will'	/i/	/i/	/e/
foide comp. of *fada* 'long'	/e/	/i/	/i/

3.3.6 Lowering of high vowels to mid-vowels

This rule lowers high vowels to mid-vowels in different contexts. It must, however, be remembered that, as has been pointed out (see 3.1), the distinction between /o/ and /u/ is not always clear, as shown by the very few minimal pairs found. The three contexts for this rule are:

(a)   before /x/, /L/, /l/, /r/
(b)   before /L/, /N/, /m/ followed by a word boundary (or by a verbal ending)
(c)   before /d/, /t/, /s/, /l′/

Context (a) seems to be implemented fairly regularly in Connacht and Donegal:

(22)   *luch* /lox/ (Cn), *luchóg* /Loxag/ (D) 'mouse'
        ucht /oxt/ (D, C) 'breast'
        currach /korəx/ (C) ~ /korax/ (D) 'coracle'
        tur /tor/ (D, C, Mk, Dn) 'arid'
        lucht /Loxt/ (D, C) '(category of) people'
        culaith /kolə/ (Cn) ~ /koliː/ (Mo, D) 'suit of clothes'
        turas /torəs/ (D, C) 'journey'

A somewhat similar lowering of /iː/ to /eː/ or /uː/ to /oː/ is found sporadically throughout the dialects, e.g. *buíochas* /beːxəs/ (M) 'gratitude' or in unstressed syllables *béilíochaí* /b′eːl′eːxiː/ (Cn) 'meals', *cleitiúchaí* /k′l′et′oːxiː/ (Cn) 'feathers'. Indeed the reverse is also found as a minor rule in Cois Fhairrge: /eː/ becomes /iː/ in a small number of words, mostly with a long *a* or *o* in the second syllable, for example: *féasóig* /f′eːsoːg′/ → /f′iːsoːg′/ 'beard'.

In Munster, this part of the rule only affects isolated words such as *lucht* /loxt/ (Dn, Mk) and /loxt/ ~ /luxt/ (Rg).

Context (b) of the rule is mostly applicable only to Ring (and to Clare). It is really aimed at words which are subsequently affected by lengthening/diphthongization such as:

(23)   *cill* /k′iL′/ → /keL′/ → /kaiL′/ (Cl) 'graveyard'
        croinn (/kreN′/ →) /kriN′/ → /kreN′/ → /kraiN′/ (Cl), gen. of *crann* 'tree'

The word *teinn* 'sick' is an exception in Clare as it is not subsequently diphthongized. This part of the rule also applies in Connemara to previously raised /e/ before a tense cluster, e.g.:

(24) *coimhlint* (/kev′l′əN′t′/ →) /kiv′l′əN′t′/ → /kev′L′əN′t′/ (→ /kaiv′l′əN′t′/) (Cn) 'conflict'
doimhne (/dev′N′ə/ →) /div′N′ə/ → /dev′N′ə/ (→ /daiv′N′ə/) (Cn) comp. of *domhain* 'deep'

Context (c) applies to Munster and Donegal. In one sense, this is a way of allowing for a series of exceptions to such examples as *troid* (M) 'fight', *cois* 'leg', *scoil* 'school' and *loit* (Mk) 'destroy', all of which are pronounced with a mid-vowel as opposed to *goid* 'steal', *soir* 'eastwards', which are pronounced with a high vowel (see 3.3.5). It is either possible to exempt mid-vowels from raising before /d′/, /t′/, /s′/, /l′/, or, as proposed here, to allow raising under the general rule, then to lower them again under the present rule: *troid* /tred′/ → /trid′/ → /tred′/ etc. The argument for this arrangement is that there is a somewhat similar minor rule required to lower high vowels in Connacht in words such as:

(25) *sileadh* /s′el′uː/ (Er) 'dripping'
fireann /f′er′əN′/ (Tm) 'male'

A further, if minor, point of interest is that the lowering before /d′/, /s′/ (/t′/, /l′/) does not take effect where there has been raising/lowering between low and mid-vowels, e.g. *goid* /gid′/ (M) 'steal' related to *gadaí* /gadiː/ 'thief' or *coise* /kis′ə/, comparative of *cas* /kas/ (Mk) 'twisted'.

It is interesting to note in passing that /e/ rather than /i/ often appears in borrowings, e.g.:

(26) *peictiúr* (C) 'picture'
peiliúr (C) 'pillow' (dialectal 'pillover')
poilseár /pel′s′eːr/ (→ /pail′s′eːr/) (Cn) 'pilchard'

Finally there is another variation between /u/ and a mid-vowel /o/ before /r/ which occurs in a limited number of words and must be marked in the lexicon. In three of the four examples in (27) an underlying /u/ is required for Munster and /o/ in Donegal and Connacht:

(27) *urchóid* /urəxoːd′/ (M) 'harm' : *orchóid* /orəxoːd′/ (D, C)
ursa /ursa/ (M) 'jamb' : *orsain* /orsən′/ (D, C)
urlár /urlaːr/ (→ /uːrlaːr/) (M) 'floor' : *orlár* /orLaːr/ → /oːrlaːr/ (Mo, D) [→ /aurlaːr/ (Cn, South Tipperary)]

urball /urəbaL/ (→ /rubəL/) (D, Mo) 'tail' : *orball* /orəbəL/ [→ /erʹəbəɫ/; see 4.2.2(ii)] (M)

3.4 Syllable lengthening before tense consonants

As was pointed out at the beginning of this chapter, it can be argued that vowels are lax or tense, but as tension is expressed as length, we have for convenience' sake spoken simply of length. These rules about to be discussed can be viewed as the spread of tension from a tense consonant, or a cluster which must be considered tense, to a preceding stressed vowel. The tension is in practice expressed as length. At this point in the derivation, all dialects still retain /R/ as well as /N/ and /L/.

Syllable lengthening is a cover-term for both vowel lengthening and diphthongization. This spread of tension to a preceding stressed short vowel is expressed either by vowel lengthening or diphthongization, depending both on the context and on the dialect. In this diphthongization a semi-vowel is required alongside the underlying stressed short vowel: a semi-vowel /j/ is placed before a slender consonant and a semi-vowel /w/ before a broad consonant. This normally results in the diphthongs /ai/ and /au/ and they are shown at this stage of the derivation in the examples given. However, in some Munster dialects, e.g. Muskerry and Ring, if a short mid-vowel follows a slender consonant it may be actually realized as /əi/ and if it follows a broad consonant as /ou/.

The most noteworthy difference between the dialects is the distribution of diphthongization. In Donegal and Mayo, the limited form of syllable lengthening is never implemented as diphthongization. In Connemara syllable lengthening is expressed as diphthongization only in the case of mid-vowels. Throughout Munster syllable lengthening takes the form of diphthongization in the case of low vowels and also, in the majority of contexts, of mid-vowels. The diphthongization is needed in Ring and Clare in words such as *iompar* /aumpər/ 'carry', *thimpeall* /hʹaimʹpʹəL/ 'around', *cill* /kʹaiLʹ/ 'graveyard'. This can be achieved by saying either that high vowels which require lengthening are also diphthongized or, as proposed in this work, that they have been previously lowered (see 3.3.6) and thus come under the general Munster rule of diphthongization.

Throughout the discussion of syllable lengthening neither the more surface change of /aː/ to /ɑː/ or of /a/ to /aː/ in Connemara (see 3.7.1) or the addition or removal of tension or other more surface rules affecting nasals and laterals [see 4.2.5(i)] are always shown in the example derivations.

There are three basic rules of syllable lengthening:

(a)   a short stressed vowel before a boundary
(b)   a short stressed vowel in a word of any shape
(c)   a short stressed vowel in a word of two or more syllables

3.4.1 Syllable lengthening 1
Here syllable lengthening occurs largely before consonants which are *originally* tense (/R(ʹ)/, /N(ʹ)/, /L(ʹ)/, /m(ʹ)/) rather than as a result of assimilation. However *ng* /ŋg(ʹ)/ must also be included. Examples are:

(28)   *barr* /baR/ → /baːR/ [→ /baːr/ → /bɑːr/ (Cn)] 'top'
       gann /gaN/ → /gɑːN/ (Cn) ~ /gaun/ (M) 'scarce'
       poll /poL/ → /pauL/ (C), /paul/ (Dn, Mk, Rg) 'hole'
       poill /peLʹ/ → /paiLʹ/ (Cn), /pailʹ/ (Dn, Mk, Rg) 'holes'
       im /imʹ/ → /iːmʹ/ (Cn, Dn, Mk) ~ /aimʹ/ (Rg, Cl) 'butter'
       cill /kʹiLʹ/ → /kʹiːLʹ/ (Cn), /kʹiːlʹ/ (Dn, Mk) ~ /kailʹ/ (Rg, Cl) 'churchyard'

In Mayo and Donegal the application of this rule is extremely restricted. For the most part it takes effect where there is a low vowel before /R/, e.g. *barr* 'top' or in certain districts of Donegal before /L/, e.g. *thall* /haːL/ (Gd) 'over there'.

In Connemara the rule is to some extent optional. Lengthening is not always required before *ng* /ŋg(ʹ)/; low vowels are excluded, as in *raing* /raŋʹgʹ/ 'rank' while high vowels present a choice as in:

(29)   *muing* /miŋʹgʹ/ ~ /miːŋʹgʹ/ (Cn) 'mane'
       long (/Loŋg/ →) /Luŋg/ ~ /Luːŋg/ 'ship'

There are also certain options before /m/. Vowel lengthening applies to low vowels in Connemara, as in *am* /am/ → /aːm/ (→ /ɑːm/) 'time' (but not in Inishmaan). The rule is optional in Connemara when /u/ is before /m/, e.g.:

(30)   *tom* (/tom/ →) /tum/ ~ /tuːm/ (Cn) 'bush'
       lom (/Lom/ →) /Lum/ ~ /Luːm/ (Cn) 'bare'

It must be noted, of course, that mid-vowels before nasals have previously been raised to high vowels, as seen in *long* 'ship' and *tom* 'bush' in (29-30).

50 *Modern Irish: grammatical structure and dialectal variation*

Furthermore, it is interesting to note that the application of the rule is in general optional at the eastern extremity of Cois Fhairrge.

In Munster, this syllable lengthening seems to be obligatory [with one notable exception *ann* /aːn/ ~ /ən/ (Dn, Rg) 'in it' depending on the sentence stress].

Finally, the question of morpheme boundaries must be touched on. In Munster, where there is a word boundary or a boundary before the verbal endings with an initial consonant, e.g. future *-f(a)idh* /həj/, conditional *-f(e)adh* /həγ/, autonomous *-t(e)ar* /tər/ etc., verbal adj. *-tha* /hə/, etc., the rule must take effect. Contrast examples (31) with (32) where the rule is required:

(31)   *bearradh* /bʹarə/ (Dn) 'shaving'
       bearrann /bʹarəN/ (Dn) 'shaves'
       bearraigh /bʹarəgʹ/ (Dn) 'shave' (imperative etc.)
(32)   *bearrfaidh sé* /bʹaːrhə/ (Dn) 'he will shave'
       bhearrfadh /vʹaːrhəx/ (Dn) 'would shave'
       bearrtar /bʹaːrtər/ (Dn) 'one shaves'
       bearrtha /bʹaːrhə/ (Dn) 'shaved'

There is, however, a tendency among younger speakers occasionally to retain the long syllable, throughout, particularly when it is diphthongized, e.g. *geallaim* /gʹaLəmʹ/(→ /gʹaləmʹ/) ~ /gʹauLəmʹ/ (→ /gʹauləmʹ/) 'I promise'.

In Connemara, while among older speakers the same types of boundaries as in Munster conditioned the rule, many speakers now apply the rule throughout the verbal inflection. In Inishmaan, the use of the long syllable, e.g. *milleann* /mʹiːLʹəN/ (rather than /mʹiLʹəN/) 'destroys', is the norm.

3.4.2 Syllable lengthening 2
In this case, irrespective of the shape of the word, syllables are lengthened before certain clusters which can be considered to be tense. There are four parts to the rule.

Firstly, a rule is necessary to lengthen a stressed short high vowel before /l/, (/r/) and a voiceless continuant (in practice: /lʹsʹ/ and occasionally /rʹsʹ/ and /lʹxʹ/):

(33)   *milse* /mʹilʹsə/ → /mʹiːlʹsʹə/ (Cn, Dn, Mk) ~ /mʹailʹsʹə/ (Rg, Cl)
       comp. of *milis* 'sweet'

soilse /sel′s′ə/ → /sail′s′ə/ (Cn, Rg, Cl) ~ /sil′s′ə/ → /si:l′s′ə/ (Dn, Mk) plural of *solas* 'light'
(*s*)*poilséar* /(s)pel′s′e:r/ → /(s)pail′s′e:r/ (Cn, Rg) 'pilchard'
geirseach /g′er′s′əx/ → /g′air′s′əx/ (~ /g′e:r′s′əx/) (Cf) 'small girl'
soilche /sel′x′ə/ → /sail′x′ə/ → /sail′əx′ə/ → /sail′i:/ (Cn), optional comparative of *salach* 'dirty'

Secondly, this rule must also lengthen a vowel before a voiced non-continuant followed by a liquid (in practice slender *br* /b′r′/ and *bl* /b′l′/):

(34) *oibre* /eb′r′ə/ → /aib′r′ə/ (Cn) gen. of *obair* 'work'
Oibreán /eb′r′a:n/ → /aib′r′a:n/ (→ /aib′r′ɑ:N/) (Cn) 'April'
oibliogáid /eb′l′əga:d′/ → /aib′l′əga:d′/ (Cn) 'obliging act'

Thirdly, this syllable lengthening is needed before a voiced consonant and a continuant (in practice /v′r′/, /v′N′/, /v′l′/):

(35) *geimhreadh* (/g′ev′r′əɣ/ →) /g′iv′r′əɣ/ → /g′i:v′r′əɣ/ (→ /g′i:v′r′ə/) (Cn) 'winter'
soibhre /sev′r′ə/ → /saiv′r′ə/ (Cn), comp. of *soibhir* 'rich'
(*Mac*) *Suibhne* /siv′N′ə/ → /si:v′N′ə/ (Cn) Surname
goibhne /gev′N′ə/ → /gaiv′N′ə/ (Cn) 'smiths'
coimhlint /kev′l′əN′t′/ → /kaiv′l′əN′t′/ (Cn) 'conflict'
oibhne /ev′N′ə/ → /aiv′N′ə/ (Cn) gen. of *abhainn* 'river'
oimhreas (see 3.3.3) /ev′r′əs/ → /aiv′r′əs/ (Cn) 'doubt'

Fourthly, the rule is required to lengthen any syllable containing a stressed short vowel before *r* followed by a voiced dental (i.e. *rl*, *rn*, *rd*):

(36) *bearna* /b′arNə/ → /b′a:rNə/ [→ /b′ɑ:rNə/ (Cn)] 'gap'
ard /ard/ → /a:rd/ [→ /ɑ:rd/ (Cn)] 'high'
tharlaigh /harLəj/ → /ha:rləj/ [→ /hɑ:rLə/ (Cn)] 'happened'
(*a*)*tornae* /torNe:/ → /taurNe:/ (Cn) 'lawyer'
ordó(i)g /ordo:g(′)/ → /o:rdo:g(′)/ (Dn, Mk) ~ /aurdo:g(′)/ 'thumb' (Cn, Rg, South Tipperary)
orlach /orləx/ → /o:rləx/ (M) ~ /aurLəx/ (Cn) 'inch'
bord /bord/ → /bo:rd/ (M) ~ /baurd/ (Cn) 'table'

In Connemara all four parts of the rule take effect. However, syllable lengthening before /rs/ is sporadic; it occurs in *geirseach* 'young girl' (both the underlying *girseach* /gʹirʹsʹəx/ and *geirseach* /gʹairʹsʹəx/ [~ /gʹeːrʹsʹəx/] are required in the dialect). Otherwise, *fairsing* 'extensive', *doirse* 'doors', *tuirseach* 'tired' etc. have no lengthening. Furthermore, it should be noticed that syllable lengthening in the case of mid-vowels is implemented as diphthongization in each part of the rule.

In Munster, all four parts of the rule apply excepting the second part. In other words, *oibre*, gen. of *obair* 'work' is /ebʹrʹə/ (→ /ibʹərʹə/). As far as the first part of the rule is concerned, there is also a hesitation here with regard to lengthening before /rs/. Although this lengthening is a minor rule in Munster it has a wider scope than in Connacht, e.g.:

(37)   *doirse* /doːrsʹə/ (M) 'doors'
        thairsi /haːrsʹə/ (M) 'over her'
        tairseach /taːrsʹəx/ (M) 'threshold'

There is, however, no lengthening needed for:

(38)   *tuirse* /tirsʹə/ 'tiredness'
        fairsing /farsʹəg/ (Mk) 'extensive'

It should be observed that the second part of the rule is quite regular in Munster, although, of course the /vʹ/ is subsequently lost:

(39)   *geimhreadh* (/gʹevʹrʹəɣ/ →) /gʹivʹrʹəɣ/ → /gʹiːrʹəɣ/ (→ /gʹiːrə/ (M)) 'winter'
        goibhne /gevʹnʹə/ → /gəivʹnʹə/ → /gəinʹə/ (→ /gəiŋʹiː/ (Mk)) 'smiths'

In the fourth part of the rule syllable lengthening is normally implemented as vowel lengthening rather than by the diphthongization required under these syllable lengthening rules in Connemara, e.g. *bord* /boːrd/ (M) beside /baurd/ (Cn) 'table'. There are, however, some cases of diphthongization in Ring and South Tipperary, e.g. *ordóg* /aurdoːg/ 'thumb'.

Finally, there is a lengthening peculiar to Ring before /hr/:

(40)   *ceathrú* /kʹaːhruː/ (→ /kʹaːˈrhuː/) (Rg) 'quarter'
        athrú /aːhruː/ (→ /aːˈrhuː/) (Rg) 'change'

This syllable lengthening must be applied prior to the metathesis because length is a condition required for metathesis (see 4.2.6).

In Donegal and Mayo, this lengthening is extremely limited; only the third part of the rule applies and even then only to a low vowel (i.e. /a/), e.g. *tairne* /taːrnʲˊə/ (Gd) 'nail', *cairde* /kaːrdˊə/ 'friends', *bearnaidh* /bˊaːrNiː/ (Gd) 'gap'.

3.4.3 Syllable lengthening 3

In this case a short syllable becomes long in either of two contexts. Firstly, before a voiced plosive followed by a liquid (in practice /gl/, /gr/, /d(ˊ)r(ˊ)/) as in the following examples:

(41)   *eaglais* /agləsˊ/ → /aːgləsˊ/ (→ /aːgLəsˊ/) (Cn) 'church'
        eagla /aglə/ → /aːglə/ (→ /aːgLə/) (Cn) 'fear'
        freagra /fˊrˊagrə/ → /fˊrˊaːgrə/ (→ /fˊrˊaːgrə/) (Cn) 'answer'
        madraí /madriː/ → /maːdriː/ (→ /maːdriː/) (Cn) 'dogs'
        paidrín /padˊrˊiːnˊ/ → /paːdˊrˊiːnˊ/ (→ /paːdˊrˊiːnˊ/) (Cn) 'rosary'

Secondly, a short syllable must be lengthened before a nasal followed by any consonant as in the following examples:

(42)   *muintir* /miNˊtˊərˊ/ → /miːNˊtˊərˊ/ (Cn), /miːnˊtˊərˊ/ (Ky, Mk)
        ~ /mainˊtˊərˊ/ (Rg) 'people'
        timpiste /tˊimˊpˊəsˊtˊə/ → /tˊiːmˊpˊəstˊə/ (Cn) 'accident'
        imleacán /imˊlˊəkaːn/ → /iːmˊlˊəkaːn/ (→ /iːmˊlˊəkaːN/) (Cn) 'navel'
        anró /aNroː/ → /aːNroː/ (D) [→ /aːNroː/ (Cn)] ~ /aunroː/ [→ /auˊroː/ (M)] 'hardship'
        teampall /tˊampəL/ → /tˊaːmpəL/ (D) [→ /tˊaːmpəL/ (Cn)] ~ /tˊaumpəl/ (M) 'Protestant church'
        brionglóidí /bˊrˊingloːdˊiː/ → /bˊrˊiːngloːdˊiː/ (Cn) 'dreaming'
        ingne /iŋˊgˊrˊə/ → /iːŋˊgˊrˊə/ (Cf) '(finger/toe) nails'
        condae /koNdeː/ → /kaundeː/ (Dn) ~ → /kuNdeː/ → /kuːNdeː/ (Cn) 'county'

In Connemara, the first part of the rule may be obligatory while the second part would seem to be optional. (In Inishmaan, the entire rule is obligatory - although some younger speakers retain a short vowel in *freagra* and *eaglais*, possibly due to schooling.) There are, however, some restrictions on the second part of the rule. First of all, it will not apply in certain words which must in some way still be marked as loan-words, e.g.:

54 *Modern Irish: grammatical structure and dialectal variation*

(43) *pionta* /pʹiNtə/ (Cn) 'pint'
 prionda /pʹrʹiNdə/ (Cn) 'print'
 prindéara /pʹrʹiNʹdʹeːrə/ (Cn) 'printer'
 tincéara /tʹiŋʹkʹeːrə/ (Cn) 'tinker'
 lampa /Lampə/ (→ /Laːmpə/) (Cn) 'lamp'

Another restriction is that apart from the case of *mp* and *nr*, e.g. *anró* 'hardship', *teampall* 'Protestant church', only high vowels (i.e. /i/, /u/) are lengthened, as in *muintir* 'people' or *condae* 'county' in (42) or in:

(44) *intinn* /iNʹtʹəNʹ/ ~ /iːNʹtʹəNʹ/ (Cn) 'mind'
 ionlach /iNLəx/ ~ /iːNLəx/ (Cn) 'spreading ground (for turf etc.)'
 unsa /uNsa/ ~ /uːNsa/ (Cn) 'ounce'
 cuntas /kuNtəs/ ~ /kuːNtəs/ (Cn) 'account'

It should also be noted that syllable lengthening is required before /ŋʹgʹ/ only when followed by a liquid as in *brionglóidí* 'dreaming', *ingne* 'nails' in (42) but not, for example, in:

(45) *ionga* /uŋgə/ (Cn) '(finger/toe) nail'
 loinge /Liŋʹgə/ (Cn) gen. of *long* 'ship'

A morpheme boundary may affect the situation. The rule does not apply at certain boundaries unless there is an underlying *nn* /N(ʹ)/ rather than *n* /n(ʹ)/ [for the change /nʹ/ → /Nʹ/ before /tʹ/ see 4.2.5(i)]:

(46) *mionta* (/mʹintə/ →) /mʹiNtə/ 'fragmented' (Cn) : *feannta* /fʹɑːNtə/ (Cn) 'flayed'
 cionta (/kʹintə/ →) /kʹiNtə/ (Cn) 'fault(s)'
 croinnte /kri(ː)Nʹtʹə/ (Cn) 'trees'

Finally, an optional minor rule is necessary, in Cois Fhairrge at least, to introduce a diphthong in the case of a low vowel in a small group of words:

(47) *caint* /kaNʹtʹ/ (→ /kaːNʹtʹ/) ~ /kaiNʹtʹ/ (Cf) 'talk'
 slainte /sLaNʹtʹə/ (→ /sLaːNʹtʹə/) ~ /slaiNʹtʹə/ (Cf) 'health'
 baint /baNʹtʹ/ (→ /baːNʹtʹ/) ~ /baiNʹtʹ/ (Cf) 'take with force'
 aimsir /amʹsʹərʹ/ (→ /æːmʹsʹərʹ/) ~ /aimʹsʹərʹ/ 'weather'

Syllable lengthening before tense consonants 55

Since in Munster syllable lengthening in the case of low vowels is implemented as diphthongization, these nouns are all obligatorily diphthongized [see (48)]. This means that we are dealing here with what is in Munster a major rule which is only needed in Cois Fhairrge as an optional minor rule (i.e. affecting a limited number of words of this shape).

In Munster the first part of the rule does not apply and the cluster is normally split up by the second epenthetic vowel, e.g. *eagla* /agələ/ 'fear' (see 2.4) while the second part of the rule applies and it is obligatory:

(48) *iompar* (/ompər/ →) /umpər/ → /uːmpər/ (Ky, Mk) ~ /aumpər/ (Rg, Cl) 'carry'
insint /inˊsˊənˊtˊ/ → /iːnˊsˊənˊtˊ/ (Ky, Mk) ~ /ainˊsˊənˊtˊ/ (Rg, Cl) 'tell'
tuincéir /tiːnˊkˊeːrˊ/ (Dn) 'tinker'
piont /pˊuːnt/ (Ky, Mk) 'pint'
bronntanas /brontənəs/ → /brauntənəs/ (M) 'gift'
lampa /Lampə/ → /Laumpə/ (M) 'lamp'
bambairne /bambərˊnˊə/ → /baumbərˊnˊə/ (Dn) 'lout'
ancaire /aŋkərˊə/ → /auŋkərˊə/ (M) 'anchor'
caint /kanˊtˊ/ → /kainˊtˊ/ (M) 'talk'
aimsir /amˊsˊərˊ/ → /aimˊsˊərˊ/ (M) 'weather'
saint /sanˊtˊ/ → /sainˊtˊ/ (M) 'greed'
baintreach /banˊtˊrˊəx/ → /bainˊtˊrˊəx/ 'widow'

However, a short vowel is not lengthened before *m* /m/ which is followed by another nasal or liquid, as such a group is generally split up by a secondary epenthetic vowel (see 2.4):

(49) *simné* /sˊimˊəˈnˊeː/ (M) 'chimney'
imleacán /imˊəlˊəkaːn/ (M) 'navel'
seamróg /sˊamˊəˈroːg/ (M) 'shamrock'

Similarly, syllable lengthening is not required before /ŋˊ/ followed by a liquid, as the cluster will already have a secondary epenthetic vowel:

(50) *ingneach* /iŋˊənˊəx/ (Mk) 'taloned'
briongloid /bˊrˊuŋəˈloːdˊ/ (Mk) 'uneasiness'

Also as in Connemara, there may be no lengthening, or optional lengthening before certain morpheme bounderies where there is a basic /n/ (rather than /N/):

(51)   *cionta* /k´untə/ (Mk) 'fault(s)'
        ciontach /k´untəx/ (Mk) ~ /k´uːntəx/ (Mk, Dn) 'guilty'

In Donegal only the second part of the rule is required and it seems that it will affect only low vowels before *nr*, *mp*, e.g.:

(52)   *scannradh* /skaːnruː/ (Tn, Mn) [→ /skæːruː/ (Gd)] 'scaring'
        anraith /aːnri/ (Mn) 'broth'
        teampall /t´aːmpəL/ (Mn, Tn) 'Protestant church'

Syllable lengthening does not seem to be required for Mayo.

3.5 Diphthongization

There are three rules here regarding diphthongization. This diphthongization is not conditioned by tense consonants or clusters and must therefore be regarded as unconnected with the diphthongization which was described under syllable lengthening in 3.4.

3.5.1 Optional diphthongization before ch/th /h/

A diphthong optionally applies before /h/ in certain words in Connacht (and to an extent in Donegal):

(53)   *meitheal* /m´ehəl/ (→ /m´eːL/) (Cf) ~ /m´aihəl/ (→ /m´aiL/) (Cf) 'working party'
        soitheach /sehəx/ → /seːəx/ → /seːx/ (Cf, Tn) ~ /saihəx/ (Mn) → /saix/ (Cf) 'vessel'

3.5.2 Diphthongization of /iː/ before the stress

A second rule is required to diphthongize /iː/ following broad consonants before the stress:

(54)   *maothán* (/mɯːˈhaːn/) → /miːˈhaːn/ → /məiˈhaːn/ (Mk) 'flank'
        caorán (/kɯːˈraːn/) → /kiːˈraːn/ → /kəiˈraːn/ (Mk) 'clod'
        taoscán (/tɯːsˈkaːn/) → /tiːsˈkaːn/ → /təisˈkaːn/ (Mk) 'draught'
        taobhán (/tɯːˈwaːn/) → /tiːˈwaːn/ → /təiˈwaːn/ 'purlin'

duibheagán (/div´ə'ga:n/ → /dijə'ga:n/ →) /di:'ga:n/ → /dəi'ga:n/ (Mk) 'abyss'
duibhré (/div´'r´e:/ → /dij'r´e:/) → /di:'r´e:/ → /dəi'r´e:/ (Mk) 'the dark of the moon'

This seems to be a major rule in Muskerry. (For an overall picture of the variation in *caorán* see Wagner 1958:170.) The rule operates subsequent both to the development of semi-vowels and to Stress-shift 2 (see 2.8.3). It appears as a minor rule in Dunquin in, e.g., (*n*)*aomhóg* (/n/)/əi'wo:g/ ~ (/n/)/e:'wo:g/ (Dn) 'coracle'.

3.5.3 Sporadic diphthongization of *é* /e:/

A diphthong is required for stressed *é* /e:/ in a limited number of words varying from dialect to dialect. There are more examples from Munster than from the other dialects:

(55) *féire* /fe:r´ə/ → /f´air´ə/ (Dn, Mk) 'pair'
 péileacán /p´e:l´əka:n/ → /p´ail´əka:n/ (Dn, Mk) 'butterfly'
 déileáil /d´e:'l´a:l´/ → /d´ai'l´a:l´/ (Dn, Mk) 'dealing'
 éist /e:s´t´/ → /ais´t´/ (Rg) 'listen'

The *é* /e:/ is stressed in all of the examples in (55). However, where the third syllable is stressed the diphthongization is still required, e.g. /p´ail´ə'kan/ [see 2.8.3(i) and Wagner 1958:212]. The picture is more varied in the case of *éirí* 'rising' and *téann* 'goes'

(56) *éirí* /e:r´i:/ (Er) : /air´i:/ (Cn, M) : /i:r´i:/ (Gd) 'rising'
 téann /t´e:N/ (Ky, Mk, D) : /t´aiN/ (Cn, Rg) 'goes'

3.6 The vowel /ɯ:/

In order to allow for the various pronunciations of words such as *saor* 'free', *saoire* 'holiday', it is easiest to begin with /ɯ:/ in the underlying form. In this way the various pronunciations can be accounted for by three rules.

3.6.1 The vowel *ao* /ɯ:/ changed to /i:/

In Connacht and in most of Donegal /ɯ:/ becomes /i:/, e.g.:

(57) *saor* /sɯ:r/ → /si:r/ (C, Gd) 'free'
 saoire /sɯ:r´ə/ → /si:r´ə/ 'holiday'

However, in certain areas of Donegal the rule does not apply when /ɯː/ comes before a broad consonant, e.g.:

(58)   saor /sɯːr/ (Rf) 'free'
         saoire /siːr′ə/ (Rf) 'holiday'

In Muskerry, and more sporadically in Dunquin, /ɯː/ becomes /iː/ (which ultimately becomes /əi/ [see 3.5.2]) in disyllabic words where the second syllable is long, e.g.:

(59)   maothán /mɯːˈhaːn/ → /miːˈhaːn/ → /məiˈhaːn/ (Mk) 'flank'

3.6.2 The vowel *ao* /ɯː/ changed to /eː/
The vowel /ɯː/ becomes /eː/ preceding a broad consonant or a word boundary. Examples are:

(60)   saor /sɯːr/ → /seːr/ 'free'
         saoghail /sɯːɣəl′/ → /seːɣəl′/ (→ /seːl′/) gen. of *saoghal* 'life'
         faoi /fɯː/ → /feː/ (→ /f′eː/) 'under'

This Munster rule must operate prior to /ɯ/ becoming /iː/, so /ɯ/ remaining before a slender consonant is then changed to /iː/.

3.6.3 The vowel *ao* /ɯː/ changed to /uː/ or /oː/
A rule converting /ɯː/ to /uː/ or /oː/ is required for a very limited number of words, e.g.

(61)   maothán /mɯːhaːn/ → /muːhan/ (→ /muːṉ/) (Cf) 'earlobe' : /məiˈhaːn/ (Mk)
         caonach /kɯːnəx/ → /kuːnəx/ (Rg) 'moss' : /kiːnəx/ (Cf), /keːnəx/ (Dn)
         faoi /fɯː/ → /feː/ (→ /f′eː/) (M), /fiː/ (C, Gd) 'under' : *fúm* /fuːm/ (C, M) 'under me'

For the full range of variants for *caonach* 'moss' see Wagner 1958:300. Examples with /oː/ rather than /uː/ are:

(62)   saonta(í) /sɯːntə/ → /seːntiː/ (Mk) 'shy' : /soːṉtax/ (Mn) [→ /suːṉtə/ (Cn)] 'naive'

sraoth /srɯː/ → /sriː/ (Cn) 'sneeze' : /sroː/ (Tm)
draoibeáilte /drˠɯːbˠaːlʹtʹə/ → /driːbaːlʹtʹə/ (Cf) 'bespattered' : /droːbaːlʹtʹə/ (Rm)
daothaint /deːhʹənʹtʹ/ ~ /doːhənʹtʹ/ (Rg) 'enough'

3.7 Low vowels

Apart from raising/lowering or lengthening or/and diphthongization there are other developments of low vowels in the different dialects. We are concerned here with three rules.

3.7.1 Treatment of low vowels in Connemara

In Connemara any /a/ which remains after syllable lengthening, irrespective of the context, now becomes long:

(63) *bainne* /baNʹə/ → /baːNʹə/ 'milk'
 asal /asəL/ → /aːsəL/ 'donkey'

At that point, there develops a three-way division of low vowels; original long vowels and those which have become long due to lengthening from tense consonants or clusters now appear as /aː/ as exemplified in (64), all other low vowels have the value /æː/ if preceded by a slender consonant, by /t/, /d/, /s/, /r/ or /h/ or by a word boundary as exemplified in (65); otherwise they will appear as /aː/ as shown in (66):

(64) *bád* /baːd/ 'boat'
 peann /pʹaːN/ 'pen'
 bearna /bʹaːrNə/ 'gap'
(65) *cead* /kʹæːd/ 'permission'
 peain /pʹæːnʹ/ 'pan'
 ais /æːsʹ/ 'back'
 tais /tæːsʹ/ 'damp'
 dair /dæːrʹ/ 'oak'
 saicín /sæːkʹiːnʹ/ 'small sack'
 raithneach /ræːnʹəx/ 'fern'
 haitín /hæːtʹiːnʹ/ 'small hat'
(66) *cas* /kaːs/ 'turn'
 bainne /baːNʹə/ 'milk'
 Gaillimh /gaːLʹə/ 'Galway'

60 *Modern Irish: grammatical structure and dialectal variation*

The change of /a/ to /aː/ must precede vowel coalescence (see 2.6) in order to give the sequence *athair* /ahərʹ/ → /aːərʹ/ → /aːrʹ/ → /æːrʹ/ 'father'. Otherwise, the lengthening in place of *h* (see 2.7) would cause *athair* to be pronounced as /ɑːrʹ/.

3.7.2 Treatment of long *a* /aː/ in Donegal

In Donegal /aː/ is most often realized as /æː/, as in, e.g., *áit* /æːtʹ/ 'place'. The environment in which this change takes place varies from one local dialect to another. In the eastern area of Gweedore, for instance, the rule has effect before any slender consonant except a tense nasal or liquid. This yields examples such as:

(67) *páiste* /pæːsʹtʹə/ (Gd) 'child'
      sáile /sæːlʹə/ (Gd) 'brine'
      Spáinn /spaːnʹ/ (Gd) 'Spain'

Furthermore, an original stressed /aː/ is often realized as /a/ before /h/:

(68) *máthair* /mahərʹ/ (Gd) 'mother'
      áthas /ahəs/ (Gd) 'joy'
      snáthad /snahəd/ (Gd) 'needle'

While this is widespread in the case of /aː/, it is probably part of a more general tendency to shorten original long stressed vowels before /h/.

3.7.3 Shortening of long *a* /aː/ before *mh* /w̃/ in Kerry

There is a rule needed for Kerry to change stressed /aː/ to /a/ before *mh* (see O'Rahilly 1940-2:119-27). The long *ámha* subsequently yields /aː/ and the short *amha* yields /au/ (see 4.1.3). The following examples contrast the Muskerry forms with those of Dunquin where the rule operates:

(69) *lámhach* /Laːwəx/ → /laːx/ (Mk) 'shot' : *lamhach* /laux/ (Dn)
      lámhacán /Laːwəkaːn/ → /laːkaːn/ (Mk) 'creeping' : *lamhacán* /laukaːn/ (→ /lauŋkaːn/) (Dn)
      lámhanán /Laːwənaːn/ → /laːnaːn/ (Mk) 'bladder' : *lamhanán* /launaːn/ (Dn)
      rámhann /raːwəN/ → /raːn/ (Mk) 'spade' : *ramhann* /raun/ (Dn)

The stress on the first syllable in *lámhacán* 'creeping' and *lamhanán* 'bladder' is because Stress-shift 2 (see 2.8.3) must be applied prior to this rule and to the removal of the middle syllable due to rules which affect the semi-vowel /w/ (see 4.1.3).

This rule may be required as a minor rule outside of West Munster, e.g. *námhaid* /**naud´**/ (Mk) 'enemy'. Furthermore a variant with *o* occurs in *nomhaid* (Rg) which, due to raising of /o/ to /u/ before the nasal /w̃/ and due to the effect of subsequent rules which apply to the semi-vowel, will result in /nuːd´/ (Rg).

3.8 Falling diphthongs

The two falling diphthongs /iːə/ and /uːə/ are the only case where a neutral vowel survives following another vocalic element. Notwithstanding, there are various tendencies which militate against the retention of these diphthongs. Yet despite this, a new diphthong /iːa/ is introduced. There are eight rules involved here.

3.8.1 Elision of second element before a nasal

The second element in the diphthongs /iːə/ and /uːə/ is frequently elided before a nasal:

(70)　*scian* /s´k´iːən/ (M) → /s´k´in/ (D) → /s´k´iːN/ (Cf) 'knife'
　　　móisiam /moːs´iəm/ (Mn) → /muːs´iːəm/ → /muːs´iːm/ (Cn) 'upset'
　　　ruainne /ruəN´ə/ → /ruːN´ə/ (C) 'shred'
　　　mian /m´iːən/ → /m´iːN/ (Cf) 'desire'
　　　gruaim /gruːəm´/ → /gruːm´/ (Cf) 'gloom'

Occasionally this reduction is also found following a nasal or before a /h/ in Connacht (except Cois Fhairrge where /h/ is removed):

(71)　*nua* /Nuːə/ → /Nuː/ (C) [→ /nuː/ (Rg)] 'new'
　　　snua /sNuːə/ → /sNuː/ (C) 'complexion'
　　　sciathán /s´k´iːəhaːN/ → /s´k´iːhaːN/ (→ /s´k´iːɑːN/) (Cf) 'wing'

For the full range of variants for *nua* see Wagner 1958:78.

This rule is mainly found in Connacht and Donegal. It is a minor rule. It is impossible to predict that in Cois Fhairrge, for instance, *pian* /p´iːəN/ 'pain' retains the diphthong but not *scian* 'knife'. Moreover, there is great variation from dialect to dialect as regards the words which are affected.

3.8.2 Change of diphthong *ia* /iə/ to *é* /e:/
The diphthong /i:ə/ remains before a slender consonant in extremely few words, e.g.:

(72)   *Briain* /bʹrʹi:ənʹ/ (gen. of man's name *Brian*)
       bliain /bʹlʹi:ənʹ/ 'year'
       riail /ri:əlʹ/ 'rule'

Normally in all dialects /i:ə/ becomes /e:/ before a palatalized consonant:

(73)   *ciall* /kʹiəL/ 'sense' gen. *céille* /kʹe:Lʹə/ [→ /kʹe:lʹə/ (M)]
       cliabh /kʹlʹi:əw/ 'pannier basket' gen. *cléibhe* /kʹlʹe:vʹə/
       grian /gʹrʹi:ən/ 'sun' gen. *gréine* /gʹrʹe:nʹə/ [→ /gʹrʹe:Nʹə/ (Gd)]
       iasc /i:əsk/ 'fish' gen. *éisc* /e:sʹkʹ/

3.8.3 Change of *é* /e:/ to /i:a/
This major rule is a Munster rule by which stressed /e:/ is changed to the new diphthong /i:a/ (or /i:ə/ in, for example, Clear Island) between a palatalized consonant or word boundary and a non-palatalized consonant:

(74)   *méar* /mʹe:r/ → /mʹi:ar/ 'finger'
       éan /e:n/ → /i:an/ 'bird'

This change is not normally required in unstressed syllables although it occurs sporadically in Muskerry (often in words marked as loan-words or in poetry) and is apparently optional in some Munster dialects, e.g. *séipéal* /sʹe:pʹe:l/ ~ /sʹe:pʹial/ (Rg) 'chapel'.

It also features sporadically as a minor rule in other dialects, e.g.:

(75)   *scéal* /sʹkʹial/ (Gd) 'story'
       céanna /kʹiaNə/ (Gd) 'same'

3.8.4 Elision of second element after removal of *dh/gh* /ɣ/
There is a rule in Connemara (and Donegal) which elides the neutral vowel in the diphthongs /i:ə/ and /u:ə/ before a following long vowel after the removal of /ɣ/:

(76)   *ruadhóig* /ru:əo:gʹ/ → /ru:o:gʹ/ (Cn) 'wax end'
       cruadhóig /kru:əo:gʹ/ → /kru:o:gʹ/ (Cn) 'urgency'

Falling diphthongs 63

In an example such as *cruadhóig* 'urgency' the obvious derivation from *cruaidh* 'hard' justifies the /ɣ/ in the underlying form which is changed to /w/ and is subsequently removed. The combination *uaó* is apparently not allowed and must be solved either by the removal of the second element of the diphthong as exemplified in (76) or by the removal of the following long vowel as in the alternative pronunciations illustrated in (77):

(77) *ruadhóig* /ruːəoːgʹ/ → /ruːəgʹ/ (Cf, Mn) 'wax end'
 cruadhóig /kruːəoːgʹ/ → /kruːəgʹ/ (Cf) 'urgency'

In a somewhat similar fashion /iːaː/ is reduced to /iːa/ in Munster:

(78) *fíáin* /fʹiːɑːnʹ/ (C) → /fiːæːnʹ/ (D) 'wild' : /fʹiːanʹ/ (M)
 lián /LʹiːɑːN/ (C) 'trowel' : /lʹiːan/ (M)
 triáil /triːɑːlʹ/ (C) 'trial' : /tʹrʹiːalʹ/ (M)

3.8.5 Change of *ua* /uːə/ to /ɯːə/ or /iːə/

There are some further rules of lesser importance which affect the diphthongs /iːə/, /uːə/. One such rule is the development of /ɯːə/ from /uːə/ in certain Donegal dialects. This is needed following a labial consonant or glide (/b/, /f/, /w/) and may be regarded as dissimilation in the feature of rounding. Examples are:

(79) *bualadh* /bɯːəlu/ → /biːəlu/ (Gd) 'hitting'
 fuáil /fɯːəlʹ/ → /fiːəlʹ/ (Gd) 'sewing'
 uaim /ɯːəmʹ/ → /wiːəmʹ/ (Gd) 'from me'

3.8.6 Insertion of semi-vowel /w/

Another is the insertion of semi-vowel /w/, with the subsequent removal of /iː/ or /uː/ in certain words, e.g.:

(80) *uaim* /uːəmʹ/ → /wuːəmʹ/ → /wemʹ/ (Cn) 'from me'
 uabhar /uːəwər/ → /wuːəwər/ → /wəuər/ (Er) 'romping'

Yet another rule turns /uːə/ into /əi/ before the stress in Muskerry and Ring, e.g. *Ruairí* /rəiʹrʹiː/ (Mk, Rg) 'man's name'.

3.8.7 Variation between *ua* /uːə/ and *ó* /oː/

An interchange of *ua* /uːə/ and *ó* /oː/ must be allowed for in certain words:

(81)   *muar* (M) 'big' : *mór* (C, D)
       fuagra (C, D) 'notice' : *fógra* (M)
       cnuasach [→ *cruasach* (C, D)] 'collection' : *cnósach* (Mk)

Although *muar* 'big' is found throughout Munster, *mór* is occasionally found in verse in, e.g., Muskerry.
   This interchange occurs also when the /uːə/ is not stressed, e.g. *comhlódar* (Cf) 'company' beside *cluadar* (Tn) with Stress-shift 1 (see 2.8.2). The interchange is also found after the development of the semi-vowels, e.g. *amhrán* /oːraːn/ 'song' (Tn) beside /uəraːn/ (Gd).

3.8.8 Variation between *ia* /iːə/ and *ea* /a/
An interchange of *ia* /iː/ and *ea* /a/ must be treated in a few words:

(82)   *ciaró(i)g* (M, C) 'beetle' : *cearóg* (Gd)
        diabhal [see 4.1.4(ii)] (D, M) 'devil' : *deabhal* (C)

3.9 Prevocalic glide

There are certain cases where the assimilation of palatalization by the normal rules which apply to this phenomenon are insufficient to explain the situation. If we take, for example, *an t-eolas* /ə(n) t′oːləs/ 'the knowledge', or *t'eochair* /t′oxər′/ (Cf) 'your key', there is no way of accounting for the external sandhi which results in /t′/ when at the outset there are only the two elements /ə(n) t/ and /oːləs/, /tə/ and /oxər′/. One method of dealing with this problem is to allow for a theoretical diphthong. This means a theoretical /u/ is prefixed to front vowels as exemplified in (83) and a theoretical /i/ is prefixed to back vowels as exemplified in (84):

(83)   *uisce* /uis′k′ə/ → /is′k′ə/ 'water'
        oiread /uer′əd/ → /er′əd/ 'amount'
        aer /ueːr/ → /eːr/ 'air'
(84)   *easbog* /iasbəg/ → /asbəg/ 'bishop'
        eochair /ioxər′/ → /oxər′/ 'key'
        eolas /ioːləs/ → /oːləs/ 'knowledge'

The actual height of the first element of the diphthong is of no importance. Once the palatalization is assimilated (*an t-iomlán* /ə(n) tiumlaːn/ → /ə(n) t′iumlaːn/ 'the whole') the prefixed glide is then no longer required. Any variation can be explained by different ordering of the rules; for instance the pronunciation /ə(n) tumlaːn/ would be accounted for by the fact that the glide was removed prior to the assimilation of palatalization. (For another treatment in terms of autosegmental phonology see Gussmann 1986.)

It is noteworthy that there are further traces of this first element in sporadic examples such as *de eallach* /gə jˈaʟəx/ (Er) 'of cattle'.

4 *The semi-vowel and consonant systems*

4.1 Semi-vowels

Some sounds in Irish have a very limited usage in actual pronunciation. A good example is the fact that /ɣ/ is needed only initially in Irish (as opposed to Scottish Gaelic where it is found non-initially). Another example is the fact that while slender *dh/gh* /j/ and slender *ch* /x'/ are found initially in all dialects, only in Donegal and Connacht are slender *dh/gh* /j/ and slender *c h* /x'/ necessary medially. Yet despite the restricted occurrence of such sounds in actual pronunciation, an underlying broad *dh/gh* /ɣ/, slender *dh/gh* /j/, broad *bh* /w/ and broad *mh* /w̃/ are required in order to explain the relationship which exists between certain forms.

4.1.1 Slender fricatives

Here the conversion of a semi-vowel slender *ch* /x'/ or slender *bh/mh* /ṽ'/ to /j/ is our main concern; but the further change *dh/gh* /j/ to /g'/ is also discussed.

4.1.1(i) *Treatment of slender* **ch** /x'/ *and slender* **dh/gh** /j/. The various developments of slender *ch* /x'/ and slender *dh/gh* /j/ in the major dialects are illustrated in Table 4.1.

In summary it can be said that slender *ch* /x'/ either must be preserved as in *cloiche* /klox'ə/ (D, Mo) or be changed to /h/ as in *cloiche* /klohə/ (M) or be changed to /j/ following an unstressed vowel. Conversely, slender *dh/gh* /j/ is changed to slender *ch* /x'/ as in *cruaidh* /kruːəx'/ (Mo).

It must be pointed out that, although the convention in Irish is to spell the plural of *éadach* 'cloth' as *éadaighe* (or more recently *éadaí*), from a morphological point of view, we are dealing with a plural formed by slendering with the addition of the vowel *-e* /ə/ (see 7.3.2), i.e. *éadaiche* (→ /eːdiː/). [The addition of an underlying /ə/ is necessary to allow for the difference between, for instance *éadach* 'cloth', plural /eːdiː/ and *bromach* 'colt', plural /bruməə/ (Cf).] Similarly, although the genitive of *bealach* 'way' is

68   *Modern Irish: grammatical structure and dialectal variation*

conventionally spelt *bealaigh*, showing the slender *gh* /j/, this is morphologically a case of a genitive formed by slendering [see 6.3.1(i)]. There are one or two noteworthy exceptions to the general rules as shown in Table 4.1. For instance in the genitive of *teach* (M, C) 'house', which is based on *tighe* (M, C) (now conventionally spelt *tí*), slender *ch* /xʲ/ is changed to /j/ rather than /h/, i.e. /tʲixʲə/ → /tʲijə/ (→ /tʲiː/).

Table 4.1 *Treatment of slender* ch /xʲ/ *and slender* dh/gh /j/ *in major dialects*

Dialect	After a short stressed vowel	After a long stressed vowel	After /ə/	Unstressed word final position
	cloiche gen. of *cloch* 'stone'	*cruaidh* 'hard'	*éadaighe* 'clothes'	*bealaigh*, gen. of *bealach* 'way'
Donegal	/kʟoxʲə/	/kruːəj/	/j/ /eːdəjə/ (→ /eːdiː/)	/j/ /bʲaləj/ (→ /bʲaliː/)
Mayo	/kʟoxʲə/	/xʲ/ /kruːəxʲ/ (except after /iː/ *fraoich* /j/ /friːj/ (→/friː/))	/j/ /eːdəjə/ (→ /eːdiː/)	/j/ /bʲaləj/ (→ /bʲaliː/)
Cois Fhairrge	/h/ /kʟohə/ (→ /kʟoː/)	/kruːəj/ (→ /kruːə/)	/j/ /eːdəjə/ (→ /eːdiː/)	/j/ /bʲaləj/ (→ /bʲalə/)
Munster	/h/ /kʟohə/	/kruːəj/ (→ /kruːəgʲ/)	/j/ /eːdəjə/ (→ /eːdiː/)	/j/ /bʲaləj/ (→ /bʲaləgʲ/)

4.1.1(ii) *Interchange between slender* **dh/gh** /j/ *and slender* **g** /gʲ/. There is a major rule in Munster which changes slender *dh/gh* /j/ to /gʲ/, e.g.:

(1)   *cruaidh* /kruːəj/ → /kruːəgʲ/ 'hard'
       d'éirigh (Seán) /dʲairʲəj/ → /dʲairʲəgʲ/ (M) '(Seán) got up'

However, between a finite verbal form and a pronoun subject, the rule does not take effect:

(2)   *d'éirigh sé* /dʲairʲəj/ (→ /dʲairʲə/) 'he got up'

Two grades of word boundary need to be distinguished and for convenience the boundary between the finite verbal form and a pronoun subject might be

Semi-vowels 69

labelled a 'weak' word boundary as opposed to a 'strong' boundary where no subject pronoun follows.

There are sporadic examples of this rule in other dialects, e.g. *Seoighe* 'Surname' as /sˈoːgˈə/ (Cn).

4.1.1(iii) *Development of slender* **bh/mh** /ṽʲ/. The various treatments of slender *bh/mh* /ṽʲ/ are illustrated in Table 4.2.

Table 4.2 *Treatment of slender* bh/mh /ṽʲ/ *in major dialects*

Dialect	After short stressed vowel	After /ə/ (non-final)	Unstressed word final position	Before consonant (except /s/)
	nimhe gen. of *nimh* 'poison'	*gainimhe* gen. of *gaineamh*, *Gaillimhe* gen. of *Gaillimh* 'Galway'	*gaineamh/ gainimh* 'sand'	*nimhneach* 'poisonous' (*nimhneas* 'poisonousness')
Donegal	/Nʲivˈə/		/ganˈavˈ/ (Mn, Gd)	/Nʲivˈnˈəx/ (→ /NʲivˈNʲəx/)
Mayo	/Nʲivˈə/	/j/ /ganˈəjə/ (→ /ganˈiː/)	/j/ /ganˈavˈ/ (/ganˈəj/ → /ganˈiː/)	/Nʲivˈnˈəx/ (→ /NʲivˈNʲəx/)
Connemara	/Nʲivˈə/	/gaːLˈəvˈə/	/j/ /ganˈəj/ (→ /ganˈə/)	/Nʲivˈnˈəs/ (→ /NʲivˈNʲəs/)
Munster	/j/ /nʲijˈə/ (→ /nʲiː/)	/j/ /gaLˈəjə/ (→ /gaˈlʲiː/)	/ganˈavˈ/	/j/ /nʲijnˈəx/ (→ /nʲiːnˈəx/)

Examples are scarce and it is necessary to use the word for 'sand' in which gender (and consequently inflection) fluctuate: see 7.1.2.

In summary, slender *bh/mh* /ṽʲ/ must either be preserved or changed to /j/. As can be seen from Table 4.2, the change to slender /j/ is needed more frequently in Munster than elsewhere.

There are some exceptions to the general rules shown in Table 4.2. In Mayo, after a neutral vowel /ə/, slender *bh/mh* /ṽʲ/ is retained in *tairbhe* /tarˈəvˈə/ 'benefit' and, presumably under Galway influence, in *Gaillimhe* /gaLˈəvˈə/, gen. of *Gaillimh* 'Galway'.

In Connemara slender *bh/mh* /ṽʲ/ is changed to /j/ in *scríbhneoir* /sˈkˈrʲiːjNʲoːrʲ/ (→ /sˈkˈrʲiːNʲoːrʲ/) 'writer' and presumably under Munster influence, in the adjective *Muimhneach* /miːjnˈəx/ (→ /miːnˈəx/) 'Munsterman'.

70 *Modern Irish: grammatical structure and dialectal variation*

In Munster, the general rule is that slender *mh/bh* (i.e. /ṽ´/) is changed to /j/ as in:

(3) *nimhe* /n´ijə/ (→ /n´iː/), gen. of *nimh* 'poison'
   aimhleas /ajl´əs/ (→ /ail´əs/) 'disadvantaage'
   deimhin /d´ejən´/ (→ /d´ain´/) 'certain'
   duibhe /dijə/ (→ /diː/) comparative of *dubh* 'black'
   goibhní /gejn´iː/ (→ /gəin´iː/ → /gəi'ŋ´iː/) (Mk) 'smiths'

There are, however, exceptions such as:

(4) *uimhir* /iv´ər´/ 'number'
   soibhir /sev´ər´/ 'rich'

Interestingly, while *soibhreas* is /sev´ər´əs/ 'wealth', the pronunciation /səir´əs/ is needed in Munster verse.

4.1.1(iv) *Random change of slender* **dh/gh** /j/ *to* /v´/. There is a very restricted minor rule which is in effect the opposite rule to that treated above. Under this rule slender *dh/gh* /j/ → /v´/ in examples such as:

(5) *guidhe* /gijə/ → /giv´ə/ (C) 'praying'
   eidhean /ejən/ → /ev´ən/ (Tm) [(→ /ev´əN/ (Cn)] 'ivy'
   tighthí /t´ijhiː/ → /t´iv´h´iː/ (→ /t´if´iː/) (Er) 'houses'
   thoigh /hej/ → /hev´/ (Dn, Mk) 'chose'

There is, in fact, another even more restricted minor rule which is the voiceless equivalent of the change /j/ → /v´/. Under this rule slender *ch* /x´/ is changed to slender *f* /f´/ in examples such as:

(6) *cluiche* /klix´ə/ → /klif´ə/ (C) 'game'
   doicheall /dex´əL/ → /def´əL/ (C) 'inhospitability'

All the rules noted concerning slender fricatives in 4.1.1(i-iv) must be applied before the merger of semi-vowels with neighbouring vowels (see 4.1.3) and before the removal of semi-vowels (see 4.1.4).

4.1.2 The voiced velar fricative
As was pointed out in 4.1, apart from word-initial position, the status of the voiced velar fricative /ɣ/ is purely theoretical. The voiced velar fricative

broad *dh/gh* /ɣ/ in the underlying forms is changed in ways which correspond to those of the palatal fricative *dh/gh* /j/. Yet broad *dh/gh* /ɣ/ is changed to /x/ and /w/, which is exactly the reverse of the changes to slender *ch* /x´/ and slender *bh/mh* /ṽ´/ to /j/ which were dealt with in 4.1.1.

There are five different ways in which the velar fricative must be changed as shown in Figure 4.1:

Figure 4.1 Changes required for broad *dh/gh* /ɣ/

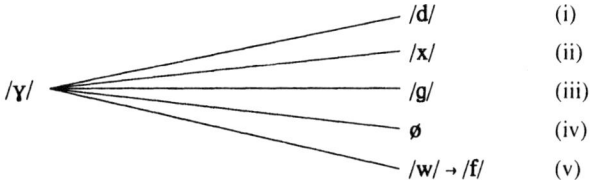

4.1.2(i) *Broad* **dh/gh** /ɣ/ *changed to* /d/. This change is required in verbal forms which are immediately followed by a personal subject pronoun, e.g.

(7) *bhriseadh sé* /v´r´is´əɣ s´e:/ → /v´r´is´əd s´e:/ (→ /v´r´is´ət s´e:/)
     (C, D) 'he used to break'

This rule operates in Connacht and Donegal but not in Munster and would appear to be optional in parts of Connemara.

4.1.2(ii) *Broad* **dh/gh** /ɣ/ *changed to* /x/. This devoicing of broad *dh/gh* /ɣ/ to /x/ is needed after the change of broad *dh/gh* /ɣ/ → /d/ treated in 4.1.2(i), so that it is now possible to state a rule that in Connemara and Munster any broad *dh/gh* /ɣ/ which remains in a finite verbal form (excluding the impersonal form) must be changed to /x/:

(8) *bhriseadh* /v´r´is´əɣ/ → /v´r´is´əx/ 'used to break'

In Donegal and Mayo /ɣ/ → /w/ [see 4.1.2(v)] → /u:/ [see 4.1.3(ii)], e.g. *bhriseadh* /v´r´is´u:/. In West Kerry this devoicing is also required in the impersonal *briseadh* /b´r´is´əɣ/ → /b´r´is´əx/ (Dn) 'one broke'.

4.1.2(iii) *Broad* **dh/gh** /ɣ/ *changed to* /g/. This rule affects the impersonal form in certain Munster dialects, e.g. *-(e)adh* /b´r´is´əɣ/ → /b´r´is´əg/ (Mk). There are further sporadic examples where this change is necessary, e.g.:

(9) *carghas* (/karɣəs/ →) /karɣəs/ → /karəɣəs/ (D) 'Lent'
Fearghal (/fʹarɣəl/ →) /fʹarɣəl/ → /fʹarəɣəl/ (D) (a man's name)
blioghan /bʹlʹiɣən/ → /bʹlʹiɣən/ (Mn) 'milking'

4.1.2(iv) Removal of broad dh/gh /ɣ/. Broad *dh/gh* /ɣ/ is removed after a stressed long vowel, e.g.:

(10) *tuagh* /tuːəɣ/ → /tuːə/ 'an axe'

On the removal of /ɣ/ a preceding short vowel is lengthened, e.g.:

(11) *leaghadh* /Lʹaɣəɣ/ → /Lʹaːɣ/ [→ /Lʹaːw/ (Cn)] 'melting'
bleaghan /bʹlʹaɣən/ → /bʹlʹaːn/ [→ /bʹlʹɑːN/ (Cn)] 'milking'
faghann /faɣəN/ → /faːN/ [→ /fɑːN/ (Cn)] 'gets'

The broad *dh/gh* /ɣ/ is needed in the underlying forms of these words in order to allow for the relationships between, e.g. *bligh* 'milk' and *bleaghan* (now conventionally spelt *bleán*) 'milking' or the relationship between *leaghann* /Lʹɑːn/ (Cn), *leáighim* /Lʹaːjəmʹ/ (Er) and *leigheann* /lʹain/ (M), /Lʹeːn/ (D) 'melts'. For further discussion of this variation between broad *dh/gh* /ɣ/ and slender *dh/gh* /j/ see 4.2.2(ii).

In Munster, following an unstressed short vowel and immediately before a word boundary, /ɣ/ is removed, e.g. *briseadh* /bʹrʹisʹəɣ/ → /bʹrʹisʹə/ 'breaking'.

It is important that the two previous rules (i.e. broad *dh/gh* /ɣ/ changed to /x/ and /g/) precede this rule so that other finite forms ending in broad *dh* /ɣ/, e.g. *bhriseadh* /bʹrʹisʹəx/ 'used to break' and (in parts of Munster) the impersonal form in the past, e.g. *briseadh* /bʹrʹisʹəg/ 'one broke' are excluded here.

4.1.2(v) Broad dh/gh /ɣ/ is changed to /w/. This rule is needed subsequent to the four rules in 4.1.2(i-iv). In this way any broad *dh/gh* /ɣ/ which has not already been altered or removed is now changed to /w/, e.g. *briseadh* /bʹrʹisʹəɣ/ → /bʹrʹisʹəw/ 'breaking', which is subsequently realized as /bʹrʹisʹuː/ (Mo) or /bʹrʹisʹə/ (Cn). The change of /w/ to /f/ is treated in 4.2.3.

4.1.3 Merger of semi-vowels with neighbouring vowels

Basically we are dealing here with two rules which involve the merging of the semi-vowels broad *bh/mh* /w̃/ and slender *dh/gh* /j/ with either a following or a preceding vowel. The semi-vowels have much in common and indeed they are dealt with here by the same two rules. The result of this merger, irrespective of which rule is involved, is that where there is a slender *dh/gh* /j/ the sound /iː/ will emerge, and where there is a broad *bh/mh* /w̃/ the sound /uː/ will emerge.

4.1.3(i) *Slender* **dh/gh** */j/ or broad* **bh/mh** */w̃/ followed by a short vowel.*
This first rule stated in its broadest terms deals with the case of slender *dh/gh* /j/ or broad *bh/mh* /w̃/ when followed by a short vowel. Essentially this rule is intended to handle examples involving slender *dh/gh* /j/:

(12) *páighe* /paːjə/ → /paːiː/) (→ /pɑːiː/) (Cn) 'pay'
      láighe /Laːjə/ → /Laːiː/ (→ /Lɑːiː/) (Cn) 'loy, spade'
      nuaidheacht /nuːəjəxt/ → /nuːiːxt/ (Cn) 'news'
      truaighe /truːəjə/ → /truːəiː/ (Cn) 'pity'
      léighim /Lʹeːjəmʹ/ → /Lʹeːmʹ/ (Cn) 'I read'

There are some important restrictions on the rule. In the first place if the slender *dh/gh* /j/ or broad *bh/mh* /w̃/ is preceded by an unstressed vowel it must come under the second general rule [see 4.1.3(ii)]. Secondly, where the preceding vowel is long only slender *dh/gh* /j/ (and not broad *bh/mh* /w̃/) is involved, e.g. *námhaid* /Naːwədʹ/ 'enemy' (C,D). Thirdly, there is a geographical restriction in that Donegal and Mayo are excluded, so that there slender *dh/gh* /j/ is retained:

(13) *páighe* /paːjə/ (D, Mo)
      léighim /Lʹeːjəmʹ/ (D, Mo)

A fourth restriction is that in the case of a short vowel preceding slender *dh/gh* /j/ the rule takes effect only if it is a high vowel, e.g.:

(14) *fioghachán* /fʹijəxaːn/ → /fʹiiːxaːn/ → /fʹiːxaːn/ 'weaving'

Where slender *dh/gh* /j/ is preceded by mid-vowels or low vowels a diphthong or, in the case of Donegal, a long vowel [see 4.1.3(iii)] is required, e.g.:

(15) *leigheas* /Lʹejəs/ → /Lʹais/ (C), /lʹəis/ (M) 'cure'
      bodhar /bawr/ → /baur/ (C) 'deaf'
      adharc /ajərk/ → /airk/ (C), /eirk/ (M) 'horn'

Finally, morpheme boundaries play a part, in the case of the adjectival suffix *-mhar* where there is variation. An example is *greannmhar* /g´r´ɑːNwər/ (Cf) beside /g´r´aNwər/ → /g´r´aNəwər/ [→ /g´r´anəwər/) (Mk) → /g´r´anuːr/ (M, Er)] 'amusing'. Another case in point is the Munster second plural past ending *-abhair* as in *dheineabhair* 'you made' /jin´əwər´/ (Dn, Rg) beside /jin´uːr´/ (Mk).

4.1.3(ii) *Slender* **dh/gh** /j/ *or broad* **bh/mh** /w̃/ *preceded by a short vowel.*
This second rule deals with the case of slender *dh/gh* /j/ or /w/ preceded by a short vowel. Essentially this rule is to handle examples such as:

(16) *talamhan(a)* /taləwən/ → /taluːn/ [→ /taːLuːN/ (Cn)] [→ /taluːnə/ (Mo)], gen. of *talamh* 'ground'
caillighe /kaL´əjə/ → /kaL´iː/, gen. of *cailleach* 'hag'
ualaighe /uːəLəjə/ → /uːəLiː/, plural of *ualach* 'load'
bealaigh /b´aləj/ → /b´aliː/, gen. *bealach* 'way'

The conventional spelling of these words would now be *talún, caillí, ualaí, bealaigh* but the retention of an underlying /w̃/ or slender *dh/gh* /j/ is demanded by the morphology in all of the forms in (16).

Once again, there are some limitations which must be placed on the general statement of the second rule.

Where the preceding short vowel is an epenthetic vowel, operation of the rule is optional, at least in parts of Connemara, e.g.

(17) *marbh* /marəw/ ~ /maːruː/ 'dead'
garbh /garəw/ ~ /garuː/ 'rough'

On the other hand, it does not seem to be optional in, e.g. *talamhan* /taluːn/ (M) [→ /taːLuːN/ (Cn)] where the semi-vowel is followed by a vowel with a subsequent consonant.

The final /w/ of the impersonal form also proves exceptional in that in Connemara the merger rule is optional, e.g. *briseadh* /b´r´is´əw/ ~ /b´r´is´uː/ (Cn) 'one broke'. In Mayo, the rule comes into play only where there is no other semi-vowel in the underlying form (i.e. Category 1 verbs; see 8.1.2), e.g. *briseadh* /b´r´is´əw/ ~ /b´r´is´uː/ 'one broke'. For Category 2 verbs see 4.2.3.

There is a further limitation when the vowel and semi-vowel are followed by a word boundary, that is to say, when they are in word final position. In this case the rule will not apply in Connemara due to the removal of semi-vowels (see 4.1.4):

(18)   *bealaigh* /bʹaləj/ → /bʹaːlə/ (→ /bʹæːLə/) (Cn), gen. of *bealach* 'way'

In Munster, however, as *dh/gh* /j/ has previously changed to /gʹ/ (e.g. *bealaigh* /bʹaləgʹ/, gen. of *bealach* 'way'), the restriction here need only apply to the weak boundary between a verb form and personal pronoun due to the removal of semi-vowels [see 4.1.4(i)]:

(19)   *d'éirigh sé* /dʹairʹəj sʹeː/ (→ /dʹairʹə sʹeː/) 'he rose'

There is one other limitation which is important. If the preceding vowel is stressed, for the rule to take effect that vowel must be a high one. This means there are examples such as:

(20)   *nimhe* /Nʹivʹə/ → /Nʹijə/ → /Nʹiːə/ → /Nʹiː/ (→ /nʹiː/) (M), gen. of *nimh* 'poison'
        tighe /tʹijə/ → /tʹiːə/ → /tʹiː/ (C, M), gen. of *teach* (C), *tigh* (M) 'house'

On the other hand mid-vowels and low vowels generally will be diphthongized, e.g.:

(21)   *loighe* /Lejə/ → /Lai/ (Cn) 'lying'
        leabhar /Lʹawər/ → /Lʹaur/ (C, M) 'book'
        adharc /ajərk/ → /airk/ (C), /oirk/ (M) 'horn'

These two general rules discussed above will come into operation after vowel separation (see 3.2), in order to allow here for differences between front and back vowels, and also subsequent to the development of fricatives, as they are needed for this rule. They must, however, be applied before Stress-shift 2 (see 2.8.3), as the long vowels which emerge here may receive the accent.

4.1.3(iii) *The diphthongs* /aj/, /ej/ *are changed to* /eː/ *and* /aw/, /ow/ *are changed to* /oː/. There is another change needed for Donegal and sporadically for Connacht which must be implemented prior to the two rules under discussion in 4.1.3(i-ii). Under this rule /ej/, /aj/ are changed to /eː/ and /aw/ and /ow/ are changed to /oː/, e.g.:

(22) adharc /ajərk/ → /eːrk/ (D) 'horn'
leigheann /Lʹejən/ → /Lʹeːn/ (D) 'melts'
tabhair /tawərʹ/ → /toːrʹ/ (D, C) 'give'
leabhar /Lʹawər/ → /Lʹoːr/ (D) 'book'
bodhar /bowər/ → /boːr/ (D) 'deaf'

A similar rule must be implemented at this point for Clare by which /aw/ or /ow/ would give /oː/, e.g.:

(23) amhrán /aw̃raːn/ → /õːraːn/ (→ /uːraːn/ (see 3.3.4) 'song'
samhradh /saw̃rəw/ → /sõːrəw/ (→ /suːrə/) 'summer'

There must be some exchange between /w̃/ and /w/ in the underlying forms. It would appear for example that Donegal *amhrán* /oːraːn/ 'song' should be derived from *abhrán*, as /oː/ is conditioned by *bh* but not by *mh*. The pronunciation /oːraːn/ (C) is exceptional in Connacht and must be a sporadic example of the Donegal rule. In the same way, Donegal *deamhan* /dʹoːn/ 'demon' would require an underlying *deabhan*, presumably influenced by *diabhal* 'devil'.

4.1.4 Removal of final semi-vowel

4.1.4(i) Main rule. This rule is required to remove a final /w/ or /j/. In Donegal or Mayo, a semi-vowel is lost after a long vowel only when followed by a personal subject pronoun: *léigh sé* /Lʹeːj sʹeː/ → /Lʹeː sʹeː/ 'he read'. On the other hand, the semi-vowel must be preserved if there is a normal word boundary, e.g.

(24) léigh Seán /Lʹeːj sʹaːn/ (D, Mo) 'Seán read'
dligheadh /dʹLʹiːw/ (D, Mo) 'law'
ceannaíodh /kʹaNiːw/ (D, C) (→ /kʹaNiːfʹ/ (Er) [see 4.2.3]) 'one bought'

After any short vowel the semi-vowel is removed.
  In Connemara, the final semi-vowel is not removed in the (past) impersonal form, e.g. *briseadh* /bʹrʹisʹəw/ 'one broke' or following an epenthetic vowel, e.g. *marbh* /marəw/ 'dead'. The rule is optional in the case of /w/ after a short stressed vowel as in *dubh* /du/ or /duw/ 'black'. In all other cases /w/ or slender *dh/gh* /j/ is removed, e.g.

(25) *léigh Seán* /l´e:j s´a:n/ → /l´e: s´a:n/ (→ /l´e: s´ɑ:N/) 'Seán read'
dligheadh /d´l´i:w/ → /d´l´i:/ 'law'
déanamh /d´i:nəw/ → /d´i:nə/ (→ /d´i:N´ə/) 'doing, making'
briseadh /b´r´is´əw/ → /b´r´is´ə/ 'breaking'

In Munster, the removal of a final semi-vowel is not required. Final /ɣ/ was removed previously [see 4.1.2(iv)]. The rule does not affect /w/ as can be seen in an example such as *déanamh* /d´e:nəw/ (→ /d´ianəw/) (M) 'doing'.

4.1.4(ii) Three Munster rules. There are three Munster rules which must be considered at this point. Firstly there is the removal of final /i:/ following a long syllable in examples such as:

(26) *páighe* (/pa:jə/ →) /pa:i:/ → /pa:/ (M) 'pay'
sléibhe (/s´l´e:v´ə/ → /s´l´e:jə/ →) /s´l´e:i:/ → /s´l´e:/ (M) gen. of *sliabh* 'mountain'
truaighe (/tru:əjə/ →) /tru:əi:/ → /tru:ə/ (M) 'pity'
cruaidhe (/kru:əjə/ →) /kru:əi:/ → /kruə/ (M) comparative of *cruaidh* 'hard'

Secondly there is the removal of final /w/ following a stressed *á* /a:/, *ao* /e:/, or *ia* /i:ə/. Examples are:

(27) *lámha* /la:wə/ → /la:ə/ (→ /la:/) (M) 'hands'
lámhacán /La:wəka:n / → /La:əka:n/ (→ /la:ka:n/) (Mk) 'crawling'
tábhacht /ta:wəxt/ → /ta:əxt/ (→ /ta:xt/) (M) 'importance'
faobhar /fe:wər/ → /fe:ər/ (→ /fe:r/) (M) 'keen edge'
saoghal (/se:ɣəl/ →) /se:wəl/ → /se:əl/ (→ /se:l/) (M) 'life'
riabhach /ri:əwəx/ → /ri:əəx/ (→ /ri:əx/) (M) 'speckled'
diabhal /d´i:əwəl/ → /d´i:əəl/ (→ /d´i:əl/) (M) 'devil'

Thirdly there is the removal of medial /j/ following a stressed vowel (except in the case of a low vowel) as in an example such as *scríbhneoir* (/s´k´r´i:v´n´o:r´/ →) /s´k´r´i:jn´o:r´/ → /s´k´r´i:n´or´/ (M) 'writer'.

4.1.5 Treatment of semi-vowel broad *mh* /w̃/ as a consonant
The semi-vowel /w̃/ has the quality of a consonant when it comes before a stressed vowel, though often, depending on the dialect, becoming a labiodental

slender /v/, particularly in Munster. However the symbol /w/ has been retained and used in the phonetic transcription throughout this account.

The semi-vowel /w̃/ must be given a consonantal quality after a stressed /a/ in West Connemara and South Mayo, e.g.:

(28)   *gamhain* /gawən´/ (West Cn, South Mo) 'calf'
         samhradh /sawrə/ (West Cn), /sawruː/ (South Mo) 'summer'
         cleamhnas /kʹlʹawnəs/ (West Cn, South Mo) 'match'

This consonantal quality is not needed in the case of *bh* /w/ as opposed to /w/ in:

(29)   *leabhar* /Lʹaur/ (Ca, Tm) 'book'
         gabhar /gaur/ (Ca, Tm) 'goat'

This internal development of *mh* /w̃/ as a consonant following stressed /a/ is also necessary as a minor rule in Munster dialects, e.g.:

(30)   *amhrán* /auˈraːn/ (Dn) ~ /avəˈraːn/ (Dn, Mk) 'song'
         amharc /avərk/ (Mk) 'sight'

4.1.6 Defricatization of the semi-vowels broad *mh/bh* /w̃/ and slender *mh/bh* /ṽʹ/

In Connemara and sporadically in other dialects /w̃/ or /ṽʹ/ may interchange with /m(ʹ)/ before /s(ʹ)/, e.g.:

(31)   *tréimhse* /tʹrʹeːvʹsʹə/ → /tʹrʹeːmʹsʹə/ (Rm) 'period'
         damhsa /daːwsə/ → /daːmsə/ (West Cn) 'dancing'
         láimhsiughadh (/Laːvʹsʹuː/ →) /Laːvʹsʹuː/ → /Laːmʹsʹuː/ (Cf) 'handling'
         domsa ~ *domhsa* /doːsə/ (M) /duːsə/ (C, D) 'to me'

In Munster dialects there is an optional defricatization of *bh/mh* or *ph* following *-m*, the form of *mo* /mə/ 'my' after a preposition ending in a vowel, e.g. *i m bolg* /əm boləg/ ~ /əm woləg/ 'in my stomach'(Mk).

It may also be mentioned in passing that there is in Connemara a defricatization of slender *bh* /vʹ/ in monosyllabic second plural personal pronouns, e.g. *sibh* /sʹibʹ/ 'you', *libh* /lʹibʹ/ (~ /lʹiːbʹ/) 'with you' as opposed to disyllabic second plural personal pronouns where the second syllable is exceptionally pronounced with a long *i* /iː/, e.g. *oraibh* /oriː/ 'on you', *asaibh* /asiː/ 'out of you'. This rule is a late one as it applies after the lengthening in place of *th*/*ch* /h/ in Cois Fhairrge (see 2.7), e.g. *fúthaibh* 'under you' /fuːhəv´/ → /fuːv´/ → /fuːb´/.

4.1.7 Treatment of /h/

4.1.7(i) *Fricatization of* /h(´)/. The close relationship between /h´/ and /x´/ has already been seen in the discussion of the slender fricatives (see 4.1.1). Here, however, we are dealing with an underlying slender *th* /h´/ which changes to slender /x´/ following a stressed vowel and under certain conditions.

This change appears to be a major and obligatory rule in Donegal and Mayo, e.g.:

(32) *caith* /kax´/ (D, Mo) 'throw'
      rith /rix´/ (D, C) 'run'
      maith /max´/ (D, Mo) 'good'

There are however some restrictions. The slender *th* /h´/ remains (eventually changing to /h/ in most dialects excepting Ring) before /iː/, in a personal verbal ending or before a consonant, e.g.:

(33) *caithfidh* /kahiː/ (D, Mo) 'will throw'
      chaith mé /xah m´eː/ (→ /xa m´eː/) 'I threw'
      caithtear /kah´t´ər/ (→ /kat´ər/) 'one throws'

Lastly, the change does not take place between two vowels where diphthongization (see 3.5.1) has taken place, e.g.:

(34) *soitheach* /saihah/ ~ /sex´ah/ (Gd) /saihəx/ ~ /sex´əx/ (Er) 'vessel'

This change is not normally found in Munster. In Connemara it is a minor rule applying, optionally, to words such as:

(35) *rith* /rix´/ (D, C) 'run'
      ráithe /rɑːx´ə/ (D, C) 'three month period'
      oíche /iːx´ə/ (D, C) 'night'

A similar change also is required as part of a different sort of development. This /hʹ/ is the result of a lenition of initial /sʹ/ or /tʹ/ when followed by a long vowel. In Connemara and Tourmakeady it must be a high back vowel, i.e. u, when /hʹ/ is the result of lenited /tʹ/. In Donegal and Mayo and in Munster (with some few exceptions) only /hʹ/ from /sʹ/ is changed before a long back vowel, e.g.:

(36)   (a) *Sheáin* /xʹaːnʹ/ 'Seán!'
       sheol /xʹoːl/ 'sailed'
       shiúil /xʹuːl(ʹ)/ 'walked'
       (a) *shiopa* /xʹupə/ (Cn) '(his) shop'
       (*nuair a*) *thiocfainn* /xʹukəNʹ/ (Cn, Tm), /hukəNʹ/ (D, M) '(when) I would come'
       (a) *thiubharfainn* /xʹuːrəNʹ/ (Cn, Tm) '(which) I would give'

There is yet another environment where /h/ will be changed to /x/ but this seems to be limited to certain dialects such as Ring. The rule is needed following a stressed vowel and preceding a word boundary or certain types of morpheme boundary, e.g.:

(37)   *gaoth* /geːx/ (Rg) 'wind'
       liath /lʹiːəx/ (Rg) 'grey'
       leath /lʹax/ (Rg) 'half'
       riothadar /rʹuxədər/ (Rg) 'they ran'

It can also occur sporadically in compounds such as *tráthnóna* /traːxnuːnə/ (Rg) 'afternoon'.

All the above changes of slender *th*/*sh* /hʹ/ to /xʹ/ will naturally take effect before /hʹ/ is changed to /h/ or indeed before any removal of /h/.

Finally, certain Donegal dialects show the reverse process, that is the substitution of /h/ for original broad *ch* /x/, e.g.:

(38)   *luchóg* /Luhag/ (Gd) 'mouse'
       Gaelach /geːlah/ (Gd) 'Irish'

4.1.7(ii) *Removal of* /h/. There are three different contexts in which /h/ must be removed: firstly, adjacent to another consonant; secondly, in word final position where the next word does not begin with a vowel, and thirdly, between two vowels.

The case of /h/ adjacent to a consonant is obviously closely connected with the whole question of devoicing (see 4.2.3). It is difficult to say quite how much voice is retained by the sonants in any particular dialect. This whole question is no doubt further connected with the rule by which /rh/ is changed to /hr/ [see 4.2.6(v)]. The discussion here is confined to the second and third contexts.

In Munster, both in word final position and between vowels, broad, *th* /h/ is quite stable. Notwithstanding this, it is generally removed following a long vowel when preceding the morpheme -*as* /əs/:

(39) *gnáthas* /gnaːs/ 'custom'
      dlúthas /dluːs/ 'density'

In Donegal, in word final position broad *th* /h/ is removed after a long vowel, but generally remains after a short vowel, e.g.:

(40) *fáth* /faː/ (D) 'reason'
      dath /dah/ (D) 'colour'
      leath /Lʹah/ (D) 'half'

In some Donegal dialects following /a/ a glottal stop is needed, e.g.:

(41) *fathach* /faʔax/ ~ /fahəx/ → /faːx/ (Tn) 'giant'

In Mayo, following /u/, the removal of /h/ is not required as it has been altered to /w/ prior to this rule, which in turn is changed to /f/ under a general rule in the dialect which changes /w/ to /f/ before a word boundary (see 4.2.3):

(42) *guth* /guh/ → /guw/ (→ /guf/) (Mo) 'voice'
      gruth /gruh/ → /gruw/ (→ /gruf/) (Mo) 'curd'

On the other hand, between vowels broad *th* /h/ must normally be removed after a long *a* in examples such as:

(43) *saláthar* /solaːhər/ → /solaːər/ (→ /solaːr/) 'provision'
      gnáthach /gnaːhəx/ → /gnaːəx/ (→ /gnaːx/ → /graːx/) (Mo) 'usual'

In the west of Connemara, /h/ is not removed medially. However, in Cois Fhairrge (and the Aran Islands) the removal of broad *th* /h/ is needed in almost all positions except in word-initial position. Examples are:

82   *Modern Irish: grammatical structure and dialectal variation*

(44)   *luath* /Lu:əh/ → /lu:ə/ (Cn) 'early'
guth /guh/ → /gu/ (Cn) 'voice'
máthair (/ma:hər´/ →) /ma:hər´/ (West Cn) → /ma:r´/ (Cf) 'mother'
cuthach /kuhəx/ (West Cn) → /ku:x/ (Cf) 'frenzy'
bóthar /bo:hər/ (West Cn) → /bo:r/ (Cf) 'road'
gearrtha (/g´a:rhə/ →) /ga:rhə/ (West Cn) → /g´a:rə/ (Cf) 'cut'

Nevertheless, at certain boundaries the removal of /h/ is optional, e.g.

(45)   *dathúil* /dahu:l´/ ~ /daul´/ (Cf) 'beautiful'
le haghaidh /l´e hai/ ~ /l´ai/ (Cf) 'for'
ná himigh /Na: him´ə/ ~ /Na: im´ə/ (Cf) [see also 6.2.3(i)] 'don't go off'.

4.2 Consonants

4.2.1 Overview of system
The following table is a basic outline of the underlying consonantal system.

Table 4.3 *Outline of consonantal system*

Broad consonant				Slender consonant			
/p/	/t/	/k/		/p´/	/t´/	/k´/	
/b/	/d/	/g/		/b´/	/d´/	/g´/	
/f/	/s/	(/x/)	/h/	/f´/	/s´/	(/x´/)	/h´/
(/w/)		(/ɣ/)		(/v´/)		(/j/)	
(/w̃/)		(/n/)		(/ṽ´/)		(/n´/)	
/m/		/N/		/m´/		/N´/	
		(/ʎ/)				(/ʎ´/)	
		/L/				/L´/	
		(/r/)				(/r´/)	
		/R/				/R´/	

The sounds bracketed in the table occur initially only as a result of lenition. The tense quality is often lost in /L(´)/, /N(´)/ or /R(´)/, depending on the dialect in question. The /h´/ is usually realized as /h/ [or /x´/, see 4.1.7(i)]. There are occasional words with an initial *bh*/*mh*, e.g. *bhíog* /v´i:g/ (Cf) 'sudden jump', *mhuing* /wiŋ´g/ (Cf) 'mane'.

There are several good reasons for the retention of a distinction between *b h* /w/ and *mh* /w̃/. In the first place, when the semi-vowel is removed its nasal quality may be retained in the vowel:

(46) *comhairle* /kõːrLə/ (Er) 'advice'
      romhat /rõːt/ (Er) 'before you'

In Connemara, Tourmakeady, Ring and in Dunquin the nasal causes the previous vowel to be raised, e.g. *romhat* /roːt/ → /ruːt/ (see 3.3.4). In addition to this, in West Connemara and Mayo, the consonantal quality is preserved in words with an original *mh* /w̃/ but not where there is an original *bh* /w/ (see 4.1.5), e.g. *sleamhain* /sʼlʼawənʼ/ 'slippery' as opposed to *leabhar* /Lʼaur/ 'book'. Finally, there are two further rules which are conditioned by this distinction between *mh* /w̃/ and *bh* /w/. In Donegal /oː/ develops in words such as *leabhar* /Lʼoːr/ 'book' only where /a/ or /o/ precedes the sound *b h* /w/ [see 4.1.3(iii)] and contrariwise in Clare /oː/ (ultimately /uː/) is required when /a/ or /o/ precedes *mh* /w̃/ in words like *samhradh* /soːrə/ (→ /suːrə/) 'summer'.

4.2.2 Slender quality

4.2.2(i) *General principles*. When the general phenomenon is being described, the traditional terms 'slender' and 'broad' are used as general terms rather than palatalization and the reasons for this were given in 0.8. The actual realization of both slender and broad quality depends a great deal and in a very complicated way on the phonetic context. Although an account of such surface realization is not attempted here, it is appropriate to mention certain general traits. One important feature is the heavy velarization or labialization which is found on broad consonants when they occur before front vowels. Another important feature is that slender labials are hardly ever phonetically palatalized.

Generally speaking, the consonants in a cluster must have the same quality, that is the entire cluster must be either broad or slender. Normally, in a consonant group a broad and slender consonant are not permitted side by side. If such a case arises due to the application of morphological rules or due to pretonic elision (see 2.5), this incongruity will be eliminated by the assimilation of the broad quality by the slender quality. There are, however, four important exceptions to the general rule.

Firstly, *dh/gh* /j/ will not spread the slender quality to a following consonant, e.g.:

(47)   *saghdadh* /**sajdə**/ (→ /**saidə**/) (Cf) 'incite'
       adhmad /**ajməd**/ (→ /**əiməd**/) (M) 'timber'
       laghdú /**Lajduː**/ (→ /**Laiduː**/) (C) [→ /**laiduː**/ (M)] 'lessen'
       meadhg /**mʹajg**/ (→ /**mʹaig**/) (C) 'whey'

Secondly, when /s/ in word-initial position precedes a slender consonant, assimilation of the slender quality will not take effect if the consonant is a labial:

(48)   *smig* /**smʹigʹ**/ 'chin'
       speal /**spʹaːl**/ 'scythe'

On the other hand assimilation is required in a medial position, e.g.:

(49)   *caismirt* /**kasʹmʹərtʹ**/ 'contention'
       taisme /**tasʹmʹə**/ (D) 'accident'

It might be assumed that this initial assimilation is a late or surface phonetic adjustment sensitive to phonetic specification rather than to such underlying distinctions as broad or slender. The lack of assimilation here is then due to the fact that slender labials are not phonetically palatalized.

Furthermore, in certain dialects, for instance Inishmaan, or optionally in Cois Fhairrge and in Dunquin, the assimilation does not take place before a velar, e.g. *scéal* /**skʹeːl**/ 'story'. Also in some Munster dialects, e.g. Iveragh, Muskerry, the initial slender *s* /**sʹ**/ of the third singular pronoun may not show the slender quality following a verbal form ending in /x/, e.g. *tugadh sé* 'let him give' /**tugəx seː**/ (Mk).

Thirdly, although there is a difference between a broad and slender /r/ or /ʀ/, that opposition is subsequently removed in certain circumstances and this must be ultimately connected with the fact that the slender quality of /rʹ/ and /ʀʹ/ will be removed before a dental or when following /s/ or in word-initial position. Examples are:

(50)   *tairne* /**taːrnʹə**/ 'nail'
       boird /**baurdʹ**/ (Cn) 'tables'
       srian /**sʹriːN**/ (Cf) 'bridle'
       rí /**riː**/ 'king'

Fourthly the opposition between slender *ch* /**xʹ**/ and broad *ch* /x/ is removed before a dental, e.g.:

(51) boichte /**boxt´ə**/ comparative of *bocht* 'poor'
      uicht /**oxt´**/ (C) gen. of *ucht* 'bosom'

In certain Donegal dialects *ch* /x/ must be changed to a vocalic *r* before a dental, e.g.:

(52) *bochta* /**bo̯rtə**/ (Gd) 'poor (people)'
      ocht /**o̯rt**/ (Gd) 'eight'

A further exception to the general rule of slender quality assimilation is the case of the impersonal form endings which have an initial /t/ or /f/. Often assimilation is optional, e.g. *ligfí* /l´ig´f´i:/ (→ /l´ik´i:/) ~ /lig´fi:/ (→ /l´ik´fi:/) 'one would let'.

A similar phenomenon must be dealt with in the case of *timpeall* 'around' in certain Munster dialects:

(53) *t(h)impeall* /t´i:m´pəl/ (Dn, Mk) : /t´im´p´əL/ (D, Mo) →
      /h´aim´p´əl/ (Rg) : /t´i(:)mpəL/ (Cf) 'around'

The assimilation may also apply across word boundaries, e.g.

(54) *(cuir) síos tine* /**s´i:s´ t´in´ə**/ 'set a fire!'

In such external sandhi, or indeed simply across morpheme boundaries, a following initial front vowel can cause a preceding consonant to become slender, e.g.:

(55) *bád iascach* /ba:d i:əskəx/ → /ba:d´ iəskəx/ (Cn) 'fishing boat'
      báidín (*bád* + *ín*) /**ba:d´i:n´**/ (Cn) 'a little boat'
      sáibhéara (*sábh* /sa:w/ + *éara*) /**sa:v´e:rə**/ (Cn) 'sawyer'

Apart from the case of initial *s*, the general assimilation of slender quality is needed at an early stage. It will take effect before syllable adjustment (see 2.3) as, when a cluster is split up, the group as a whole must have already assimilated the slender quality. Indeed, the adjusting of syllables and the assimilation will come into play as often as 'incongruous' clusters arise. In almost all cases (there are one or two exceptions), the entire cluster must have established its quality prior to the vowel separation.

86 *Modern Irish: grammatical structure and dialectal variation*

The rule which removes the slender quality from slender /r´/ and slender /R´/ before a dental must normally be thought of as applying *before* vowel separation (see 3.2) as shown in Table 4.4

Table 4.4 *Munster and Connemara derivations of* boird *'tables'*

Rule ordering	Munster	Connemara
underlying form	/bər´d´/	/bər´d´/
raising (see 3.3.5)	/bɯr´d´/	
removal of slender quality	/bɯrd´/	/bərd´/
vowel separation (see 3.2)	/burd´/	/bord´/
vowel lengthening (see 3.4.2)	/buːrd´/	
dipthongization (3.4.2)		/baurd´/
realization	/buːrd´/	/baurd´/

Interestingly, there is one exception, where the removal of the slender quality from slender r /r´/ and slender rr /R´/ is required after vowel separation. In the comparative of *ard* 'high', in Donegal and Mayo the slender quality is removed from /r´/ *before* vowel separation (i.e. following the normal rule order), while in Connemara and Munster the slender quality is removed *after* vowel separation (the exceptional rule ordering). These two rule orderings are illustrated in Table 4.5.

Table 4.5 *Derivations of* oirde, *comparative of* ard *'high'*

Rule ordering	Donegal/Mayo	Rule ordering	Connemara	Munster
underlying form	(/ər´d´ə/)	underlying form	/ər´d´ə/	/ər´d´ə/
raising (see 3.3.5)		raising		/ɯr´d´ə/
removal of slender quality	/erd´ə/	vowel separation	/er´d´ə/	/ir´d´ə/
vowel separation (see 3.2)	/ord´ə/	removal of slender quality	/erd´ə/	/ird´ə/
vowel lengthening (see 3.4.2)		vowel lengthening		/iːrd´ə/
diphthongization (see 3.4.2)		diphthongization	/aird´ə/	
realization	/ord´ə/	realization	/aird´ə/	/iːrd´ə/

4.2.2(ii) *Fluctuation between broad and slender quality.* There is a tendency for consonants to fluctuate between broad and slender quality in certain words, depending on the particular dialect. This phenomenon may best be dealt with in the lexicon. Nevertheless, certain trends can be observed and it seems there are three particular environments where this variation is most likely.

Firstly, a *t* /t/ or *f* /f/ in word-initial position tends to change its quality, e.g.

(56)   *teora(inn)* /tʹoːrə/ (Ky, Mk) 'boundary' : /toːrəNʹ/ (Cf)
       tobar /tobər/ 'well' : /tʹobər/ (Rg)
       tuigim /tigʹəmʹ/ (M, D) 'I understand' : /tʹigʹəmʹ/ (C)
       foghlaim /foːLəmʹ/ (Cf) 'learning' : /fʹoːLəmʹ/ (West Cn)
       fuinneo(i)g /fiNʹoːgʹ/ (C) → /fiNʹag/ (D) 'window' : /fʹiʹNʹoːg/ (M)
       [→ /fʹiʹNʹuːg/ (Dn, Rg)]
       faoi /fiː/ (C, D) 'under' : /fʹeː/ (M) (see also 3.6.2)

This type of variation is presumably triggered by the assimilation which occurs between the article and a following vowel, e.g.:

(57)   *an t-éan* /ə(N) tʹeːN/ 'the bird'
       an fhead /ə Nʹad/ 'the whistle'

Furthermore there is the fact that lenited /tʹ/, i.e. /h/, does not ultimately in most dialects distinguish between slender and broad, e.g.:

(58)   *tuig* /tigʹ/ : *ní thuigim* /Nʹiː higʹəmʹ/ 'I don't understand'

At this point the root is then reinterpreted as being *tig* /tʹigʹ/.

Secondly, a medial broad *dh/gh* /ɣ/ and slender *dh/gh* /j/ tend to vary. Examples are:

(59)   *adhmad* /aːməd/ (C, D) 'timber' : *aidhmad* /aiməd/ (M)
       leaghaim /Lʹɑːmʹ/ (Cn) 'I melt' : *leighim* /lʹaimʹ/ (M) /Lʹeːmʹ/ (D)
       leáighim /Lʹaːjəmʹ/ (Er)
       rogha /rau/ ~ /rou/ (M) 'choice' : *roghain* /raunʹ/ (C) : *roighe* /reː/ (D)
       Fearghal /fʹarɣəl/ → /fʹarəgəl/ (D) man's name : /fʹarəjəl/ → /fʹariːl/ (M)

We may note in passing that even in the orthographical tradition a broad *dh* or *gh* have commonly represented *dh/gh* /j/ in such words as *gadhar* /gair/

'dog', *saghas* /**sais**/ 'sort'. In Donegal a rule might deal with an internal lenition together with a slendering of the consonant, e.g.:

(60) *sagart* /**sajərt**/ (Gd) 'priest'
      agam /**ejəm**/ (Tn) 'at me'

Where there is a non-reverting lenited initial consonant [see 6.2.5(i)] slendering of /ɣ/ would be needed, e.g.:

(61) *dhá* /**jæː**/ (Gd) 'two'
      a dhath /**ə ja**/ (Gd) 'nothing'

Thirdly, slender quality fluctuates in the case of a medial liquid or nasal. Examples are:

(62) *dúnaim* /**duːnəmʹ**/ (M) 'I shut' : *dúinim* /**duːnʹəmʹ**/ (Cn)
      baileaghadh (→ *bailiú*) /**baːlʹuː**/ 'gathering' : *balú* /**baːʟuː**/ (Cf)
      foláir /**folaːrʹ**/ → /**f(ə)ˈlaːr**/ (M) 'necessary' : *fleár* (/**felʹaːr**/ → /**fəˈlʹaːr**/ →) /**fʹlʹaːr**/ (Cn)
      amáireach /**əˈmaːrʹəx**/ (Dn) (→ /**əˈmɑːrʹəx**/ (Cn)) 'tomorrow' : *amárach* /**əmaːrəx**/ (Rg, Tm, Er) [→ /**əmæːrah**/ (Gd)]
      urball /**urəbəʟ**/ (→ /**rubəʟ**/) (D, Mo) 'tail' : *eireaball* (/**erbəʟ**/ [see 3.3.6] → ˌerəbəʟ →) /**erʹəbəl**/ (M)
      furast(a) /**furəst**/ (D) → /**fəˈrustə**/ → /**frustə**/ (C) 'easy': *friste* / **firʹisʹtʹ(ə)**/ → /**fʹrʹisʹtʹ(ə)**/ (M)

In the final example the cluster *st* is also made slender.

Often, as in *dúnaim*, a slender quality is developed in all the verbal forms, excluding the verbal noun. This points to the fact that it is due to the influence of a rule which causes the final *l* in *oscail* 'open' to be slender [see 6.3.1(ii)1]. Pairs, such as *cosain* (M) and *coisin* (Cn) 'defend' or *fulaingt* /**felʹəNʹtʹ**/ ~ /**foʟən**/ (in petrified usages) (Cf) 'suffering', show how the slender quality seems to spread through forms where a cluster arises such as *fuilngním* 'I suffer' and may eventually permeate the entire inflection of the verb, including even the verbal noun. In general it would appear that this fluctuation is a phenomenon which is needed late in the derivation. It is required subsequent to the introduction of the epenthetic vowel (see 2.2) as illustrated by *eireaball* (M) 'tail' (normally slendering is applied prior to the introduction of the epenthetic vowel but in this case that ordering would yield *eiribeall*) and examples such as *fleár* (C), *frist(e)* (M) would indicate that it is required before Stress-shift 1 (see 2.8.2).

4.2.3 Devoicing
Essentially, two general principles are involved here: adjacent consonants must agree in the matter of voicing, and the unvoiced consonant will dominate. However, there is one important addendum; in the case of sonants, i.e. *l, n, r,* the assimilation of a voiced consonant by an unvoiced one normally only takes place when /h/ is the unvoiced consonant. There are two important rules for devoicing to note here.

Firstly, there must be a rule which causes devoicing as a result of /h/ (which itself is, in turn, often removed), e.g. *leag* /L´ag/ 'lay' : *leagfaidh* 'will lay'. In some parts of Connemara the sonants (*l, n, r*) are devoiced, but in many dialects they retain full voicing. An example where a plosive is devoiced is:

(63) *leag* /L´ag/ 'lay': *leagfaidh* /L´aghəj/ → /L´akhəj/ → /L´akəj/
       (→ /L´æːkə/ (Cn) ~ /L´akiː/ (D, Mo) ~ /l´akəgˊ/ (M)) 'will lay'

Generally, this devoicing as a result of a following /h/ is found throughout the dialects. Exceptionally, in some Donegal dialects, for example Gweedore, /w/ will not be devoiced, e.g. *scríobhfaidh* /sˊkˊrˊiːwiː/ (Gd) 'will write', *lobhtha* /Lowə/ (Gd) 'rotten'.

It may be noted that there is a sporadic variation among the dialects between a voiced and unvoiced dental plosive (i.e. *d* or *t*) following *l* or *n*. This is, however, probably best left to the lexicon. Examples are:

(64) *cárta* (most of M, Cn) 'card' : *cárda* (D, M, East Galway, South Tipperary)
      contae (most of M) 'county' : *condae* (D, C, Dn)
      cuartaíocht/cuairtíocht (D, C) 'visiting' : *cuardaíocht* (M)
      canta (Mk) 'chunk of bread' : *canda* (Cn)

Secondly, the voiced versus unvoiced contrast is unnecessary following *f* /f/, *s* /s/ or *ch* /x/. Examples are:

(65) *scríobhta* /sˊkˊrˊiːfdə/ (Cf) 'written'
      bocht /boxt/ 'poor'
      creistiúint (*creid + s + ú + n + t*) /kˊrˊəsˊtˊuːNˊtˊ/ (Cf) [see 4.2.6(i)] 'believing'

90 *Modern Irish: grammatical structure and dialectal variation*

       tuiscint (*tig* + *s* + *n* + *t*) /t´is´k´əN´t´/ (C) [see 4.2.6(i)] 'understanding'
       absalóid /absəlo:d´/ (Ih) → /aspəlo:d/ (Tm, Im) 'absolution'

Although the combination *ft* /ft/ is rare in Irish, it is noteworthy that the cluster does arise in Donegal where *f* /f/ seems to strengthen *t* /t/ in words such as:

(66)   *geata* /g´atə/ → /g´aftə/ (D) ~ /g´autə/ (Gd) 'gate'
       ratan /ratən/ → /raftən/ (Mn) 'rafters'
       lata /Latə/ → /Laftə/ → /Lautə/ (Gd) 'loft'
       scata /skatə/ → /skaf´t´ə/ (with slendering) (Gd) 'crowd'

In Connemara /t/ is retained in such words, e.g.:

(67)   *geata* /g´æ:tə/ (C) 'gate'
       lota /Lotə/ (C) 'loft'

In Munster on the other hand /t/ is sometimes strengthened to give /xt/, e.g. *lota* /lotə/ → /loxtə/ 'loft' (M), *rata* /ratə/ → /raxtə/ (M) 'rafter'.

    This removal of the contrast between voiced and unvoiced consonants can occur across word boundaries, e.g. *an bád seo* /ə ba:t´ s´o/ 'this boat'. Of course, as this is a closely knit syntactic unit there is normally no pause involved.

    There is yet another sort of devoicing which is primarily required in the North. In this case the final consonant of certain types of syllable is devoiced. In many parts of Donegal a glottal stop occurs after a short syllable with a final lax consonant, particularly when followed by a pause. This glottal stop largely devoices the preceding consonant, e.g.:

(68)   *fuin* /fin´h?/ (Tn) 'knead'
       mhol /wolh?/ (Tn) 'praised'
       dhuibh /ɣif?/ (Tn) gen. of *dubh* 'black'
       cion /k´in?/ (Tn) 'affection'
       scuir /skir?/ (Tn) 'overlap'
       dubh /duw?/ (Tn) 'black'

There is some need for a similar devoicing in Connacht. In the first place, in Erris following a long vowel, a final /w/ in verbal forms (when not followed by a personal pronoun subject) must be devoiced, e.g.:

(69) *bíodh* /bʹiːw/ → /bʹiːf/ (Er) 'let it be'
chóireodh /xoːrʹoːw/ → /xoːrʹoːf/ (Er) 'would arrange'

In a similar fashion in Mayo /w/ is devoiced in word final position following a short stressed vowel in words such as:

(70) *tiubh* /tʹuw/ → /tʹuf/ (Er, Tm) 'thick'
duibh /divʹ/ → /difʹ/ (Er) gen. of *dubh* 'black'
guth (/guh/) → /guw/ → /guf/ (Er, Tn) 'voice'

The full devoicing, at least of verbal forms, must take effect subsequent to the merger of semi-vowels with neighbouring vowels (see 4.1.3), as illustrated by : *bhailigheadh* (→ *bhailíodh*) /walʹəjəɣ/ → /walʹəjəw/ → /walʹiːw/ → /walʹiːf/ 'used to gather'. In other words, a long vowel is needed in order to provide the requisite context for devoicing to occur.

A further type of devoicing is required for West Connemara. In this case, medial *l*, *n* and *r*, are devoiced in a certain limited number of words. Examples are:

(71) *baladh* /baːlʰə/ (Lm) 'smell'
loine /Linʹʰə/ (Lm) 'churn–dash'
tórainn /toːrʰənʹ/ (Lm) 'boundary'
tórramh /toːrʰə/ (Lm) 'wake'

Furthermore *l*, *n*, *r* and *m* are at least partly devoiced adjoining /h/, particularly in the tenses marked for the future and in the verbal adjectives:

(72) *bhuailfeadh* /wuəlʹhʹəx/ (Lm) 'would hit'
d'fhanfadh /danhəx/ (Lm) 'would remain'
cumfaidh /kumhə/ (Lm) 'will compose'
curtha /kurhə/ (Lm) 'put'
aithne /æːhnʹə/ (→ /æːnʹhə/) (Lm) 'acquaintance'
aithrí /æːhrʹiː/ (→ /æːrʹhiː/) (Lm) 'repentance'

For the metathesis see 4.2.6(v).

Finally, there is a devoicing of final *g* /g (ʹ)/ when it follows a neutral vowel (excluding an epenthetic vowel). This change, with some few exceptions, is a general feature of Donegal and Connacht. Examples are:

92 *Modern Irish: grammatical structure and dialectal variation*

(73)   *Nollaig* /**NOLəg´**/ → /**NOLək´**/ (D, C) 'Christmas'
        Nollag /**NOLəg**/ → /**NOLək**/ (D, C) gen. of *Nollaig* 'Christmas'
        reilig /ril´əg´/ → /ril´ək´/ (D, C) 'graveyard'
        tháinig /haːn´əg´/ → /haːn´ək´/ (D, Er) 'came'
        carraig /karəg´/ → /karək´/ (D, north Mo) 'rock'

The addition of a morpheme does not block the rule: *reilige* /ril´ək´ə/ (C) gen. of *reilig* 'graveyard', *Nollaigeacha(í)* /**NOLək´əxiː**/ (Cn) 'Christmases'.

The rule does not apply in Munster except in some words where *ng* /ŋ (´)/ is lost before a final /g (´)/ [see 4.2.5(iv)], e.g. in:

(74)   *tarrang* (/tarəŋg/ →) /tarəg/ → /tarək/ 'draw'
        thuirling (/huːrl´əŋ´g´/ →) /huːrl´əg´/ → /huːrl´ək´/ 'descended'

However, there is no devoicing in *folang* (/foləŋg/ →) /foləg/ 'suffering'. The verbal endings seem to block the limited devoicing:, e.g. *tairringím* /tarə'g´iːm´/ 'I draw'.

4.2.4 Voicing

A final /t/ following a neutral vowel is voiced (for a full discussion see McKone 1981). This is not a feature of Munster but is required for Connacht:

(75)   *agat* → *agad* (C) 'at you'
        malairt → *malraid* [see 4.2.6(ii)] (C) 'change'
        conairt → *conraid* [see 4.2.6(ii)] (Er) 'pack of hounds'

In the use of second singular of the prepositional pronouns, the rule has a wider context in Donegal in that it is a feature of the final *t* in all second singular prepositional pronouns (with the exception of *leat* 'with you' and *ort* 'on you'):

(76)   *ionat* /**uNəd**/ 'in you'
        agat /ejəd/ (Tn) 'at you'
        duit /did/ 'to you'
        frít /f´r´iːd´/ 'through you'

4.2.5 Liquids and nasals

4.2.5(i) *Tense versus lax.* It is clear from such rules as syllable lengthening (see 3.4) that there must be in the lexicon a distinction between tense and lax consonants in the case of liquid and nasals, i.e. /N (´)/, /L (´)/ etc., as opposed to /n (´)/, /l (´)/ etc. This contrast has a role to play in lenition [see 6.2.1(iii)]. Apart from lenition the opposition tense versus lax need not be preserved. In certain environments the contrast will be completely removed. In the following, six of those various contexts are discussed.

Firstly, the sound /r (´)/ survives in certain Munster dialects (and sporadically elsewhere) as a form of lenited *r* (for a full discussion of this phenomenon see Ó Siadhail and Wigger 1975:115 and Ó Murchú 1986). Examples are:

(77)   *do rogha rud* /də r´au rud/ (C) 'your choice'
        a rí /ə r´iː/ (Dn, Mk) 'o king!'
        do rugadar /də r´ugədər/ (Dn, Mk, Ky) 'they gave birth'

While in the case of /R/ normally, except in certain cases in Donegal, the tension is removed (i.e. /R/ becomes /r/) subsequent to vowel lengthening, there is a close relationship between tension and slender quality. Since slender *r* will not ultimately appear either in word-initial position or before dentals (see 4.2.2(i)) and as /R´/ is removed, even in Donegal, the easiest arrangement is to say that it is from /R´/ rather than /r´/ that the slender quality is removed. It is of no significance whether this /R´/ is in the underlying form or whether it arises because of a following dental. In this arrangement /r´/ will remain where it is lenited in word-initial position. The fact that only a limited number of phrases are involved can be explained by alternative rule orderings. In the examples above, *do rogha rud* /də r´au rud/ 'your choice' etc., lenition is required after the removal of the slender quality ; elsewhere removal of slender quality is needed following lenition.

Secondly, in many parts of Connemara /l/ and /n/ become tense (i.e. /L/ and /N/) and thus a tripartite system is needed : /L/ and /L´/, /l´/; /N/ and /N´/, /n´/. The examples in (78) illustrate *l* and examples in (79) illustrate *n*:

(78)   *ball* /baːL/ (Cn) 'place'
        baladh /baːlə/ → /baːLə/ (Cf) 'smell'
        buille /buL´ə/ (C) 'blow'
        buile /bil´ə/ (C) 'anger'
(79)   *bonn* /buːN/ (Cn) 'sole'
        buan /buːn/ → /buːN/ (Cn) 'lasting'
        Spáinn /spaːN´/ (C) 'Spain'
        (tai)spáin /spaːn´/ (C) 'show!'

In some Donegal dialects, Gweedore for example, a /n'/ becomes /N'/ when between vowels as in:

(80)   *duine* /din'ə/ → /diN'ə/ 'person'
        gloine /glin'ə/ → /gliN'ə/ 'glass'
        gainimh /gan'əv'/ → /gaN'əv'/ 'sand'

In Munster the opposition between tense and lax *l* and *r* is lost, so that a two-part system emerges with /l/, /l'/ and /n/, /n'/. However, in certain parts of Munster, for example Muskerry and Ring (see Ó Cuív 1951:51-2), /N'/ between vowels or in word-final position becomes /ŋ'/, e.g.:

(81)   *coinne* /kiN'ə/ → /kiŋ'ə/ (Mk, Rg) 'appointment'
        binn /b'i:N'/ → /b'i:ŋ'/ (Mk, Rg) 'melodious'

This change from /N'/ to /ŋ'/ must, of course, be implemented before the difference between /N'/ and /n'/ is removed.

Thirdly, it should be noted that *m* /m (')/ and *ng* /ŋ (')/ must be regarded as tense seeing that syllable lengthening occurs preceding them (see 3.4).

Fourthly, tension is removed before *s* as in, e.g.:

(82)   *inseacht* /i(:)N's'əxt/ → /i(:)n's'əxt/ (C) : /iN's'əxt/ (Tn) 'telling'

Fifthly, both *n* and *l* are normally tense when beside a dental except before *s* in Connacht and parts of Donegal and before *t* in Donegal and Mayo:

(83)   *baint* /ban't'/ → /baN't'/ (Cn) 'cutting'
        sneachta /s'n'axtə/ → /s'N'axtə/ (D, C) 'snow'
        tharlaigh /ha:rLi:/ (D, Mo) 'happened'
        óinseach /u:n's'əx/ (C) : /o:N's'əx/ (Tn) 'foolish woman'

Lastly, in most Connemara dialects /n'/ becomes /N'/ following /v'/ as in:

(84)   *doimhne* /daiv'N'ə/ (Cn) comparative of *domhan* 'deep'
        goibhne /gaiv'N'ə/ (Cn) 'smiths'

This tensing of /n'/ also occurs in North Donegal, e.g.:

(85)   *doimhne* /div'N'ə/ (Gd) comparative of *domhan* 'deep'
        cuimhne /kiv'N'ə/ (Gd) 'memory'

In South Donegal and Mayo, however, *doimhne* /div´n´ə/ (Tn, Mn, Er, Tm) and *cuimhne* /kiv´n´ə/ (Tn, Mn, Er, Tm) are required. Although in Munster, the distinction between /n´/ and /N´/ is generally removed, the pronunciation in Muskerry of examples such as the following with /ŋ´/ points to the fact that /n´/ must also be changed to /N´/ in Munster:

(86) *oibhní* /ev´əN´iː/ → /ejN´iː/ → /əiN´iː/ → /əi'ŋ´iː/ (Mk) 'rivers'
      goibhní /gev´N´iː/ → /gəjN´iː/ → /gəiN´iː/ → /gəi'ŋ´iː/ (Mk) 'smiths'
      Suibhne /siv´N´ə/ → /sijN´ə/ → /siːN´ə/ → /siːŋ´ə/ (Mk) a surname

4.2.5(ii) *Denasalization*. Primarily we are dealing here with a rule by which *n* followed by a consonant is changed to *r*. There are two parts to this rule.

Firstly, in word-initial position *n* is changed to *r* following any consonant except *s* (or /h/ due to lenition of an original *s*). Examples are:

(87) *cnoc* /knuk/ → /kruk/ (D, C) 'hill'
      mná /mnaː/ → /mraː/ (D, C) [→ /mrɑː/ (Cn)] 'women'
      gnaoi /gniː/ → /griː/ (D, C) 'liking'
      tnúth /tnuːh/ → /truːh/ (D, C) [→ /truː/ (Cf)] 'desiring'
      an tsneachta /ə t´#n´axtə/ → /ə t´#r´axtə/ gen. of *sneachta* 'snow'
      sneachta /s´N´axtə/ (Mo) 'snow'
      shneachta /hn´axtə/(Mo), lenited form of *sneachta* 'snow'

As can be seen from *an tsneachta* 'of the snow', the rule takes effect across the boundary between the article and its noun. It is worth noting that nasalization of a following vowel may be preserved from the original nasal, e.g.:

(88) *cnoc* /krũk/ (Er) 'hill'
      gníomh /g´r´ĩːw/ (Er) 'deed'
      mná /mrãː/ (Er) 'women'
      sa tsnámh /sə trãːw/ (Er) 'into the deep'

Secondly, in medial position *n* becomes *r* for the most part only when it follows another nasal as in:

(89) *imní* /im´n´iː/ → /i(ː)m´r´iː/ (Cn) 'worry'
      cuimhne /kiv´n´ə/ ~ /kiːv´r´ə/ ~ /kim´n´ə/ ~ /kim´r´ə/ (Cf) 'memory'
      ingne /iŋ´g´n´ə/ → /iŋ´g´r´ə/ (Cf) '(finger/toe) nails'

96   *Modern Irish: grammatical structure and dialectal variation*

cloigne /kleg′n′ə/ (Cn) 'heads'
macnas /maknəs/ (Tm) : /makrəs/ (Ln) 'wantonness'

The first part of the rule is needed for Donegal and Connacht (including Inishmaan and Inishmore and to a large degree for Inisheer and Clare). The second part is often optional. Examples from Donegal are:

(90)   *Doiminic* /dim′r′ək′/ (Gd) (man's name)
       damnú /damruː/ (Gd) 'damnation'

It is however required sporadically over a far wider area as can be seen in the examples:

(91)   *léimnigh* /l′eːm′r′əg′/ (Dn) 'leaping'
       géimnigh /g′eːm′r′əg′/ (Dn) 'lowing'

Curiously, there are random cases when the opposite change is needed, that is *r* becomes *n*, for instance in the Dunquin taboo formation: *(a) Chríost* /x′n′iːst/ (Dn) 'Christ!' or South Tipperary *préamhacha* /p′n′iːəxə/ 'roots' (see Ó Maolchathaigh 1963) but *daúis* /da′nuːs′/ (Rg).

Finally, there is a deal of dissimilation involving liquids in isolated words such as:

(92)   *baineann* /bir′əN/ (Cf) 'female' : /bin′ən/ (M)
       (dá) réir /r′eːr′/ ~ /l′eːr′/ (Cf) 'according to it'

A minor rule within Cois Fhairrge is the interchange of /l/ and /rl/ in words with a final /əx/ such as:

(93)   *muicealach* /mik′əLəx/ ~ /mik′ərLəx/ (Cf) 'botcher'
       péicealach /p′eːk′əLəx/ ~ /p′eːk′ərLəx/ (Cf)
       'a vain person'
       béalbhach /b′eːLuːx/ ~ /b′eːrLuːx/ (Cf) 'bridle-bit'

4.2.5(iii) *Introduction of* **n** *beside an original nasal fricative.* The need for retention of nasalization adjacent to nasals would seem to be related to the age of a speaker, the oldest speakers retaining nasalization, at least in uncommon words. Even in words where the nasal fricative /w̃/ is subsumed into a diphthong /au/, nasalization may be preserved as a feature, e.g. *amhlaidh*

/auLə/ (Cf) 'thus'. In a limited number of words a rule is required to convert that nasalization into *n*, e.g.:

(94) *damhsa* /dausə/ ~ /dauNsə/ (Cf) 'dancing'
lámhacán (/Laːwəkaːn/ → /lawəkaːn/ →) /Laukaːn/ → /lauŋkaːn/ (Dn) 'creeping'
pǎmhsaer /pauseːr/ ~ /paūseːr/ ~ /pauNseːr/ (Im) 'flower'

4.2.5(iv) *Velarized nasal.* This rule removes /g(′)/ after /ŋ(′)/. The /ŋ(′)/ arises either as a result of /g(′)/ being nasalized in eclipses or it develops from a dental /n/ in front of a velar plosive. In certain dialects after the assimilation operates, the plosive, if voiced, is removed. In Mayo, this /g(′)/ is lost in every context, e.g.:

(95) *ceangal* /k′aŋgəl/ → /k′aŋəl/ (Mo) 'binding'
loinge /Liŋ′g′ə/ → /Liŋ′ə/ (Mo) gen. of *long* 'ship'

This does not happen in Donegal, Connemara or Munster. There is a minor rule in Munster which turns *ng* /ŋ(′)g(′)/ into *g* /g(′)/ when following a neutral vowel and before a word boundary in a word such as *tarrang* /tarəŋg/ → /tarəg/ (→ /tarək/) (see 4.2.3) 'drawing'. In contrast to this, in Connacht and Donegal it is the nasal which must be preserved in this context. Examples are:

(96) *scilling* /sˈk′iL′əŋ′g′/ → /sˈk′iL′əN′/ (D, C) 'shilling'
fuiling /fel′əŋ′g′/ → /fel′əN′/ (D, C) 'suffer'
tarraing /tarəŋ′g′/ → /tarəN′/ (D, C) 'draw'

The rule applies even when endings are added, e.g.:

(97) *scillinge* /sˈk′iL′əŋ′g′ə/ → /sˈk′iL′əN′ə/ gen. of *scilling* 'shilling'
scillingeacha /sˈk′iL′əŋ′g′əxə/ → /sˈk′iL′əN′əxə/ [→ /sˈk′iL′N′əxə/ → /sˈk′iL′əxə/; see 4.2.5(v)] 'shillings'

This removal of voiced velar (i.e. *g*) following a nasal can be viewed as an extension of the general rule which operates in word-initial position (see 6.2.1(viii)).

4.2.5(v) *Lateral and nasal assimilation.* There is a development of /d(′)/ and /n(′)/ to /l(′)/ and /n(′)/ when they occur beside another /l(′)/ or /n(′)/. Examples of this change are:

98 *Modern Irish: grammatical structure and dialectal variation*

(98) *maidne* /madˈənˈə/ → /madˈnˈə/ → /maNˈə/ (D, C) gen. of *maidin* 'morning'
áilne /aːlənˈə/ → /aːlNˈə/ → /aːLˈLˈə/ → /aːLˈə/ comparative of *álainn* 'beautiful'
cad 'na thaobh? /kad nə heːw/ → /kanəheːw/ (Ky, Mk) 'why?'
codladh /kodləɣ/ → /kolləɣ/ → /koLLəɣ/ → /koLəɣ/ 'sleep' (for development see 4.1.2)

It may be noted in passing that a change in the opposite direction is needed for Ballymacoda, e.g. /L/ → /ld/. That rule is required after /ld/ is changed to /L/ but prior to the Munster removal of the distinction between /L/ and /l/, so that the sequence must be *codladh* /kodlə/ → /koLə/ → /koldə/ 'sleep'.

There is another rule of importance by which *n* or *l* is removed before *r*. Examples are:

(99) *anró* /aunroː/ → /auroː/ (Mk, Rg) 'hardship'
scannradh /skaunrə/ → /skaurə/ (Mk, Rg) 'scaring'
bainríon /baunriːn/ → /bauriːn/ (Mk, Rg) 'queen'
lonnrach /luːnrə/ → /luːrə/ (Mk) 'shining'
ceannrach /kˈaunrəx/ → /kˈaurəx/ (Mk) 'halter'
síolrach /sˈiːlrəx/ → /sˈiːrəx/ (Mk, Rg) 'offspring'
dealramh /dˈaulrəw/ → /dˈaurəw/ (Dn, Mk) 'likeness'

Interestingly, both *l* and *n* are dropped before *r* in Muskerry (whereas in Dunquin only *l* seems to be dropped and then only occasionally). In Donegal the rule would appear to be needed only for, e.g.:

(100) *scannradh* /skaNruː/ → /skaruː/ (D) 'scaring'
bainríon /banriːn/ → /bariːn/ (Gd) 'queen'
sonnraithe /suːNri/ → /soːRi/ (Tn) 'noted'

4.2.5(vi) *The intrusive dental*. The type of assimilation which is common for laterals and nasals is rarer in the case of /r/ beside /l/ or /n/. We are concerned here with a plosive dental which will separate /l/ or /n/ from a following /r/. By all appearances this rule is entirely optional. Most often, this is a voiceless dental plosive /t̪/ which devoices the following *r*. In part of Connemara and in Mayo a sort of semi-devoicing is required rather than /t̪/. Examples are:

(101)　*bainríon* /baNriːən/ → /baNṭṛiːən/ (Cn, Mo) 'queen'
　　　　eanraith /aNrə/ → /aNṭrə/ ~ /aNṛə/ (Cn, Mo) 'broth'
　　　　anró /aNroː/ → /aNṭroː/ ~ /aNṛoː/ (Cn, Mo) 'hardship'

There are, however, some words where full voicing is preserved, e.g.

(102)　*lonnradh* /LuNrə/ → /LuNdrə/ (Cf) 'shining'
　　　　malrach /maːLrəx/ → /maːLdrəx/ (Cf) 'young boy'
　　　　lionnrach /L'iːNrəx/ → /L'iːNdrəx/ (Cf) 'fluid from a sore'

The cluster is normally unaltered (except that vowel lengthening can occur, see 3.4). Sometimes *rl* will arise due to metathesis [see 4.2.6(ii)], particularly in Mayo, in words where /d/ is required in Connemara, e.g.:

(103)　*galra* /gaːLdrə/ (Cn) ~ /garLə/ (Mo) 'disease'
　　　　olra /oLdrə/ (Cn), /ulrə/ (Tm) (→ /urlə/) (Er) 'eagle'
　　　　biolra /b'ildrə/ (Cn), /b'irLə/ (Er) 'watercress'

These exemplified derivations would presuppose a rule changing an underlying *galar* to *galra*, *iolar* to *iolra* [see 4.2.6(ii)] before the intrusion of /d/ and before the metathesis *lr* to *rl*.

4.2.5(vii) *Adjacent vibrant and sibilant*. There are two basic contrary rules: firstly, that /s'/ adjacent to /r/ becomes /s/; secondly, that /s/ adjacent to /r/ becomes /s'/.

As has been seen [4.2.2(i)] /r/ is never slender when following a sibilant. The opposition between /s/ and /s'/ is also removed in this environment. In essence, these changes involve the position of the tip of the tongue; either the /r/ retracts the /s/ or the /s/ brings the /r/ forward. Where the tip of the tongue is retracted the result is a postalveolar sibilant (i.e. /ʃ/), which is further back than /s'/.

Table 4.6 illustrates the variation in the major dialects.

As may be deduced from Table 4.6, the first rule applies in Donegal, the second in Mayo. In the west of Connemara, the second rule is optional, while in Cois Fhairrge the first one is optional. In Munster the first rule obtains in initial position.

In Cois Fhairrge (and West Connemara), there is also a metathesis [see 4.2.6(iii)] which affects the combination *sr* in words such as:

100 *Modern Irish: grammatical structure and dialectal variation*

(104)   *lasrachaí → larsachaí* /Laːrsəxiː/ ~ /Laːrʃəxiː/ (Cf) 'flames'
        pisreoig → pirseoig /pʹirsoːgʹ/ ~ /pʹirʃoːgʹ/ (Cf) 'superstition'
        glaisreo → glairseo /gLaːrsuː/ ~ /gLaːrʃuː/ (Cf) 'hoar-frost'

Table 4.6 *Realization of adjacent vibrant and sibilant in major dialects*

Underlying form	/sʹrʹ/	/sr/	/rʹsʹ/	/rs/
Example	*srian* 'reins'	*sráid* 'street'	*tuirseach* 'tired'	*comharsa* 'neighbour'
Donegal	/sr/	/sr/	/rs/	/rs/
Mayo	/ʃr/	/ʃr/	/rʃ/	/rʃ/
West Connemara	/ʃr/	/sr/ ~ /ʃr/	/rʃ/	/rs/ ~ /rʃ/
Cois Fhairrge	/ʃr/ ~ /sr/	/sr/	/rʃ/ ~ /rs/	/rs/
Munster	/sr/	/sr/	/rʃ/	/rs/

The two rules illustrated in the table above affect the result of the metathesis in the normal way.

4.2.5(viii) The slender vibrant (/rʹ/). Apart from the removal of slender quality, there are two other noteworthy rules affecting /rʹ/.

Firstly, in Gweedore, there is a major rule which converts /rʹ/ to /j/. Some examples are:

(105)   *Máire* /mæːrʹə/ → /mæːjə/ (Gd) woman's name
        bádóir /bæːdarʹ/ → /bæːdaj/ (Gd) 'boatman'
        iascaire /iːəskərʹə/ → /iːəskəjə/ (Gd) 'fisherman'
        gáirí /gæːrʹiː/ → /gæːjiː/ (Gd) 'laughing'
        fir /firʹ/ → /fij/ (Gd) 'men'

Where /j/ follows a neutral vowel and is at the end of a word, it combines with that neutral vowel to give /iː/, e.g. *soi[dh]bhir* /seːvʹərʹ/ → /seːviː/ 'rich'. Although there is a similarity between the latter change and that of *bealaigh* (/bʹaləxʹ/ →) /bʹaləj/ → /bʹaliː/ [see 4.1.3(ii)] gen. of *bealach* 'way', they do not, as a whole, operate in a parallel fashion, as can be seen in:

(106)   *fir* /firʹ/ → /fij/ (Gd) 'men'
        nigh /Nʹij/ → /Nʹiː/ (D) 'wash!'

iascaire /iːəskərʲə/ → /iːəskəjə/ 'fisherman'
caillighe /kaʟʲəjə/ → /kaʟʲiː/, gen. of *cailleach* 'hag'

The development of /ð/ from slender *r* /rʲ/ is widely known in Scotland. There are, however, occasional examples recorded for Donegal, e.g.:

(107)   *cladhaire* /kʟeːrʲə/ ~ /kleːðə/ (Tn) 'coward'
        oighreog /eːðag/ (Tn) 'ice'

Somewhat similar to this is the sporadic change from slender *r* /rʲ/ to /dʲ/ in various dialects in such words as:

(108)   *dréimire* /dʲrʲeːmʲərʲə/ ~ /dʲrʲeːmʲədʲə/ (Cf) 'ladder'
        báire /baːrʲə/ → /baːdʲə/ (Dn) 'goal'
        mochóirí /muxoːrʲiː/ ~ /muxoːdʲiː/ (Mk) 'early risers'

4.2.6 Metathesis

There are several different cases where the order of neighbouring sounds must be altered. Five rules governing some of these changes are proposed here:

4.2.6(i) s *following a plosive*. An *s* following a plosive is switched about so that it then precedes the plosive, e.g.

(109)   *creidsiúint* → *creistiúint* /kʲrʲedʲ + s +úː + nt/ → /kʲrʲesʲtʲuːɴʲtʲ/ (C, M) 'believing'
        tuigsint → *tuisciúint* /tigʲ + s + n + t/ → /tisʲkʲəɴʲtʲ/ (M) (→ /tʲisʲkʲəɴʲtʲ/) (C) 'understanding'
        absalóid /absəʟoːdʲ/ (Ih) → *asbalóid* /aspəʟoːdʲ/ (Im, Tm, Mk) 'absolution'
        gíogsán → *gíoscán* /gʲiːg + s + aːn/ → /gʲiːskaːn/ (C) [→ /gʲiːskɑːɴ/ (Cn)] 'squeaking'
        bocsa /boksə/ (D) → *bosca* /boskə/ (C, M) 'box'

The rule applies generally to the dialects. However, in Donegal velar plosives (i.e. /g (ʲ)/ or /k (ʲ)/) are excluded so that *bocsa* /boksə/ (Gd) 'box' and *tuigseannach* /tikʲsʲənah/ 'understanding' are required. Certain borrowings do not come under the rule:

(110) stáitse 'stage'
       bitse(ach) 'bitch'
       peáitse (Cf) 'page' : páiste 'child'
       meaits 'match' : maiste (Rm) 'spill'

4.2.6(ii) /l/ *or* /n/ + /ə/ + /r/. The combination vowel + /l/ or /n/ + /ə/ + /r/ changes about so that the /r/ will follow directly the /l/ or /n/. Furthermore, the then adjacent /l/ or /n/ or /r/ may be subsequently transposed as in:

(111) galar /galər/ → /galrə/ → (/garlə/) (Er) 'disease'
       iolar /ulər/ → /ulrə/ (/urLə/) (Er) 'eagle'
       malairt /malər′t′/ → /malrəd′/ → /malhrəd′/ ~ /maːLt̪rəd′/ (Cf) 'change'
       conairt /konər′t′/ → /kunhrət′/ → /kunhrəd′/ (Er) 'pack of hounds'

This metathesis is confined to Connacht and is most pervasive in Erris, where examples with /n/, such as *conairt* 'pack of hounds', are found. (For the substitution of *d* for *t* in final position after a neutral vowel in *malraid* 'change', *conraid* 'pack of hounds', see 4.2.4.)

4.2.6(iii) sr /sr/ → **rs** /rs/. There is an optional rule in Cois Fhairrge which causes *sr* /sr/ to be changed to *rs* /rs/ in medial position, e.g.:

(112) lasrachaí /Laːsrəxiː/ ~ larsachaí /Laːrsəxiː/ (Cf) 'flames'
       glaisreo /gLaːʃruː/ ~ glairseo /gLaːrsuː/ (Cf) 'hoar-frost'

4.2.6(iv) C/r/V̆'CV → CV̆/r/'CV. There is a minor rule which is required in Munster dialects which will change the combination *consonant* + *r* /r/ + *short vowel* + *consonant* + *stressed vowel* (i.e. C/r/V̆'CV) to consonant + neutral vowel + r + consonant + stressed vowel (i.e. CV̆/r/'CV) provided the newly created cluster is permitted by the syllabic rules. Examples are:

(113) brollach /brə'lax/ → /bər'lax/ (Dn, Mk) 'breast'
       bradán /brə'daːn/ /bər'daːn/ (Dn, Mk) 'salmon'
       graibhéal /grə'v′eːl/ → /garə've:l/ (Mk) 'gravel'
       cruithneacht /krəŋ'haxt/ (Mk) → /kər″n′axt/ (Ky) 'wheat'

4.2.6(v) /h/ *beside a liquid*. There is a rule by which /h/ beside a liquid is transposed as in examples such as:

(114) aithrí /ahrʹiː/ → /arʹʰiː/ (M) ~ /arhʹiː/ (Tn) → /æːrhʹiː/ (Lm) 'repentance'
aithne /ahnʹə/ → /anʰə/ (Tm) → /æːnʰə/ (Lm) 'acquaintance'
iothlainn /ohləNʹ/ → /olhəNʹ/ (Lm) 'haggard'

In the examples in (114) an original short vowel precedes *l*, *n*, and *r*. In Cois Fhairrge *h* has already been removed [see 4.1.7(ii)]. In Munster the metathesis is not required before *n* or *l* and only occasionally before *r* because a rule introducing a secondary epenthetic vowel (see 2.4) has already taken effect at this point in the derivation so that the cluster does not arise.

(115) aithne /ahənʹə/ (M) 'acquaintance'
iothla /ihələ/ (Mk) ~ /ahələ/ (Rg) 'haggard'
fothram /fohərəm/ (M) 'noise'

In Erris there is apparently no metathesis following a short vowel, e.g. *aithrí* /ahrʹiː/ 'repentance'. In Donegal metathesis is recorded, e.g. *raithneach* /ranʰəx/ (Tn) 'fern', *aithris* /arʹhəsʹ/ (Mn) 'narrate'.

It would seem that following a long vowel this rule of metathesis is necessary before *r* in any dialect where /h/ is still retained at this point in the derivation. There is more variation before *l* or *n*:

(116) saothrughadh /sɯːhruː/ → /serʰuː/ (M) ~ /siːrhuː/ (D, Mo, west C) 'earning'
bóithre/í /boːhrʹə/ → /boːrʹhə/ (M) ~ /boːrʹhiː/ (Mo, west C) 'roads'
féithleog /fʹeːhlʹoːg/ → /fʹeːlʹʰoːg/ (Mk) 'sinew'
traithnín /traːhnʹiːnʹ/ (Er) → /traːnʹʰiːnʹ/ (Tm) 'blade of grass'
cáithnín /kaːhnʹiːnʹ/ → /kaːnʹʰiːnʹ/ (Mk) 'flake'

To some extent, this metathesis might simply be seen as varying degrees of the devoicing of liquids (see 4.2.3). Indeed /r̥/ and /n̥/ are required for Teelin (see Quiggin 1906:89, 98), e.g.:

(117) aithne /æn̥ʹə/ (Mn) 'acquaintance'
aithrí /ær̥ʹiː/ (Mn) 'repentance'
saothrughadh /sɯːr̥hu/ (Mn) 'earning'
parrthas /paːr̥həs/ (Mn) 'paradise'
tuartha /tuːər̥ə/ (Mn) 'bleached'

4.2.7 Expressive clusters

The increase in the number of consonants in a word-initial cluster is sometimes used to alter the meaning slightly or to lend a greater expressiveness to the word. It is difficult to say how productive this phenomenon is. Often, as in the following examples, the words involved are pejorative. Two cases are dealt with here.

4.2.7(i) Initial s. There is the largely optional prefixing of /s/ to a single or double consonant group, e.g.

(118)   *(s)máirtíneach* (Cf) 'cripple'
        (s)líbíneach (Cf) 'messer'
        (s)lapaire (Cf) 'a pudgy person'
        (s)crománach (Cf) 'tall stooped person'
        (s)cluitéara (Cf) 'a glutton, sponger'
        geataire 'long rush' : *sceatachán* (Mk) 'splinter, slightly built person'

A similar variation throughout the dialects is exemplified in (119). In many cases, there is no semantic significance:

(119)   *preab* (Gd) 'spadeful' : *spreab* (Cf)
        corróig (Cn) 'hip' : *scorróg* (Gd)
        poilséir (Cn) 'pilchards' : *spoilséirí* (Rg)

Interestingly, *s* is often prefixed to the name of an animal to give extra force to a command, e.g.:

(120)   *scut amach* (Cf) 'out with you, cat'
        scearc amach (Cf) 'out with you, hen'

The examples in (120) are derived from *cut* 'cat' and *cearc* 'hen'.

4.2.7(ii) Initial /pʹ/. There is the prefixing *p* /pʹ/ to an initial /lʹ/ in examples like Cois Fhairrge *(p)leidhce, (p)leota, (p)leidhb* 'fool'. This may be related to lenition; see 6.2.5(i).

PART II

MORPHOLOGY

5 *Introduction to morphology*

The three chapters in Part II give an overview of the general morphological rules of Irish, and of the morphology of the noun and the verb. This introduction outlines very briefly the approach employed, explains the concept of extension and finally comments on the question of regularity within the morphology.

5.1 The approach

The morphology and the phonology of Modern Irish are intrinsically connected. This means that the morphological patterns must be seen in the light of the phonological rules described in Part I. Let us illustrate this with an example. On the surface a noun like *margadh* 'market' has three different inflectional patterns in the singular; Table 5.1 shows the various pronunciations:

Table 5.1 *Inflectional patterns of* margadh *'market'*

	Donegal/Mayo	Connemara	Munster
unmarked *margadh*	/marəguː/	/maːrəgə/	/marəgə/
genitive *margaidh*	/marəgiː/	/maːrəgə/	/marəgəgʹ/

However, the descriptive approach used here would state that there is one underlying pattern, one which is shared with many masculine words such as *bád* 'boat' : unmarked *margadh* /**marəgɣ**/ *bád* /**baːd**/, genitive *margaidh* /marəgəj/ *báid* /baːdʹ/.

The actual realizations of a final *-adh* as /uː/ in Donegal/Mayo or /ə/ in Connemara/Munster and a final *-(a)idh* as Donegal/Mayo /iː/, Connemara /ə/ or Munster /əgʹ/ are regular and predictable phonological rules. In other words, our patterns are based on a more abstract form. From the example in Table 5.1, it would appear that it is simply a question of saying that the pattern is based on the historical form *margadh* /**marəgəɣ**/, gen. *margaidh* /**marəgəj**/, and that phonological rules are merely the historic developments within the given dialects. In the case of *margadh*, gen. *margaidh*, the underlying forms together with the phonological rules coincide with the historical forms and their development. Though this is very often the case, it is not always so. Living grammatical patterns are always in a state of change, rearranging and adjusting, and the choice of underlying forms (i.e. *margadh* -/əɣ/, gen. *margaidh* -/əj/) is determined by what explains the various developments most economically. In order to explain the behaviour in Dunquin of nouns such as *geata* 'gate', *sneachta* 'snow' with the genitive forms *geataidh* /gʹatəgʹ/ and *sneachtaidh* /snʹaxtəgʹ/, we have to propose as underlying unmarked forms for Dunquin *geatadh* /gʹatəɣ/ and *sneachtadh* /snʹaxtəɣ/. These are not historical forms but this is the most economical way of expressing such a local analogy.

It is important to note in the discussion of the morphology that the forms given are often not the final realization; in general a cross reference to the relevant phonological rules is given in brackets, for example: *cruinnigheann* (→ *cruinníonn*) /krinʹiːjən/ 'gathers' [for development see 4.1.3(ii)].

5.2 The concept of extension

The addition of a morpheme and its effect on the relevant syllable is viewed here as an extension. We may take as an example the formation of the words Cois Fhairrge *síonach*, genitive of *síon* 'stormy weather' and *brisim* first singular habitual present of *bris* 'break'. In each of these cases we can think of the basic form of the word as being extended by a consonantal morpheme *ch* /x/ and *m* /m/ respectively:

(1) *síon* + *ch* /x/ *síonch* /sʹiːnx/
     bris + *m* /mʹ/ *brism* /bʹrʹisʹmʹ/

The new consonant clusters are not among those permitted in an Irish word; in other words the clusters *nch* and *sm*, in this position, violate the canonical form of an Irish word. The word is automatically rearranged and the syllables adjusted under a general rule of syllabic adjustment exemplified in Table 5.2 (see 2.3). This viewpoint differs from the historical one (and indeed the traditional synchronic one). The historical view treats forms such as *seachnóidh* 'will avoid', future of *seachain*, as contracted forms of *seachanóidh* (< *seachan* + *óidh*).

Table 5.2 *Examples of syllabic adjustment*

Original word	Morpheme added	Syllabic adjustment
síon	ch /x/	síonach
bris	m /m´/	brisim

Here we start with a basic form *seachn-*; the future is then *seachn-* + *óidh* → *seachnóidh*. In the imperative (or past) the basic form *seachn-* will be adjusted to *seachan* as the cluster *-chn* in final position is not permitted. Ultimately, *seachan* becomes *seachain* 'avoid' due to a rule which makes the *n* slender in the context [see 6.3.1(ii)1]. In other words, beginning with the form *seachn-*, the various morphemes are added, and if at any point a cluster arises which is incompatible with the patterns of sounds permitted in Irish (the canonical form) then the syllabic adjustment rule breaks up the inappropriate cluster.

5.3 Regularity

Undoubtedly the relationship between the actual phonetic shape of a verbal form and its grammatical function is more straightforward than that which exists between the phonetic shape of a noun and its grammatical function. We can illustrate this with some examples. In *tabharfad* 'I will give' the ending *d* indicates the features, first person singular, future (in conjunction with *f*), and in some dialects (particularly in Connacht) a responsive. These functions are unique to *-d*. On the other hand, in *sróine* genitive of *srón* 'nose', while the slendering and the addition of *e* /ə/ signify the genitive in this instance, they do not always do so. They could equally well signify the comparative as in *báine* comparative of *bán* 'white'. Apart from the irregular verbs (see 8.3) the verb is far more predictable than the noun.

In certain cases, given particular endings, e.g. *ín*, *óir*, etc., and given the gender of the noun, a morphological pattern is predictable. Yet there is a great deal of unpredictability, especially in the case of the plural and the verbal noun. Nevertheless, even with such unpredictability it is possible to lay out certain patterns. Ultimately, though there are patterns of regularity, the actual applicable pattern for a given word must often be specified in the lexicon. In this sense such morphological rules are minor ones (see 1.3).

6 *General morphological rules*

6.1 General discussion

It cannot be said that these rules are the product of any particular grammatical function but they are, so to speak, simply 'available' for use in certain syntactic or semantic circumstances. This means that, on one level, these morphological rules resemble the phonological rules (see Part I) inasmuch as they are not directly connected with the syntax or with the semantics. In that sense, these rules might be regarded as phonological rules which have limited functions. Nevertheless, these morphological rules differ from the phonological ones in that they are not simply determined by the phonetic environment but are affected by grammatical and lexical considerations.

The general morphological rules are broadly similar in the various dialects, even though differences may occur in the way in which they are employed. They are discussed here under two main headings: firstly, initial mutations – those which affect the beginning of the first syllable – and secondly, final changes – those which affect word endings.

6.2 Initial mutations

6.2.1 General description

Initial mutations are shown in Table 6.1. There is obviously regularity in these phonetic changes. In the process of lenition plosives become continuants (the non-sonant dentals then become back sonants) and there is a loss of tension in laterals, vibrants and nasals. In the case of eclipsis, the rules involve nasalization of voiced plosives and voicing of voiceless consonants. The initial mutations can in fact be expressed by a series of ordered rules (see Ó Siadhail and Wigger 1975:25-7 and Ó Dochartaigh 1977/9 in Refs:457-94). These are not repeated here, but some additional commentary on the table is required.

112 *Modern Irish: grammatical structure and dialectal variation*

Table 6.1 *Initial mutations*

Basic consonant	Lenited consonant		Eclipsed consonant	
	phonemic symbol	spelled	phonemic symbol	spelled
plosives				
c /k/	/x/	*ch*	/g/	*gc*
g /g/	/ɣ/	*gh*	/ŋ/	*ng*
t /t/	/h/	*th*	/d/	*dt*
d /d/	/ɣ/	*dh*	/N/	*nd*
p /p/	/f/	*ph*	/b/	*bp*
b /b/	/w/	*bh*	/m/	*mb*
fricatives				
s /s/	/h/	*sh*	---	---
f /f/	ø	*fh*	/w/	*bhf*
nasals				
n /N/	/n/	*n*	---	---
m /m/	/w̃/	*mh*	---	---
lateral				
l /L/	/l/	*l*	---	---
vibrant				
r /R/	/r´/	*r*	---	---

Although they are not shown in the table, slender consonants behave largely in the same way, e.g. slender *c* /k´/ becomes /x´/ when lenited and becomes /g´/ when eclipsed. As was pointed out in 0.7, lenited slender *m/b* and *d/g* are transcribed as /v´/ and /j/.

6.2.1(i) *Lenition of r.* There is a limited lenition of initial *r* which is expressed by palatalization, e.g. *(do) rugadar* /də r´ugədər/ (Dn, Mk) 'they bore'. This is for the most part recorded for an older generation of speakers in Munster (see Ó Siadhail and Wigger 1975:115 and Ó Murchú 1986). There are nevertheless sporadic examples outside of Munster, e.g. *d o roghain* /də r´aun´/ (Cf) 'your pick'. See also 4.2.5(1).

6.2.1(ii) *Non-lenition of* **st, sp, sc, (sm)**. Lenition does not affect an initial *st*, *sp*, *sc*, e.g. *mo scéal* 'my story' (beside *mo dhoras* 'my door'). An initial *sm* is not lenited in most dialects although it does occur in at least some Munster dialects, e.g. *shmut* /hmut/ (Dn) (lenited form of *smut*) 'stump, small portion'.

6.2.1(iii) *Lenition of* n, l. As the lenition of *n* /N´/ and *l* /L´/ is expressed as loss of tension, obviously it is only found where tense forms of *l* and *n* exist, that is to say outside Munster.

6.2.1(iv) *Lenition of* f. Although in the case of lenition *f* disappears, i.e. *f* becomes ø, a palatalized *f* leaves a palatal offglide which in sandhi affects a previous consonant, e.g. *an fheoil* /ən´ oːl´/ 'the meat'. The mutation of *f* is somewhat unstable, as can be seen in examples from Cois Fhairrge such as *feoil fuar* 'cold meat', *a leithéide de focal* 'such a word', where lenition would be expected following a feminine noun or the preposition *de* 'of'. It may also be remarked in passing that the change *f* → ø may be thought of as passing through a middle stage *h*. The change *f* → *h* → ø is a well established phonetic progression and such pairs as *féin* and *fhéin* /heːn´/ 'self' probably reflect this progression [see 6.2.5(iii)].

6.2.1(v) *Restrictions on* d, t, s, r, l, n. Although lenited *t* or *s* (whether slender or not) may all give /h/ except in Ring, they are distinguished at one level and they also provide the environment for some phonological rules [see 4.1.7(i)].

Sometimes, in circumstances where lenition is normal, it may not occur where homorganic consonants are involved:

(1) *an diabhail* (Cf) 'of the devil'
     an-socair (Cf) 'very steady'
     aon teach (Cf) 'any house'
     bean slachtmhar (Cf) 'a handsome woman'

On the other hand, where the second element is employed attributively or in a compound, lenition is the norm, e.g.:

(2) *móin dhubh* (Cf) 'black peat'
     sloitín dhraíocht (Cf) 'a wand'
     mionshodar (Cf) 'a slow trot'

In the case of *l, n, d, t* there is no apparent lenition as in, e.g.

(3)   *an leic* /ə(N) L′ek′/ (Cf) 'the flagstone'
        an chéad duine (Cf) 'the first person'
        an chéad truip /ə x′eːd trip′/ (Cf) 'the first trip'

However, these might be interpreted as a secondary *sandhi* development, that is /N′l′/ → /N′L′/, /dɣ/ → /d/, /th/ → /t/, etc.

6.2.1(vi) *Lenition in English loan-words.* It should also be noted that /ḍ/ or /ṭ/ remain unlenited and *s* or *f* are unlenited in loan-words from English, e.g. *Máirín Frainc* (Gd), *Paidí Saera Jeaic* (Gd) as opposed to *Connie Mhéaraí Mhicí, Máire Bhilí.*

6.2.1(vii) *Words which resist lenition.* In Gweedore, Connemara and Dunquin, and presumably on a wider basis throughout the dialects, the words *méid* 'amount', *Dé* (in names of days) resist lenition. The word *t(o)igh* 'at the house of' seems also to resist lenition.

6.2.1(viii) *Eclipsis of* **g**. Eclipsis is achieved in the case of *g* by nasalization. However, under a general rule the voiced velar (i.e. *g*) is removed following a nasal and, as can be seen in Table 6.1, the actual realization is /ŋ/.

6.2.1(ix) *Eclipsis of* **s**. A limited form of eclipsis of *s* is recorded from East Galway (Ó Tuathail 1939:281-4) and Clear Island (Breatnach 1940:87-8) where /s/ → /z/ and /s′/ → /j/.

6.2.2 Grammatical functions of lenition
It is not possible to give a full account here of the circumstances where lenition occurs, but the following overview is organized under three headings: (i) proclitics (ii) compounds and (iii) attributive combinations. The proclitics differ from the compounds and attributive combinations in that mutation (including a zero mutation) is an intrinsic characteristic and in that they are very weakly stressed.

6.2.2(i) *Proclitics.* The proclitics listed in the next sections lenite a following verb, noun or adjective:

6.2.2(i)1 *In a verb phrase:*

(4)   *ní* /N′iː/ 'not'
        cha(n) /xa(n)/ ~ /ha(n)/ 'not' (D) (also eclipsis; *chan* before *fh*)

do /də/ preverbal particle for past tense, etc.
-r (*gur* /gər/, *ar* /ər/, *nár* /na(ː)r/, *níor* /N′iːr/, i.e. negativers, question particles and complementizers in past tense)
má /maː/ 'if'
ó /oː/ 'since'
a /ə/ direct relative particle
a /ə/ or /də/ preverbal particle in verbal noun complement

6.2.2(i)2 *In a noun phrase:* (a) The article *an(t)* /əN(t)/ (unmarked case for a feminine and genitive for masculine noun) lenites. The restrictions on *d, t, s, l, n, r* described above [see 6.2.1(v)] apply here, e.g. *muintir an tí* 'the people of the house', *an tine* (fem) 'the fire'. When the article is preceded by a preposition there are three possibilities: lenition, eclipsis or no change. This is discussed in 6.2.4(iv).

(b) The possessive pronouns *mo* /mə/ 'my', *do* /də/ 'your' (sing.), *a* /ə/ 'his' lenite.

(c) All simple (i.e. non-compounded) prepositions except *go* 'to', *ag* 'at', *chun* 'towards', *i* 'in', *(e)idir* 'between', *le* 'with' and *seachas* 'apart from' lenite. The preposition *as* lenites sporadically in Dunquin, e.g. *as sheomra* 'out of a room'; in Connacht and Donegal it does not lenite. The prepositions *ar* 'on' and *thar* 'over' lenite e.g.:

(5) *thar dhuine eile* 'past another man'
    ar bhád 'on a boat'

However, they do not lenite where they form part of a petrified adverbial phrase:

(6) *thar sáile* (C, D) 'overseas'
    thar barr (C, M) 'excellent'
    ar maidin 'in the morning'

This gives rise to semantically differentiated pairs:

(7) *ar dóigh* (Gd) 'excellent'
    ar dhóigh (Gd) 'in a way'
    ar fad (Cf) 'entirely'
    ar fhad (Cf) 'in length'

The preposition *gan* 'without' tends to lenite abstract nouns, e.g. *gan mhaitheas* (Dn) 'worthless', *gan bhrón* (Cf) 'without sorrow'. On the other hand the *d, t, s, l, n, r* restriction [see 6.2.1(v)] applies. Furthermore in Munster *gan* does not seem to lenite a verbal noun, e.g. *leanaí gan baisteadh* (Dn) 'unbaptized children' beside *páiste gan bhaisteadh* (Cf) 'unbaptized child'.

(d) The vocative particle *a* /ə/ 'o' lenites, e.g. *a Mháire* 'o Máire'.

6.2.2(i)3 *Following forms of the copula:* Forms of the copula which end in *-r, -bh* lenite. The form *ba* (past/conditional) also sometimes lenites. In Donegal, Connacht, and more sporadically in Munster, nouns tend not to be lenited.

(8)   *Ba mac a bhí ann* (Cf) 'It was a son'
      Dá ba clocha a bheadh ansan (Dn) 'If it were stones that were there'

Before an adjective the use of lenition seems to depend on the initial consonant: *d, t, s, l, n, r,* are often left unlenited e.g. *Ba deas...* (Cf, Gd) 'It would be nice...' but always *Ba mhaith...* 'It would be good...'. The comparative form *níosa* 'than' also causes lenition in Dunquin except before *f* where a glide /vʹ/ occurs [see 6.2.4(v)].

6.2.2(i)4 *Continued lenition:* In a few cases the lenition passes on from the word immediately following the proclitic to a subsequent adjective or attributive noun:

(a) Following *Tá... ina* 'is' [see 10.3.1(i)] in certain phrases, e.g:

(9)   *Tá sé ina lá gheal* (Cf) 'It is bright daylight'
      Nuair a bhí mé i mo ghasúr bheag (Cf, Gd) 'When I was a small child (Cf)/boy (Gd)'

In some dialects of Donegal (particularly among older speakers) the rule is broader. An adjective is regularly lenited following any singular noun which is preceded by a preposition (except *as* 'from' or *le* 'with'): *don chapall dhubh* 'to the black horse'. Traces of this broader rule are seen in Cois Fhairrge in a petrified phrase such as *a chomhairle féin don mhac dhanartha* (lit. his own advice to the self-willed fellow) 'a wilful man will have his way'.

(b) Following proper names after prepositions:

(10) *ar Sheán Ó Fhíne* (Cf) 'on Seán Ó Fíne'
ar Thadhg Ó Shúilleabháin (Mk) 'on Tadhg Ó Súilleabháin'
don Lochán Bheag (Cf) 'to Lochán Beag'
ag Pádraig Ó Bhroin (Mk) 'at Pádraig Ó Broin'
faoi Sheán Mhór (Cf) 'under Seán Mór'

In Muskerry presumably by analogy lenition occurs following prepositions which do not cause lenition, e.g. *ag* 'at'.

(c) Following *Uí* in surnames

(11) *tigh Phádraig Uí Fhíne* (Cf) 'at Pádraig Ó Fíne's place'

(d) Following *agus/is* 'and' in co-ordinate structures, particularly in careful or stylized speech or in set phrases with attributive names:

(12) *thar fhréamhacha agus chuirp na gcrann* (D) 'over the roots and trunks of the trees'
fear shiúil lae agus chollata na hoíche (Mk) 'a travelling man by day and a sleeping man by night'
na diail mhóra agus bheaga (Ky) 'the big and small devils'
aois Mhurchú is Mheanchair (Cf) 'a very great age'

(e) Following the comparative of an adjective (in poetic style):

(13) *ba dheise dheirge* (Cf) 'most beautiful and red'

(f) Following the co-ordinative preposition *(e)idir... agus/is* 'both...and':

(14) *idir chorp, chleite is sciathán* (Cf) 'entirely'
idir gheimhreadh is shamhradh (Dn) 'both winter and summer'

(g) Following an adverb intervening between a noun and adjective:

(15) *Gaeilge iontach mhaith* (D) 'very good Irish'

This is not the case in the other major dialects, e.g. *Gaeilge réasúnta maith* (Cf) 'reasonably good Irish'.

118   *Modern Irish: grammatical structure and dialectal variation*

6.2.2(ii) *Compounds.*
6.2.2(ii)1 *General principle:* We are dealing here not only with true compounds but with cases where an adjective or noun is employed attributively preceding a noun. This includes adjectives such as *sean-* 'old', *droch-* 'bad' and numerals in general. It must be added immediately that *trí* 'three', *cheithre* 'four', *c(h)úig* 'five' and *sé* 'six' only lenite a following noun when the singular is used, and of the ordinals *seacht* 'seven', *(h)ocht* 'eight', *naoi* 'nine' and *deich* 'ten' normally cause eclipsis rather than lenition although sporadically in Dunquin lenition is found, e.g. *naoi bhraon* 'nine drops', *deich mhíle* 'ten miles'.

6.2.2(ii)2 *Restrictions on* d, t, s, r, l, n: The restriction regarding lenition between the dentals *d, t, s, r, l, n* tends to apply here:

(16)   *an-dona* (Cf) 'very bad'
       aon suim (Cf) 'any interest'
       cúilteach (Cf) 'return (of a house)'
       caoldroim (Cf) 'small of back'
       leasdeartháir (Dn) 'stepbrother'
       mórtimpeall /muːərtʹiːmʹpəl/ (Dn) 'around about'

Nevertheless there are many exceptions such as *ardthráthnóna* (Cf) 'midafternoon' and *caolsheans* (Cf) 'slender chance'. Furthermore between *n* (and sometimes *l*) and a following lenited *s* an intrusive *t* is often required:

(17)   *lántsásta* /ˈLɑːnt ˈhɑːstə/ → /ˈLɑːN ˈtɑːstə/ (Cf) 'fully satisfied'
       aon tseans /ˈeːnt ˈhʹans/ → /ˈeːnʹ ˈtʹans/ (Dn) 'any chance'
       cúiltseomra /ˈkuːLˈtˌhuːmrə/ → /ˈkuːLʹ ˌtʹuːmrə/ (Cf) 'backroom extension'

Finally, *t* or *d* tend not to be lenited following *th*, e.g. *athd(h)áir* /aˈtaːrʹ/ (Dn), /atɑːrʹ/ (Cf) 'recurrent heat in cattle'; *lea(th)taobh* 'one side'. Such examples may, however, no longer be felt to be compounds.

6.2.2(ii)3 *Continued lenition:* From the point of view of lenition compounds differ little from proclitics (the major difference being the very weak stress on proclitics). As in the case of proclitics the lenition may extend across the noun phrase:

(18) *dhá bhád bheaga* 'two small boats'
cheithre sheomra mhóra 'four big rooms'
trí lá fhichead 'twenty-three days'
sé lampa dhéag 'sixteen lamps'

As seen in (18) following *dhá* 'two' on to *sé* 'six' the lenition of a singular noun extends to a following adjective and to *déag* '-teen' and *fichead* 'twenty-' (Dunquin and Muskerry occasionally have *ar fhichid*). Presumably, originally by analogy, an adjective *déag* '-teen' or *fichead* 'twenty-' are also lenited following *seacht* 'seven' to *naoi* 'nine', which in fact cause eclipsis, e.g. *seacht mbosca mhóra* 'seven big boxes'.

There is here one minor distinction between the dialects. In Gweedore *déag* '-teen' is always lenited in these circumstances, e.g. *sé lampa dhéag* 'sixteen lamps', *trí chathaoir dhéag* 'thirteen chairs'. On the other hand in Connemara and Munster *déag* '-teen' is only lenited following a vowel, e.g.:

(19) *dhá ghlao dhéag* (Dn) 'twelve calls'
aon pháiste dhéag (Cf) 'eleven children'
dhá fhear déag (Cf) 'twelve men'

In Cois Fhairrge there is a sporadic exception with *aon...déag* : *aon lá d(h)éag* 'eleven days'.

6.2.2(iii) *Attributive phrases*. There are two basic rules governing lenition in attributive phrases.

6.2.2(iii)1 *Lenition under certain morphological conditions:* An attributive phrase is joined together by the use of lenition on nouns or adjectives which follow the head noun of the phrase if it is:

(a) masculine and marked for genitive case:

(20) *lár an phoill bháite* (Cf) 'middle of the engulfing sea'
i bpáirt an duine bhoicht (Dn) 'in regard to the poor person'

(b) masculine and marked for vocative case:

(21) *a dhuine bhocht* (Cf) 'poor person!'

(c) feminine and unmarked for case:

(22)   *ruaig mhór thinnis* (Cf) 'bad bout of sickness'

(d) plural with a final consonant:

(23)   *na fóid dhubha* (Dn) 'black sods'
        fir mhóra 'big men'
        tomaíl fhraoigh (Cf) 'clumps of heather'
        lachain bheaga 'small ducks'
        beithígh bhána (M, C) 'white cattle'
        leoraís mhóra 'big lorries'

In practice we are dealing with a final slender consonant or *s*. The fact that a final /j/ in *beithígh* /bʹehiː/ is lost in subsequent developments is immaterial. In Dunquin, where a historical dative is used as an unmarked case, there is a varied usage, e.g. *fearaibh mhuara gharbh* 'big rough men' beside *fearaibh muara graíthe láidir* 'huge big strong men'.

6.2.2(iii)2 *Lenition of definite attributive noun:* A definite noun used attributively is lenited, e.g. *cathaoir Thomáis* 'Tomás's chair', *in aghaidh Bhaile Átha Cliath* (C) 'against Dublin'. Diachronically speaking this is a relatively late rule and there are exceptions in petrified phrases such as *Lá Fhéil Pádraig* 'St. Patrick's day' (D, C), *pota Pádraig* (Cf) 'a St Patrick's day drink', *críoch Banba* (Cf) 'the land of Banba'. Where the attributive component consists of two nouns which are in genitive relationship, lenition is usually but not constantly found. It should be noted that in compound prepositions such as *as cionn* 'above' the second element consists of a noun. Lack of lenition is frequent where one of the nouns is not a proper noun. Examples of lenition are given in (24) and of non-lenition in (25).

(24)   *as cionn Gharrdha na Raithní* (Cf) 'above Garrdha na Raithní'
        téad bharr an ualaigh (Dn) 'the rope for securing the top of the load'
(25)   *le ais Garrdha na Muc* (Cf) 'beside Garrdha na Muc'
        in n-aice geata an tséipéil (Cf) 'beside the chapel gate'
        lár mí an Mheithimh (Dn) 'the middle of June'

6.2.2(iii)3 *Restrictions on lenition:* There is a great deal of option here in the various dialects, and many restrictions on this rule, sometimes including the *d, t, s, l, n, r* restriction. It often depends on how much the noun phrase in question is felt as a semantic unit. Cases which tend to restrict the rules stated in 6.2.2(iii)1-2 and which involve the syntactic structure of the phrase are listed here:

(a) An attributive noun which is a partitive genitive:

(26) *adharc pocaide* (Cf) 'a billy-goat's horn'
óinseach mná (Cf, Dn) 'a fool of a woman'
a chuid cainte 'his talk'

An attributive noun which is a partitive genitive (either involving measurement or material) is not lenited.

(b) An attributive noun qualified by an adjective:

(27) *oíche gaoithe móire* (Cf) 'a night with a high wind'
fir baile mhóir (Cf) 'men from big towns'

An attributive noun qualified by an adjective is often left unlenited, as in (27), where, following *oíche* 'night' (feminine) and *fir* 'men' (plural ending in a consonant), we might expect lenition.

(c) When the head noun of the noun phrase has verbal force, e.g. *a g ceannacht muca* 'buying pigs', or prepositional force, e.g. *i n-áit bainne* (Gd) 'in place of milk', the second noun tends not to be lenited.

On the other hand, there is in all dialects a substantial group of verbal noun phrases where the second noun is lenited, e.g. *ag fáil bháis* 'dying'. Though these phrases may predominantly (or originally) contain feminine verbal nouns, there are many which contain masculine verbal nouns, e.g. *a g ól bhainne* (Cf) 'drinking milk' or *ag cur sheaca* (Cf, Dn) 'freezing'. Although this phenomenon is very widespread in some dialects, for example Rosmuck (see Ní Dhomhnaill 1969/70:1-9), what is noteworthy is that there is a core of phrases common to all dialects such as: *ag fáil bháis* 'dying' (with the second noun in the genitive) or *ag cur fhataí (phr(e)átaí)* 'sowing potatoes'. It appears that many such phrases contain common verbs such as *fáil* 'get', *cur* 'put' and the lenition serves to bond the phrase with a particular meaning.

122 *Modern Irish: grammatical structure and dialectal variation*

6.2.3 The insertion of *h* and hiatus

Although the insertion of *h* is not included in Table 6.1 it is part of the system of initial mutations. It seems that following proclitics there are three possibilities: lenition, eclipsis or no change. It can be said that this *h*, which only follows proclitics with a final vowel, belongs to the third possibility (i.e. no change) and serves as a sort of hiatus marker which prevents vowel elision. But it also serves to complement lenition.

6.2.3(i) *The grammatical functions of* **h** *insertion.* The grammatical functions of *h* insertion are largely shared by the dialects. However, where there is a rule removing *h* between vowels [see 4.1.7(ii)] it has also a certain effect on *h* insertion. There is a certain amount of hesitancy, e.g. *Ní hiad* (Cf) beside *Ní iad* (Cf) 'It is not them'. In such an example there is a deal of redundancy. Where there is no redundancy, e.g. *a hathair* 'her father', beside *a athair* 'his father', the *h* is more stable. The proclitics which cause no change and after which *h* is inserted before a vowel are described in 6.2.3(i)1-6:

6.2.3(i)1 *The insertion of h following verbal proclitics:* There is *h* insertion following *ná* 'not' (negative imperative particle and, in Munster, negative complementizer or negative question particle):

(28)   *Ná hól* 'Don't drink'
        Ná híosfá? (M) 'Wouldn't you eat?'

6.2.3(i)2 *Insertion of h following forms of the copula*: There is *h* insertion following *ní* 'is not' and *cé* 'who/what is' (but not normally before a prepositional pronoun in either case). [The form *ba* 'was' may or may not cause lenition (see (8) above and 10.2.1).] Compare examples (29) and (30):

(29)   *Ní hé* 'It is not'
        Cé hé féin? 'Who is he?'
        Cé hiontas...? (Cf) 'It is no surprise' (lit. What surprise?)
(30)   *Ní air...* 'It is not on it...'
        Cé air? 'On what?'

6.2.3(i)3 *Insertion of h following nominal proclitics:* There is *h* insertion following the article *na* /nə/ 'the' (except in the genitive plural), *a* /ə/ 'her' and the prepositions *go* /gə/ 'to', *le* /lʹə/ 'with' [except where *n* is employed to fill a hiatus; see 6.2.4(v)] and *sa* /sə/ 'in the (plural)' in Dunquin:

(31)　　*na hóige* 'of the youth'
　　　　na hamadáin 'the fools'
　　　　a hathair 'her father'
　　　　go hÓrán Mór 'to Oranmore'
　　　　le hinsint (Dn) 'to tell'
　　　　sa háiteanna sin (Dn) 'in those places'

6.2.3(i)4 *Insertion of h following adjectival proclitics:* There is *h* insertion following the adverbial particle *go* /gə/ '-ly', the equivalence particle *chomh* /xə/ (D, C) /xoː/ (M) ~ *go* (Er, Gd) 'as' and the counting particle *a* /ə/:

(32)　　*go haisteach* 'strangely'
　　　　chomh hard 'as high'
　　　　bus a hocht 'the eight [o'clock] bus'

6.2.3(i)5 *Insertion of h in petrified attributive compounds:* There is *h* insertion following *Ó* /oː/ in surnames and *Dé* /dʹe(ː)/:

(33)　　*Ó hEidhin* (surname)
　　　　Dé hAoine 'Friday'

6.2.3(i)6 *Insertion of h following numerals which precede a plural form:* There is *h* insertion before a plural form following *trí* 'three', *cheithre* 'four', *c(h)úig* 'five' and all the ordinals (except *céad* 'first').

(34)　　*trí huaire* 'three times'
　　　　an deichiú hualach 'the tenth load'
　　　　an dara huair (D, C) 'the second time'

Eclipsis is the rule in Dunquin before a limited number of nouns (of measurement) which take the plural, e.g. *sé norlaí* 'six inches'. The special plural form *bliana* 'years' is very exceptional in that following *c(h)úig* 'five' it is lenited in Gweedore and Connemara *c(h)úig bhliana* 'five years' and it is eclipsed in Dunquin *chúig mbliana* 'five years'.

The numerals are somewhat exceptional insofar as they can receive a stronger stress than the proclitics described in 6.2.3(i)1-5. Nevertheless, the use of lenition shows that phonologically the numeral and the noun are felt to be a unit.

6.2.3(ii) h insertion and the question of hiatus.

6.2.3(ii)1 *Impersonal form*: Normally, at least in Gweedore, Cois Fhairrge and Dunquin, where lenition would occur in personal forms, an *h* is inserted before the impersonal forms (barring the conditional) of verbs which begin with a vowel:

(35)   *nuair a híslítear* 'when one lowers'
       ní húsáidtear 'one doesn't use'

Lenition may be avoided in the case of impersonal forms (once again barring the conditional):

(36)   *ní maitear na fiacha* (Cf) 'the debts are not forgiven'
       nuair a cuirfear (Dn) 'when it will be put'
       má buaitear air (Dn) 'if he is defeated'
       ó doirfear í (Dn) 'from the time it will be bulled'

We can say that *h* is here a way of avoiding vowel coalescence following proclitics where lenition is not permitted. In a similar fashion the prefixing of *h* to the past impersonal in examples such as *hardaíodh* 'one raised', 'it was raised' can be explained as an attempt to fill the hiatus between (*do*) and *ardaíodh* where no lenition is normally permitted: (*do*) *tugadh* 'one gave, it was given'.

However, it must be said that, presumably influenced by the personal forms and the conditional impersonal form, lenition of all impersonal forms (except the past) has become the norm in Cois Fhairrge and Gweedore (though not in Dunquin):

(37)   *má chaithtear* (Cf) 'if one loses'
       an mhaith a mhaoitear (Cf) 'the good which one begrudges'
       Ní bhuailtear é (Gd) 'one doesn't strike it'

The past impersonal does not normally take lenition: *moladh é* 'people praised him'. There are some exceptions, largely among irregular verbs such as Cois Fhairrge *tháinigeadh* 'one came', *chuadhadh* 'one went' or Dunquin (optionally) *chaitheadh poll a dhéanamh* 'one had to make a hole'.

6.2.3(ii)2 *Hiatus avoidance and lenition:* The insertion of *h* is not the only way of preventing vowel coalescence. Apart from a permanent eclipsis [i.e.

len, see 6.2.4(v)] or the development of *bh* /w/ /v´/ instead of *fh* [i.e. *ní bhfuair* 'didn't get' or Dunquin *níosa bhfearr* 'better', *sa bhfarraige* 'in the sea'; see 6.2.4(iv)] a doubling of a proclitic may serve the same purpose. The doubling of the past proclitic *do* in, for example, Dunquin and Ring, is one such example: *do dho ól → do dh'ól → dh'ól* 'drank'.

However, this *dh* /ɣ/ (or /j/ before front vowels) now intrudes before vowels following proclitics which cause lenition, e.g. *ní dh'ólann* (Dn) 'does not drink'. This means that *dh* /ɣ/ or /j/ before vowels is now part of the lenition rules for Dunquin.

Finally it may be mentioned in passing that in the copula forms *babh é* /bə v´e:/ 'it was', /v´/ serves to block vowel coalescence (see 10.2.4) and this might alternatively be achieved by a similar doubling of *ba* i.e. *ba bha é →* /bə v´e:/.

6.2.4 Grammatical functions of eclipsis

Eclipsis has in general more limited and more specialized grammatical functions than lenition and is therefore easier to describe. Eclipsis differs from lenition in that it is always triggered by either proclitics or numerals. The differences between the dialects are minimal except in the case where the noun follows a preposition with the article.

6.2.4(i) Verbal proclitics. There is eclipsis following the positive question particle *an* /ən/, the positive complementizer *go* /gə/, the indirect relative particle *a* /ə/ [see 12.1.1(ii)], *d(h)á* /da:/ → /(ɣ)a:/ 'if' and *mara/muna* 'if not' (see 12.1.2) and *cá?* or *cé?* (Con) 'where?'.

(38)   *An mbriseann sé...* 'Does he break...'
       ...go bpógann... '...that kisses...'
       an fear a mbíonn a mhac ann 'the man whose son is (usually) there'
       Dá n-íosfadh sé é... 'If he were to eat...'
       Mara mbacfaidh sé leis... (C) 'If he doesn't bother with it...'
       Cá bhfuil sé? 'Where is he?'
       Cé ngeobhainn é (Cf)'Where would I get it?'

Furthermore eclipsis follows the negative question particle and complementizer *nach* /nax/ in Connacht and Donegal and the negative particle in Donegal *cha(n)*. In the case of *cha* 'not' the usage varies from dialect to dialect in Donegal (see Ó Buachalla 1977:92-141, Ó Dochartaigh 1975/6:317-34 and Wagner 1986:1-10). In Gweedore (except in *cha bhíonn* 'is not wont to be' and *chan fhuil* 'isn't') eclipsis is the rule. Elsewhere lenition is widespread and the form *chan* always lenites. Examples are:

(39) *Nach mbeidh?* (D,C) 'Won't it be?'
  Nach dtiocfaidh sé? (D,C) 'Will he not come?'
  Cha dtáinig sé (Gd) 'He didn't come'
  Chan fhuil (Gd) 'It isn't'

6.2.4(ii) *Eclipsis following nominal proclitics.* Apart from the case of prepositions followed by a singular article [which is considered in 6.2.4(iv)] a noun is eclipsed following the plural article (when the noun is in genitive relationship) *na* 'of the', the possessive adjective *ár* /aːr/ (M), /ar/ (D), /ə/ (C) 'our', *bhúr* /wuːr/ (M), /mur/ (D), /ə/ (C) 'your' (pl.) and *a* /ə/ 'their' and following the preposition *i* 'in':

(40) *lucht na dtithe móra* 'the people of the big houses'
  ár mbád 'our boat'
  bhúr gcathaoir 'your chair'
  a gcuid 'their portion'
  i n-áit 'in place of'

Exceptionally in Gweedore or Cois Fhairrge *i(n)* 'in' does not normally eclipse a personal name in the second substantive identificatory construction [see 10.3.1(i)], e.g. *Bean mhaith tighe a bhí in Brighid* (Cf) 'Brighid was a good housewife'.

6.2.4(iii) *Eclipsis following numerals.* The numerals *seacht* 'seven', *(h)ocht* 'eight', *naoi* 'nine' and *deich* 'ten' cause eclipsis.

(41) *seacht ndoras* 'seven doors'
  (h)ocht bpeann 'eight pens'
  naoi bpíosa 'nine pieces'
  deich ngloine 'ten glasses'

On the other hand, in Dunquin there is a mixed usage here, tending in the case of *seacht* 'seven' and *hocht* 'eight' to show no change, e.g. *seacht clais* 'seven furrows', *hocht clocha* 'eight stones (of weight)' – except in set phrases; in the cases of *naoi* 'nine' and *deich* 'ten' there is a tendency to lenite singulars [see 6.2.2(ii)1] and only sporadically to eclipse plural nouns.

Furthermore in Dunquin the numbers *trí* 'three' to *sé* 'six' may cause eclipsis to the initial vowel of a following noun which expresses a measurement, e.g. *cheithre n-unsa* 'four ounces', *chúig mbliana* 'five years'.

6.2.4(iv) Preposition followed by singular article. Basically here we are dealing with a choice between eclipsis and lenition. We must bear in mind that, where lenition is the rule, it is blocked here before *d, t, l, n, r* [see 6.2.1(v)] and that before lenited *s* the article has the form *an t* /ənt/ 'the', e.g. *faoin ts[h]úil*. (The orthographical convention is not to show the *h* following the *s*.) In broad terms it can be said that there is lenition in Donegal and that in Connacht and Munster there is eclipsis. However, this statement must be qualified.

Firstly, in Donegal lenition seems to be employed consistently:

(42) *ar an bhád* (D) 'on the boat'
      fríd an fhuinneog (D) 'through the window'
      faoin doras (D) 'under the door'
      san fhuinneog (D) 'in the window'
      leis an ts[h]agart (D) 'with the priest'
      faoin ts[h]úil (D) 'under the eye'

In Connacht the rule is generally eclipsis; however, eclipsis is blocked before *d* or *t*. Following the two prepositions *do* 'to' /gə/ and *de* /gə/ 'of, off' lenition is the rule. Examples of eclipsis are given in (43) and of lenition in (44).

(43) *ag an mbean* (C) 'at the woman'
      thríd an mbliain (C) 'throughout the year'
      sa gcladach (C) 'at the sea-shore'
(44) *den fhear* (C) 'off the man'
      don bhó (C) 'to the cow'
      tuirseach den ts[h]aoghal (C) 'tired of the life'
      siar don ts[h]eomra (C) 'back to the room'

Another feature of Connacht is the fact that, presumably, historically speaking on the analogy of the unmarked form of a singular feminine noun following the article, e.g. *an ts[h]úil* 'the eye', the lenition is found in all usages of the singular feminine noun with an initial *s*, e.g. *faoin ts[h]úil* 'under the eye'.

128 *Modern Irish: grammatical structure and dialectal variation*

In Munster, once more, the general rule is eclipsis. In Dunquin, Ring (and Ballymacoda) at least eclipsis is also found following the compound preposition *go dtí* 'to':

(45) *roimis an gcoileach* (M) 'before the cock'
ón mbord (M) 'from the table'
ar an gcnoc (M) 'on the hill'
ar an dtaobh (M) 'on the side'
ag an ndoras (M) 'at the door'
leis an bhfarraige (M) 'with the sea'
ón sochraid (M) 'from the funeral'
go dtí an ndoras (Dn) 'to the door'

However, there are three prepositions to be considered. Following the preposition *sa* (the most frequent realization of *insa(n)* 'in the') lenition is for the most part the rule:

(46) *sa bhaile* (M) 'at home'
sa cheártain (M) 'in the forge'
sa ts[h]éipéal (Mk)/*ts[h]áipéal* (Dn) 'in the chapel'

A further feature is the development of a glide /w/ (or /vʹ/) [see 6.2.4(v)] between *sa* and *fh* (the orthographical convention is not to show the *h*):

(47) *sa bhf[h]airrge* (M) 'in the sea'
sa bhf[h]eirm (M) 'in the farm'
sa bhf[h]alla 'in the wall'

In Dunquin, in a few phrases expressing a rate of measurement, eclipsis rather than lenition is found:

(48) *sa mí* (Dn) 'per month'
sa mbliain (Dn) 'per year'
sa mbreis (Dn) 'extra'

A noteworthy internal difference in Munster is the fact that in Muskerry following the two prepositions *do* /də/ 'to' and *de* /do/ 'off', which combine with the article as *don/den* /dən/, lenition is the rule (though it is blocked by a following *d, t, l, n, r*), whereas in Dunquin eclipsis is the rule following *don/den* /dən/:

(49)　　*den fhear* (Mk) 'of the man'
　　　　den bhiolar (Mk) 'of the watercress'
　　　　don doras (Mk) 'to the door'
　　　　don ts[h]lí (Mk) 'to the way'
　　　　don dtír (Dn) 'to the country'
　　　　den seachtain (Dn) 'of the week'

On the other hand where *'on* /ən/, the abbreviated form of *don/den*, is employed in Dunquin, lenition is the rule (though it is blocked by a following *d, t, l, n, r*):

(50)　　*'on ghort* (Dn) 'to the field'
　　　　'on diabhal (Dn) 'to the devil'
　　　　'on bhanc (Dn) 'to the bank'
　　　　'on ts[h]oitheach (Dn) 'to the vessel'

Finally there is a system in Ring (see Breatnach 1960/1:217-22) where, in the case of a noun with an initial *p* or *c*, the use of lenition or eclipsis depends on whether the preposition ends in a vowel or not. Where the preposition ends in a consonant *p* and *c* are eclipsed:

(51)　　*ar an bpáirc* (Rg) 'on the field'
　　　　as an gcoláiste (Rg) 'out of the college'
　　　　thar an gcearta (Rg) 'beyond their rights'

On the other hand where the preposition ends in a vowel lenition is required:

(52)　　*age 'n chúinne* (Rg) 'at the corner'
　　　　ón pharóiste (Rg) 'from the parish'
　　　　den cheann óg (Rg) 'off the young one'

In the case of *sa* 'in the' lenition is normal in Ring, e.g. *sa chúinne* 'in the corner', where in neighbouring South Tipperary eclipsis is recorded, e.g. *sa gcathair* 'in the city'.

6.2.4(v) *Eclipsis and hiatus.* There are two phenomena which, though they are sometimes treated as cases of eclipsis, are probably better regarded as further devices within the language to avoid vowel coalescence.

Firstly, there is the *n* in, e.g. *faoina* 'under his/her/their', *lena* 'with his/her/their'. This *n* appears as /n/ rather than /ɴ/ in those dialects which preserve the difference and therefore must be distinguished from *ina* /əNə/ 'in his/her/their', where there is a genuine eclipsis. The *n* /n/ is a device used to prevent the occurrence of a hiatus when a proclitic with a final vowel comes before any of the particles *a* /ə/ or before a verbal noun in the case of *le* (e.g *len ithe* 'to eat'). This use of *n* and other elements gives rise to parallel sets such as Dunquin *dona* or *dá* 'to his/her/their' or Cois Fhairrge *lena* 'with his/her/their' beside *leis na* (or *le na*) 'with the (plural)'. This tendency to use *n* to obviate either vowel coalescence or a hiatus is even found in certain compound prepositions in Connacht:

(53)　　*go dtí n-a bhean* (Cf) 'to his wife'
　　　　le haghaidh n-a mbricfeasta (Cf) 'for their breakfast'

(This is paralleled by the wide use of the *s* before a plural noun in Dunquin: *leis na daoine* (Dn) 'with the people', *go dtís na seanoibreacha* (Dn) 'to the old works'.)

Secondly, a phenomenon resembling eclipsis is found following the negative particle *ní* 'not' in forms of the irregular verb *fágh-*, e.g. *ní bhfuair* 'didn't get', *ní bhfuighidh* 'will not get' [see 8.3.2(v)] and in Munster, following *sa* 'in the' or *níosa* (comparative particle) in the case of nouns with an initial *f*, e.g. *sa bhfómhar* 'in the autumn' [see 6.2.4(iv)], *níosa bhfearr* 'better'. Nevertheless this is probably best regarded as the development of a glide /w/ (or /vʹ/) which prevents a hiatus (i.e. *ní fhuair* /Nʹiː uːərʹ/ → /Nʹiː wuːərʹ/).

6.2.4(vi) *Continued eclipsis*. Eclipsis does not generally continue across the noun phrase, as is so often the case with lenition, particularly where an attributive usage is involved. However, there are some examples of continued eclipsis in the case of numerals, for the most part following the plural article *na* 'the' or the possessive adjective *a* 'his/her/their'.

As far as the plural article *na* 'the' is concerned there is a definite tendency to avoid eclipsis on following numerals, as the following examples show:

(54)　　*fear na fíche blian* (Dn) 'the man of twenty years'
　　　　fear na trí bhó (Cf) 'the man who has three cows'

The use of continued eclipsis seems to be limited to some petrified phrases and sometimes only the attributive element is eclipsed:

(55)   *seamróg na gceithre gcluas* (Dn) 'four-leaved shamrock'
         beithíoch na gceithre gcos (Cf) 'four-legged beast'
         beithíoch na cheithre gcos (Cf) 'four-legged beast'

Following the possessive *a* 'his/her/their' the numeral is eclipsed in the normal fashion, e.g. Cois Fhairrge *a gcúig cinn de mhuca* 'their five pigs'. However, in the case of *dhá* 'two' which, when not preceded by the article, is permanently lenited [see 6.2.5(ii)] eclipsis may be extended to the qualified noun:

(56)   *iad ag marcaíocht ar a dhá gcapall* (Cf) 'they riding on their two horses'
         Thá beirt acu súd ina dhá ndochtúir (Dn) 'Two of those are doctors'

Finally, there are occasional examples from Muskerry of eclipsis being continued where a preposition is followed by the article:

(57)   *ar an nduine mbocht* (Mk) 'on the poor person'
         ag an láir mbán (Mk) 'by the white mare'

6.2.5 Non-reversion of initial mutations

There are basically two cases where the sound resulting from lenition or eclipsis does not revert to the radical sound: firstly where the basic form of a word is changed, giving rise to sporadic differences between the dialects, and secondly where a weakly stressed element is normally lenited.

Table 6.2 *Initial changes due to reinterpretation of mutation 1*

Translation	Basic form	Mutated form	Reinterpreted basic form
footing turf	*cróigeadh* (D)	*(leis an) gcróigeadh*	*gróigeadh* (C)
skull	*plaosc* (M)	*(ar an) bplaosc*	*blaosc* (C, D)
return	*pill* (D, Mo)	*(níor) phill*	*fill* (M, Cn)
cliff	*aill* (D, C)	*(an) aill* (fem.)	*faill* (M)

6.2.5(i) Change in basic form. In this case a word may be given initial mutation under certain grammatical circumstances, and the new form which arises as the result of the mutation is then reinterpreted as the basic form, e.g.

cróigeadh 'footing turf' when eclipsed gives *gcróigeadh* which is then reinterpreted as *gróigeadh*. In this way it is possible to achieve a difference between Donegal *cróigeadh* and Connemara *gróigeadh*, both meaning 'footing turf'.

The noun *aill* 'cliff' is feminine, and following the article in the unmarked case, lenition is the rule. At this point, either *an aill* 'the cliff' is reinterpreted as *an (f)aill*, giving the new basic form *faill*, or alternatively *an fhaill* is reinterpreted as *an aill*, giving the basic form *aill*. Similarly it might be argued that there is a basic form *pill* 'return' and, because of the non-lenition of *f* [see 6.2.1(iv)] *níor fill* 'didn't return' is reinterpreted as *níor phill*, giving a reinterpreted basic form *pill* (see Table 6.3). It would not always be possible to decide from a synchronic viewpoint which might serve as an underlying basic form for all dialects.

Table 6.3 *Initial changes due to reinterpretation of mutation 2*

Translation	Basic form	Mutated/non-mutated form	Reinterpreted basic form
cliff	*faill* (M)	*(an) fhaill* (fem.)	*aill* (C, D)
return	*fill* (M, Cn)	*(níor) fill*	*pill* (D, Mo)

A similar process can obviously also occur with the initial consonants of verbal forms. For instance, in certain varieties of Donegal Irish, e.g. Teelin, both *deachaigh* and *teachaigh* are found as dependent forms of *chuaigh* 'went' and *dearn* and *tearn* as dependent forms of *rinn* 'made'. The forms *teachaigh* 'went' and *tearn* 'made' presumably develop because of negative forms like *cha deachaigh* 'didn't go' and *cha dearn* 'didn't make'. Since, on the one hand, *cha* in these varieties of Donegal Irish does not mutate *d*, and on the other hand eclipses *t* (i.e. *t → d*), the original *cha deachaigh*, *cha dearn* is reinterpreted as *cha dteachaigh*, *cha dtearn*. This, of course, gives rise to the new or alternative basic forms *teachaigh*, *tearn*.

Table 6.4 *Initial changes due to reinterpretation of mutation 3*

Translation	Basic form	Mutated form	Reinterpreted alternative basic form
went (dependent form)	*deachaigh*	*(cha) dteachaigh*	*teachaigh*
made (dependent form)	*dearn*	*(cha) dtearn*	*tearn*

Historically speaking, this type of change plays a big part in the development of loan-words. The English word *wall* is borrowed as *bhalla* 'wall' and then the initial /w/ is either taken as lenition (i.e. *mo bhalla* 'my wall' therefore *balla* becomes the basic form) or as eclipsis (i.e. *ar an bhfalla* 'on the wall' therefore the basic form becomes *falla*). In fact in Munster *falla* 'wall' is found, whereas in Connacht and Donegal the form is *balla*.

As lenited *b* and *m* are both ultimately realized as /w/ or /v′/, *g* and *d* as /ɣ/ or /j/ and *t* and *s* as /h/, they are perhaps more likely to undergo such changes:

(58) *beach* (M) 'bee' : *meach* (Cn)
   geis (Cn) 'taboo' : *deas* (Mk)
   tunc (Cf) 'shove' : *sunc* (Mk)

Another cause of difference in the basic forms, which is very similar to this, is the 'wrong' separation of the *n* or *t* from the article:

(59) *an neascóid* (Cf) 'boil' : *eascóid* (Mk)
   an tsiocair (Gd) 'cause' : *tiocair* (Cf)

Sometimes it is necessary to envisage a two-stage process in the change, for example /m′/ → /v′/ → /f′/ as in Cois Fhairrge *meitheal* ~ *feitheal* 'working party'. This type of two-stage process might also explain an expressive cluster [see 4.2.7(ii)] such as *pleidhce* beside *leidhce* 'fool' (i.e. *p* → *f* → ø).

Table 6.5 *Initial changes due to reinterpretation of mutation 4*

	Basic form	Lenition	Non-reversion of lenition
Stage 1	*meitheal* /m′/	*a mheitheal* /v′/	*mheitheal* /v′/
	New basic form	Expected eclipsis	Removal of eclipsis
Stage 2	*mheitheal* /v′/	*ar an mheitheal* /v′/	*feitheal* /f′/

Finally there are examples of variation between the dialects which cannot be understood as initial mutations, e.g. *glaoch* ~ *blaoch* (Cf) 'call', *dias* ~ *déas* (Cf) 'ear of corn' beside *lias* (Mk).

134 *Modern Irish: grammatical structure and dialectal variation*

6.2.5(ii) Weakly stressed words. Weakly stressed words tend to be permanently lenited. The following are some examples:

(60)   *dhá* 'two'
       cheithre 'four'
       chomh 'as'
       cheana /**haNə**/ 'already'
       le /**l′ə**/ 'with'
       thar 'over, past'

The environment may have a certain influence here. The prepositional pronouns *dom, dhom, 'om* 'to/for me'; *duit, dhuit, 'uit* 'to/for me' etc. are a case in point. All three forms occur in Cois Fhairrge. The lenited forms *dhom, dhuit* etc. are undoubtedly the most frequent and are obligatory between vowels, e.g. *go mbeannaí Dia dhuit* 'may God bless you'. The unlenited forms are rare and probably confined to certain environments. This obligatory use of lenition is also found sporadically within words:

(61)   *dearmhad* (→ /**d′aru:d**/) (M) 'forgetting' : *dearmad* /**d′arəməd**/ (D, C)
       carghas (→ /**ka:ri:s**/) (Cf) 'Lent' : *cargas* /**karəgəs**/ (D)
       Fearghal (K) (→ /**f′ari:l**/) (M) man's name : *Feargal* /**f′arəgəL**/ (D)

6.2.5(iii) Interchange of f and h. In both types of mutation described in 6.2.5(i-ii) there are examples of *f* and *h* interchanging. Examples are:

(62)   *féin* (Dn, Mk) 'self' : *héin* (D, C, Ring)
       féach or *héach* (Dn, Ring) 'see' : *feacha* or *heacha* (Cf)
       cé/hé/fé ar bith (Cn) 'whatever'

This probably is a reflection of the series *f* → *h* → ø discussed in 6.2.1(iv). This series may also explain the variation between *tríd* (Dn), *thríd* (Cn) and *fríd* (D) 'through him/it'.

6.3 Final mutations

Two rules which affect the ends of words are dealt with here. They are what might be called 'all-purpose' rules in that they are employed for various grammatical functions and apply equally to verb, noun, adjective and prepositional pronoun. Only words with a final consonant are affected by these rules: either the quality of that consonant is changed (i.e. replaced by its slender or broad counterpart) or an extra vowel is added, increasing the number of syllables. Both rules can be combined in a given grammatical function.

6.3.1 Slendering and broadening
For convenience' sake, this rule is referred to as slendering and broadening. It may, of course, be thought of as one rule: the addition or the removal of the marked slender quality. The following are some of the main grammatical applications of slendering and broadening.

6.3.1(i) *The noun and adjective.* Here gender, case and number are involved and the nouns and adjectives to which the rules apply cannot usually be predicted. There are also nouns and adjectives where no changes are made or endings added (particularly in the plural). All we can speak of here are the grammatical circumstances where these rules may apply in some dialects.

In all of the examples given in examples 63-7 there is either slendering, e.g. *gasúr* 'child', gen. *gasúir*, where the genitive singular is formed by making the final *r* slender (/r/ → /rʹ/), or broadening, e.g. *athair* 'father', gen. *athar*, where the genitive singular is formed by making the final *r* broad (/rʹ/ → /r/). In some of the examples slendering or broadening combine with other types of final mutation such as vowel addition (see 6.3.2), e.g. *scuab* 'broom', gen. *scuaibe*, where the genitive system is formed by making the *b* slender (/b/ → /bʹ/) and adding a neutral vowel. In such examples the changes which combine with slendering or broadening are in parenthesis. In an example such as *bealach* 'way', gen. *bealaigh*, the actual surface realizations vary among the dialects and they are labelled accordingly. The following examples illustrate the various functions of slendering: in (63) the genitive singular, in (64) the plural, in (65) the dative singular, in (66) the vocative singular and in (67) comparative or abstract noun:

(63)   *gasúr* 'child'   *gasúir*
           /gasuːr/   →   /gasuːrʹ/
           asal 'donkey'   *asail*
           /asəl/   →   /asəlʹ/
           bealach 'way'   *bealaigh*
           /bʹaləx/ → /bʹaləxʹ/ [→ /bʹaləj/ → /bʹaləgʹ/ (M) ~ /bʹaliː/ (D, Mo) ~ /bʹæːlə/ (Cn)]

scuab 'broom' *scuaibe*
/skuːəb/ → /skuːəb´/ (→ /skuːəbˊə/)
gealach 'moon' *gealaí*
/gˊalək/ → /gˊalək´/ (→ /gˊaləxˊə/ → /gˊaləjə/ → /gˊaliː/)
banbh 'piglet' *bainbh*
/banw/ → /banvˊ/ (→ /banˊvˊ/ → /banˊəvˊ/)
samhradh 'summer' *samhraidh*
/sawrəɣ/ → /sawrəj/ [→ /saurəgˊ/ (M) ~ /sauriː/ (D, Mo)
~ /saurə/ (Cn)]
athair 'father' *athar*
/ahərˊ/ → /ahər/
Éirinn 'Ireland' *Éireann*
/eːrˊəNˊ/ → /eːrˊəN/
tinidh 'fire' *tineadh*
/tˊinˊəj/ → /tˊinˊəɣ/ (→ /tˊinˊuː/) (Mo)

(64) *bád* 'boat' *báid*
/baːd/ → /baːdˊ/ (M, C)
leanbh 'child' *linbh* (Cf)
/Lˊanw/ → /Lˊanvˊ/ (→ /Lˊanˊvˊ/ → /Lˊinˊəvˊ/)
Éireannach 'Irishman' *Éireannaí*
/eːrˊəNəx/ → /eːrˊəNəxˊ/ [→ /eːrˊəNəxˊə/ → /eːrˊəNəjə/ → /eːrˊəNiː/
(C, D)]
cathair 'city' *cathracha*
/kahrˊ/ → /kahr/ (→ /kahrəxə/)

(65) *cos* 'leg' *cois*
/kos/ → /kosˊ/
gealach 'moon' *gealaigh*
/gˊalək/ → /gˊalək´/ [→ /gˊaləj/ → /gˊæːlə/ (Cn) /gˊaliː/ (D, Mo) ~
/gˊaləgˊ/ (M)]

(66) *Séamas* man's name *Séamais*
/sˊeːməs/ → /sˊeːməsˊ/
bacach 'beggar' *bacaigh*
/bakəx/ → /bakəxˊ/ [→ /bakəj/ → /baːkə/ (Cn) /bakiː/ (D, Mo)
/bakəgˊ/ (M)]

(67) *bán* 'white' *báine* 'whiter'
/baːn/ → /baːnˊ/ (→ /baːnˊə/)
Éireannach 'Irish' *Éireannaí* 'more Irish'
/eːrˊəNəx/ → /eːrˊəNəxˊ/ (→ /eːrˊəNəxˊə/ → /eːrˊəNəjə/ → /eːrəNiː/)

Final mutations 137

fearúil 'manful'   *fearúla(cht)* 'more manful, manfulness'
/fʹaruːlʹ/ → /fʹaruːl/ (→ /fʹaruːlə(xt)/)
cóir 'just'   *córa* 'more just'
/koːrʹ/ → /koːr/ (→ /koːrə/)

6.3.1(ii) *The verb*. The slendering/broadening process is very limited within the verbal system; there is a variety of endings and particles which serve to express the different verbal categories. However, there are two cases where the slendering/broadening rule applies to the final consonant of the verb.

6.3.1(ii)1 *Final* l, n, r: A final *l*, *n* or *r* which is in the second syllable and which is in word-final position or before a final /t/ is made slender. The endings are already added to the verbal root at this point. (If we think of *t* of the verbal noun and the *te* of the verbal adjective as being added subsequent to the *l*, *n* and *r* becoming slender, then we need not make mention of a final /t/.) Examples are *oscail* 'open!', *labhairt* 'speaking', *féachaint* 'looking'. The following table shows the development of these examples from the roots *oscl-*, *labhr-* and *féach*:-

Table 6.6 *Development of* oscl-, labhr-, féach

roots	oscl-	labhr-	féach-
ending or consonant extension			féachn
syllabic adjustment	oscal	labhar	féachan
slendering	oscail	labhair	féachain
addition of *t* for verbal noun		labhairt	feachaint
result	oscail	labhairt	féachaint (M)

There is a tendency for this slendering to intrude on verbs with a final *-áil* which exhibit a deal of hesitation when endings are added, e.g. Cois Fhairrge *thiomálfainn* ~ *thiomáilfinn* 'I would drive'. The broad *l* is more frequent.

It would seem that slendering and the addition of *t* are concomitant. There is a small number of verbal nouns, including all those ending in *-achan*, which do not become slender:

138 *Modern Irish: grammatical structure and dialectal variation*

(68)   *leagan* (C) 'lay' : *leogaint* (Gd)
       tligean 'condemn, cast' (C), 'cast up' (D)
       ligean (Cf, Er) 'let' : *ligint* (Cf, Dn) : *leogaint* (Mk)
       lagachan (C) 'weakening'
       aipeachan (C) 'ripening'

6.3.1(ii)2 *Broadening in verbal noun:* In some verbs which have a root which ends in a slender consonant, that consonant is broadened before a verbal noun ending, in particular before *-adh*. Examples are:

(69)   *bualadh* 'hitting' : *buaileann* 'hits'
       bleaghan (→ *bleán*) (C) 'milking': *bligheann* (→ *blíonn*) 'milks'
       cur 'putting' : *cuireann* 'puts'
       bánaghadh (→ *bánú*) 'dispersing' : *bánaigheann* (→ *bánaíonn*) 'disperses'
       múnadh (Cn) 'teaching' : *múineann* 'teaches'
       cathamh (Er) 'throwing' : *caitheann* 'throws'
       ceannacht (< *ceannagh* + *t*) 'buying' : *ceannaigheann* → *ceannaíonn* 'buys'
       dúsacht (< *dúsagh* + *t*) (Er) 'waking' : *dúisigheann* (→ *dúisíonn*) 'wakens'
       dúnadh (Cn) 'shutting' : *dúineann* 'shuts'

This broadening of the verbal root in verbal nouns seems to be most widespread in Erris.

Ultimately this variation in broad and slender quality may be responsible for a more general instability in the quality of consonants [see 4.2.2(ii)].

6.3.1(iii) *The prepositional pronoun.* Prepositions are inflected for person and number when their object is a pronoun. These inflected forms are called prepositional pronouns. The slendering/broadening process is utilized in the inflection of the prepositional pronouns. Despite all the irregularity and variation between dialects which these forms entail, operations can be observed similar to those found generally in the morphology and in the phonology. As shown in Table 6.7, slendering is widely used to signify the third person singular forms. In some cases a slender ending is added and this is illustrated in Table 6.8. The actual examples in the table are from Connemara but the general principles are shared by the dialects.

Final mutations 139

Table 6.7 *Slendering in third person of Connemara prepositional pronouns*

Preposition	3rd singular masculine	3rd singular feminine	contrasted with first singular etc.
ag 'at'	*aige*	*aice*	*agam* etc.
/eg´/	/eg´ə/	/eg´ + hə/ → /ek´ə/	/aːgəm/
ar 'on'	*air*	*oirthi*	*orm* etc.
/er´/	/er´/	/er´ + hə/ → /orə/	/orəm/
roimh 'before'	*roimhe*	*roimpi*	*romham* etc.
/riv´/	/riv´ə/	/rim´ + p´ə/	/ruːm/
as 'out of'		*aisti*	*asam* etc.
/aːs/		/as + t´ə/	/aːsəm/
i 'in'		*inti*	*ionam* etc.
/ə/		/iN + t´ə/	/uNəm/

Although traditionally 'on' is written as *ar* and 'at' as *ag* we are in fact dealing here with *oir* /er´/ and *oig* /eg´/; see also 3.3.3.

Table 6.8 *Addition of slender ending to third singular of Connemara personal pronouns*

le 'with'	*leis*	*léithi*	*liom* etc.
/l´ə/	/l´ə + s´/	/l´eː + hə/	
thrí 'through'	*thríd*	*thríthi*	*thríom* etc.
/hriː/	/hriː + d´/	/hriː + hə/	
thar 'over'	*thairis*	*thairte*	*tharam* etc.
/haːr/	/har + s´/	/har + t´ə/	

The endings *-m, -t* (e.g. *le* 'with', *liom* 'with me', *leat* 'with you') in the first and second singular and *-nn, -bh* (e.g. *linn* 'with us', *libh* 'with you') in the first and second plural are constant. This slendering is the main morphological device used and it is employed to distinguish between the third singular feminine and the third plural so that there is an opposition either between:

(a) *-thi* /hə/ and *-thu* /hə(b)/, e.g. *aice* 'at her' : *acu* 'at them'

(b) *-pi* /p´ə/ and *-pu* /pə(b)/, e.g. : *roimpi* 'before her' : *rompu* 'before them'

(c) *-ti* /t´ə/ and *-tu* /tə(b)/, e.g. *inti* 'in her' : *iontu* 'in them'

6.3.2 Vowel addition

This rule concerns the addition of a short vowel to the end of a word. As the stress never transfers to this vowel, it is always a neutral vowel (i.e. /ə/).

6.3.2(i) Use in nouns and adjectives. This vowel addition plays an important role in the morphology of the noun and adjective and is often combined with slendering or broadening in order to form genitive or plural forms.

Undoubtedly there is a great variation and irregularity in the plural forms and the vowel addition is often simply a part of a plural ending. Nevertheless the majority of the plural endings can be analysed as a series composed of consonant extension and vowel addition. Some examples are:

(70)   *cos* 'leg', plural *cos + a /ə/*: *cosa*
         scéal 'story', plural *scéal + t + a /ə/*: *scéalta*
         cathair 'city', plural *cathr + ch + a /ə/*: *cathracha*
         lus 'plant', plural *lus + nn + a /ə/*: *lusanna*

For a full discussion of the plural formation see 7.3.

6.3.2(ii) Variation between -a/e /ə/ and -(a)í /iː/. In plural endings there is a great deal of variation in Connacht between *-a/e /ə/* and *-(a)í /iː/*. (This *-(a)í /iː/* is not derived from *-(a)ighe /əjə/*.) An example of this variation would be Erris *bróga* or *brógaí* depending on where in the sentence it occurs.

Generally in Irish it would seem that *-(a)í /iː/* is the only possible ending in the following cases:

(a)   words ending in *-a/e*, e.g. *cóta* 'coat', plural *cótaí*
(b)   words ending in *-ín*, e.g. *cipín* 'small stick', plural *cipíní*
(c)   words ending in *-(e)acht*, e.g. *Gaeltacht* 'Irish-speaking area', plural *Gaeltachtaí*
(d)   words ending in *-ú(i)r*, e.g. *dochtú(i)r* 'doctor', plural *dochtúirí*
(e)   words ending in *-óir*, e.g. *bádóir* 'boatman', plural *bádóirí*
(f)   words ending in *-éir*, e.g. *búistéir* (M) 'butcher', plural *búistéirí*

There is a further group of words, some of which require *-(a)í /iː/* in all dialects, e.g. *rud* 'thing', plural *rudaí*, *buachaill* 'boy', plural *buachaillí*, and some of which are peculiar to one major dialect, e.g. *bád* 'boat', plural *bádaí* (D).

There is therefore a new morpheme *-(a)í /iː/* which is required. This morpheme is especially common following consonant extension (see 7.3.3) and it would appear that it is more widespread in the north, as can be seen in the following:

(71)   -anna /ənə/ (M)
         -anna(í) /ənə/ ~ /əNiː/ (Im)
         -annaí /əNiː/ (Cn)
         -anna /ənə/ and -annaí /əNiː/ (depends on sentence position) (Er)
         -annaí /əNiː/ (D)

A rule is required in Connacht and Donegal to give -(a)í /iː/ rather than -a/e /ə/ in certain plural forms of the noun (as opposed to the adjective, where -a/e /ə/ is the rule). Yet there are several restrictions on this rule which must be mentioned:

(a) In Erris the ending is determined by the syntactic context: where an attributive element follows, /ə/ is retained, e.g. bróga móra 'big shoes' beside brógaí 'shoes'.

(b) In Donegal the number of syllables in a word may influence the choice: monosyllabic nouns often taking -a/e /ə/ rather than -(a)í /iː/, e.g. bróg 'shoe', plural bróga (Gd); cos 'leg', plural cosa (Gd).

(c) In Donegal, following a consonant extension in ch /x/, the morpheme -a /ə/ is retained, e.g. éan 'bird', plural éanacha (Tn), áit 'place', plural áiteacha (Tn). In some Donegal dialects /əj/ rather than /ə/ is used when no attributive element follows, e.g. éanacha /eːnəhəj/ (Gd), áiteacha /æːtʹəhəj/ (Gd).

(d) In special plural forms for counting [see 7.3.5(iii)] there is a tendency to preserve -a/e /ə/, e.g. seacht mbliana 'seven years' beside bliantaí (Gd) 'years'.

(e) Where there is a special vocative plural form, -a /ə/ is also retained, e.g. feara 'men' (Cn).

(f) Following consonant extension with th /h/, only -a /ə/ is permitted, e.g. tír 'country', plural tíortha (Cn) 'countries'.

Yet despite the general rule replacing the morpheme /ə/ by /iː/ and the restrictions outlined in (a-f) above, it is not possible to predict fully the usage of -(a)í /iː/ rather than -a/e /ə/. Sometimes, it will depend on the individual word, e.g. láimh 'hand', plural lámha (Cf) 'hands' beside lámhaí (Rm); cois 'leg', plural cosa (Cf) beside cosaí (Rm) 'legs'.

6.3.2(iii) Use in verbs. In the verbal system the only use of vowel addition is found in the present subjunctive [see 8.2.3(i)]:

(72)   go gcuire (cuir + e /ə/) 'that...may put'
        go mbeannaí (beannaigh + e /ə/) 'that... may bless'.

7 *The noun*

The noun is discussed in this chapter under three headings, Gender (see Ó Siadhail 1984b:173-7), Inflection and Formation of the plural. While gender, case and number are distinct features, sections 7.1-7.3 also show that they are also inextricably interconnected.

7.1 Gender

7.1.1 Single gender
Parallels are often drawn between the relationship of natural time to tense and that of biological sex to gender. Despite some obvious exceptions such as *stail* (fem.) 'stallion' and *cailín* (masc.) 'girl', where morphological patterns override biological distinctions, Irish has a close correspondence between sex and gender. In general nouns describing males – either humans or higher animals - are masculine, e.g. *fear* (masc.) 'man', *tarbh* (masc.) 'bull'. Furthermore, occupations historically associated with men are normally masculine, e.g. *sagart* (masc.) 'priest'. Conversely, nouns describing females are generally feminine, e.g. *bean* (fem.) 'woman', *cearc* (fem.) 'hen'.

The general correspondence of sex with gender is overruled by certain word-endings, some of which may function as final morphemes, e.g. *-as*, *-án*, *-an*, *-ín*, *-(e)adh*, *-(e)amh*. The type of endings (with a few exceptions) listed in (1), the agent suffixes in (2) and the suffix *-ch* in derivatives of place-names or surnames as illustrated in (3) all determine that a noun is masculine.

(1)   *-as* : *doras* 'door'
          -án : *cupán* 'cup'
          -(e)an : *leagan* 'version'
          -ín : *cailín* 'girl'
          -(e)adh : *moladh* 'praise'

-(e)amh : *caitheamh* 'use (up), throw (away)'
-ás : *sólás* 'consolation'
-úr : *casúr* 'hammer'
-ún : *náisiún* 'nation'
-éad : *firéad* 'ferret'
-éal : *buidéal* 'bottle'
-éar : *suipéar* 'supper'
-(e)ad : *droichead* 'bridge'
-ar : *bóthar* 'road'
-ste : *páiste* 'child'

(2) *-óir/eoir* : *bádóir* 'boatman'
-(a)ire : *cabaire* 'prattler'
-(a)í : *scéalaí* 'storyteller'
-éir/éara : *búistéir* (M, D), *búistéara* (C) 'butcher'

(3) *Éireannach* 'Irishman'
Árannach 'Aran islander'
Cúlánach 'a person whose surname is Ó Cúláin'

On the other hand, word-endings listed in (4), all of which may function as word final morphemes, except *-aois/ís*, *-áid*, *-óid*, and the word-ending *-ch* in most mass nouns as exemplified in (5) determine that a noun is feminine:

(4) *-ó(i)g/eo(i)g* : *lasóg* 'small light'
-(e)acht : *Gaeltacht* 'Irish-speaking area'
-seach : *cláirseach* 'harp'
-éis : *móiréis* (Cn) 'haughtiness'
-áil(t) : *spáráil* 'sparing'
-aíl : *feadaíl* 'whistling'
-(a)irt : *bagairt* 'threat(ening)'
-(a)ilt : *meilt* 'grinding'
-(a)int : *caint* 'talk(ing)'
-aois/-ís : *mailís* 'malice'
-áid : *úsáid* 'use'
-óid : *neascóid* 'boil'

(5) *-(e)ach* : *báisteach* 'rain'
praiseach 'mess'

There is, however, a further subtlety to be noted: where *-ín* is used as a diminutive suffix, the gender of the original noun is retained, e.g. *fear*

Gender 145

(masc.) 'man', *feairín* 'little man'; *bean* (fem.) 'woman', *beainín* 'little woman'. Where the addition of the morpheme *-ín* creates a completely new lexical item, it is always masculine, e.g. *céir* (fem.) 'wax' beside *céirín* (masc.) 'poultice', *paidir* (fem.) 'prayer' beside *paidrín* (masc.) 'rosary'.

Apart from those endings which determine the gender, there is little or no predictability. Nevertheless, a general tendency has emerged for masculine nouns to end in a broad consonant and feminine nouns in a slender consonant, e.g. *fear* (masc.) 'man' but *muintir* (fem.) 'folk'. In the light of this trend certain developments may be interpreted as part of a levelling process, for example the substitution of an historical dative for a nominative, as in the feminine nouns *fuinneoig* for *fuinneog* 'window' or *muic* for *muc* 'pig', which is found in some Connacht dialects and indeed among younger speakers in Kerry dialects and in Ring and Ballymacoda (see Ó Cuív 1951:63). Similarly, the use of *-éara* rather than *-éir* in Connacht dialects, as in *búistéara* beside *búistéir* 'butcher', and the treatment of monosyllabic nouns with a final *-acht* as masculine in Connacht dialects, e.g. Cois Fhairrge *fuacht* (masc.) 'cold', may also be interpreted as a levelling.

7.1.2 Double gender

Some nouns exhibit what can be described as double gender in that in certain inflectional circumstances they behave as masculine nouns and in others as feminine ones. The commonest case is where, following an indefinite noun, the initial of an adjective is lenited as befits a feminine noun, while the noun itself is inflected as a masculine noun (see Table 7.1).

Table 7.1 *Examples of double gender 1*

Masculine	Feminine
an leoraí (Gd) 'the lorry'	*leoraí mhór* (Gd) 'a big lorry'
an t-aistir (Cf) 'the journey'	*aistir mhaith* (Cf) 'a good journey'
an méid (Cf) 'the amount'	*méid mhaith* (Cf) 'a good amount'
an t-eolas (Cf) 'the knowledge'	*eolas mhaith* '(Cf) 'a good knowledge'
an cleachtadh (Cf) 'practice'	*cleactadh mhaith* (Cf) 'much practice'
an radharc (Ky) 'the sight'	*radharc bhreá* (Ky) 'a good sight'

Examples like *aistir* 'journey(ing)' and *méid* 'amount' might be said to conform to the levelling process in that the initial of the adjective is lenited after a slender consonant. In addition *méid* may be influenced by *oiread* 'much', which also has a double gender. The behaviour of the nouns *eolas* 'knowledge' and *cleachtadh* 'practice' is harder to explain though the former may be influenced by *aithne* (fem.) 'acquaintance' and the latter by *taithí* (fem.)'experience'. Although *an leoraí* 'the lorry' or *an radharc* 'the sight' do not show lenition, the fact that they retain *an* 'the' (rather than the feminine *na* 'the') in the genitive singular, e.g. *doras an leoraí* (Gd) 'the door of the lorry', or that a typically masculine genitive with slendering is retained, e.g. *fad mo radhairc* 'the length of my vision', indicates that they are masculine.

Another case of double gender is that in which the nominative and genitive may show opposing genders, as shown in Table 7.2.

Table 7.2 *Examples of double gender 2*

Masculine unmarked case	Feminine in genitive case
an talamh (Cf) 'the land'	*an talaimh* (Cf), *na talún* (Cf) 'of the land'
deatach géar (Cf) 'intense smoke'	*baladh na deataí* (Cf) 'the smell of smoke'
an t-am (Gd) 'the time'	*i rith an ama ~ i rith na hama* (Gd) 'all the time'
Feminine unmarked case	Masculine in genitive case
an gheimhreadh (Ky) 'the winter'	*i lár an gheimhridh* (Ky) 'in the middle winter'

In the case of *talamh* 'land' double gender is due to the choice between the synchronically expected *talaimh* and the historical form *talún* (<*talamh+n*) which must be synchronically reinterpreted as a feminine genitive. *Deatach* 'smoke' is a mass noun and a feminine gender is expected (as is the case in other dialects). *Am* 'time' may be influenced by *aimsir* (fem.) 'time, weather'.

There are also cases where the inflection belongs to a 'masculine' pattern but the usage of the article befits a feminine noun, e.g. *ag léamh na leabhair* (Cf) 'reading the book', *cois na rásúir* (Cf) 'the razor's handle'. The feminine usage of articles (*na* rather than *an*) is presumably influenced by the fact that both *rásúr* 'razor' and *leabhar* 'book' are normally referred to by the feminine pronoun *sí* 'it' (see 7.1.3). In the case of *leabhar* a complete feminine declension develops among some speakers in Rannafast: *leabhar mhaith* 'a good book', *clúdach na leabhra* 'the book's cover'.

There is furthermore a deal of variation in gender among the dialects. The noun *loch* 'lake' is a particularly good example; the genitive singular fluctuates from dialect to dialect between the feminine *na locha*, *na loiche* and the masculine *an locha* with no discernible pattern (see Wagner 1958:69). Other examples are:

(6)   *asal* 'donkey' feminine (D) : masculine (C, M)
       condae 'county' feminine (D, Mk) : masculine (C, Ky)
       paróiste (Mk) *paráiste* (D) 'parish' feminine : masculine (C, Ky)
       páighe 'pay' feminine (C, D) : masculine (M)
       ainm 'name' feminine (M) : masculine (D, C)
       mí 'month' feminine (C, D) : masculine (M)
       tubaist (M) *tubaiste* (C, D) 'disaster' feminine (M) : masculine (C, D)
       gaineamh ~ gainimh 'sand' feminine (Er, M) : *gaineamh* masculine (Cn, Tn)

Such variation is difficult to explain. The treatment of *coláiste* 'college' as feminine in Donegal may be accounted for as being influenced by *scoil* 'school' which is feminine. The extra vowel in *tubaiste* (D, C) may cause it to conform to the norm for final *-ste*. The historical feminine *gaineamh* may become masculine due to the fact that the preponderance of nouns ending in *-eamh* are masculine. Diachronically, variation in examples such as *loch* 'lake', *ainm* 'name' and *mí* 'month' may reflect a certain hesitancy in assigning a gender and inflectional pattern to what was originally a neuter noun.

7.1.3 Gender agreement of anaphorical pronouns
In the case of humans, sex determines pronoun usage irrespective of grammatical gender, e.g. *fear* (masc.) 'man' is referred to by a masculine pronoun, *cailín* (masc.) 'girl' or *bean* (fem.) 'woman' by a feminine one.

In the case of higher animals where no gender marker is used, pronoun usage follows grammatical gender, e.g. *tarbh* (masc.) 'bull' is referred to by a masculine pronoun, *stail* (fem.) 'stallion' and *bó* (fem.) 'cow' by a feminine pronoun. Exceptionally, *capall* (masc.) 'horse', and *rón* (masc.) 'seal' are referred to by a feminine pronoun in Cois Fhairrge and Kerry respectively.

Where animals require a gender marker to distinguish sex such as *cat fireann/baineann* (masc.) 'male/female cat', *coileach/cearc fuiseoige* (fem.)

'male/female lark', the gender of the unmarked generic term determines the gender of the anaphoric pronoun. Thus *cat fireann/baineann* is referred to by a masculine pronoun while *coileach/cearc fuiseoige* is referred to by a feminine pronoun as *cat* 'cat' is masculine and *fuiseo(i)g* is feminine 'lark'.

There is a limited number of inanimate nouns which may be personalized and regarded as female and these are optionally referred to, in Connemara at least, by a feminine pronoun. These nouns largely describe machines and implements, e.g. *meaisín* (masc.) 'machine', *rásúr* (masc.) 'razor', modes of conveyance, e.g. *bád* (masc.) 'boat', *carr* (masc.) (Cf) 'car', and certain garments, e.g. *geansaí* (masc.) 'jersey'. The word *leabhar* 'book' is optionally referred to by a feminine pronoun in all major dialects. Otherwise, the anaphoric pronoun follows the gender of the inanimate noun, e.g. *doras* (masc.) 'door' is referred to by a masculine pronoun while *cathaoir* (fem.) 'chair' is referred to by a feminine pronoun. However, in Gweedore it is the norm to use a masculine pronoun when referring to any inanimate noun (see also 10.2.5). Finally, there is a number of inanimate nouns, e.g. *áit* 'place', *uair* 'time' which, although they are feminine, are referred to by a masculine pronoun, at least in Connemara and Kerry.

7.2 Inflection

7.2.1 Inflectional patterns

The inflectional patterns of the noun are varied and complicated. Depending on the dialect, on the usage and on the particular noun, the spectrum of possibilities stretches from a straightforward system with one case in the singular and plural to the more complex system with cases (nominative, vocative, genitive and dative) in the singular and plural. (The genitive and dative plural are petrified in that they only occur in specific circumstances and these are discussed in 7.3.5.) Although there is a great deal of variation, certain patterns emerge.

Basically, it can be said that there are three morphological devices (or various interactions of these devices) which are required to form cases in both the singular and plural. They are slendering or broadening (see 6.3.1), vocalic addition (see 6.3.2) and consonantal extension.

The inflection of the noun is best described by setting up three categories, which in turn have a number of subtypes.

7.2.1(i) *Category 1: consonant quality changes.* The characteristic of the first category is that the genitive is formed by slendering or broadening. The use of a broadened consonant to form the genitive is quite restricted.

7.2.1(i)1 *Genitives formed by slendering:* These genitives may be divided into three subtypes:

Subtype A:

The distinctive feature of this subtype, exemplified in (7), is the formation of the genitive or general plural form by slendering.

(7)   *fear* 'man'

	Singular	Plural
unmarked	*fear*	*fir/fearaibh* [see 7.3.5(ii)]
voc.	*fir*	*feara(ibh)* (petrified)
gen.	*fir*	*fear* (petrified)
dat.		*fearaibh* (petrified)

Subtype B:

The distinctive feature of this subtype, exemplified in (8) and (9), is that the nominative or general plural form is made by the addition of /ə/, as in *focla*, or by the addition of *cha* (in practice appearing as *-acha* when the rules of the syllabic adjustment are applied; see 2.3), as in *tamallacha*. Obviously, there is dialectal variation; *focal*, for instance, in many Munster dialects belongs to Subtype A above.

(8)   *focal* 'word'

	Singular	*Plural*
unmarked	*focal*	*focla*
gen.	*focail*	*focal* (petrified)
dat.		*foclaibh* (petrified)

(9)   *tamall* 'spell'

	Singular	Plural
unmarked	*tamall*	*tamallacha*
gen.	*tamaill*	*tamall* (petrified)
dat.		*tamallaibh* (petrified)

Subtype C:

The characteristic of this subtype, exemplified in (10) and (11), is that it combines in the unmarked (and dative) plural the features of the two previous subtypes i.e. both slendering and vowel addition and often involving the elision of a syllable.

(10)   *solas* 'light'

	Singular	Plural
unmarked	*solas*	*soilse*
gen.	*solais*	*solas* (petrified)
dat.		*soilsibh* (petrified)

(11)   *tobar* 'well'

	Singular	Plural
unmarked	*tobar*	*toibreacha*
gen.	*tobair*	*tobar* (petrified)
dat.		*toibribh* (petrified)

7.2.1(i)2 *Genitive formed by broadening*: An example of a genitive singular distinguished by broadening of the final consonant is given in (12).

(12)   *máthair* 'mother'

	Singular	Plural
unmarked	*máthair*	*máthaireacha*
gen.	*máthar*	*máthar* (petrified)
dat.		*máthairibh* (petrified)

7.2.1(ii) *Category 2: vowel addition.* The characteristic of Category 2 is the addition of a vowel in the genitive singular and there are six subtypes:

Subtype A:

The final consonant of the genitive singular becomes slender prior to the addition of the vowel as in (13). Although this example shows the petrified forms of the genitive and dative plural, for the sake of clarity they will be omitted in subsequent examples.

Inflection 151

(13) *muc* 'pig'

	Singular	Plural
unmarked	*muc*	*muca*
gen.	*muice*	*muc* (petrified)
dat.	*muic*	*mucaibh* (petrified)

Subtype B:

This subtype is distinguished by broadening of the final consonant before the addition of /ə/ in the plural, as exemplified in (14).

(14) *binn* 'gable'

	Singular	Plural
unmarked	*binn*	*beanna*
gen.	*binne*	

Subtype C:

The distinctive feature of this subtype is the simple addition of /ə/ in the genitive. The plural is formed by the addition of a vowel as in (15) or by consonant and vowel extension as in (16).

(15) *Gaeltacht* 'Irish-speaking area'

	Singular	Plural
unmarked	*Gaeltacht*	*Gaeltachtaí*
gen.	*Gaeltachta*	

(16) *am* 'time'

	Singular	Plural
unmarked	*am*	*amanna(í)*
gen.	*ama*	

Subtype D:

In this subtype, as well as the addition of /ə/ in the genitive singular, the final consonant is broadened. The plural is formed by consonant and vowel extension and the final consonant may also be broadened, as exemplified in (17) (for the vowel change see 3.3.3).

(17)   *greim* 'grip, bite'

	Singular	Plural
unmarked	*greim*	*greamanna(í)*
gen.	*greama*	

Subtype E:

In this subtype, as well as the addition of /ə/ in the genitive singular, the final consonant is broadened and the plural is formed by vowel addition, as exemplified in (18).

(18)   *bádóir* 'boatman'

	Singular	Plural
unmarked	*bádóir*	*bádóirí*
gen.	*bádóra*	

Subtype F:

This subtype simply adds /ə/ in the genitive singular and the plural is formed by making the final consonant slender and by the addition of /iː/, as in (19).

(19)   *saighdiúr* 'soldier'

	Singular	Plural
unmarked	*saighdiúr*	*saighdiúirí*
gen.	*saighdiúra*	

7.2.1(iii) *Category 3: consonant addition.* Category 3 is distinguished by the fact that the genitive singular is formed by the addition of a consonant and the syllable is adjusted as required (see 2.3) and there are five subtypes.

Subtype A:

In this subtype the genitive is formed by the addition of *-ch* /x/. In practice, due to syllable adjustment (see 2.3), *-ach* is added. The final consonant is almost always broadened and, as in *cathrach*, the plural is made by consonant and vowel extension.

(20)   *cathair* 'city'

	Singular	Plural
unmarked	*cathair*	*cathaireacha(í)*
gen.	*cathrach*	

Subtype B:

In this subtype the final consonant is broadened in the plural.

(21)   *coróin* 'crown'

	Singular	Plural
unmarked	*coróin*	*corónacha(í)*
gen.	*corónach*	

Subtype C:

This subtype is distinctive in that the final consonant is made slender before the addition of *-ch* in the genitive singular as shown in (22):

(22)   *speal* 'scythe'

	Singular	Plural
unmarked	*speal*	*spealta*
gen.	*speileach*	

Subtype D:

In this subtype the unmarked noun ends in a vowel; in the genitive singular a consonant /n/ or /ɴ/ is added and in dialects (largely Munster) where a dative singular is preserved /n'/ [as exemplified in (23)] or /d'/ is added. The unmarked plural is formed by adding /n'/ or by consonant and vowel extension, e.g. *comharsanna(í)* 'neighbours'. The genitive plural found in petrified phrases is, as is the case in this category generally, similar to the genitive singular.

(23)   *lacha* 'duck'

	Singular	Plural
unmarked	*lacha*	*lachain*
gen.	*lachan*	*lachan* (petrified)
dat.	*lachain*	

Subtype E:

In this subtype, which consists of example (24), the unmarked singular form ends in a vowel, the genitive singular adds /x/ and in dialects (largely Munster) where the dative singular is found *-gh* /g′/ [see 4.1.1(ii)] is added. The unmarked plural is very distinctive in that the medial *r* is palatalized and in Donegal and Mayo is followed by vowel extension, i.e. *caoirí*. Furthermore, it would seem that in Dunquin palatal *r* of the plural intrudes on the genitive singular, giving *caoireach* /kiːr′əx/.

(24)   *caora* 'sheep'

	Singular	Plural
unmarked	*caora*	*caoire*
gen.	*caorach*	*caorach* (petrified)
dat.	*caoraigh*	

7.2.2 Variations in inflection

Most of the inflectional differences between the major dialects, and indeed variations within those dialects, can be explored under the following five headings:

(a)   a levelling process that causes nouns with a final slender consonant to be feminine and nouns with a final broad consonant to be masculine;
(b)   the erosion of Category 2;
(c)   a simplification to a system with only an unmarked singular and a plural;
(d)   the proliferation of genitives with *-ch* and *-dh*;
(e)   movements within Category 2;
(f)   addition of a morpheme.

7.2.2.(i) *Levelling process.* There is a movement from Subtype A to Subtype B within Category 2.

(25)   *bróig* (Cf) 'shoe' : *bróg* (Gd)
         cois (Cf) 'foot' : *cos* (Gd)
         láimh (Cf) 'hand' : *lámh* (Gd)
         cluais (Cf) 'ear' : *cluas* (Gd)
         ceird (Cf) 'skill' : *ceard* (Gd)

Often this movement is optional such as Cois Fhairrge *muc ~ muic* 'pig', *leac ~ lic* 'flagstone' or the ending *-óig ~ óg* (the former being now the norm). This is not confined to Cois Fhairrge; younger speakers in Dunquin tend to substitute *muic* for *muc*, *cois* for *cos* 'foot' etc. (see also Ó Cuív 1951:63). Indeed, there are examples in Mayo and in Donegal such as *ceird* (Mo) 'skill' compared with *ceard* (D) or *uibh* (D) 'egg' compared with *ubh* (Cf).

There is also a movement from Subtype D of Category 3 to the broadening type in Category 1 and in the case of final *nn* to Subtype B in Category 2:

(26)   *caraid*, gen. *carad* (Cf) 'friend' : *cara*, gen. *carad* (Dn)
         gualainn, gen. *gualainne* (C, D) 'shoulder' : *guala*, gen. *gualann* (Dn)

There is a simplification of Subtype E of Category 2 which can be seen as part of the general levelling process. Agent nouns with the termination *-éir* in Munster and Donegal end in *-éara(í)* in Connacht:

(27)   *ministéir* (M, D) 'minister' : *ministéara* (Cn)

It must be noted that agent nouns ending in *-óir* and masculine nouns ending in *-ín* still run counter to the levelling process, as does the general retention of the final broad consonant as the unmarked form in the feminine noun in Subtype A of Category 2, e.g. *muc* 'pig', *cos* 'foot' etc. in Donegal or in all dialects in the case of *craobh* 'branch', *srón* 'nose' etc.

7.2.2(ii) *Erosion of Category 2*. The tendency for Category 2 to diminish is most noticeable in Connemara; nevertheless there are examples to be found in Mayo and in Munster.

There is a simplification of Subtype C. In Connacht and in Dunquin disyllabic nouns ending in *-acht* have merely an unmarked form in the singular and in the plural:

156 *Modern Irish: grammatical structure and dialectal variation*

(28)   *Gaeltacht*, gen. *Gaeltachta* (D) 'Irish-speaking area' : gen. *Gaeltacht* (C)

On the other hand, monosyllabic words remain in this subtype in Munster while in Connemara these move to Subtype A (i.e. *fear* 'man') of Category 1:

(29)   *fuacht*, gen. *fuachta* (M) 'cold' : gen. *fuaicht* (Cn, Gd)

There is a simplification of Subtype B which is caused by the addition of /ə/ to the singular unmarked form; diachronically, this is due to the generalization of the genitive form. Examples are:

(30)   *béice* (Cf) 'shout' : *béic* (Mo)
       oifige (Cf) 'office' : *oifig* (Mo, M)
       sochraide (Cf) 'funeral' : *sochraid* (Dn)
       Gaeilge (C) 'Irish' : *Gaeilig* (D)
       míorúilte (Cf) 'miracle' : *míorúilt* (D)

Furthermore there is a simplification of Subtype E. In Cois Fhairrge, for example, the genitive singular form is now rare and mainly preserved in petrified phrases such as (31). Otherwise there is no special genitive form.

(31)   *gotha an chrochadóra* (Cf) 'a villainous look', *gotha* 'appearance' + gen. of *crochadóir* 'hangman'

There is also a movement from Subtype F of Category 2 to Subtype C of Category 1. This applies to agent nouns ending in *-úr*:

(32)   *táilliúr*, gen. *táilliúra* (Cf) 'tailor' : *táilliúr*, gen. *táilliúir* (Er)
       saighdiúr, gen. *saighdiúra* ~ *saighdiúir* (Cf) 'soldier'
       dochtúr, gen. *dochtúra* ~ *dochtúir* (Cf) 'doctor'

There is also a movement from Subtype A and Subtype B to Category 3 Subtype A or Subtype B. These nouns end in /l/, /N/ or /r/. This movement away from Subtype A is illustrated by (33) and from Subtype B is exemplified by (34):

(33)   *srón*, gen. *sróine* ~ *srónach* (Cf) 'nose'
(34)   *súil*, gen. *súile* (Dn) 'eye': gen. *súlach* (Cf)

toil, gen. *toile ~ toileach* (Dn) 'will': gen. *tolach* (Cf)
spéir, gen. *spéire ~ spéireach* (Dn) 'sky'
tír, gen. *tíre ~ tíorach* (Dn) 'country'

It must be observed nevertheless that there are some important countertendencies. Firstly, in Donegal and North Mayo words with a final /l/, /r/, /n/ move from the broadening type in Category 1 to Subtype E of Category 2:

(35)   *athair*, gen. *athar* (M, Cn) 'father' : gen. *athara* (Gd, Er)
       máthair, gen. *máthar* (M, Cn) 'mother' : gen. *máthara* (Gd, Er)
       tórainn, gen. *tórann* (Cn) 'boundary' : *teorainn*, gen. *teoranna* (Er)
       abhainn, gen. *abhann ~ oibhne* (C) 'river' : gen. *abhanna* (Gd)
       iothlainn, gen. *iothlann ~ iothlanna* (~ *iothlainne*) (Cf) 'haggard'

Secondly, there are some examples of movement from Subtype A of Category 1 to Subtype C of Category 2, as shown in (36):

(36)   *dinnéar*, gen. *dinnéir* (Er) 'dinner' : gen. *dinnéara* (Gd)

Thirdly, Subtype B of Category 2 is productive, as can be seen in the loanwords in (37).

(37)   *brois*, gen. *broise* 'brush'
       beilt, gen. *beilte* 'belt'
       jib, gen. *jibe* 'jib-sail'

7.2.2(iii) *Simplification to a system with only an unmarked singular and plural.* The simplification of Subtype D Category 3 is achieved in two stages. Firstly, the Dunquin three-case system in the singular in a word such as *teanga*, gen. *teangan*, dat. *teangain* 'tongue' becomes *teanga*, gen. *teangan* and ultimately is reduced to a one-case system with the one unmarked form *teanga*. The latter is the case in Cois Fhairrge in words such as *teanga* 'tongue', *ionga* 'nail', though the genitive forms *teangan*, *iongan* may be retained in petrified phrases such as *ag déanamh teangan* 'chatting' or *scamhacha iongan* 'agnail'.

The simplification of Subtype A in Category 1 is often achieved by the addition of /ə/.

158 *Modern Irish: grammatical structure and dialectal variation*

(38) *úlla* (C, D) 'apple' : *úll* (M, C in petrified phrases) 'apple'
dorna (Cn) 'fist' : *dorn* (M)
mionna (C, D) 'oath' : *mionn* (M)
rása (C, D) 'race' : *rás* (M)
leachta (Cn) 'cairn' : *leacht* (M)

As can be seen from the examples in (38), this phenomenon may occur as a result of back-formation from plurals formed by adding *-í*, e.g. *rás*, plural *rás(t)aí* becomes *rása*, plural *rás(t)aí* on the model of *pota*, plural *potaí* 'pot'.

The simplification of nouns in Subtype B of Category 2 [see (30)] has already been discussed as part of the erosion of that category. Similarly the simplification of Subtype E of Category 2 [see (31)] has been previously considered as contributing to the general levelling process. Both of these reductions also illustrate the development of a system with only an unmarked singular and plural.

Undoubtedly, *ch* is the most productive of the consonants in Category 3 as witnessed by its use in loan-words such as:

(39) *traein*, gen. *traenach* (Cf) 'train'
cruib, gen. *cruibeach* (Cf) 'crib (of a cart)'
stil, gen. *stileach* (Cf) 'still'
rásúr, gen. *rásúrach* (Cf) 'razor'

Its productiveness can also be observed in the movements within the inflectional patterns, *tír*, gen. *tíre* ~ *tíorach* (Dn) 'country' [see (34)]. While *ch* intrudes, the use of *n* and *d* disappears [see 7.2.1(iii)].

The intrusion of the use of *-dh* in Category 3 is a feature of Mayo and partly of Donegal as in :

(40) *feoil*, gen. *feoladh* /**fʹoːluː**/ (Er) 'meat' : *feola* (M, Cn)
fuil, gen. *foladh* /**foluː**/ (Mo) 'blood' : *fola* (M, Cn)

7.2.2(iv) Movements within Category 2. Some of these movements within Category 2 have been touched on under the previous four headings and are only summarized here:

Subtype A moves to Subtype B [see (25)] or to Subtype C, e.g. *cluas*, gen. *cluaise* ~ *cluasa* (Dn) 'ear'. There is also movement between Subtype D and Subtype B, e.g. *colainn*, gen. *colla* ~ *colainne* (Er) 'body' and see also *abhainn* 'river' and *iothlainn* 'haggard' in (35).

7.2.2(v) *Addition of a morpheme.* Less frequent patterns or less frequent plural formations are sometimes avoided by the addition of a morpheme such as *-óg* which then follows Subtype A Category 2. Examples are:

(41)   *luchóg* (D) 'mouse' : *luch*, pl. *luchain* (Cn)
         beachóg (Tn) 'bee' : *beach* (Tn in set phrases) : *meach*, pl. *meachain* (Cn)

7.3 Formation of the plural

7.3.1 Long and short plurals

Basically 'short' plurals are formed by slendering [see 6.3.1(i)] while 'long' plurals are formed by the use of either vowel addition or by consonant extension and vowel addition combined. The 'long' plurals can also employ slendering with either vowel addition or with consonant extension and vowel addition combined. It is very difficult to predict how the plural of any given noun is formed; nevertheless the phonetic environment and the function of the plural play a certain part in determining the formation.

Viewed from a diachronic point of view, there is a gradual separation taking place between the plural form and the inflectional patterns as a whole. This progressive detachment of the plural form is for the most part, due to the proliferation of 'long' plurals, in particular *-acha(í)* and *-anna(í)*. There is a substantive shift in Category 1 from Subtype A to Subtypes B and C. In other words, rather than *bád*, plural *báid* 'boat', we find Cois Fhairrge *bád*, plural *báid ~ báideachaí* (Cf) and *bádaí* (Gd). A further factor in the general tendency towards 'long' plurals is that when a noun shifts from one pattern to another it introduces a plural form from the original pattern into the new one. In Gweedore or Erris, seemingly *máthair* 'mother' has moved from the broadening type in Category 1 to Subtype E of Category 2 (i.e. *máthair*, gen. *máthara*) and the plural *máithreacha(í)* is transferred, thus preventing any new plural on the model of *bádóir*, gen. *bádóra*, plural *bádóirí* 'boatman' from emerging.

The proliferation of 'long' plurals often leads to a noun having two or more optional plural forms. For example, *luicht, luchtannaí* and *luchtaíl* are recorded as plural forms for the noun *lucht* 'load' (Cf). Sometimes a differentiation of usage arises, as in *solais* (Er) 'lightning' as opposed to *soilse* (Er) 'lights', both plural forms of *solas* 'light', or *boinn* (Cf) 'coins' as opposed to *bonnaíocha, (bonnúchaí* etc.) (Cf) 'soles', both plural forms of

160 *Modern Irish: grammatical structure and dialectal variation*

bonn 'coin, sole'. The retention of older forms of plural in counting is discussed in 7.3.5(iii).

7.3.2 Vowel addition

To a large extent, this type of plural is formed by the addition of a neutral vowel /ə/. This is particularly the case in Subtypes A and B of Category 2, e.g. *muc*, plural *muca* 'pig', *binn*, plural *beanna* 'gable', etc. It is, of course, also found in Category 1, e.g. *focal* , plural *focla* (Cn, Gd) 'word' or *solas*, plural *soilse* 'light'. This neutral vowel combined with palatalization will also allow for the plural of, e.g., *éadach*, plural *éadaighe* /eːdiː/ (Cf) 'clothes' or trisyllabic surnames or names of peoples such as *Sasanach*, plural *Sasanaighe* /saːsəniː/ (C, D) 'Englishman'. This neutral vowel is, of course, the same as that used with consonant extension in, for example, *scéal* + *t* + *a* 'stories', *cathr* + *ch* + *a* 'cities', *bus* + *nn* + *a* 'buses'.

It has been already noted that *í* /iː/ is often employed instead of /ə/ [see 6.3.2(ii)].

7.3.3 Consonant extension and vowel addition combined

The root is extended by the addition of a consonant. If the ensuing cluster does not conform to the canonical form, it is split by a neutral vowel under the rules of syllable adjustment (see 2.3). If *-ch* /x/ or *-nn* /N/ are added then, under the same rules of syllable adjustment, these become syllabic.

It is possible, with some exceptions, to predict whether *-nn* /N/ or *-ch* /x/ will be chosen. Normally *-nn* /N/ is added to monosyllables and *-ch* /x/ to polysyllables, e.g. *busanna(í)* 'buses', *reiligeacha(í)* (C, D) 'graveyards'. Some of the exceptions are *áiteacha(í)* (C, D) beside *áiteacha* or *áiteanna* (Dn) 'places', *éanacha(í)* (C, D) 'birds', *uibheacha(í)* (C, D) 'eggs'. The use of *-nn* /N/ with polysyllables is rare except in words with a double stress, as in *measíneannaí* /ˈmæˈsˈiːnˈəniː/ (Cf) 'machines'. The basic rule of *-nn* /N/ with monosyllables and *-ch* /x/ with polysyllables is clear in recent loan-words, e.g. *bálanna* (C, D) 'balls', *peaicitseacha(í)* (C, D) 'packages'.

As well as the *-ch* /x/ and *-nn* /N/ discussed in the previous paragraph, *t* /t(ˈ)/, *r* /r(ˈ)/, *m* /m/, *n* /n/ and *s* /s/ are the consonants most frequently employed in consonant extension. These are essentially secondary consonant extensions insofar as they must always be followed by either *-ch* /x/ or *-nn* /N/. The consonant additions *-ch* /x/ and *-nn* /N/ are mutually exclusive, whereas there are combinations of the secondary consonants, for instance *t* + *r*. In (42) there are examples of *t*, which is the most common secondary consonant extension and which is regularly found after monosyllables with a long syllable ending in *l* or *n*:

(42) *cuan*, plural *cuanta(í)* 'bay'
      scéal, plural *scéalta(í)* 'story'
      cú, plural *cúití* (Cf) 'greyhound'
      rása, plural *rás(t)aí* (Cn) 'race'
      léine, plural *léinte(achaí)* (Cn) 'shirt'

Consonant extension with *r* is rare and is required mostly for nouns ending in plosives:

(43) *ceist*, plural (in set phrases) *ceastracha* (Gd) 'question'
      carraig, plural *carraigreachaí* (Cf) 'rock'
      stéig, plural *stéig(r)eachaí* (Cf) 'gut'
      leaba(idh), plural *leabrachaí* (Im) 'bed'
      leac, plural *leacracha(í)* (Cf, Gd) 'flagstone'

Consonant extension with *n* is needed rarely following *m*:

(44) *ainm*, plural *ainm(n)eachaí* (Cf) 'name'
      anam, plural *anamnacha* (Cf) 'soul'

In a few nouns ending in *s* a consonant extension with *g* is required:

(45) *clais*, plural *clasgannaí* (Cn) 'furrow'
      cis, plural *ceasgannaí* (for vowel change see 3.3.3) (Cn) 'hurdle'

The combination *tr* occurs mostly after monosyllables ending in *l* or *n*:

(46) *tonn*, plural *tonntracha* (Cf) 'wave'
      aill, plural *alltrachaí* (Cf) 'cliff'

It may be noted in passing that the type of secondary consonant extension used in the formation of plurals resembles that found in the formation of adjectives or nouns, e.g. *giortach* (*gior* + *t* + *ch*) 'skimpy', *fiosrach* (*fios* + *r* + *ch*) 'curious'. In the case of adjectives or nouns, however, the range of consonants employed is wider and has more combinations, e.g. *cráidhcamas* (*cráidh* + *c* + *m* + *s*) (C) 'hardship'; *dorchadas* (*dorcha* + *d* +*s*) (C) 'darkness'.

In nouns describing time, there is a tendency for the addition of *nn* and *t* before vowel addition as in:

(47) *uair*, plural *uaireantaí* (C) 'hour'
      lá, plural *laethantaí* (C) 'day'
      am, plural *amann(t)aí* (Cf) 'time'

The consonant *th* /h/ is also used as an extension. Although it is not possible to state the phonetic environment in which this occurs, it is largely the same words which are involved in every dialect. Firstly, agent nouns with a final /əjə/ as in:

(48) *gadaighe* (/gadəjə/ →) /gaːdiː/, plural *gadaighthe* /gadəhə/ (M) → /gaːdiː/ (Cf) 'thief'
      gadaighe (/gadəjə/ →) /gadiː/, plural *gadaighthiú* (/gadəjhˊuː/ →) /gadəxˊuː/ (Er)

Secondly, there is a small group of words, mostly with a final *r*, where *th* /h/ forms part of the extension:

(49) *leabhar*, plural *leabhartha(í)* 'book'
      tír, plural *tíortha* 'country'
      spéir, plural *spéartha* 'sky'
      leaba(idh), plural *leabthacha* /Lˊæpəxiː/ 'bed'

Thirdly, there is a group of words which are shortened in Munster before *th* /hˊ/ or *t* /tˊ/ :

(50) *ní*, plural *nithe* 'thing'
      rí, plural *rithe* 'king'
      slí, plural *slite* 'way'

These might alternatively be allowed for by basing, for example, *rí* 'king' on *righe*, as *gadaí* 'thief' is derived from *gadaighe*. Against that, however, we must weigh the fact that the long vowel is retained in other dialects such as Cois Fhairrge *rí*, plural *rítí* 'king'.

It can be observed in passing that this use of *th* /h/ in plural formation is connected to that found in noun and adjective formation such as *ceannaigh* + *th* + *eoir* /kʹanəhoːrʹ/ (Dn) 'buyer' or *bearrtha* 'shaved'.

The consonant *s* also has a particular function. It is found optionally in Dunquin in a handful of words:

(51)   *uair*, plural *uaireasta* ~ *uaireanta* (Dn) 'hour'
       lá, plural *laethasta* ~ *laethanta* (Dn) 'day'
       méar, plural *méarasta* ~ *méaranta* (M) 'finger'

Once again this use is paralleled by the *s* which occurs in the formation of adjectives such as *dlisteanach* (*dligh* + *s* + *t* + *n* + *ch*) 'lawful' or *cóiriste* (*cóir* + *s* + *te*) (D) 'mended'.

Another minor use of *s* before vowel addition is found in Connemara in words associated with card playing:

(52)   *triuf*, plural *triufasaí* (Cn) 'club'
       mámh, plural *mámhasaí* (Cn) 'trump'
       drámh, plural *drámhasaí* (Cn) 'non-trump'

Interestingly, rather than -*th* /h/, *s* /s/ may be employed to form the plural of an agent noun ending in /iː/. We find *gadaí* (from a underlying *gadaighe* on the basis of the plural in other dialects), plural *gadaíos* (Cf) 'thief'. Diachronically, the *s* in *triufasaí* and *gadaíos* must be due to the influence of English. It is also noteworthy that this *s* also turns up in children's speech, e.g. *sméara*, plural *sméaraí* ~ *sméaraíos* (Im) 'blackberry' or plural *sméartha* ~ *sméaras* (Cf).

One further point should be observed. In the case of certain nouns there must be two roots, a long and a short one. The long root forms the basis of the singular while the plural is formed from the short root. Examples are *léine* 'shirt', *culaith* 'suit', *talamh* 'ground'. The plural of these nouns is based on *léin-*, *cul-* and *tal-* respectively:

(53)   *léine* (M, Cn) *léinidh* (D), plural *léinteacha* 'shirt'
       culaith, plural *cultacha* 'suit'
       talamh, plural *taltaí* (Cn) *tailte* (Mk) 'land'

Finally, there are one or two nouns which form their plural with *bh* + vowel addition, e.g. *gé* 'goose', plural *géabha* (Cn) or tantum plurale *aobha* 'liver' [compared with *aonna* (Dn)].

7.3.4 Other long plurals

There is a type of plural in Connemara which is formed by the addition of -*aíl* /iːlʼ/. Most of the nouns involved are monosyllabic. All of these examples are optional plurals in Cois Fhairrge except perhaps *plump* and *bruth*:

(54)   *múr*, plural *múraíl* (Cf) 'shower'
       slám, plural *slámaíl* (Cf) 'large amount'
       bruach, plural *bruachaíl* (Cf) 'bank'
       plump, plural *plumpaíl* (Cf) 'bang'
       bolgam, plural *bolgamaíl* (Cf) 'mouthful'
       bruth, plural *bruthaíl* (Cf) 'heat'

Sometimes consonant extension and vowel addition follow -*aíl*, e.g. *múraíolacha* 'showers'. This ending -*aíl* is, of course, also found in verbal noun formation such as *feadaíl* (*fead* + *aíl*) 'whistling'. Occasional examples of -*ál* are also required before consonant extension and vowel addition, e.g. *trucálacha* (Cf) 'belongings', which is presumably influenced by the plural of what are basically verbal nouns such as *cruinneálachaí* 'gatherings', *pábhálachaí* 'pavings'.

There are some nouns which form their plurals in -*ú* /uː/. Examples are:

(55)   *gearrchaile*, plural *gearrchailiú* (C) 'young girl'
       cleite, plural *cleitiú* (Er, Im [in petrified phrases]) 'feather'
       faithne, plural *faithniú* (Er) 'wart'

There are also several nouns in which *í* or *ú* occur before consonant extension and vowel addition. While it is apparent that from a historical point of view endings such as -*aíocha(í)* or -*úcha(í)* originate in nouns such as *samhradh*, plural *samhraidheacha* /**sauriːxə**/ 'summer' or *seire*, plural *seireadhacha* /**sʼerʼuːxə**/ 'hough', it is now an established ending which has spread beyond nouns with an underlying *dh*. In order to allow for examples like *uisce*, plural *uiscíocha* (Dn) 'water' or *eanga*, plural *eangaíochaí* (Cf) 'notch', we must presume that the combination of vowel addition -*(a)í* /iː/ + consonant extension -*ch* /x/ + vowel addition -*aí* /iː/ now affects a limited, if unpredictable, number of nouns. Similarly, an example such as *sine*, plural *siniúchaí* (Cf) 'teat' must be now interpreted as an independent ending -*úchaí* employed for a certain group of words.

7.3.5 Marked plural forms

Normally, there is only one unmarked form in the plural. Nevertheless there are other marginal forms to be noted, particularly in Munster. The genitive plural is, in the case of Subtype A in Category 1 and 2, the same as its unmarked singular (e.g. *fear* 'man', *muc* 'pig', etc.) and in the case of Category 3 the same as the genitive singular (e.g. *lachan* 'ducks', *carad* (C) 'friends', *caorach* 'sheep'). Exceptionally *súil* 'eye' has a genitive plural *súl*. There are also sporadic examples of consonant extension without vowel addition:

(56) *ag cur ceisteann* (Dn) 'asking questions'
      beirt níonach (D) 'two daughters'
      Muintir na Rosann (D) 'the people of the Rosses'

While the use of *-ch*, e.g. *níonach* 'daughter' rather than *-ch* + a neutral vowel, e.g. *níonacha*, is now confined to petrified phrases, it was a regular feature in the speech of an older generation of Donegal speakers.

7.3.5(i) *The use of genitive plural.* The genitive plural only survives in petrified usages which contain names of animals, as exemplified in (57), names of parts of the body, as exemplified in (58) and numbers or partitive words in (59):

(57) *ag iascach ronnach* (Cn) 'fishing mackerel'
      ál lachan (Cn) 'a brood of ducks'
      tinneas na muc (Cn) 'pig sickness'
      mil bheach (Dn) 'bee honey'
(58) *os cionn na gcluas* (Cn) 'above the ears'
      scamhacha iongan (Cn) 'agnail'
      radharc mo shúl (Cn, D) 'my eyesight'
(59) *triúr mac* 'three sons'
      do chuid leitreach (Dn) 'your letters'

(Where the noun does not belong to Subtype B of Category 1 or 2, an unmarked plural is used following personal numbers, e.g. *triúr buachaillí* 'three boys'.)

7.3.5(ii) *The use of dative plural.* In Munster there is also a limited use of a dative plural. The ending *-bh* /v′/, with subsequent syllabic adjustment (see 2.3), is added to the unmarked singular or in the case of consonant exten-

166 *Modern Irish: grammatical structure and dialectal variation*

sions to the unmarked plural. This form is most often used when there is no definite article before the noun, as exemplified in the first five cases in (60):

(60)   *a trí nó a ceathair de cheannaibh* (M) 'three or four'
péire de bhrógaibh (M) 'a pair of shoes'
in áiteannaibh (M) 'in places'
ó chianaibh (M) 'a while ago'
ina choinnibh (M) 'against it'
desna brógaibh (M) 'off the shoes'
agesna fiacha (M) 'at the debts'

Sometimes this form is used as a 'nominative' as in *fearaibh* 'men', *bochtaibh* 'poor people' (see also Ó Cuív 1951:63), or as a vocative plural as in *a fhearaibh!* (Dn, Cf) 'men!'.

7.3.5(iii) *Use of plural forms in counting.* Often the plural form employed following a cardinal number (see Ó Siadhail 1982:102-6) is an older one which is only preserved in this usage. In Cois Fhairrge, for instance, we find the forms:

(61)   *cinn*, plural of *ceann* 'one', normally *ceanna*
bliana, plural of *bliain* 'year', normally *blianta*
pingne, plural of *pingin* 'penny', normally *pingneachaí*
scóir, plural of *scór* 'score', normally *scórtha*
uaire, plural of *uair* 'time', normally *uaireantaí*
uibhe, plural of *ubh* 'egg', normally *uibheachaí*

In Kerry a similar distinction is made in the case, for example, of:

(62)   *seachtaine*, plural of *seachtain* 'week', normally *seachtainí*
orlaigh, plural of *orlach* 'inch', normally *orlaighe*
réal(t)a, plural of *réal* 'sixpence', normally *réalacha*

Where there are optional plural forms, the (historically) shorter form tends to be obligatory following cardinal numbers; e.g. *troigh* (Cf) 'foot' with optional plural forms *troighthe* or *troigheannaí*, but only *sé troighthe* 'six feet' is possible.

There are also three types of petrified phrases in which a plural form is required and these contain what we may for convenience label as 'sum of the parts', 'seven for many', and 'set of three' phrases:

(63)   *chúig cúigí na hÉireann* (M) 'the five provinces of Ireland'
       na seacht dteangain (C) 'many languages'
       lá de na trí laethe... (D) 'one of the three days...'

Apart from those types of petrified phrase, plural forms are used after numerals in the case of words inherent to the counting system:

(64)   *ceann* 'head/one' *trí cinn* 'three' (lit. three heads)
       fiche 'twenty' *trí fichid* 'sixty' (lit. three twenties)
       fear 'man' *trí feara déag* (C, M) 'thirteen men'
       cloigeann 'head/person' *deich gcloigne* (D) 'ten persons' (lit. ten heads)

Besides the 'counting' nouns illustrated in (64), plural forms after numerals are required for all dialects in the following feminine nouns of measurement which do not contain more than two syllables and which have plurals formed by vowel addition:

(65)   *uair* 'time'
       seachtain 'week'
       bliain 'year'
       pingin 'penny'
       scilling 'shilling'
       troigh 'foot'
       slat 'yard'

The series is, in most dialects, filled out by using a plural after a cardinal number in the case of *orlach* 'inch' and *punt* 'pound'. This provides the common core of nouns with which a plural form is employed following a cardinal. However, due to the semantic element involved, there are examples of various other nouns of measurement being used in the plural. There are differences here between the major dialects. At least some of those nouns of measurement are illustrated in the following; examples from Connacht are given in (66) and from Kerry in (67):

(66)   *chúig chlocha* (C) 'five stones (of weight)'
       sé lámha déag (C) 'sixteen hands (high)'
       trí scóir (C) 'three score'
       cheithre stóir (C) 'four stories'

trí boird fhichead (C) 'twenty-three loads (of seaweed)'
cheithre duail (C) 'four strands'
trí galúin (C) 'three gallons'
trí hualaí (C) 'three loads'
cheithre málaí déag (C) 'fourteen bagfuls'
(67) trí nóimintí (Ky) 'three minutes'
trí báid (Ky) 'three boatfuls'
trí turais (Ky) 'three times'

8 *The verb*

8.1 Phonetic shape

8.1.1 General discussion
The inflection of the verb is affected by the use of various morphological and syntactic devices:

(a)   Broadening of a root final consonant, e.g. *bualadh* 'hitting' beside *buail* 'hit!', *siúl* 'walking', *siúil* 'walk!';
(b)   Addition of an ending to signify person, number etc., e.g. *cuirim* 'I put', from *cuir* 'put!';
(c)   Placing before the verb an element which carries grammatical information other than person, number etc., e.g. *(do) chuir* (M) 'put' (past);
(d)   Use of personal pronouns which are also found outside the verbal system to denote person, number etc., e.g. *cuireann muid* (C, D) 'we put';
(e)   Use of periphrasis where a verbal noun is unmarked for person, number and tense, which are then attached to an auxiliary verb, e.g. *tá sé ag bualadh* 'he is hitting'.

There is no absolute distinction between morphology and syntax. Those listed as (a) and (b) above are largely morphological while (e) is generally regarded as syntactical. This section deals with the morphological or inflectional side of matters; the use of periphrasis by which certain features of aspect and passivity are expressed by auxiliary verbs will be discussed in 11.3.

The inflectional system is similar for the great majority of verbs in Irish. There are fewer than a dozen verbs where the actual root of the verb varies, e.g. *téirigh* 'go' beside *téann* 'goes', *chonacthas* 'one saw' beside *feiceann* 'sees' as opposed to the regular verb *cuir* 'put' beside *cuireann* 'puts', *cuireadh* 'one put'. The verbs where the actual root changes have a high frequency. They are traditionally known as the irregular verbs (see 8.3.2).

8.1.2 Verb categorized by the shape of the root

It is sufficient to speak of one conjugation as, excepting one variation in the future, the same set of endings apply to all verbs. Nevertheless, it is interesting to categorize the verb according to the shape of the root. In some cases the shape of the root alters when an ending is added. These changes must be viewed as part of the phonological system and indeed the phonological rules, described in Part I of this book, account for most of them.

There are two categories: Category 1 where the root has the shape *consonant + vowel + consonant* and Category 2 where the root has the shape *consonant + vowel + consonant (+ vowel) + consonant*. These two categories are further subdivided in Tables 8.1 and 8.2.

Table 8.1 *Category 1 verbs*

Second consonant	Short vowel	Long vowel
plosive	*leag* 'lay'	*póg* 'kiss'
fricative	*sroich* 'reach'	*pós* 'marry'
liquid/nasal	*gearr* 'cut'	*múin* 'teach'
a cluster	*measc* 'mix'	*fáisc* 'squeeze'
/h/	*rith* 'run'	*báith* 'drown'
/w/	*lobh* 'rot'	*snámh* 'swim'
/j/	*nigh* 'wash'	*léigh* 'read'
zero		*reo* 'freeze'

Table 8.2 *Category 2 verbs*

Description of underlying form	Underlying form	Surface form with second vowel short	Surface form with second vowel long
second and third consonant form cluster	*seachn*	*seachain* 'avoid'	
second and third consonant separate	*foghlaim, tiomáin, glasáil*	*foghlaim* 'learn'	*tiomáin* 'drive', *glasáil* 'lock'
third consonant is *-gh* /j/	*ard + gh* /j/, *éir + gh* /j/	*ardaigh* 'raise', *éirigh* 'rise'	

In an example such as *ardaigh* 'raise' the *-gh* /j/ is regarded here as a consonant extension which, following the application of the syllabic adjustment rules (see 4.2.3), appears as *-(a)igh* /əj/. The same is true of some personal endings described in 8.2.4. For convenience, in the following discussion the post-syllabic adjustment form *-(a)igh* /əj/ is given in the examples.

8.1.3 Effect of phonological rules on the inflection

It is interesting here to point to the effect which the general phonological rules have on the inflectional system of the verb. Generally speaking it is rules regarding voice, tension and the development of semi-vowels which have most bearing on the shape of the verbal root. The roots with a final devoiced consonant (excepting *-ch/th* /h/) are the most consistent. On the other hand roots with a final *-dh/gh* /j/, *-mh/bh* /w/ and *-ch/th* /h/ are most variable in behaviour. The five most important phonological rules which affect the roots are presented in the following examples. The examples in (1) show devoicing, which was described in 4.2.3, and those in (2) illustrate syllable lengthening before tense consonants, which is described in 3.4:

(1)   *leagfaidh* /Lʹag + həj/ → /Lʹakəj/ (for development see 3.4) 'will lay'
      lobhfaidh /Low + həj/ → /Lofəj/ (for development see 3.4) 'will rot'
      nighfidh /Nʹij + həj/ → /Nʹixʹəj/ (Er) (for development see 3.4) 'will wash'
      leagtha /Lʹag + hə/ → /Lʹakiː/ (C) 'laid'
      lobhtha /Low + hə/ → /Lofə/ (M, C) 'rotten'

(2)   *gearrfaidh* /gʹaʀ + həj/ → /gʹaːrhəj/ *recte (?)* (C) (for development see 4.1) 'will cut'
      gearr /gʹaʀ/ → /gʹaːr/ 'cut'
      meallfaidh /mʹaL + həj/ → /mʹaːLəj/ (C) (for development see 4.1) 'will coax'
      meall /mʹaL/ → /mʹaːL/ (C) 'coax'

(For the further change of /aː/ → /ɑː/ in Connemara: see 3.7.1.) There are, three further rules which change the root. The examples in (3) show the removal of *-th/ch* /h/ [see 4.1.7(ii)], those in (4) the merger of semi-vowels with neighbouring vowels (see 4.1.3) while those in (5) illustrate the removal of a final semi-vowel (see 4.1.4):

(3)   *ritheadar* /rih + dər/ → /riːdər/ (Cf) 'they ran'
      rite /rih + tʹə/ → /ritʹə/ 'run'
      sroichfidh /srexʹ + həj/ → /srexʹə/ → /srehə/ → /sreː/ (Cf) 'will reach'

172 *Modern Irish: grammatical structure and dialectal variation*

(4) *nigheann* /nʲij + ən/ → /nʲiːn/ 'washes'
lobhann /low + ən/ → /loːn/ (D) 'rots'
cruinnigheann /krinʲəj + ən/ → *cruinníonn* /krinʲiːn/ (M, C) 'gathers'
(5) *nigh* /nʲi/ (Cn) 'wash'
cruinnigh /krinʲə/ (Cn) 'gather'

8.1.4 Use of *-óidh/eoidh* /oːj/ and *-(a)igh* /əj/ in Category 2 verbs
There are two important points which must be made concerning Category 2 verbs.

Firstly, in the future of Category 2 verbs we require *-óidh/eoidh* /oːj/ [or /əhəj/ for Donegal; see 8.2.1(i)] rather than simply *-fa(i)dh* /-əj/. Category 2 verbs with a final *-(a)igh* /əj/, e.g. *cruinnigh* 'gather', drop the *-(a)igh* /əj/ before the future ending:

(6) *cruinnigheann* /krinʲ + əj + ən/ (→ *cruinníonn* /krinʲiːn/) 'gathers'
cruinnigh /krinʲəj/ (for development see 4.1) 'gather'
cruinneoidh /krinʲ + oːj/ (for development see 4.1.3(ii)) 'will gather'

Secondly, in the case of other Category 2 verbs, in whose roots there is neither a final *-gh* /j/ nor a vowel in the second syllable, *-(a)igh* /əj/ is introduced before any ending and *-óidh/eoidh* /oːj/ is employed in the future:

(7) *seachn* /sʲaxn/ → *seachain* /sʲaxənʲ/ 'avoid!'
seachnaigheann /sʲaxn + əj + ən/ (→ *seachnaíonn* /sʲaxniːn/) 'avoids'
seachnóidh /sʲaxn + oːj/ 'will avoid'

Where these verbs have no ending, a vowel is inserted because the cluster cannot occur in word-final position (see syllabic adjustment, 2.3) and the final consonant becomes slender [see 6.3.1(ii)] as in:

(8) *seachain* /sʲaxn/ → /sʲaxən/ → /sʲaxənʲ/ 'avoid'
oscail /oskl/ → /oskəl/ → /oskəlʲ/ 'open!'

Furthermore, where the actual ending begins with a consonant such as in the third plural past -/dər/, or in the verbal adjective, these verbs show a hesitancy in regard to the inclusion of /əj/. This is shown by such options in Cois Fhairrge as:

(9) *cheangladar ~ cheanglaigheadar* (→ *cheanglaíodar*) 'they bound'
ceangailte ~ ceanglaighthe (→ *ceanglaithe*) 'bound'

Undoubtedly, the latter option is now the more frequent form. There are occasional examples of verbs of this sort showing other inflections where *-(a)igh* /əj/ and *-óidh/eoidh* /oːj/ [or /ahəj/ (D)] are optional:

(10) *labhraighim* /**Laurəjəm´**/ (→ *labhraím*) /**Lauriːm´**/) ~ *labhraim* (Cf) /**Laurəm´**/ 'I speak'
labhaireoidh /**Laur´oː**/ ~ *labhairfidh* /**Laur´ə**/ (Cf) 'will speak'
cornaigheann /**kaurNəjən**/ [→ *cornaíonn* /**kaurNiːN**/ ~ *cornann* /**kaurNən**/ (Cf)],'rolls'
cornóidh /**kaurNoː**/ ~ *cornfaidh* /**kaurNə**/ (Cf) 'will roll'
codlófaidh /**koləhəj**/ ~ *codalfaidh* /**kodəliː**/ (Tn) 'will sleep'

8.1.5 Variation in the use of *-(a)igh* /əj/ and *-óidh/eoidh* /oːj/ or /ahəj/ (D)
Apart from the general overview of the use of *-(a)igh* /əj/ and *-óidh/eoidh* /oːj/ given above, variations within and between the major dialects can best be treated further in the context of two counter-tendencies, the more extensive use of *-(a)igh* /əj/ and *-óidh/eoidh* /oːj/ or /ahəj/ (D) or the removal of these elements.

8.1.5(i) *The more extensive use of* -(a)igh /ə/ *and* -óidh/eoidh /oːj/ *or* /ahəj/
The ending *-(a)igh* /əj/ intrudes on Category 2 verbs where no ending was required, as in:

(11) *chodail ~ chodlaigh* (Dn) 'slept'
d'aithin ~ d'aithnigh (Cn, Dn) 'recognized'

Another feature of this extensive use is the intrusion of the ending /ahəj/ on the future of verbs with an original long *a* in the second syllable in:

(12) *pacálófaidh* /**pakələhəj**/ (Gd) 'will pack'
tiománófaidh /**t´umənəhəj**/ (Gd) 'will drive'

Furthermore the ending *-óidh/eoidh* /oːj/ or /ahəj/ (D) intrudes on Category 1 verbs, as in:

(13) *fanófaidh* /**faːnəhəj**/ (Gd) 'will wait' : *fan* (Gd) 'wait'
dóirtófaidh /**doːrt´ahəj**/ (Gd) 'will pour' : *dóirt* (Gd) 'pour'

174 *Modern Irish: grammatical structure and dialectal variation*

>   *meascófaidh* /mˈaskahəj/ (Gd) 'will mix' : *measc* (Gd) 'mix'
>   *fáisceofaidh* /faːsˈkˈahəj/ (Gd) 'will squeeze' : *fáisc* (Gd) 'squeeze'
>   *éisteofaidh* /eːsˈtˈahəj/ (Gd) 'will listen' : *éist* (Gd) 'listen'
>   *bhearr(aigh)* /vˈaːr/ ~ /vˈarəgˈ/ (Dn) 'shaved'
>   *lean(aigh)* /lˈan/ ~ /lˈanəgˈ/ (Dn) 'follow'
>   *fanfaidh ~ fanóidh* (Cf, Gd) 'will wait'

Finally in Dunquin both -*(a)igh* /əj/ and -*óidh/eoidh* /oːj/ intrude on Category 1, as in:

(14)   *loirgím* /lorˈəgˈiːmˈ/ ~ *loirgim* /lorˈəgˈəmˈ/ (Dn) 'I look for'
        loirgeod /lorˈəkˈoːd/ (Dn) 'I will look for'
        dheargódh /jarəkoːx/ (Dn) 'it would redden'
        dheargóidíst /jarəgoːdˈiːsˈdˈ/ (Dn) 'they would redden'

Interestingly, such verbs sometimes, as in *loirgeod* 'I will look for' and *dheargódh* 'would redden' in (14), transfer the devoicing which pertains originally to the ending -*f(a)idh* /həj/ (see 4.2.3).

8.1.5(ii) *The removal of* -(a)igh /əj/ *and* -óidh/eoidh /oːj/. In some Donegal dialects the element -*(a)igh* is removed in what is traditionally called the present habitual or in the impersonal form in the past, as in:

(15)   *cruinneann* /krinˈəN/ (Gd) : *cruinnigheann* /krinˈəjəN/
        (→ *cruinníonn* /krinˈiːN/) (Tn, Cn, M) 'gathers'
        cruinneadh /krinˈuː/ (Gd) : *cruinnigheadh* /krinˈəjəɣ/ (→ *cruinníodh* /krinˈiːɣ/) (for development see 4.1.3) (Tn, C, M) 'one gathered'

Furthermore in Cois Fhairrge -*(a)igh* /əj/ and -*óidh/eoidh* /oːj/ are optionally removed in the inflection of verbs which have /uːə/ in the root or which end in -*th* /h/, e.g.:

(16)   *cruadhaigheann* (→ *cruadhaíonn*) /kruːəiN/ ~ *cruadhann* /kruːəN/ (Cf) 'hardens'
        cruadhóidh /kruːəoː/ ~ *cruadhfaidh* /kruːə/ (Cf) 'will harden'
        cruthaigheannn (→ *cruthaíonn*) /kruːiːN/ ~ *cruthann* /kruːN/ (Cf) 'proves'
        cruthóidh /kruːoː/ ~ *cruthfaidh* /kruː/ 'will prove'

Sporadically -*óidh*/*eoidh* /oːj/ is replaced in the future by -*f(a)idh* /həj/. The following example contains the first singular future personal ending -*ód* and -*fad* (see 8.2.4):

(17)   *cabhród* ~ *cabhrfad* /**kaurhəd**/ (Dn) 'I will help'

Finally, it is noteworthy that /j/ becomes /vˊ/ [see 4.1.1(iv)] in the occasional Munster verb, e.g. *bhailigh* /walˊəvˊ/ 'gathered'. This is possibly influenced by, though distinct from, a verb where there is a basic /w/ such as *seasamh* 'stand', where the present /sˊasiːɴ/ is presumably based on *seasaimheann* /sˊasəvˊəɴ/ (for development see 4.1.1(iii)) 'stands' and the past has a /vˊ/ in *sheasaimh* (Dn) 'stood'.

8.2 Grammatical categories

8.2.1 Tense

The major distinction between the verb and the noun is the fact that the verb may show tense. It is best to think of Irish as having two marked tenses: the future and the past. Both the future and the past exhibit particular grammatical morphemes, which clearly indicate tense, whereas the present does not. We may therefore consider the present to be unmarked.

8.2.1(i) *The future tense.* The formation of the future depends both on the person involved and, indeed, on the phonetic shape of the verb. In the impersonal form the future is marked by 'f' (which is a cover-sign for much dialectal variation: see Quin 1969 and Ó Buachalla 1985), e.g. *molfar* 'one will praise' (beside the present *moltar* 'one praises'). On the other hand -*f(a)idh* /həj/ is the most widespread ending in personal forms and, as discussed in 8.1.4, -*óidh*/*eoidh* /oːj/ is used for certain categories of verbs:

(18)   *pógfaidh* /**poːɡ** + **həj**/ → /**poːkəj**/ (for development see 4.1) 'will kiss'

   cruinneoidh /**krinˊ** + **oːj**/ (for development see 4.1) 'will gather'

However, in Gweedore, where the form is required *in pausa,* and it would seem in much of Donegal, the semi-vowel in -*óidh*/*eoidh* /oːj/ is broadened to give /oːɣ/ and -*f(a)idh* /həj/ is suffixed. Preceding the /h/ the /ɣ/ is devoiced. An example is:

176 *Modern Irish: grammatical structure and dialectal variation*

(19) *cruinneoidh* /kriN′ + oːɣ + həj/ → /kriN′axəj/ 'will gather'

The development /oː/ → /a/ in unstressed syllables is normal for Donegal.

It is important to note that /j/ in the endings /həj/ or /oːj/ is dropped where personal suffixes are employed, e.g. *pógfad* /poːkəd/ 'I will kiss'.

Undoubtedly, the sounds /f/ and /h/ in the future morpheme are closely connected and, as might be expected, there is a deal of variation in the dialects (see Ó Buachalla 1985). In several Cork dialects (Berehaven, West Carbery, East Carbery) /f/ rather than /h/ occurs in personal forms and in Cois Fhairrge both /f/ and /h/ are found in the impersonal forms, e.g. *brisfear* /bˊrˊisˊfˊər/ ~ /bˊrˊisˊhər/ (~ /bˊrˊisˊɑːr/) 'one will break'. On the other hand /h/ is virtually invariant in the future in Donegal.

8.2.1(ii) *The past tense.* The past tense is marked by the use of the proclitic morpheme *do* /do/ which causes lenition, e.g. *do phós* (Dn) 'married'. Nevertheless, with the exception of older speakers (as in the case of the last example), in most Munster dialects, the actual proclitic *do* /də/ is removed as is the case in all the major dialects. The lenition, however, remains and functions as a past tense marker, e.g. *phós* 'married'. The *d* /d(ˊ)/ is however retained before a vowel, irrespective of whether the verb itself has an initial vowel or an initial *f* is lenited:

(20) *d'ól* /doːL/ 'drank'
      d'éist /dˊeːsˊtˊ/ 'listened'
      d'fhás /daːs/ 'grew'

The proclitic is slender before a front vowel. In the case where a verb begins with *fr* or *fl* the proclitic is usually employed, e.g. *d'fhreagair* /dˊrˊagərˊ/ 'answered', *d'fhliuch* /dˊlˊux/ 'wet'. However, before *fl* there is some hesitation and *fhliuch* /lˊux/ 'wet' is an option in Cois Fhairrge and is normal in Gweedore and other Donegal dialects.

In some Munster dialects the *d'* itself can be lenited, e.g. *dh'fhaigheadh* /ɣaix/ (Dn) 'used to get', *dh'áirimh* /ɣaːrˊəvˊ/ (Dn) 'counted' [see 6.2.3(ii)2].

The majority of preverbal particles, where there is no habitual aspect (see 8.2.2), have a final *r* /r/ in the past:

(21) *níor phós* /Nˊiːr foːs/ 'did not marry'
      nár phós /Naːr foːs/ 'that did not marry'
      ar phós...? /ər foːs/ 'did... marry?'

It is worth mentioning in passing that the use of *r* in Dunquin is on the wane, e.g. *ní phós...* '... did not marry'.

There are, on the other hand, three particles which generally do not take a final *r*: *ó* 'since', *má* 'if' and *a* 'that, who' (direct relative particle), e.g:

(22) *ó phós...* (C, D) 'since... married'
ó d'fhás... (C, D) 'since... grew'
má phós... (C, D) 'if... married'
má d'fhás... (C, D) 'if...grew'
a phós (C, D) '... who married'
a d'fhás (C, D) '... who grew'

In certain Munster dialects, for instance Muskerry, these particles replace *do*: *má fhás* 'if... grew', *ó imigh* 'since... went away'. In other Munster dialects, Dunquin for instance, the proclitic *do* is subject to lenition: *má dh'fhás* 'if... grew', *a dh'imigh* 'which went off'.

It could be argued that *ó* 'since' and *má* 'if' should be analysed as *ó* + *a* (the direct relative particle) and *má* + *a* (direct relative particle) in the same way as, e.g., *mar* + *a* (direct relative particle) 'as'. The particle *a* would then quite regularly be elided following the long vowel of *ó* 'since' and *má* 'if'. If this analysis were accepted then *a* 'that, who' (the direct relative particle) would be the only particle which does not take a final *r* in non-habitual aspect.

For the non-lenition of the impersonal form following *do* or *-r*, e.g. *pósadh é* 'he was married', *níor pósadh é* 'he wasn't married' and in several dialects the concomitant prefixing of /h/ with non-lenition, e.g. *hiarradh orm* (Cf, Gd) 'I was asked', see 6.2.3(ii)1.

8.2.2 Combination of tenses and aspect

The matter of aspect must be considered at this point as it has an important implication for the tense system and also determines the set of personal endings which are employed. We are not concerned here with various aspects which may be achieved by the use of an auxiliary verb in combination with a verbal noun, such as the continual aspect, the prospective aspect or the perfective aspect. These are fully discussed in 11.3.1. What is of importance here is the 'habitual' aspect.

Although we may use the convenient label 'habitual', strictly speaking, habituality is only apparent when it is combined with a past tense, e.g. *d'fhásadh* 'used to grow', *phógadh* /**foːgəx**/ 'used to kiss'. In the unmarked tense, traditionally called the present tense, an absolute distinction between

178 *Modern Irish: grammatical structure and dialectal variation*

habitual and non-habitual is only possible in the case of the substantive verb, where *tá/tánn* (Ky, Mk) 'is' is opposed to the habitual *bíonn* 'is wont to be'. In the case where the past (*do* + lenition) and the future (/f/ or /h/ which devoices: see 4.2.3) and the 'habitual' aspect endings are combined, e.g. *d'fhásfadh* 'would grow', *phógfadh* /foːkəx/ 'would kiss', the result is what is traditionally the conditional mood, which has a syntactic function quite unrelated to the concept of habituality. Nevertheless, the similarity of the actual endings involved seems to justify on formal grounds the retention of the habitual aspect as a grammatical category.

There are four basic rules concerning how the habitual aspect is indicated:

(a) A *t* /t(ʹ)/ is inserted in an impersonal form where the future tense is not involved, e.g. *póstar* 'one is married', *d'fhástaí* 'one used to grow'.

(b) A *t* /t(ʹ)/ is inserted before the second person singular ending when the past is involved, e.g. *bhristeá* (M, C) 'you used to break'.

(c) An ending -*dh* /ɣ/ [→ /x/; see 4.1.2(ii)] is added where the past tense is involved and there is no personal ending, e.g. *d'fhásadh* 'used grow', *d'fhásfadh* 'would grow'.

(d) An ending -*nn* /N/ (-*(e)ann* /əN/ after syllabic adjustment; see 2.3) is added where the tense is unmarked and there is no personal ending, e.g. *fásann* 'grows'. More marginally in some Donegal dialects, particularly in positive responsives, there is the ending -*dh* /j/, -(*a*)*idh* /əj/ after syllabic adjustment; see 2.3, e.g. *tuigidh/ní thuigeann* (Tn) 'understands/doesn't understand'.

The personal endings are dealt with in 8.2.4.

8.2.3 Mood

The conditional mood was discussed above and analysed as a combination of the future and past together with habitual aspect. In other words, the so-called 'conditional mood' is an amalgam of tense and aspect. If this formal analysis is accepted, there remain two other types of mood, the subjunctive and the imperative. Once again, we are concerned here only with mood expressed by specific inflectional devices.

8.2.3(i) *The subjunctive.* The term subjunctive is used here to denote forms of the verb employed to express an optative mood and, more marginally, in subordinate constructions (see 12.1.4). The fact that the interrelation of mood and subordination is a linguistic phenomenon well established in many languages lends support to the use of the term subjunctive.

The optative usage of the subjunctive is now largely confined to petrified phrases and its subordinating functions have for the most part been taken over by the future or by forms combining the habitual aspect and the past (see 12.1.4).

Their commonest form, referred to as the present subjunctive, is made by adding a vowel *-a/e* /ə/ to the verbal root and when it functions as an optative it is preceded by the particle *go* /gə/ 'that', which causes eclipsis, or *nár* 'that... not', which lenites:

(23) *Go gcuire Dia an t-ádh ort!* (*go* + nasalization + *cuir* + *e*) (C) 'That God may make you lucky!'
Go mbeannaí Dia dhuit! (*go* + nasalization + *beannaigh* + *e*) (C) 'That God may bless you!'
Nár éirí sin leat! (*nár* + *éirigh* + *e*) (C) 'May you not succeed with that!'
Nár theaga sé (*nár* + lenition + *teag* + *a*) (C) 'May he not come!'

Where personal endings are required the future endings are added (see 8.2.4).

What is called the past subjunctive is now limited to subordination and it is formally the same as the combination of the habitual aspect and the past tense traditionally referred to as the past habitual.

8.2.3(ii) *The imperative.* The imperative has no special characteristics except that a personal ending can be added in the plural (see 8.2.4) and that the negative particle *ná* /Na:/ which prefixes *h* [see 6.2.3(i)], rather than *ní*, is used:

(24) *Ól an bainne!* 'Drink the milk'
Ná hólaigí an t-uisce (C) 'Don't (plural) drink the water'

8.2.4 Personal/impersonal endings

8.2.4(i) *General description.* The personal endings are to a great extent dependent on a particular combination of tense, aspect and mood. It should be noted that not all of the various combinations have personal endings.

180 *Modern Irish: grammatical structure and dialectal variation*

The relationship between synthetic and analytic forms is discussed in 8.2.4(ii).

In many cases the endings are consonant extensions, e.g. *-dh* /ɣ/ in the past impersonal form. When the syllabic adjustment rules are applied, any unacceptable cluster is broken up, e.g. *brisdh* /bʹrʹisʹɣ/ → *briseadh* /bʹrʹisʹəɣ/ [for subsequent developments see 4.1.2(iii) and (v)].

Table 8.3 shows the three main endings in the impersonal forms.

Table 8.3 *Impersonal form endings*

Habitual aspect combined with past	Past	Unmarked tense/future/imperative
-í /iː/ *bhristí* 'one used to break' *bhrisfí* 'one would break'	*-dh* /ɣ/ *briseadh* 'one broke'	*-r* /-rʹ/ *bristear* 'one breaks' *brisfear* 'one will break'

In Cois Fhairrge the future impersonal ending /aːr/ is widespread.

Table 8.4 illustrates the personal endings where habitual aspect and past tense combine, that is to say, in what are traditionally called the habitual past and (when further combined with the future marker) the conditional.

Table 8.4 *Personal endings in habitual combined with past*

		Habitual combined with past	Habitual combined with past (+ future marker)
Person	Endings	Habitual past	Conditional
first singular	*-nn* /Nʹ/	*bhrisinn* 'I used to break'	*bhrisfinn* 'I would break'
second singular	*-á* /aː/ ~ *f(e)á* /f(ʹ)aː/ ~ *th(e)á* /haː/	*bhristeá* 'you used to break'	*bhrisfeá* 'you would break'
first plural	*-mís(t)* /ˈmʹiːsʹ/ ~ /ˈmʹiːsʹdʹ/ (M) ~ /misʹtʹ/ (Tn, Mn)	*bhrisimís(t)* 'we used to break'	*bhrisfimís(t)* 'we would break'
third plural	*-dís(t)* /ˈdʹiːsʹ/ ~ /ˈdʹiːsʹdʹ/ (M), /dʹiːsʹ/ (C)	*bhrisidís(t)* 'they used to break'	*bhrisfidís(t)* 'they would break'

Table 8.5 presents the personal ending used in the past tense. Some of the personal endings are in specific dialects confined to echo forms. This concept is explained in 8.2.4(ii).

Table 8.5 *Personal endings in past*

Person	Ending	Form
first singular	-s /s/ (M, C and D echo form)	*bhriseas* 'I broke'
second singular	-s /sʹ/ (M, echo form)	*bhrisis* 'you broke'
first plural	-mair /mərʹ/ (M) -mar (West Cn)	*bhriseamair, bhriseamar* 'we broke'
second plural	-bhair (M) /wər(ʹ)/ (Ky), /uːrʹ/ (Mk)	*bhriseabhair* 'you broke'
third plural	-dar /dər/ (M, C)	*bhriseadar* 'they broke'

Again, in Table 8.6, where the personal endings required for the future tense are shown, some of the endings are limited to echo forms.

Table 8.6 *Personal endings in future*

Person	Endings	Form
first singular	-d /d/ (M, C and D in echo forms)	*brisfead* 'I will break'
second singular	-r /rʹ/ (M, C echo), -s /sʹ/ (C echo)	*brisfir, brisfis* 'you will break'
first plural	-m /m/, míd /mʹiːdʹ/ (M)	*briseam, brisfimíd* 'we will break'
third plural	-d /dʹ/ (M)	*brisid* 'they break'

Table 8.7 presents the ending in the unmarked tense traditionally known as the present habitual. For convenience these endings are tabularized separately from the future but it should be observed that the endings -r /rʹ/ ,-míd /mʹiːdʹ/ and -d /dʹ/ are shared.

As was pointed out in 8.2.3(i) the future personal endings apply also to the present subjunctive and this can be seen in the following example, which shows the optative usage of the personal ending -r /rʹ/ in the second singular:

(25)   *Go mairir is go gcaithir...*(Ky)
        'May you enjoy and use...'

Finally there is a personal ending in the second plural imperative. The ending -gí /gʹiː/ is the norm in Donegal and Connacht, e.g. *brisígí* 'break' (plural). However, the ending *í* /iː/ is found in set phrases and in irregular verbs, e.g.

182 *Modern Irish: grammatical structure and dialectal variation*

teagaí (Cf) 'come' (plural). In Munster the most common ending is *íg* /iːgʹ/ (see Ó Murchú 1969b).

Table 8.7 *Personal endings in unmarked tense*

Person	Endings	Habitual present
first singular	*-m* /mʹ/	*brisim* 'I break'
second singular	*-r* /rʹ/ (M, C echo), *-nns* /nʹs/ (C echo)	*brisir, brisinns* 'you break'
first plural	*-míd* /mʹiːdʹ/ (M)	*brisimíd* 'we break'
third plural	*-d* /dʹ/ (M)	*brisid* 'they break'

8.2.4(ii) *Options in personal endings*. Generally speaking, it can be said that the use of synthetic forms in Irish is incompatible with additional use of an independent pronoun subject. In other words only *cuirim* 'I put' (and not *cuirim mé), *chuirfinn* 'I would put' (and not *chuirfinn mé) etc. are possible.

There is one exception to this general rule. In some Munster dialects older speakers employed the third plural subject pronoun following a synthetic form in any tense. An example is:

(26)   *Mhuise, tugaid siad orm é* (Mk)
       'Indeed they call me it'

From a diachronic point of view it might be claimed that there is a gradual shift from synthetic forms to analytic forms, e.g. from *bhriseas* 'I broke' to *bhris mé* 'I broke'. Nevertheless, all dialects show a mixture of synthetic and analytic forms (see Greene 1972:62-3). In general, it can be said that the smallest number of synthetic forms is found in Donegal, where they are largely confined to the first and second singular when habitual aspect and past tense combine, e.g. *bhrisfinn* 'I would break', *bhrisfeá* 'you would break', and also to the first singular of the unmarked tense, e.g. *brisim* 'I break'. In central and south Donegal the first plural *muist* /misʹdʹ/ is also possible. On the other hand, Munster has the greatest number of synthetic forms. Naturally, there is variation within Munster: Muskerry probably has a higher tally than Kerry, Ring or Clare. Where both the synthetic and the analytic forms coexist in a dialect, there seem to be four possibilities:

(a)   free variation
(b)   variation with the more frequent use of the synthetic form as an echo form

(c) use of the synthetic form solely as an echo form
(d) use of the synthetic form in a restricted sense or register.

It is difficult to assess the frequency or the exact local variations, but forms such as *bhriseadar* ~ *bhris siad* (Im) 'they broke', or *bhriseamar* ~ *bhris muid* (Rm) 'we broke' seem to be in free variation, though one might predict that eventually the analytic form will win out.

In Dunquin there is a deal of free variation in the second singular future, e.g. *brisfir* or *brisfidh tú* 'you will break'. Nevertheless, it appears that in echo forms only *brisfir* is normally permitted.

When a verb or its auxiliary *déan* 'do' [see 11.3.2(i)] is 'echoed' in the same utterance in Connacht, and to a much more limited extent in Munster and Donegal, certain synthetic forms are optional:

(27) *Bhris tú an chathaoir, ar bhrisis?* (C)
 'You broke the chair, did you?'
(28) *...dúirt liom póg a bhaint dhi rud a rinneas* (C)
 '...she said to kiss her which I did'
(29) *Ar bhris tú an chathaoir?*
 'Did you break the chair?
 Bhriseas (C)
 'I did'

The forms *bhrisis* 'you broke' in (27), *rinneas* 'I did' in (28) and *bhriseas* 'I broke' in (29) are referred to as echo forms and can only be accompanied by an assertive adverbial phrase as seen in:

(30) *Ar bhris tú an chathaoir?*
 'Did you break the chair?'
 Bhriseas, go deimhin! (C)
 'Yes, indeed I did!'

The unison and addition syntax normal in response (see 9.2.8) is also permitted after an echo form:

(31) *Brisfidh mé an chathaoir*
 'I will break the chair'
 Tá mé ag rá go mbrisfis agus go leor eile! (C)
 'I'll say you will and much more besides!'

In Connacht these synthetic optional echo forms occur in the first and second singular of the future and past:

(32)   *brisfead* (C) 'I will break'
       brisfir (C) 'you will break'
       bhriseas (C) 'I broke'
       bhrisis (C) 'you broke'

What from a historical viewpoint is a new synthetic form has developed in the second singular of the unmarked tense, e.g. *brisinns* /b′r′is′in′s/ 'you break'. In Connemara at least, the *-s* /s′/ of the past and the *-r* /r′/ of the future second singular interchange to give two extra echo forms *brisfis* 'you will break' and *bhrisir* 'you broke'.

In Donegal, there are traces of this echo system, particularly in the first person singular of the past or future, though recorded examples from Teelin, for instance, appear to be confined to the irregular verbs:

(33)   *An dtug tú?*
       'Did you give?'
       Thugas (Tn)
       'I did'
(34)   [*An*] *ndéanfaidh tú?*
       'Will you do?'
       Dhéanfad (Tn)
       'I will'

In Dunquin, it would seem that an echo system has developed in the third plural of the future and unmarked tenses, e.g. *deinid* (Dn) 'they do', *gheobhaid* (Dn) 'they will get'.

The synthetic first plural ending where the habitual aspect is combined with the past tense, *-muist* /mis′d′/, is required for Faulmore, Erris, but is extremely rare and seems in Faulmore at least to be confined to verse, prayers etc. Again the ending *muist* /mis′d′/ is found in Cois Fhairrge but only in the petrified phrase *feiceamuist!* 'let's see (if you can)!'.

Once again, from a diachronic viewpoint, other options within the dialects may occur, due to the survival of what diachronically are older forms alongside later developments, e.g. *brisfeam* (Dn) beside the much more frequent *brisfimid* 'we will break'. In other cases, the variation is due to more recent developments, e.g. *an dtuigeas tú* (Dn) beside *a n dtuigeann tú?* (Dn) 'do you understand?'; *ghlacfas muid* (Gd) beside *ghlacfadh muid* 'we should'. In the preceding examples there is not, strictly speaking, an inflectional option, since the form is followed by a pronoun; yet the responses do not have a final *-s*. We might say that forms such as *an dtuigeas* or *ghlacfas* are halfway between being synthetic and analytic.

8.3 Root variation and irregular verbs

8.3.1 General discussion

There are eleven verbs (including the substantive verb) where various roots are employed for different combinations of tense, aspect and mood. In some cases the different roots required are phonetically closely related, e.g. *feic-* and *fac-* or *beir-* and *béar-*, even though this phonetic relationship eludes synchronic explanation. On the other hand, in some verbs, there is no apparent relation, e.g. *deir-* and *abr-* or *té-*, *rach-* and *cuaigh-*. These eleven verbs are best described as being defective verbs in which different roots interweave in a complementary fashion.

A further feature of these defective or 'irregular' verbs is that, apart from root variation in the normal verbal categories, there can be special forms to express syntactic features such as complementation, negation or questioning. In non-defective or 'regular' verbs such syntactic functions are expressed solely by the use of preverbal particles. These special forms are traditionally called 'dependent forms' (as opposed to 'independent' or statement form). They too are formed by root variation, e.g. *choinic* (Cf) 'saw' but *ní fhaca(idh)* (Cf) 'did not see', *bheireann* (Gd) 'gives' but *cha dtabhrann* (Gd) 'does not give'.

A characteristic of the substantive verb is that when no tense is specified the habitual aspect is absent, so that there is an opposition between *tá* 'is' and *bíonn* 'is wont to be'.

8.3.2 The irregular verbs

The degree of defectiveness among the irregular verbs varies greatly. Apart from differences between independent and dependent forms, defectiveness can be described in terms of variation of the following roots:

(a) Those with habitual aspect and no future marker (traditionally the present and habitual past)

186   *Modern Irish: grammatical structure and dialectal variation*

(b)   Those marked for future tense (the future and traditionally the conditional)
(c)   Those marked for the past without habitual aspect (i.e. the past tense)
(d)   Those in imperative mood
(e)   Those used in nominal and adjectival forms (traditionally the verbal noun and adjective).

In this outline of the irregular verbs, in 8.3.2(i)-(xii) examples are given for (a)-(e) from Gweedore, Erris, Cois Fhairrge and Dunquin. There is much local variation within the major dialects and the most that can be achieved here is an account of these four areas. Where there was a significant difference between Gweedore and Teelin, the latter is included and there is occasional reference to noteworthy features of other dialects. The underlying ending *-gh* /j/ is not realized before a personal pronoun subject but otherwise is realized as *-(a)igh* /əgʹ/ (M) and /iː/ (D, Mo): see 4.1.3. For convenience, in this account the underlying *-(a)igh* is retained, e.g. *rinnigh* (Mo), *dearnaigh* (Dn). Furthermore the verbal adjective suffix *-tha* /h/ and the future marker /h/ devoice certain preceding consonants, e.g. *teagtha* /tʹæːkiː/ (Cf) 'come'. Otherwise, the roots are given in an approximate spelling with a surface phonemic transcription.

8.3.2(i) *The verb* déan *'do'*. The verb *déan* 'do, make' has most root variation in the past. There is also a limited root variation with *ní* (Gd, Cf) and *din* (Dn). Apart from the *déan ~ díon* option (and its various realizations), in other respects this verb does not show great irregularity:

(35)   Ind. *ní-* /Nʹiː/, dep. *déan-* /dʹen/ (Gd)
       déan- /dʹeːn/ ~ *díon-* /dʹiːn/ (Er)
       díon- /dʹiːN/ ~ *dion-* /dʹiN/ ~ *ní-* /Nʹiː/ (Cf)
       din- /dʹinʹ/ (Dn)
(36)   *dhen-* /jen/ (Gd)
       déan- /dʹeːn/ ~ *díon-* /dʹin/ (Er)
       díon- /dʹiːN/ ~ *dion-* /dʹiN/ ~ *ní* /Nʹiː/ (Cf)
       déan- /dʹian/ (Dn)
(37)   Ind. *rinn* /riNʹ/, dep. *dearn* /dʹæːrN/ (Gd)
       Ind. *rinn* /riNʹ/ ~ *rinnidh* /riNʹəj/, dep. *dearnaigh* /dʹaːrNəj/ (Er)
       Ind. *rinne*, dep. *dearnaigh* /dʹaːrNəj/ (Cf)
       Ind. *dhin* , dep. (rare) *dearnaigh* /dʹaːrNəj/ (Dn)

(38) *dean-* /dʲen/
 deán- /dʲæːn/ (Tn)
 déan- /dʲeːn/ ~ *díon-* /dʲiːn/ (Er)
 díon- /dʲiːN/ ~ *dion-* /dʲiN/ (Cf)
 din- /dʲinʲ/ (Dn)
(39) *dean-* /dʲen/ (Gd)
 deán- /dʲæːn/ (Tn)
 déan- /dʲeːn/ ~ *díon-* /dʲiːn/ (Er)
 díon- /dʲiːN/ ~ *dion-* /dʲiN/ (Cf)
 déan- /dʲian/

In Gweedore the verbal noun *déanamh* /dʲeNuː/ is used with the meaning 'do, make'; while *déanamh* /dʲæːNuː/ is found in set phrases such as *tá mé ag déanamh* 'I think'.

8.3.2(ii) The verb feic- 'see'. The use of *cí-* (Dn) and *tí-* (Gd) in (40) and (41) is noteworthy. (There is a rare use of *cí* in *chítear dom* (Cf) 'it seems to me'.) Otherwise the verb shows root variation in the past between the independent and dependent forms.

(40) *tí-* /tʲiː/, dep. *feic-* /fʲekʲ/ (Gd)
 feic- /fʲekʲ/ (Er, Cf)
 cí- /kʲiː/ ~ (rare present *fic* /fʲikʲ/) (Dn)
(41) *tif-* /tʲifʲ/ ~ *tiú-* /tʲuː/, dep. *feic-* /fʲekʲ/ (Gd)
 tíf- /tʲiːfʲ/, dep. *feic-* /fʲekʲ/ (Tn)
 feic- /fʲekʲ/ (Er, Cf)
 cí- /kʲiː/ (Dn)
(42) Ind. *chanaic* /hanʲəkʲ/, dep. *facaidh* /fakəj/ (Gd)
 Ind. *chanaic* /hanʲəkʲ/, dep. *faca* /fakə/ (Er)
 Ind. *chainic* /xanʲəkʲ/ ~ /haːnʲəkʲ/ ~ *choinic* /xinəkʲ/, dep. *facaidh* /faːkəj/ (Cf)
 Ind. *chonaic* /xnikʲ/, dep. *feacaidh* /fʲakəj/ (Dn)
(43) *feic-* /fʲekʲ/ (rare all dialects)
(44) *feic-* /fʲekʲ/ (Gd, Er, Cf)
 fic- /fʲikʲ/ (Dn)

8.3.2(iii) The verb téigh- 'go'. The verb *téigh-* 'go' displays a very high degree of root variation throughout the system. The most significant dialect difference is the use of *gobh-* /gow/ in Connacht and Donegal:

188 *Modern Irish: grammatical structure and dialectal variation*

(45) *té-* /tʼeː/ (Gd, Er, Dn)
 teigh- /tʼai/ (Cf, Rg)
(46) *ragh-* /raɣ/ (/raɣ + həj/ → /raxəj/) (Gd, Er, Cf)
 gobh- /gow/ (Cf)
 raigh- /rai/ (no future marker) (Dn)
(47) Ind. *chuaigh* /xuːəj/ dep. *deachaigh* /dʼaːxəj/ (Gd)
 Ind. *fuaidh* /fuːəj/, dep. *deachaigh* /dʼaxəj/ (Er)
 Ind. *chuaigh* /xuəj/, dep. *deachaigh* /dʼæːxəj/ (Cf)
 Ind. *chuaigh* /xuəj/, (rare) dep. *deighigh* /dʼai/ (Dn)
(48) *gobh-* /goː/ (Gd)
 téirigh /tʼe(ː)rʼəj/ (Er)
 gobh- /go/ ~ *téirigh* /tʼairʼəj/ (Cf)
 téir(igh)- /tʼeːrʼ(əj)/ (Dn)
(49) Noun: *goil* (D, C)
 dul (Dn; Gd,Cf in petrified phrases)
 Adjective: *dulta* (Dn)
 gobh- (?Gd, ?Er, Cf)

8.3.2(iv) *The verb* **tag-** *'come'*. The verb *tag-* 'come' has also a high degree of root variation. It may be said that, while the variants are not synchronically explicable, they are transparently related. The forms in the future marked tenses (51) and in the past (52) are fairly constant throughout the dialects. A lot of variation is based on the instability of the quality of the initial *t* :

(50) *tig-* /tʼigʼ/ (Gd, Er)
 teag- /tʼæːg/ ~ *tig-* /tʼigʼ/ (Cf)
 tag- /tag/ (Dn)
(51) *tiug-* /tʼug/ (/tʼug/ + /h/ → /tʼuk/) (Gd, Er, Cf)
 tug /tug/ ~ (rare) *tag-* /tag/ (Dn)
(52) *tháinig* /haːnʼəgʼ/ (M) ~ /haːnʼəkʼ/ (Gd, Er) → /hɑːnʼək/ (Cf) see 4.2.5
(53) *tair-* /tarʼ/ (Gd)
 tig- /tʼigʼ/ ~ sing. *taraigh* /tarəj/ ~ *tearaigh* /tʼaːrəj/ (Er)
 tear- /tʼæːr/ ~ *teag-* /tʼæːg/ ~ sing. *teara* /tʼæːrə/ ~ *teag(a)* /tʼæːgə/ (Cf)
 tar- /tar/ ~ *tag-* /tag/ ~ sing. *tair* /tarʼ/ (Dn)
(54) Noun: *teach-* (Gd, Er, Cf, Dn) ~ *tíoch-* /tʼiːx/ (C)
 Adjective: ? (Gd), ? (Er), *teag-* /tʼæg/ ~ *tag* /taːg/ (Cf), *tag-* /tag/ (Dn)

8.3.2(v) ***The verb* fágh- 'get'**. The verb *fágh-* 'get' exhibits a deal of root variation. The other major root is *gheobh-* /ɣow/ which, because of the final *-bh* /w/, is subject to a number of phonological rules.

(55)   *fagh-* /faɣ/ [/faɣ/ + vowel → /fɑː/ (Er) → /fæː/ (Gd)]
       fagh- /faɣ/ (/faɣ/ + vowel → /fɑː/ → /fɑː/) ~ (rare) *gheobh-* /jow/ +
       vowel → /jau/ ~ *gheof-* /jof/ (Cf)
       faigh- /faj/ (→ /fai/) (Dn)
(56)   Ind. *gheobh-* /jow/ (/jow/ + vowel → /joː/), dep. *fuigh* /fij/ (/fij/ +
       vowel → /fiː/) (no future marker) (Gd)
       Ind. *gheobh-* /jow/ (/jow/ + (future marker /h/ → /jof/), dep. *fuigh*
       /fij/ (/fij/ + vowel → /fiː/) (Er)
       gheobh- /jow/ (/jow/ + vowel → /jau/ ~ /jow/ + future marker /h/ →
       /jof/) ~ *fuigh-* /fij/ (/fij/ + vowel → /fiː/ ~ *faigh-* /faj/ (/faj/ + vowel →
       /fai/) (Cf)
       gheobh- /jow/ (/jow/ + vowel → /jau/) ~ *faigh-* /faj/ (/faj/ + vowel →
       /fai/) (no future marker) (Dn)
(57)   *fuair-* /fuːərʹ/ (Gd, Er, Cf, Dn)
       Impersonal form: *fuar-* (Gd, Er, Dn)
       fríth- /fʹrʹiːh/ (Cn)
(58)   *fá-* /fɑː/ (Gd, Er) [→ /fɑː/ (Cf)], *faigh-* /faːgʹ/ ~ sing. /faːgʹ/, /fegʹ/ (Dn)
(59)   Noun: *fá* -/fɑː/ (Gd, Er, Cf, Dn)
       Adjective: *fá* -/fɑː/ (Gd, Er) [→ /fɑː/ (Cf)], *fach* /faːx/ (Dn)

Following the negative particle all the forms with an initial *f* are mutated in accordance with rules of eclipsis rather than the expected lenition. While in practice it appears as eclipsis, it is, in fact, best analysed as a glide /w/ preventing hiatus caused by lenition [see 6.2.4(v)]. In the future marked tenses all the forms listed for Cois Fhairrge may function as either 'independent' or 'dependent' forms and the roots *fuigh-* and *faigh-* are always mutated even in the rare case where they are used without a preverbal particle.

8.3.2(vi) ***The verb* tug 'give'**. The verb *tug* 'give' has three discernible roots: *tug*, *tabhr-* and *bheir*. Most of the 'irregularity' is caused by the appearance of these roots (or their variants) in different tenses and in independent and dependent forms:

(60)   Ind. *bheir-* /vʹerʹ/, dep. *tobhr-* /tawr/ (→ /toːrʹ/) (Gd)
       tug- /tug/ (Er, Dn)
       tug- /tug/, ind. (set phrases) *bheir-* /vʹerʹ/ (Cf)

190 *Modern Irish: grammatical structure and dialectal variation*

(61) Ind. *bhéar-* /v′eːr/, dep. *tabhr-* /tawr/ (→ /toːr/) (Gd)
Ind. *bhéar-* /v′eːr/, dep. *tubhr-* /tuwr/ (→ /tuːr/) (Er)
tiubhar- /t′uwr/ (→ /t′uːr/) ~ (rare) *bhéar-* /v′eːr/ (Cf)
tubhar- /tuwr/ (→ /tuːr/) (Dn)
(62) *thug-* /hug/ (Gd, Er, Cf, Dn)
(63) *tabhr-* /tawr/ (→ /toːr/) (Gd, Er)
tabhr- /tawr/ (→ /toːr/ ~ *tug* /tug/) (Cf)
tubhr- /tuwr/ (→ /tuːr/) (Dn)
(64) Noun: *tabhr-* /tawr/ (→ /toːr/) (Gd, Er)
tabhr- /tawr/ (→ /toːr/) ~ *tiubhr-* /t′uːr/ ~ *teabhr-* /t′awr/ (→ /t′oːr/) (Cf)
tubhar /tuwr/ ~ (→ /tuːr/) (Dn)
Adjective: *tug-* /tug/ (Gd, Er, Cf, Dn) ~ *tabhr-* /tawr/ → /toːr/ (Gd in set phrases)

The development of *t(e)abhr-* /t(′)oːr/ is regular for Donegal but exceptional in Connacht (see 4.1.3(iii)).

8.3.2(vii) The verb deir 'says'. The verb *deir* 'says' has three discernible roots *deir, abr-, rá-*, which are interwoven. However, *deir-* has the variants *déar-* and *dúr-* which elude synchronic explanation:

(65) Ind. *deir-* /der′/, dep. *abr-* /abr/ (Gd)
Ind. *deir-* /d′er′/, dep. *deir-* /d′er′/ ~ *abr-* /abr/ (Er)
deir- /d′er′/ ~ (rarer) *déar-* /d′eːr/ ~ *diar-* /d′iːər/ ~ *abr-* /abr/ (Cf)
deir- (Dn)
(66) Ind. *déar-* /d′eːr/, dep. *abr-* (Gd)
Ind. *déar-* /d′eːr/, dep. *déar-* /d′eːr/ ~ *abr-* (Er)
déar- /deːr/ ~ *diar* /d′iːər/ ~ *abr-* (Cf)
déar- /d′eːr/ → /d′iːar/ (Dn)
(67) *-úr(t)-* /uːr(t)/ (Gd, Er, Cf)
dúr- (Dn)
(68) *abr-* /abr/ (Gd, Er, Cf, Dn)
(69) *rá(-)* /raː/ (Gd, Er, Dn) → /rɑː/ (Cf)

In Cois Fhairrge the *d* in *deir-* is removed following preverbal particles which lenite, e.g. *ní 'eireann* /N′iː er′ən/ 'says not'.

8.3.2(viii) The verb beir 'bears'. The verb *beir* 'bears' displays a limited degree of root variation. Apart from the change to *béar-* in tenses marked for the future (71) and the substitution of *rug* in the past (72), it behaves fairly regularly throughout. There is no distinction between independent and dependent forms.

(70) *beir-* /bʹerʹ/ (Gd, Er, Cf, Dn)
(71) *béar-* /bʹeːr/ (Gd, Er, Cf, Dn)
(72) *bheir-* /vʹerʹ/ (Gd)
 rug /rug/ (Er, Cf)
 bheir /vʹerʹ/ ~ (older speakers) *rug* /rʹug/ (Dn)
(73) *beir* /bʹerʹ/ (Gd, Er, Cf, Dn)
(74) Noun: *breith* /bʹrʹe(h)/ (Gd, Er, Cf, Dn)
 Adjective: *beir-* /bʹerʹ/ (Gd, Er, Cf, Dn)

The loss of *rug* 'bore' in some dialects is due to its association with birth. The verb *rugann* 'gives birth' is a 'regular' verb in Gweedore. In the impersonal, dialects may make a distinction between *rugadh* (Gd, Er, Cf, Dn) 'was born' and *beireadh air* (Gd), *rugús air* (Cf) 'he was caught'.

8.3.2(ix) The verb clois/cluin 'hears'. There is a geographic variation between *clois* and *cluin-*, the former a southern feature, the latter a northern one and both are found in Connemara. The past form *chualaigh* is shared by the dialects. There are no distinctions between independent and dependent forms.

(75) *cluin-* /klinʹ/ (Gd, Er)
 clois- /klosʹ/ ~ *cluin-* /kʟinʹ/ (Cf)
 clois- /kʟosʹ/ (Dn)
(76) *cluin-* /klinʹ/ (Gd, Er)
 clois- /klosʹ/ ~ *kluin-* /klinʹ/ (Cf)
 clois- /klosʹ/ (Dn)
(77) Personal: *chualaigh* /xuələj/ (Gd, Er, Cf, Dn)
 Impersonal: *cluin-* /kʟinʹ/ (Gd)
 clois- ~ *chuala-* (Tn)
 ? (Er)
 clois- kʟosʹ/ ~ *cluin-* /kʟinʹ/ (Cf)
 chuala- /xuələ/ (Dn)
(78) *cluin/clois* [rare in all dialects; distribution as in (75-6)]
 clois- kʟosʹ/ ~ *cluin-* /kʟinʹ/ (Cf)
 chuala- /xuələ/ (Dn)

8.3.2(x) The substantive verb tá 'be'. The substantive verb is complex in that there is considerable root variation. The independent forms have the three roots *bí, be-* and *tá.* In the past tense the dependent form *raibh* is synchronically opaque. When the tense is specified the habitual aspect is absent and all major dialects have the independent form *tá(-)* /taː/ (~ /haː/) (Dn) and the dependent form *fuil(-).*

(79) *bí-* /bʹiː/ (Gd, Er, Cf, Dn)
      be- (Gd, Er, Cf, Dn) (Future markers /f/ or /h/ only in the conditional second singular or in the impersonal forms.)
(80) Ind. *bhí* /vʹiː/, dep. *robh* /roː/ (Gd)
      Ind. *bhí*, dep. *robh* /ro/ (Er, Cf)
      Ind. *bhí*, dep. *roibh* /revʹ/ (Dn)
(81) *bí-* (Gd, Er, Cf, Dn)
      Noun: *bheith* /vʹeh/

In Dunquin there is a series of optional allegro forms in the past following complementizers, *go raibh* /gəv/ 'that was', *ná raibh* /naːvʹ/ 'that was not' and following the negative, *ní raibh* /nʹiːvʹ/ 'was not'. These are most frequent preceding vowels. They are apparently not employed in tags, e.g. *Ní 'bh sé féin ró-mhaith ... ní roibh* (Dn) 'He wasn't too well ... he wasn't'.

8.3.2(xi) The verb ith 'eat'.
The verb *ith* 'eat' is regular except where marked for the future tense (i.e. future or conditional). In that case *íos-* /iːs/ is the root. The root *íos-* is also found in the unmarked 'present' tense in Gweedore and Cois Fhairrge. More marginally, in the past the root *uaidh* /uəj/ is found in Clare.

8.3.2(xii) The verbs gaibh 'seize' and inis 'tell'. The above eleven verbs show root variation in all major dialects. Two further verbs must be considered.

Firstly, there is the case of the verb *gabháil* 'seize, move' etc. This verb is used in Cois Fhairrge to fill out the verb *téigh-* 'go'. In Dunquin, however, the verb generally has a root *gaibh-* /gaivʹ/. It is regularly *gaibheann* /gain/ 'moves', *ghaibheadh* /ɣaix/ 'used to move' etc. [see 4.1.1(iii)]. In the tenses marked for the future, forms similar to those of the verb *faigh* 'get' are used. The noun and adjective are based on *gabh-* /gobh-/.

Secondly, the verb *in(i)s* 'tell' has two sets of forms in Dunquin, one based on a root *ins* /in´s/, the other on a root *nis* /n´is´/. However, the tenses marked for the future are based on *neos* /n´oːs/ (→ /n´uːs/).

8.3.3 Other features of irregular verbs

8.3.3(i) *The ending* -nn /N/ *not required.* In some irregular verbs the ending *-nn* /N/ (realized as *-(e)ann* following syllabic adjustment; see 2.3) is optional in the unmarked tense, e.g. *deir* 'says', *an gcluin tú mé?* (Gd, Cf) 'do you hear me?' or in the petrified phrase *thig(e)* (Gd) ~ *tig* (Cn) *liom* 'I can'.

In general, it can be said that the use of these flexionless forms is more characteristic of Donegal and many of the irregular verbs have such forms:

(82) *tí* (D) 'see'
bheir (D) 'give'
deir (D) 'say'
ní (D) 'does'
cluin (D) 'hear'
tig (D) 'comes'

The form *téid* 'goes' is slightly exceptional in that a final *d* must be added to the root.

In all major dialects no ending is required with *tá* or *fuil* 'is'; on the other hand, in Dunquin and Muskerry *tánn* and *fuileann* can be used in the second person, *táid* in the third plural [see also (26)]:

(83) *tánn tú/sibh* (Dn, Mk) 'you are'
táid siad (Dn, Mk) 'they are'
an bhfuileann tú? 'are you?'

In some Munster dialects the form *taoi* 'you are' (sing) is current.

8.3.3(ii) *Zero endings.* In Dunquin and Muskerry the first person singular in the past tense has a zero ending in the verbs *cí-* 'see', *clois* 'hear', *deir* 'say':

(84) *chnoc* /xnuk/ 'I saw'
ní fhaca /n´akə/ 'I didn't see'
chuala /xuːəLə/ 'I heard'

194 *Modern Irish: grammatical structure and dialectal variation*

>   *dúrt* /**duːrt**/ (Dn), *duart* /**duːərt**/ (Mk) 'I said'
>   *thána* /**haːnə**/ ~ *thánag* /**haːnəg**/ (Dn) 'I came'

Somewhat similarly, the defective verb *feadar* 'know', which, while its meaning is unmarked for tense, is only found with non-habitual aspect past personal endings, e.g.:

(85)   *ní fheadar* /**nˊadər**/ 'I don't know'
       an bhfeadaraís? /**ə vˊadəˈriːsˊ**/ 'do you know?'
       ...ná feadramair '... which we do not know'

8.3.3(iii) *Impersonal endings in* **-thas** /**həs**/ *in irregular verbs.* In some irregular verbs the ending *-th* /**h**/+ *s* /**s**/ rather than *-dh* /**ɣ**/ (for development see 4.1.2) may be employed in the non-habitual aspectual past. This is most widespread in Munster; for example, it is used in Dunquin with *clois* 'hear', *cí-* 'see', *deir* 'say', *téigh-* 'go' and with the substantive verb; the final consonant of the root is always broad:

(86)   *cualathas* /**kuələhəs**/ (Dn) 'one heard'
       Ind. *conacthas* /**knokəhəs**/, dep. *facthas* /**fakəhəs**/ (Dn) 'one saw'
       dúrthas /**duːrəhəs**/ (Dn) 'one said'
       cuadhthas /**kuəhəs**/ ~ *chuadhthas* /**xuəhəs**/ (Dn) 'one went'
       Ind. *bhíothas* /**vˊiːhəs**/, dep. *rabhthas* /**rauhəs**/ (Dn) 'one was'

Furthermore all of these except *facthas* 'one saw' are optional forms in Dunquin. There is a tendency for the normal ending *-dh* /**ɣ**/ (→ /**x**/; see 4.1.2) to take over. The forms with *th* + *s* (→ *-thas*) are found in all major dialects but they are least common in Cois Fhairrge, where only *facthas* is obligatory. (In the set phrase *b'fhacthas dhom* 'it seemed to me', it is often used with the copula.) Occasionally the endings *-dh* (/**ɣ**/ → /**uː**/ ; see 4.1.2) and *th* + *s* (→ *-thas*) are fused in Cois Fhairrge to give *-ús*:

(87)   *rugús air* (Cf) 'he was caught'
       teagús (Cf) 'one came'

8.3.3(iv) *Fusion of endings in impersonal.* Throughout the dialects there is a tendency for the distinctive *-s* of the past tense impersonal ending *-th* + *s* (→ *-thas*) to intrude on the present (even in regular verbs), e.g. *feicears* in the phrase *feicears dhom* (Cf) 'it seems to me', *doirtars* (Dn) 'one pours'.

The contrary tendency is for *-tar* to intrude on the past tense, e.g. *bhíothar* /vˊiːhər/ (Er) 'one was'. In Dunquin the fused ending *-tars* /tərs/ is optional in most irregular verbs alongside *-dh* /ɣ/ (→ /x/) or *th* + *s* (→ *-thas* /həs/), e.g. *bhíothars* 'one was'.

8.4 Nominal and adjectival forms

8.4.1 Introductory remarks

The verbal noun and adjective, are, so to speak, halfway between being nominal forms and belonging to the inflectional system of the verb. They do not carry tense, aspect, mood or person and must therefore be employed with an auxiliary verb. In many ways their function and formation are similar to ordinary nouns. Indeed some nouns which have no verbal forms can be given the functions of a verbal noun, e.g. *ag imní* 'worrying' or *a g feadaíl* 'whistling' where **imníonn (sé)*, **feadann sé* do not exist. The formation of verbal nouns also resembles that of 'ordinary' nouns in that consonant extension is used and in the fact that there is a low degree of predictability. It is often not possible to say simply by the shape of a verb how the verbal noun will be formed. That information must be supplied in the lexicon. Yet despite all the similarities, since almost every verb has an associated verbal noun and adjective, it must be dealt with as part of the inflectional system of the verb.

8.4.2 Verbal nouns

8.4.2(i) *Basic rules.* Although the formation of the verbal noun is quite irregular and although there is a great deal of variation, both between and within dialects, there are three basic rules.

The first rule is that, where there are two syllables a *t* /tˊ/ is added to a slender liquid or nasal [which is slender because of a general rule; see 6.3.1(ii)] or following *-ch* /x/:

(88) *seachain* + *t* 'avoiding'
 bagair + *t* 'threatening'
 oscail + *t* 'opening'
 éisteach + *t* 'listening'

A *t* /tˊ/ is also added following a nasal which is the result of consonant extension:

(89)   *lig + n + t ligint* 'letting'
       tuig + s + n + t tuigsint (→ *tuiscint*) (M) 'understanding'

Exceptionally, there are some verbal nouns which have a final *n* which is not made slender; see 6.3.1(ii). There is also a group of monosyllabic roots which must be included under this rule, e.g.:

(90)   *bain + t* 'cutting'
       roinn + t 'dividing'
       ceil + t 'concealing'

Furthermore, a number of verbs which have a suffixed *-áil* in the noun also come under this rule:

(91)   *feic + eáil + t* → *feiceáilt* (Gd, Cf) 'seeing'
       fág + áil + t → *fágáilt* (Gd) 'leaving'
       tóg + áil + t → *tógáilt* (Gd) 'raising'

The second rule is that no ending is normally added either to verbs which have a final *-áil* or to a limited group of monosyllabic verbal roots:

(92)   *glasáil* 'locking'
       péinteáil 'painting'
(93)   *ól* 'drinking'
       fás 'growing'
       cur (~ *cuir*) 'putting'
       scor (M) 'terminating'

The third rule affects all verbal roots not already dealt with under rules one and two. This rule involves the most frequent ending *-dh* /ɣ/, which is added to the verbal stem, and in some cases the final consonant of the stem is made broad:

(94)   *pós + dh* → *pósadh* 'marrying'
       bris + dh → *briseadh* 'breaking'
(95)   *buail* 'hit', *bual + dh* → *bualadh* 'hitting'

This broadening is regular in the case where *-gh* /j/ has been added to the root to form the stem:

(96) *ard* + *gh* → *ardaigh* 'raise'
ardaigh → *ardagh* → *ardaghadh* (→ *ardú*) 'raising'

(For the phonetic realization of *-adh* as /ə/, or /uː/ in Erris and Donegal, see 4.1.)

8.4.2(ii) *More marginal formations.* Apart from the three main rules described in 8.4.2(i), there are some more marginal consonantal extensions with *-mh* /w/, *-n* /n/, *-ch* /x/ and *-m* /m/:

(97) *seasamh* (*seas* + *mh*) 'standing'
léigheamh (*léigh* + *mh*) 'reading'
leagan (*leag* + *n*) (C) 'laying'
ligean (*lig* + *n*) (C, Tn) ~ *ligint* (*lig* + *n* + *t*) (Gd, Cf, M) 'letting'
screadach (*scread* + *ch*) (Cf) 'crying out'
leanacht (*lean* + *ch* + *t*) (Cn) 'following'
titim (*tit* + *m*) 'falling'
seinnim (*sinn* + *m*) (C) 'playing music'

There are further consonantal extensions in which other combinations occur such as are illustrated in the following:

(98) *béiceadhach* (*béic* + *dh* + *ch*) (Cf) → *béiciúch* 'shouting'
lagachan (*lag* + *ch* + *n*) (C) 'weakening'
filleadhaint (*fill* + *dh* + *n* + *t*) → *filliúint* (Cf) 'returning'
tuigsint (*tuig* + *s* + *n* + *t*) → *tuiscint* [see 4.2.6(i)] (M) 'understanding'
mairstint (*mair* + *t* + *s* + *n* + *t*) (Gd) 'living'
féadachtáil (*féad* + *ch* + *t* + *áil*) (Cf) 'being able'

There is a tendency for chains of consonantal extension to develop, just as we saw in the case of the plural endings (see 7.3.3). This tendency is particularly strong in Connemara. Once again semantic distinctions are possible between short and long forms, e.g. *casadh* (Cf) 'turning, playing music' beside *casachtáil* (Cf) 'meeting' or *caitheamh* 'use(up), throw' beside *caitheachtáil* (Cf) 'compulsion'.

The following are some examples of the variation between short and long endings:

(99) *bacadh* (+*dh*) (Cn) 'hindering' : *bacaint* (+ *n* + *t*) (Gd)
seasamh (+*mh*) (M, C) 'standing' : *seasacht* (+ *ch* + *t*) (Gd)

dúiseacht (+ *ch* + *t*) (M, Cn) 'waking' : *dúiseachtáil* (+ *ch* + *t* + *áil*) (Cn)

Besides this tendency for long forms to develop, there are some other sources of variation within the dialects. Firstly, there is a frequent variation between broad and slender consonants in the extension, e.g. *éirighe* /**air′əjə**/ → *éirí* /**air′iː**/ ~ *éireagha* /**air′əɣə**/ → *éiriú* /**air′uː**/ (Cf) 'arising'. Secondly, there is a certain variation in the use of *-mh* /w/ and *-dh* /ɣ/, e.g. *dealramh* (Dn) beside *dealradh* (Rg) 'appearing'. Thirdly, the endings *-ch* + *t* and *n* + *t* tend to change, e.g. *inseacht* (Cn) beside *insint* (M) 'telling'. Finally, the endings *-áil* and *-n* + *t* vary, *tógáil* (Gd) beside *tógaint* (Dn) 'raising'.

8.4.3 The verbal adjective

8.4.3(i) *Basic rules.* Generally speaking, the adjective is formed by the addition of *ta*/*te* /t(′)ə/ or *tha* /hə/ to the root of the verb. The choice of ending depends on the shape of the root. There are three major rules which are given here in the order in which they apply:

Rule 1: *-tha(í)* /hiː/ is added to a root with a final plosive.
Rule 2: *-tha* /hə/ is added to a final *-(r)r* /r/, or *mh*/*bh* /w/ or *-(a)igh* /əj/.
Rule 3: *-te* /t′ə/ is added where neither of the preceding rules has been applied.

Rule 1 applies generally to Connacht. Examples are:

(100) *pógtha* /**poːg** + **hiː**/ → /**poːkiː**/ (C) 'kissed'
       scuabhtha /**skuːəb** + **hiː**/ → /**skuːəpiː**/ (C) 'swept'
       rodtha /**rod** + **hiː**/ → /**rutiː**/ (C) 'rotten'
       pioctha /**p′uk** + **hiː**/ → /**p′ukiː**/ (C) 'picked'

It also applies to Gweedore but only voiceless plosives are given this ending: *cnoptha* /**krop** + **hiː**/ → /**kropiː**/ (Gd) 'shrunk' as opposed to *fágtha* /**faːg** + **hə**/ → /**fæːkə**/ (Rule 2) (Gd) 'left'.

It would seem that Rule 2 applies in all dialects. Where there is a final single *r*, however, there tends to be a deal of option:

(101) *cur* (*cuir*) 'put', *curtha* (Dn, Cf) ~ *curta* (Cf) ~ *cuirthe* /**kir′əhə**/ (Dn) ~ *cuirte* (Rule 3) (Dn) 'put'
       riar 'supply', *riartha* ~ *riarta* (Cf) 'supplied'

Nominal and adjectival forms 199

Examples of Rule 2 applying to a final *mh/bh* /w/ are:

(102)   *snámh* /snaːw/ 'swim': *snámhtha* /snaː hə/(Gd) → *snáfa* /snaːfə/ 'swim'
   scríobh /sʹkʹrʹiːw/ 'write': *scríobhtha* /sʹkʹrʹiːwhə/(Gd) → *scríofa* /sʹkʹrʹiːfə/

This rule is, however, optional in Cois Fhairrge, so that Rule 3 also yields *snámhte* /snaːfdə/, *scríobhta* /sʹkʹrʹiːfdə/. Some verbs, such as *lobh* /low/ 'rot', have only *lobhtha* → *lofa*. In other cases the option creates a semantic distinction, e.g. in Cois Fhairrge *gobh* 'grip, go' has the verbal noun *gofa* /gofə/ (Rule 2) meaning 'gripped' or 'dressed' while *goibhte* /gotʹə/ (Rule 3) means 'gone'.

In Dunquin, it would seem that where the root ends with a nasal or liquid and is followed by *-gh* /j/, the addition of *-the* /hə/ is optional:

(103)   *foghlam + gh + the* /fauləməhə/ (Rule 2) (Dn) ~ *foghlaimte* /fauləmʹtʹə/ (Rule 3) (Dn)
   cosn + gh + tha /kosnəhə/ (Rule 2) (Dn) ~ *cosainte* /kosənʹtʹə/ (Rule 3) (Dn)

In general in Donegal and Connacht the tendency appears to be to retain *-gh* /j/ throughout the conjugation of such verbs:

(104)   *ceangl + gh + the* → *ceanglaithe* (Rule 2) (D, C) ~ *ceangailte* (Rule 3) (D, C) 'tied'
   oscl + gh + the → *osclaithe* (Rule 2) (D, C) ~ *oscailte* (Rule 3) (D, C) 'open'

The ending *gh + the*, which is realized in Dunquin as /əhə/, also tends to intrude on monosyllables which have a final plosive, e.g. *fágtha* /faːkəhə/ 'left', *stadtha* /statəhə/ 'stopped' etc. beside forms such as *tógtha* /toːkə/ 'raised', *scuabtha* /skuːəpə/ 'swept', which also still occur.

In verbs where neither Rule 1 or 2 has applied *-te* /tʹə/ is added under rule 3. Examples are:

(105)   *nigh* /Nʹij/ + *te* → *nite* /Nʹitʹə/ 'washed'
   cráidh /kraːj/ + *te* → *cráite* /kraːtʹə/ 'tormented'
   bris /bʹrʹisʹ/ + *te* → *briste* /bʹrʹisʹtʹə/ 'broken'

cur /kur/ + ta /tə/ → curta /kurtə/ 'put'
ceangl /kʹaŋgl/ + te → ceangailte /kʹaŋgəlʹtʹə/ 'tied'
scríobh /sʹkʹrʹi:w/ + te → scríobhta /sʹkʹrʹi:ftə/ 'written'
sábháil /sa:wa:lʹ/ + te → sábháilte /sa:wa:lʹtʹə/ 'saved'

In verbs such as *trobhann* 'ploughs', *toghann* 'chooses', a new root /trau/ (Cf) ~ /tro:/ (Gd), /tau/ (Cf) ~ /te:/ (Gd) is also required. In that case Rule 3 applies:

(106) *trobhte* /tʹrʹautʹə/ (Cf) ~ /tʹrʹo:tʹə/ (Gd) 'ploughed'
toghte /tautʹə/ (Cf) ~ /te:tʹə/ (Gd) 'chosen'

In Donegal the consonantal extension before this ending may be *-s* /sʹ/ rather than *-gh* /j/ (for one interpretation of this phenomenon see Ó Buachalla 1980). This occurs normally when the root terminates in /l/, /m/, /r/ or /j/:

(107) *ceangl + s + te → ceanglaiste* /kʹaŋgləsʹtʹə/ (Gd) 'tied'
ceann + s + te → ceannaiste /kaNəsʹtʹə/ (Gd) 'bought'
cóir + s + te → cóiriste /ko:rʹəsʹtʹə/ (Gd) 'repaired'
cruaigh + s + te → cruaiste /kruəsʹtʹə/ (Gd) 'hardened'

8.4.3(ii) *The verbal adjective and the genitive of the verbal noun.* The genitive form of the verbal noun is often similar to the verbal adjective; nevertheless, the rules for its formation are somewhat less complex. Examples of Rule 1 are rare enough, e.g. Cois Fhairrge *galún taosctha* /ti:ski:/ 'bailing vessel'. Under Rule 2, what are, from a diachronic viewpoint, older forms obtain, e.g. *scríobhtha → scríofa* (not *scríobhte*) 'written' from *scríobh* 'write'. The consonantal extension *-gh* /j/ does not intrude on these forms in verbs such as *díbirt* 'banish', *imirt* 'play', *cuimilt* 'rub'. Examples are the set phrases:

(108) *droim díbeartha* (Cf) 'a driving back'
gléas imeartha (Cf) 'instrument of play'
oighear chuimealta (Cf) 'file'

On the other hand, where *-gh* /j/ appears in the stem it may also be needed to occur in the genitive of the verbal noun:

(109) *leasaigh* 'manure'
leasughadh → leasú 'manuring'
an iomarca leasaighthe /Lʹæ:i:/ (Cf) 'excessive manuring'

Many verbal nouns belong to the normal inflectional patterns such as those ending in *-áil*, *-án*, *-int* or those with zero ending, e.g. *fás* genitive *fáis* 'growth'. Sometimes the normal pattern is opposed to a form similar to the verbal adjective and thus creates a semantic difference as in *ól* 'drink', genitive *óil* (Dn), beside the form *ólta*, where *ól* functions as a verbal noun. In Cois Fhairrge disyllabic verbal nouns ending in *-int*, *-im*, *-lt*, *-an*, and *-aí* are given no normal genitive form.

8.4.3(iii) *Plural of the verbal noun*. The plural of the verbal noun seems to follow the normal pattern for plural formation (see 7.3):

(110)   *fás*, plural *fásannaí* (Rm) 'growth'
imeacht, plural *imeachtaí* 'going on'
leagan, plural *leaganachaí* (Cn) ~ *leaganacha* (Gd) 'turn of speech'
geallúint, plural *gealluintí* (C, M) 'promise'
titim cainte, plural *titimeachaí cainte* (Cn) 'idiom'
imirt, plural *imirteachaí* (Cf) 'playing'
creathadh, plural *creaití* (Cf) 'shake'

In the case of verbal nouns where *-dh* /ɣ/ is employed (for development see 4.1.3) the plural form is widely *-íocha(í)*:

(111)   *briseadh*, plural *brisíochaí* (Cf) 'break'
pósadh, plural *pósaíocha* (Cf) ~ *póstaíochaí* (Gd) 'marriage'

On the other hand *-(aí)* /iː/ is retained in some plurals, particularly in set phrases:

(112)   *stracadh*, plural *stracaí* (Cf) 'bite' (fishing)
loscadh sáile, plural *loscaí sáile* (Cf) 'soreness from brine'
bualadh cloiche, plural *bualaí cloiche* (Cf) 'bruises from stones on the feet'.

PART III

SYNTAX

9 *Introduction to syntax*

The purpose of this introduction is to give a very brief outline of the basic word order which is shared by Irish dialects and then to describe eleven important syntactic rules which affect the basic word order and which have a bearing on the discussion in the chapters that follow. Chapters 10 and 11 are devoted to a discussion of the copula and of complementation and modal and auxiliary verbs, while Chapter 12 describes processes of subordination which do not involve the types of complementation dealt with in Chapter 11 and explores a number of marginal syntactic constructions where differences among dialects emerge, in particular the various usages of *diabhal* 'devil' as a syntactic device.

9.1 Basic word order

If we leave aside the fact that a main sentence can be preceded by presetential negative or question markers (*ní/níor*, *an/ar*, *nach/nár*, etc.) and that embedded sentences can be subordinated by complementizers (*go/gur*, *nach/nár*, etc.), a relativizer (*a*) or by various other subordinators, the basic word order is:

Figure 9.1 Sentence order in Irish

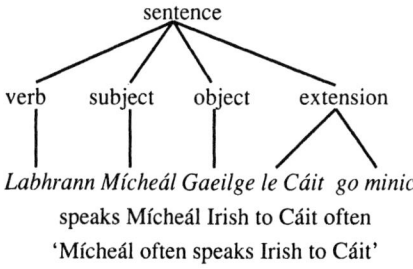

The order verb, subject, object is followed by what may be, for convenience, called the extension. The extension consists of either an adverbial phrase and/or a prepositional phrase.

The order of hierarchy within the extension is more problematic. In the first place it would be difficult to find an example containing all the possible types of adverbial phrases and prepositional phrases. Furthermore, many adverbial phrases consist of prepositional phrases. Attempts have been made (e.g. Ward 1974) to establish the unmarked hierarchy as;

(a)   directionals
(b)   positional locatives
(c)   adverbs of manner
(d)   prepositional phrase
(e)   expression of time

(1)   *Bhí sé thiar ansin go haerach ar an mbóthar inné* (C)
      'He was back there in a carefree manner on the road yesterday'

However, the matter is much more complex. The distinction between some of the elements listed above is not tenable and (d) is a purely formal category as opposed to (a), (b), (c) and (e). An adverbial phrase often consists of a prepositional phrase, e.g. *ar an bpoinnte* 'on the spot, immediately'. There is a further problem concerning the degree of 'boundness' between the verb and a prepositional/adverbial phrase, for example between *bhí sé* 'he was' and *ar an mbóthar* 'on the road'. The words *bhí sé* have no meaning on their own; the substantive verb must be accompanied by a prepositional/local adverbial phrase, e.g. *Tá sé ann* 'He is there'. However, in the case of an eventive noun a prepositional/temporal adverb is sufficient, e.g. *Bhí timpiste aréir* 'There was an accident last night'. In order to establish an unmarked order it would be necessary to distinguish between 'bound' and 'free' components and indeed to establish a scale of 'boundness'. For example, *Thug sé faoi deara* 'He noticed' would seem to be more closely bound and less liable to separation than *Bhí sé ar an mbóthar* 'He was on the road'. It is not proposed here to discuss the problem further but rather to point out the difficulty and the fact that it can influence the word order.

There is, however, another important factor. There is a high degree of interchangeability among the elements of the extension when those elements are relatively short. Conversely, a relatively long element tends to be moved to the end of the sentence simply to avoid breaking the flow or putting a strain on the memory. In other words interchangeability may occur in example (2) where there is a short extension such as *ariamh* 'never':

(2)   *Ní raibh sé sásta ariamh ~ Ní raibh sé ariamh sásta*
      'He was never content'

but is unlikely to occur in:

(3)   *Ní raibh sé sásta le blianta beaga anuas*
      'He hasn't been content in recent years'

9.2 Major variations in basic order

The most frequent and most major deviations from the basic order are fronting and clefting, both of which are fully described in 10.3.5(i). Other major variations are:

(a)   movement of pronouns to sentence-final position
(b)   narrative fronting
(c)   deletion following finite verbal forms
(d)   repetition of topic
(e)   avoidance of finite complementation
(f)   sentence-initial adverbial phrases
(g)   omission of the substantive verb in responses following *agus/is* 'and' or *ná* 'nor'
(h)   use of *agus/is* 'and' or *ná* 'nor' in responses
(i)   rightward movement of subject
(j)   parenthetical interjection between verb and subject
(k)   the semi-negative or 'only' construction

9.2.1 Movement of pronouns to sentence-final position

There is a general rule within Irish that an unmarked or normal grade of pronouns (*mé* 'me' as opposed to *mise* 'me', *mé féin* 'myself' or *mise mé féin* 'me myself') and prepositional pronouns (*agam* 'at me', as opposed to *agamsa* 'at me', *agam féin* 'at myself' or *agamsa mé féin* 'at me myself') moves to the end of a sentence. The following pairs of examples illustrate the rule:

(4)   *Bhris sé an chathaoir leis an ord aréir*
      'He broke the chair with the sledgehammer last night'

(5)   *Bhris sé aréir leis an ord í*
      (lit. He broke last night with the sledgehammer it)
      'He broke it last night with the sledgehammer'
(6)   *Léigh sé an leabhar go cúramach*
      'He read the book carefully'
(7)   *Léigh sé go cúramach í*
      'He read it carefully'
(8)   *D'inis sé an scéal do Bhríd*
      'He told the story to Bríd'
(9)   *D'inis sé do Bhríd é*
      'He told it to Bríd'
(10) *Bhí an sagart ag mo mháthair inné*
      (lit. The priest was at my mother last night)
      'My mother had the priest yesterday'
(11) *Bhí an sagart inné aice*
      'She had the priest yesterday'

This general rule is not absolute and must, moreover, be modified in the following circumstances:

9.2.1(i) *In the subjectless verbal noun complements.* It would appear that where a subjectless verbal noun complement [see 11.1.6(i)] is not followed by a prepositional phrase the order is optional:

(12) *Chonaic mé ag damhsa é ~ Chonaic mé é ag damhsa* (C)
      'I saw him dancing'
(13) *Chuala mé iad ag caint faoi* (C)
      'I heard them talking about it'
(14) *Nuair a chluinfeá a' cainnt ortha é* (D)
      'When you would hear him talking about them'

9.2.1(ii) *In complex verbs.* Where the verb is so closely connected with the following preposition that the whole must be considered as a complex, the prepositional pronoun need not move to the end:

(15) *Sín agam an leabhar* (C)
      'Pass me the book'
(16) *Tabhair dom an ceann sin* (C)
      'Give me that one'

Major variations in basic order 209

9.2.1(iii) *Where intervening elements are relatively long.* If the intervening elements would be felt to be too long the pronoun does not always move to the end of the sentence:

(17)   *Chonaic mé thú ar an mbóthar a bhfuil an teach mór air* (C)
        'I saw you on the road which the big house is on'

This must be considered part of the tendency to keep cumbersome or long elements to the right of the sentence. In the case of certain sentences where there are several elements following the initial verb, the pronoun need not necessarily be moved to final position but seemingly can occur after any of the elements as in:

Figure 9.2 Possible positionings of normal grade pronoun

Fágadh é ina loighe ar an talamh taobh thiar den scioból aréir (C)

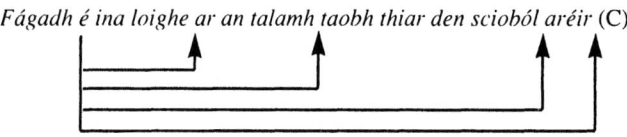

'It was left lying on the ground behind the barn last night'

9.2.1(iv) *Constraints.* There are some constraints (see Chung and McCloskey 1987) on the move to final position. A pronoun may, in certain types of prolepsis before a finite complement, move rightward but not to final position:

(18)   *Chuala mé é ráite go mbíodh sé ann ~ Chuala mé ráite é go mbíodh sé ann* (C)
        'I heard it said that he used to be there'

but not

(19)   **Chuala mé ráite go mbíodh sé ann é*

One further constraint on final position which is worth mentioning is the case of objects or subjects in verbal noun complements [see 11.1.2(ii)]. The pronouns may not normally occur in final position in sentences of the sort:

(20)   *Ba mhaith liom thú é a cheannacht* (Gd)
        'I would like you to buy it' (lit. it to buy)

(21)   *B'fhearr liom thú é a dhéanamh anois (Gd)*
        'I would prefer you to do it now'

9.2.2 Narrative fronting

The type of fronting which involves the use of the copula where the fronted element is followed by a relative clause is discussed in 10.3.5. However, in a narrative style, there is, in all dialects, a type of fronting where no relative clause is involved. Most commonly, the subject or object is the element fronted as in the examples:

Subject:

(22)   *Rópa ná gabhann ní choibhreodh sé ar an ngabhaltas é* (C)
        'Neither rope nor pen would keep it on the holding'
(23)   *Éifeacht níl ins an ghníomh sin* (D)
        (lit. Effect there isn't in that action)
        'There is no effect in that action'

Object:

(24)   *Súil ní rabhadar ag tóigeáil de* (C)
        'An eye, they weren't taking off him'
(25)   *A leithéid de thorann agus de mhacalla ní chuala tú ó lá do bheirthe* (C)
        'Such a noise and such an echo, you didn't hear from the day you were born'
(26)   *...agus stad níor dhein sí nó gur chuaigh sí go dtí doras an scióbóil* (M)
        '...and a stop he didn't make until he came to the door of the stable'

When such a sentence is embedded in a complement, the complementizer follows the fronted element as in:

(27)   *Nár gheall tú dhom deoir nach rachadh ar do bhéal go ceann fada an lá?* (C)
        (lit. Didn't you promise me a drop wouldn't go on your mouth for many the day)
        'Didn't you promise me that a drop you wouldn't touch for many a day?'

This positioning of the complementizer is similar to that in the case of the repeated topic (see 9.2.4). This contrasts with the non-requirement of the complementizer in the negative usage of *diabhal* 'devil' etc. [see 12.2.3 (iv)].

9.2.3 Deletion following finite verbal forms

In certain circumstances deletion of the subject is possible following a verb when it is clear that its subject is identical with that of the preceding verb.

The commonest case is that of responsives. Apart from where there is particular emphasis (*Tá sé!* 'Yes, he is!') or where the pronoun is included in the verbal form (*Táim* 'I am'), this deletion is obligatory;

(28) *Tá sé sásta*
'He is content'
Tá
'Yes (he is)'
(29) *Níl sé ag teacht*
'He is not coming'
Mara bhfuil...
'If [he] isn't...'

A similar deletion is possible where a verb is echoed within a single utterance:

(30) *Do riug sí ar an gciotal, ach má dhin, d'ardaigh an táilliúir...* (Mk)
'She took the kettle, but if [she] did, the tailor raised ...'
(31) *D'iarr mé air é a dhéanamh, rud nach dtearn* (Gd)
'I asked him to do it which [he] didn't'

In a narrative style where the subject has already been specified, it may be omitted several times. The phenomenon is well known from all dialects and is illustrated here by:

(32) *...agus nuair a tháini sé i n-aon chóngar don ghabha arís, chuir a phíce i n-acharann ion agus chun tailimh é; d'ardaigh a phíce chun é shá tríd, ach níor dhin* (Mk)
'...and when he came at all near to the smith again, [he] caught him with his pike and brought him to the ground; raised his pike to pierce him, but didn't'

It would seem that in such a narrative style an already explicit object may be deleted along with the subject as in :

(33)　*Bhuail sé buille don tuairgín ar an Olltach agus do mhairbh* (Mk)
　　　'He dealt a blow of the pounder to the Ulsterman and killed [him]'
(34)　*Bhí tobac aige á lorg, ach ní bhfaigheadh* (Mk)
　　　'He was seeking tobacco but wouldn't get [it]'

9.2.4 Repetition of the topic

A syntactic feature, which would seem to occur in all dialects, is the repetition of the topic. This device is employed typically where the topic contains a relative clause as in:

(35)　*An leitir dheiridh a scríobh an bhean bhocht abhaile anseo ag an Athair Éamonn, bhainfeadh sí na deora as na clocha glasa* (C)
　　　'The last letter the poor woman sent home here to Father Éamonn, it would move a heart of stone' (lit. it would extract tears from the grey stones)

Although the repetition of the topic probably occurs most frequently in spontaneous style, it is often found in narrative, particularly where the relative clause is as lengthy as in (35). When it appears as a finite complement, the complementizer follows the preposed topic as in:

(36)　*Dúirt sé an mhuintir ar leo an áit i dtosach go mbíodh ceithre chapall faoina gcóiste acu* (M)
　　　'He said – the people who owned that place originally – that they had a four-horse carriage'
(37)　*Dúirt sé linn an mhuintir a rachadh leis an tSaorstát go bhfaigheadh siad arm agus éide agus...* (D)
　　　'He said to us – the people who would side with the Freestate – that they would get a weapon and a uniform and...'

This repetition of the topic is the norm for the 'maxim' type sentence containing *an té* 'he who':

(38)　*An té nach mbíonn críonna, ní mhairfidh sé i bhfad* (C)
　　　'He who isn't cunning, [he] won't survive long'

It is also particularly useful to avoid confusion in sentences of the sort (see Wigger 1972b):

(39) *Chonaic mé an fear a bhris an fhuinneoig ar maidin* (C)
      'I saw the man who broke the window this morning'

Here the adverbial clause *ar maidin* 'this morning' can refer to *chonaic mé* 'I saw' or to *a bhris an fhuinneoig* 'who broke the window'. The confusion is avoided by the repetition of the topic and is implemented in three main ways:

9.2.4(i) *Initial absolute topic with pronominal repetition.*

(40) *An fear a bhris an fhuinneoig, chonaic mé ar maidin é*
      'The man who broke the window, I saw him this morning'

9.2.4(ii) *Final absolute topic with pronoun in advance.*

(41) *Chonaic mé ar maidin é, an fear a bhris an fhuinneoig*
      'I saw him this morning, the man who broke the window'

9.2.4(iii) *Repetition of subject and main verb along with pronominal repetition of topic.*

(42) *Chonaic mé an fear a bhris an fhuinneoig, chonaic mé ar maidin é*
      'I saw the man who broke the window, I saw him this morning'

9.2.5 Avoidance of finite complementation

In spontaneous speech the main verb, which would normally be followed by the complementizers (*go/gur* 'that', *nach, ná* (M) / *nár* 'that...not') is sometimes appended. Two types of verbs are principally involved:

9.2.5(i) *Verbs of thinking, saying, perceiving etc., e.g. (43-6).*

(43) *Tá siad anseo, sílim* (C)
      'They are here, I think'

alongside:

(44) *Sílim go bhfuil siad anseo* (C)
      'I think they are here'

and

(45)   *Bheadh sé sásta, déarfainn*
        'He would be content, I'd say'

alongside:

(46)   *Déarfainn go mbeadh sé sásta*
        'I'd say he would be content'

9.2.5(ii) *Epistemic modals, e.g. (47-50)*: see **11.2.2(ii)**.

(47)   *Beidh sé ag teacht amáireach, caithfidh sé* (C)
        'He will be coming tomorrow, it must be'

alongside:

(48)   *Caithfidh sé go mbeidh sé ag teacht amáireach* (C)
        'It must be that he is coming tomorrow / He must be coming tomorrow'

and

(49)   *Bheadh sí ansin, b'fhéidir* (C)
        'She'd be there'

alongside:

(50)   *B'fhéidir go mbeadh sí ansin* (C)
        'Maybe she'd be there'

9.2.6 Sentence-initial adverbial phrases
There are certain adverbial phrases which can be placed either initially or finally in the sentence. They are mainly either sentential adverbs, i.e. ones which refer to the sentence as a whole, or non-aspective temporal adverbial phrases.

9.2.6(i) *Sentential adverbial phrases.*

(51)   *Ar aon chuma, níor bhac sé leis ~ níor bhac sé leis ar aon chuma*
        (C)

'At any rate, he didn't bother with it' ~ 'He didn't bother with it at any rate'
(52) Ar ndóigh, bhí Mícheál sásta ~ Bhí Mícheál sásta, ar ndóigh (C)
'Of course, Mícheál was content' ~ 'Mícheál was content, of course'

The adverbial phrases *ar aon chuma* 'at any rate' and *ar ndóigh* 'of course' clearly apply to the sentence as a whole.

9.2.6(ii) *Non-aspective temporal adverbial phrases.*

(53) Amach anseo, tiocfaidh feabhas air ~ Tiocfaidh feabhas air amach anseo
'Sometime in the future, it will improve' ~ 'It will improve sometime in the future'
(54) Le céad bliain anuas, ní raibh Gaeilge ar bith anseo ~ Ní raibh Gaeilge ar bith anseo le céad bliain anuas (C)
'For the last hundred years, there was no Irish here' ~ 'There was no Irish here for the past hundred years'

Again the non-aspective adverbial phrases apply to the entire sentence.

9.2.7 Omission of the substantive verb in fronting

The relative of the substantive verb may be optionally omitted when the noun, adjective or adverb expressing frequency or measurement is fronted, whether in a question or otherwise. This appears to be common to all dialects:

(55) Cén aois atá sé? ~ Cén aois é? (C)
'What age is he?'
(56) Is minic atá sé ráite agam ~ Is minic ráite agam é (C)
(lit. It is often it is said by me)
'I have often said it'
(57) Cén t-achar atá sé anseo? ~ Cén t-achar anseo é? (C)
'How long is he here?'
(58) Is ar éigin atá pingin aige ~ Is ar éigin pingin aige (C)
(lit. It is hardly that there is a penny at him)
'He barely has a penny'

As (55-8) show, after the application of the optional rule which removes the relative of the substantive verb, the conjunctive pronouns (*tú* 'you', *sé* 'he, it', *sí* 'she, it', *siad* 'they') are automatically replaced by the disjunctive (*thú* 'you', *é* 'him, it', *í* 'her, it', *iad* 'them'), which in turn is moved to sentence-final position (see 9.2.1). This optional rule also has a bearing on the behaviour of *diabhal* 'devil' etc. (see 12.2.3).

9.2.8 Use of *agus/is* 'and' or *ná* 'nor' in responses
The verb need not be repeated in a response which is both in unison with a statement or question and which employs *agus/is* 'and' to increase or *ná* 'nor' to decrease the amount mentioned:

(59)   *Shiúil sé sé mhíle* (C)
       'He walked six miles'
       Shiúil agus deich míle (C)
       'He did and (probably) ten miles'
(60)   *Níor cheannaigh sé trí bhuidéal*
       'He didn't buy three bottles'
       Níor cheannaigh ná buidéal
       'He didn't nor did he buy even one'

Presumably these responses are based on the underlying sentences (61-2):

(61)   *Shiúil sé agus shiúil sé deich míle*
       'He walked and he walked ten miles'
(62)   *Níor cheannaigh sé ná níor cheannaigh sé buidéal*
       'He didn't buy nor he didn't buy a bottle'

The verb is similarly omitted where the subject is increased:

(63)   *Tá mé fuar*
       'I am cold'
       Tá agus mise
       (lit. [You] are and me)
       'So am I'
(64)   *Níl mé sásta*
       'I am not satisfied'
       Níl ná mise
       (lit. [You] are not nor me)
       'Neither am I'

9.2.9 Three further dislocations

9.2.9(i) Rightward movement of subject. In narrative style the subject may be moved rightward, so that typically the extension (i.e. an adverbial or prepositional phrase) occurs between the verb and the subject as in:

(65) *Tagann chugham isteach an sagart paróiste...* (M)
(lit. Comes to me in the parish priest)
'The parish priest comes in towards me...'
(66) *Do bhí acu tamal math dhon uíhe...* (M)
'They had (lit. there was at them) a good part of the night...'
(67) *...agus tháinig faoina mbráid le léamh úrscéal Sheáin Óig* (M)
'...and Seán Óg's novel came before them to be read'
(68) *...ghluais chugam aníos trasna an ghleanna ceol píbe...*(M)
'...pipe music came to me across the valley...'

While this construction is frequent in Munster, fewer examples are found in the other major dialects:

(69) *D'imigh isteach an fathach Muinille i dteach Finn* (C)
(lit. Went into the giant Muinille in Fionn's house)
'The giant Muinille went to Fionn's house'
(70) *Nuair a nocht chuige an caisleán ba deise a chonaic sé ariamh...* (D)
'When the nicest castle he ever saw appeared in his direction...'

It would seem that this construction occurs only following intransitive verbs of motion, appearance or existence. Quite often the subject is cumbersome, as in (70).

9.2.9(ii) Parenthetical interjections between verb and subject. Adverbs are not normally allowed to come between the verb and the subject. However, a small group of parenthetical interjections of the sort *muise* 'indeed', *mh'anam* 'certainly' ('upon my soul'), *ar ndóigh* 'of course', etc. may intervene, as seen in:

(71) *Tá, ar ndóighe, saighdiúirí ar a' bhealach ón Chlochán Glas* (D)
'There are, of course, soldiers on the way from Clochán Glas'
(72) *Níl, leoga, tú gabhail 'na bhaile mar sin* (D)
'You're not indeed going home like that'

The following responsive shows a similar parenthetical intervention:

(73)   *Aireoir mh'anam – tú píosa maith* (Cf)
          'Yes, you will indeed – hear a great deal'

9.2.9(iii) *The semi-negative or 'only' construction* In sentences expressing the notion 'only', the subject is often moved to the right of the extension (i.e. adverbial or prepositional phrase) as in :

(74)   *Níl air ach báisteach* (C)
          'It is only going to rain'
(75)   *Níl ann ach an bheirt againn* (C)
          'There is only the two of us'
(76)   *Ní raibh an uair sin ar an mbealach seo ach corr-theach fánach* (C)
          'There was at that time on this way only an occasional house here and there'

However, while this rightward movement is found in all dialects, it appears to be optional in many circumstances:

(77)   *Ní dheachaigh ann ach an bheirt acu / Ní dheachaidh ach an bheirt acu ann* (D)
          'Only two of them went there'
(78)   *Níl ann ach an triúr againn / Níl ach triúr againn ann* (D)
          'There are only three of us'
(79)   *Ní raibh ach aon phláta amhain 'dir é féin agus an táilliúir* (M)
          (lit. There was but a single plate between himself and the tailor)
          'He and the tailor had only a single plate between them'
(80)   *Ní raibh fanta istigh ach an garsún so go dtugaithí 'An Ciarraíoch' air, agus an t-uan* (M)
          (lit. There was remaining inside only this boy they called 'The Kerryman' and the lamb)
          'Only this boy whom they called "The Kerryman" and the lamb remained inside'.

10 *The copula*

10.1 Two verbs 'to be'

There are in Irish two verbs 'to be': the copula *is* and the substantive verb *tá*; a distinction which bears some resemblance to, for example, Spanish (see Ó Máille 1912). Although this chapter is devoted to the copula, it will be necessary to describe some usages of the substantive verb, particularly where its intrusion on the copula system (see Ó Siadhail 1983) leads to variation among the dialects.

10.2 Forms of the copula

This account of the copula begins with a brief overview of the commonest forms and variants of the copula. Basically, it has two sets of forms: one which serves as a present or future and another which serves as a past or conditional. The past/conditional set is the more marked set in that it may not generally be deleted (see 10.4). The bracketed forms in Table 10.1 are used before vowels (or *l* or *r* following *fh*). In order not to complicate the table unnecessarily, the more marginal forms combining with *cé* 'who' and *do* 'to' and *ó* 'from' are omitted. An optional *dob(a)* (the past marker *do* + *ba*) rather than *ba* for certain Munster dialects has also not been included.

Although the forms in Table 10.1 for the most part occur in descriptions of Galway and Kerry dialects, this tabulation is somewhat idealized and neither reflects the multiplicity of forms which are recorded or offers a picture of the most frequently used forms in any given dialect. In the following section we outline certain tendencies which lead to both the fusion and the proliferation of forms.

10.2.1 Distinction between present/future and past/conditional blurred

The past/conditional forms in the tabulation are followed by a lenition in brackets, whereas the present/future forms are not. There is in fact a certain redundancy. This allows for the possibility of non-lenition in the past where

220 *Modern Irish: grammatical structure and dialectal variation*

the forms are obviously distinct, as in the case of *is* and *ba*, in an example such as:

(1)   *Ba saol dona a bhí ann* (Cf)
      'Life was hard then'

Table 10.1 *Forms of copula*

Present/Future	
Is 'He is'	
Ní 'He isn't'	
An (Ab) 'Is he?'	*bádóir é* 'a boatman'
Nach 'Isn't he?'	
... *go (gob)* '...that he is'	
... *nach* '...that he isn't'	*amhlaidh é* 'thus'
Más 'If he is'	
Mara (Marab) 'If he isn't'	
Past/Conditional	
Ba 'He was'	
Níor (Níorbh) 'He wasn't'	*b(h)ádóir é* 'a boatman'
Ar (arbh) 'Was he?'	
Nar (narbh) 'Wasn't he?'	
...*gur (gurbh)* '...that he was'	*amhlaidh é* 'thus'
...*nar (narbh)* '...that he wasn't'	
Dá mba/Má ba 'If he was'	
Marar/mararbh 'If he wasn't'	

Non-lenition is not possible in all usages of copula. It is less likely in, for instance, prepositional phrase constructions [see 10.3.3(i)]. More often, however, the redundancy results in a fusion of the two sets of forms with the use of lenition to mark the past/conditional set. This fusion is particularly prevalent in Dunquin, where the final *r* sound of the past/conditional forms tends to be be dropped so that *ní cheart* 'it could not be right' tends more and more to replace *níor cheart*. In this way the contrast between present/future *ní ceart* 'it is not right' and past/conditional *ní cheart* 'it was not right' is made by lenition. Another example of the two sets of forms merging is the frequent use of *ar* and *gur* as present/future question particle and complementizer in Cois Fhairrge:

(2) *An ceann áirid é?* (Cf)
    'Is it a certain one?'
(3) *Ar fíor sin?* (Cf)
    'Is that true?'
(4) *Ní mó ná go fiú a ghoil chomh fada leis* (Cf)
    'It is hardly worth going as far as it'
(5) *Deir sé gur táilliúr é* (Cf)
    'He says he is a tailor'

10.2.2 Distinction between preconsonant and prevowel forms blurred

The prevowel forms shown in brackets in Table 10.1 are often used inconsistently, e.g. *ab amhlaidh* beside *an amhlaidh* (Cf).

10.2.3 Use of preverbal particles and complementizers with the copula

As seen in Table 10.1 negation, interrogation and complementization are expressed by various forms of the copula, e.g. *ní* 'is not', *an?* 'is?', *go* 'that... is', etc. However, the preverbal particles and complementizers, e.g. *ní* (+ lenition), *an* (+ eclipsis), *go* (+ eclipsis), etc., are also found. From a historical viewpoint, the preverbal particles and complementizers are intruding on the copular system. A blatant example of this spread is seen in the frequent Cois Fhairrge use of preverbal particles with the past/conditional *ba*, as shown in Table 10.2.

Table 10.2 *Preverbal particles with* ba

Ba 'He was' *Ní ba* 'He wasn't' *An mba...?* 'Was he?' *Nach mba...?* 'Wasn't he?' *...go mba* '...that he was' *...nach mba* '...that he wasn't' *Dá mba/Má ba* 'If he was' *Mara mba* 'If he wasn't'	*scoláire é* 'a scholar'

As can be seen, the preverbal particles and complementizers cause eclipsis. (The negation particle does not lenite but the predominating eclipsis spills over so that *ní mba* is also a common form.) Similarly, the preverbal particles' mutation system extends into the copular system as in: *An gcuimhin leat?* (Dn)

222 *Modern Irish: grammatical structure and dialectal variation*

'Do you remember?'. Yet another example of this intrusion is the use of *n á* alongside *nach* (or *nách*) as the negative question particle, the negative complementizer and negative particle in Dunquin. (The influence of *ná* is also seen in the form *nár* rather than *nar* in the past/conditional set.)

10.2.4 Prevention of elision of vowel in *ba* 'was'

There seems particularly in Cois Fhairrge a reluctance to elide the vowel in the past/conditional form *ba* /bə/ 'was' before monosyllabic pronouns with an initial vowel and before *eo* 'this', *in* 'that', *iúd* 'that' (see 10.3.4) or before *éard* 'what that...' [see 10.3.5(ii)]. This elision is avoided by the insertion of /j/ or /vʹ/.

(6)   *Ba iúd* /bə juːd/ *iad* (Cf)
        'Those were they'
(7)   *Ba in* /bə jinʹ/ *Gaeilgeoir maith* (Cf)
        'That was a good Irish speaker'
(8)   *Ba é* /bə vʹeː/ *cheana* (Cf)
        'It was indeed'
(9)   *Ba éard* /bə vʹeːrd/ *a bheadh ann drochobair* (Cf)
        'What that would be is bad work'

From a diachronic point of view the insertion of /j/ is the preservation of the historic form *badh* (rather than *ba*) in sandhi and the inserted /vʹ/ must have spread from the prevocalic series *níorbh, arbh, gurbh, narbh* (see Table 10.1). The use of /j/ following *ba* in turn gives rise to a new series *níor-dh, ar-dh, gur-dh, nar-dh,* as can be seen in:

Table 10.3 *Generalized forms of copula*

is é /sʹeː/ 'is'
ab é /bʹe/ 'is?'
nab é /nabʹ e/ 'that... isn't'
gob é /gobʹ e/ 'that... is'

(10)   *Níor-dh é* /Nʹiːr j eː/ *an t-am céanna é* (Cf)
        'It was not the same time'
(11)   *Meas tú ar-dh* /ər jeː/ *é* (Cf)
        'Do you think it was?'

10.2.5 Use of generalized forms *is é, ab é, nab é, gob é*

Table 10.1 outlined the two basic sets of forms of the copula. However, in Gweedore (and it would seem in much of Donegal) a general all-purpose set of forms is used for most functions of the copula. It should be noted that *é* is reduced to /e/ in the non-statement forms.

The origin of this use of the pronoun *é* 'it' (irrespective of number or gender) in those generalized forms is further discussed in 10.3.4.

The following are some examples using the generalized system:

(12)   *Ab é Sharkeys iad?* (Gd)
'Are they Sharkeys?'

(13)   *Nab é Pádraig a rinn é?* (Gd)
'Isn't it Pádraig who did it?'

(14)   *Deir siad gob é a phéinteáil an doras* (Gd)
'They say that it is he who painted the door'

It must be noted, however, that the forms in Table 10.1 are retained in the exclamatory usage with adjectives [see 10.3.2(i)] in equational use [see 10.3.2.(ii)] and in prepositional phrase constructions [see 10.3.3(i)]:

(15)   *Nach maith é!* (Gd)
'Isn't he good!'

(16)   *Ní hionann iad* (Gd)
'They are not the same'

(17)   *Deir sé gur fearr leis imeacht* (Gd)
'He says he prefers to go (away)'

On the other hand, tag questions in these usages sometimes employ generalized forms. The growth of the generalized forms is still in progress so that there is a deal of fluctuation:

(18)   *Nach maith é!*
'Isn't he good!'

(19)   *Nach maith / Nab é!* (Gd)
'Isn't it!'

10.3 Overview of syntax of copula

For the sake of clarity, we begin with a taxonomical description of the copula and then proceed to give some account of attempts which have been made to present the copula as a more unified system. The initial description is given under the following headings:

(a) linking of nouns/pronouns
(b) linking of nouns/pronouns and adjectives
(c) use in prepositional phrases
(d) use with *seo, sin, siúd* etc.
(e) use in fronting.

10.3.1 Linking of nouns and pronouns
There are basically two types of sentences, the classificatory copula sentence and the identificatory copula sentence:

10.3.1(i) *The classificatory copula sentence.*

(20) *Is scoláire mé* (C)
 'I am a scholar'
(21) *Is mangach é* (C)
 'It is a pollock'
(22) *Is Éireannach é* (C)
 'He is an Irishman'

Here we have *copula + classificatory indefinite noun + pronoun*. The third slot can also be taken by a definite noun which is here defined as a proper noun or one which is preceded by either the article or a possessive adjective:

(23) *Is múinteoir í Cáit* (C)
 'Cáit is a teacher'
(24) *Is scoláirí iad na fir sin* (C)
 'Those men are scholars'
(25) *Is sagart é m'uncail* (C)
 'My uncle is a priest'

It must, however, be noted immediately that there is a Munster/Connacht rule which inserts *é* 'he, it', *í* 'she, it', *iad* 'they' (according to the gender and number) before a definite noun. This is a general rule throughout the copulative system and applies equally in identificatory sentences or cleft sentences. It will be referred to as the *é, í, iad* insertion rule.

A further feature of classificatory copula sentences is the possibility of fronting for emphasis an adjective which qualifies a noun:

(26)   *Is duine deas é*
        'He is a nice person'

If the quality of 'his being nice' is emphasized, a fronted version is required and the noun is then made definite:

(27)   *Is deas an duine é*
        'He is a nice person'

Certain sentences are normally emphatic and by their nature seem to require such emphasis:

(28)   *Is bocht an rud é*
        'It is a *sorry* affair'

Presumably example (28) is derived from:

(29)   *Is rud bocht é*
        'It is a sorry affair'

The subject of the copula sentences, either classificatory or identificatory, is never non-specific. Despite the grammarian's penchant for generic sentences of the sort *Is iasc bradán* 'A salmon is a fish', *Is éan smólach* 'A thrush is a bird', there is little, if any, evidence from natural speech that a generic non-specific subject is allowed. This idea is normally expressed by using the article in a generalizing fashion, e.g. *Is iasc é an bradán* 'The salmon is a fish'. Alternatively, the construction *Iasc atá sa mbradán* (C) (lit. '[It is] a fish which is in the salmon') occurs in Connacht and Donegal [see discussion of examples (33-5)] or *Iasc is ea an bradán* [see 10.3.5(iv)] may be used.

A classificatory sentence can also be expressed by means of the substantive verb. There are two constructions. The first consists of the *substantive verb + pronoun/definite noun + preposition* i 'in' + *possessive adjective referring to the pronoun/definite noun + classificatory noun*:

(30)   Tá mé i mo scoláire
         (lit. I am in my scholar)
         'I am a scholar/I have become a scholar'
(31)   Tá sé ina mhangach
         (lit. It is in its pollock)
         'It has become a pollock'
(32)   Tá sé ina Éireannach
         (lit. He is in his Irishman)
         'He has become an Irishman'

This construction is much more dynamic than the classificatory copula sentence. This is apparent when we contrast the translations of (30-2) with (20-2). There is an implication of not only 'being' but of 'becoming'. In (31) and (32), where the classificatory noun is felt to have an innate quality, only the translation using the verb 'become' seems possible.

The second classificatory construction using the substantive verb consists of (*deletion of copula*) + *classificatory indefinite noun* + *relative of substantive verb* + *preposition* i 'in' + *pronoun/definite noun*:

(33)   Scoláire atá ionam (C)
         (lit. [It is] a scholar which is in me)
         'I am a scholar'
(34)   Mangach atá ann (C)
         (lit. [It is] a pollock which is in it)
         'It is a pollock'
(35)   Éireannach atá ann (C)
         (lit. It is] an Irishman which is in him)
         'He is an Irishman'

This second substantive verb construction would appear to derive from the first one by a process of fronting. It would seem that, formally at least, the second could be interpreted as a cleft [see 10.3.5(i)] of the first. In other words *Tá mé i mo scoláire* (lit. I am in my scholar) is clefted to give [*Is*] *scoláire atá ionam* (lit. It is a scholar which is in me). However, the second construction does not have the same dynamic semantic implications. Example (35) translates well as 'He is an Irishman' where (32) must mean 'He has become an Irishman'. This semantic difference would lead us to conclude that although the second construction originates in a clefting of the first, synchronically it is better to regard the second substantive verb construction as a separate type.

At this point it is important to note the differences between the dialects. The first substantive verb classificatory construction is possible in all dialects. On the other hand, the second substantive verb construction seems not to be a feature of Munster Irish, but it is optional in Connacht and the norm in Gweedore. In other words a classificatory copula sentence of the sort (20-2) may be optionally replaced by (33-5) in Connacht and (33-5) are the most frequent type of classificatory sentence in Gweedore. The classificatory copula type still occurs in Gweedore:

(36)   [*Is*] *Bean dheas í sin* (Gd)
        'She is a nice woman'
(37)   *Ab é Sasanach é?* (Gd)
        'Is he an Englishman?'

Nevertheless, the statement with a basic grade pronoun and no adjective as in (20-2) is now almost invariably expressed by (33-5).

10.3.1(ii) *The identificatory copula sentence.*

(38)   *Is mé an múinteoir* (C)
        'I am the teacher'

Here we have *copula + pronoun/definite noun + pronoun/definite noun*. This is referred to as an identificatory sentence, as it expresses the identity of two nouns/pronouns, e.g. *mé* is equal to *múinteoir*, as opposed to the classificatory sentence that simply states the class to which a specific subject belongs.

    Here again the Munster/Connacht '*é, í, iad* insertion rule' applies:

(39)   *Is é Seán an múinteoir* (C)
        'Seán is the teacher'
(40)   *Is iad na daoine sin na múinteoirí* (C)
        'Those people are the teachers'

A further element of the rule is that repetition of the third person pronoun is required following the second definite noun/pronoun:

(41)   *Is é an múinteoir é* (C)
        'He is the teacher'
(42)   *Is í an scoláire í* (C)
        'She is the scholar'

(43)   *Is iad na sagairt iad* (C)
        'They are the priests'

It is important to note that this 'echoic' element of the rule operates on the basic grade *é, í, iad* and not on the contrast grade (*eisean*), on the emphatic grade (*é féin*), on the emphatic contrast grade (*eisean é féin*), or on *é seo, é sin* [see (90-3)] etc:

(44)   *Is eisean an sagart*
        'He is the priest'
(45)   [*Is*] *Ise an múinteoir*
        'She is the teacher'
(46)   [*Is*] *Iadsan na scoláirí*
        'They are the scholars'

Two possible explanations have been offered for this echoic element of the rule. The first (see Ahlqvist 1972) regards it as having its origins as an emphatic repetition which became obligatory. The second (see Stenson 1981:114) regards it as a device which was developed to avoid the ambiguity which a sentence such as *Is í an bhean a bhí tinn* would contain in the absence of the 'echo'. It would either mean 'It is the woman who was sick' (a cleft of *Bhí an bhean tinn* 'the woman was sick') or 'She is the woman who was sick'.

There is, in Connemara at least, an exclamatory use of the identificatory sentence *Is é an múinteoir é*, which can, in a certain context, mean 'He is the teacher!', 'He is the teacher for you!', 'He is a great teacher'. This use is quite marginal. In the Gweedore dialect, and this is probably true of much of Donegal, the contrast grade is the norm in identificatory sentences, e.g. *Eisean an múinteoir* 'He is the teacher', *Iadsan na scoláirí* 'They are the scholars', rather than *Is é an múinteoir é, Is iad na scoláirí iad*.

It is interesting to note in passing an example such as:

(47)   *Tá sé ar an duine is sine acu* (Gd)
        'He is the oldest (person) of them'

When an order of preference is expressed an idiom using the verb *tá* 'is' + *ar* 'on, (among)' can replace the identificatory copula sentence:

(48)   *Is é an duine is sine acu é*
        'He is the oldest of them'

10.3.2 Linking of nouns/pronouns and adjectives

10.3.2(i) *Exclamatory use.*

(49) *Is maith é!*
      'He is (so) good!'
(50) *Nach deas é!*
      'Isn't it nice!'
(51) *Deir sé gur deas é!*
      'He says it's nice!'

Here we have *copula + adjective + pronoun/definite noun*. The range of adjectives permitted here is extremely limited. Only adjectives describing a permanent quality and expressing a subjective estimation are allowed.

Once more the '*é, í, iad* insertion rule' applies here. The rule operates in Munster and Connacht:

(52) *Nach deas é an teach sin!* (C)
      'Isn't that house nice!'
(53) *Nach maith í Bríd!* (C)
      'Isn't Bríd good!'

The insertion rule is not found in Donegal so (52) and (53) are realized as:

(54) *Nach deas an teach sin!* (Gd)
(55) *Nach maith Bríd!* (Gd)

It is noteworthy that it is precisely this exclamatory use which is excluded in cleft sentences, as will be seen further in 10.3.5(i). Other functions, such as contrast, can be achieved by the fronting of adjectives in such circumstances. This is interesting because, from a diachronic point of view, this use of the copula is the limited survival of an older system in which the copula was more generally used to link nouns/pronouns with an adjective. It seems, therefore, that the retention of the older system in an exclamatory function is partly explained by the desire to confine cleft sentences to a contrastive function.

10.3.2(ii) *Equational use.*

(56) *Is ionann an dá rud* (C)
      'The two things are identical'
(57) *Is mar a chéile iad*
      'They are alike'

Once again here we have *copula + adjective + pronoun/definite noun*. In this case only a very few adjectives expressing equation or similarity are possible. Perhaps due to its compound nature *mar a chéile* (lit. like one another) may be used, in Cois Fhairrge, at least, with the substantive verb, for example: *Tá siad mar a chéile*. While **Tá siad ionann* does not seem to be allowed, the substantive verb is the norm with the adverbial phrase *ionann's* 'almost', for example: *Tá sé ionann's déanta* 'It is almost done'.

We might also include here the use of *Is cosúil le...é, Is geall le...é* 'It is like...' while noting that the use of the substantive in the case of *cosúil le* (*Tá sé cosúil le...* 'It is like... ') is permitted.

10.3.2(iii) *Comparative use.*
10.3.2(iii)1 *Comparative in ná construction:*

(58) *Is deise an seomra seo (ná)...* (Gd)
      'This room is nicer (than)...'

In this instance we have *copula + comparative form of adjective + noun/pronoun*. However, alongside this use of the copula we have the parallel construction employing the substantive verb:

(59) *Tá an seomra seo níos deise (ná)...*
      'This room is nicer (than)...'

A noteworthy feature of the latter construction is that *níos* is to an extent simply a particle. Yet the fact that it is still partly in the copula system is borne out by the now largely optional form of *ní ba* (*ní* 'a thing' + past/ conditional relative of the copula) in sentences where the verb is either in the past or the conditional. Furthermore, where the noun is indefinite the use of the relative of the present/future of the copula *is* is possible, though now less frequent:

(60) *Tá ceann is fearr/níos fearr ná sin agat*
'You have a better one than that'

10.3.2(iii)2 *Comparative qualifying noun:*

(61) *Tá an seomra is fearr anseo* (C)
'The best room is here'

In these sentences, there is the sequence *definite article + noun + comparative form of adjective*. The intermediate position (i.e. between its status as the copula and as a particle) of the *is* is also apparent here as *is* may be retained even when the verb of the sentence is in the past or conditional, e.g. *Bhí an seomra ab'fhearr/is fearr anseo* 'The best room was here'.

10.3.2(iii)3 *Comparative with de:*

(62) *Ní fearrde thú é* (C)
'You aren't the better for it'
(63) *Níor dhonaide é é* (C)
'He wouldn't be the worse for it'

A few comparative forms, for example *fearr* 'better', *measa, dona* 'worse' may add *-de* in this usage.

10.3.3 Use in prepositional phrases

10.3.3(i) *Prepositional phrase construction:*

(64) *Is maith liom é* (C)
'I like it'
(65) *Ní eolas dom é* (C)
(lit. it is not knowledge to me)
'I am not aware of the fact'
(66) *Nach bocht orm é!* (C)
(lit. Isn't it poor on me)
'Amn't I in a pitiful condition!'

Normally this construction consists of *copula + adjective/noun + preposition*. (This formula, however, does not cover all cases and it is difficult to classify *féidir* in *is féidir liom* 'I can'.)

There is also an impersonal usage (corresponding in part to the impersonal form in the verbal system) where the preposition is deleted. In such examples we can infer that some phrase containing the preposition and *duine* 'person' is understood:

(67) *Is féidir [le duine] é a bhriseadh* (C)
      'It is possible [for a person] to break it / One can break it'
(68) *Níor cheart [do dhuine] é a dhéanamh*
      'It would not be right [for a person] to do it / One should not do it'
(69) *Is deacair [le duine] é a ól*
      'It is difficult [in a person's opinion] to drink / It is difficult to drink'

In this construction there is a closed category in the case of the prepositions *do* 'to' and *ar* 'on'. The extent of the category naturally varies from dialect to dialect. For example, *Níor chás dúinn* 'It would be no harm for us' may be confined to Munster dialects or *Ní eolas dúinn* 'We are not aware of' to Connacht. However, the count for the preposition *ar* is probably higher than for the preposition *do*. On the other hand, the case of the preposition *le* is more extensive. Apart from the set phrases *Is cuimhne liom* 'I remember', *Is cuma liom* 'I don't mind', apparently in Cois Fhairrge at least, it is possible to employ *le* with any member of a class of adjectives which express an estimation:

(70) *B'éadrom leis í* (C)
      'He considered it light'
(71) *Shílfeá gurbh íseal leat é* (C)
      'You might think you considered it low'
(72) *Más gearr leat é* (C)
      'If you consider it short'

Although the range of these copulative prepositional phrases differs from one dialect to another, it is safe to say that there is a tendency to replace them with constructions involving the substantive verb. Furthermore, it would seem that it is in Donegal that the replacement is greatest, for example, Gweedore: *Tá cuimhne agam ar...* 'I remember...' for *Is cuimhne liom...* or *Tá dúil agam i...* 'I like...' for *Is maith liom....* Fronting of prepositional phrase sentences is dealt with in 10.3.5(i).

10.3.3(ii) *Idiomatic use with* le.

(73)   *Is le Cáit an carr* (C)
        'The car is Cáit's / Cáit owns the car'

There is little to remark at this point except to notice that this copula construction using *le* 'with' may occur only with a definite noun. It is not possible to say **Is le Cáit carr* 'Cáit owns a car', which must be rendered as *Tá carr ag Cáit* (lit. There is a car at Cáit) 'Cáit has/owns a car'.

10.3.3(iii) *Idiomatic use with* as, ó *'from'*.

(74)   *Is as Baile Átha Cliath Máire* (C)
        'Máire is from Dublin'

Usage here can vary according to dialect. In Munster, and it would seem optionally in Donegal, the subject can be identified by the preposition *d o* 'to':

(75)   *Is as Baile Átha Cliath do Mháire* (D)
        'Máire is from Dublin'
(76)   *Ní ón nDaingean é* (M)
        'He is not from Dingle'

The use of *ó* 'from' rather than *as* 'out of' is usual in Munster.

10.3.3(iv) *Idiomatic use with* do *'to'*.

(77)   *...an chailleach sin is máthair dó* (C)
        '...that hag who is mother to him'
(78)   *Fear darb ainm dó Máirtín* (C)
        'A man whose name is Máirtín'

This idiom, it would seem, is confined to petrified phrases containing a name or kinship word. It is perhaps commonest in Munster:

(79)   *Domhnall Ó Cinnéide is ainm dó* (Ky)
        'Domhnall Ó Cinnéide is his name'

(80)   ...*a mháistreas...gurbh ainm dhi Bess Rice* (Ky)
        '...his schoolmistress...whose name was Bess Rice'

Perhaps this idiomatic use should be regarded as a permanently fronted version of the prepositional phrase construction [see 10.3.3(i)] that is to say based on a sentence *Is máthair dó an chailleach sin* (lit. is mother to him that hag) or *Is ainm dhi Bess Rice* (lit. is name to her Bess Rice). This interpretation is corroborated by the Cois Fhairrge *Fear darb ainm dó Máirtín* where such an order occurs, albeit in a petrified relative clause, with a curious doubling of the preposition *do* 'to' in *darb* 'to whom is' and *dó* 'to him'.

10.3.4 Use with *seo, sin, siúd* etc

(81)   *Seo lampa*
        'This here is a lamp'
(82)   *Sin geata*
        'That (there) is a gate'

In this case, although the traditional spellings are *seo, sin, siúd* etc., they must be analysed as *is eo, is in, is iúd* etc. From an historical point of view, these forms are thought to have their origin in *acso*, which can be interpreted as *voici* (*vois ici*) 'see here'. This original meaning is probably still retained in such expressions as *Seo, seo* 'Look here now!', 'Now, now!'. The copula is in fact used here merely as a device which enables the formation of questions, negations and indirect speech:

(83)   *Ab eo lampa?*
        'Is this a lamp?'
(84)   *Deir sé gurb eo lampa*
        'He says this is a lamp'
(85)   *Deir sé nach eo lampa*
        'He says this is not a lamp'

Here once more the Munster/Connacht *é, í, iad* insertion rule operates and a glide /w/ can develop, e.g. Cois Fhairrge *seo é* /s'ow eː/.

(86)   *Seo é an lampa* (C)
        'This is the lamp'

(87) *Sin í Bríd* (C)
      'That is Bríd'

The *é, í, iad* insertion rule does not apply in Donegal.

(88) *Seo an lampa* (D)
      'This is the lamp'
(89) *Sin Bríd* (D)
      'That is Bríd'

There is also a usage throughout the dialects of *seo* 'here', *sin* 'that', *siúd* 'that' (with distance) along with a third person pronoun:

(90) *Is é seo an lampa* (C)
      'This thing here is the lamp'
(91) *Ab í sin Bríd?* (C)
      'Is that woman (lit. she there) there Bríd?'
(92) *Ab é seo Mícheál?* (C)
      'Is this fellow (lit. he here) Mícheál?'
(93) *Deir sé gurb iad sin a bhris é* (C)
      'He says that it is those [people] there who broke it'
(94) *Níl sé seo sásta*
      'This fellow (lit. he here) isn't content'

It could be argued that generalized all-purpose forms current throughout the copula system in Gweedore and much of Donegal (see Table 10.3) originate here. In other words the third singular masculine pronoun *Ab é* in an example such as (92) has been generalized and has spread to all uses of the copula. This means that in Cois Fhairrge there is a distinction between (95) and (96):

(95) *Ab eo é Pádraig?* (Cf)
      'Is this Pádraig?'
(96) *Ab é seo Pádraig?* (Cf)
      'Is this fellow here Pádraig?'

In Donegal, on the other hand, due to the generalization of *ab é* and the non-application of the *é, í, iad* insertion rule, there is no such distinction possible. Both meanings are rendered as:

(97)   Ab é seo Pádraig? (Gd)
        'Is this (fellow) Pádraig?'

It is interesting to note that a somewhat parallel generalization of a singular masculine pronoun occurs in Kerry in questions such as:

(98)   Cé hé mise?/Cé hé mé féin? (Ky)
        'Who am I?'

In this instance we might expect:

(99)   Cé mise (Gd)
        'Who am I?'
(100)   Cé mé féin? (Cf)
        'Who am I?'

10.3.5 Use in fronting

10.3.5(i) *Cleft sentences*. As is illustrated in (102-5), the subject, object, prepositional phrase or adverbial phrase in a sentence like that in (101) can be fronted by the copula, which is then followed by a relative clause.

(101)   Bhí an fear ag péinteáil cathaoir inné
        'The man was painting a chair yesterday'
(102)   (Is é) an fear a bhí ag péinteáil cathaoir inné
        'It is the man who was painting a chair yesterday'
(103)   (Is) cathaoir a bhí an fear a phéinteáil inné
        'It is a chair the man was painting yesterday'
(104)   (Is) ag péinteáil cathaoir a bhí an fear inné
        'It is painting a chair that the man was yesterday'
(105)   (Is) inné a bhí an fear ag péinteáil cathaoir
        'It is yesterday that the man was painting the chair'

It is also possible to front an adjective. The adjective in (106) is fronted in (107):

(106)   Tá sé tinn
        'He is sick'

(107)   *(Is) tinn atá sé*
        'He is *sick*'

This fronting seems to be confined to a contrastive function and implies that 'he is sick' - not simply tired or emotional or drunk. In a sentence such as *Tá sé go deas* 'It is nice' the adjective *deas* would hardly be fronted to give **Nach deas atá sé* as this exclamatory function demands a straight copula sentence *Nach deas é!* 'Isn't it nice!' [see 10.3.2(i)].

It is also possible to front an entire adjectival phrase, as seen in the examples:

(108)   *Agus chan sásta imeacht as an oileán a bhí sé* (D)
        (lit. and not satisfied to depart from the island he was)
        'And he was not satisfied to depart from the island'
(109)   *...ní ba mheasa ná a chuid eile ba duthcha dó a bheith* (D)
        (lit. not worse than the rest was natural for him to be)
        '...it wasn't natural for him to be worse than the rest'

There is another sort of fronting which is syntactically identical to the clefting just described. While it might be claimed that there is a sort of contrast implied, nevertheless it serves to present new material. An example of this presentational fronting, from the beginning of a Donegal folktale, is:

(110)   *Fear a bhí thíos anseo in Anagaire a bhí an-tógtha le h-imirt chártaí agus...* (D)
        '[There was] this man down here in Annagry who was very taken up with card playing and...'

In a similar way responsives to *wh*- questions are introduced by clefting:

(111)   *Cé thiocfas isteach?* (C)
        'Who will come in?'
(112)   *[Is í] Bríd [a thiocfas isteach]* (C)
        '[It is] Bríd [who will come in]'

In certain prepositional phrase constructions fronting can also occur:

(113)   *Is fearr liom an fear sin* (C)
        'I prefer that man'

238 *Modern Irish: grammatical structure and dialectal variation*

(114) *(Is é) an fear sin is fearr liom* (C)
'It is that man I prefer'

(115) *Is cóir disi a thíocht anoir* (C)
'It is right for her to come from the east'

(116) *Disi is cóir a thíocht anoir* (C)
(lit. It is for her it is right to come from the east)
'She should come from the east'

The subject of a verbal noun complement may be fronted (see de Bhaldraithe 1956/7b: 245):

(117) *Thusa a ba chóir a bheith ann* (C)
'It is you who should be there'

This is presumably a fronted version of:

(118) *Ba chóir thusa a bheith ann* (C)
(lit. It would be right you to be there)
'You should be there'

Alternatively an entire verbal noun complement may be fronted:

(119) *B'fhéidir gurb é a chaitheamh amach a rinne sibh* (C)
(lit. May be that it is throwing it out you did)
'Maybe you threw it out'

This is presumably a fronted version of:

(120) *B'fhéidir go ndearna sibh é chaitheamh amach*
'Maybe you threw it out'

A Munster example is:

(121) *An é [a] chaitheamh isteach sa Pheriplegethón is ceart?* (M)
'Is it right to throw him into the Periplegethone?'

It should be noted that the Munster/Connacht *é, í, iad* insertion rule applies in cleft sentences:

(122) *Is é an fear a bhí ann* (C, M)
'It is the man who was there'
(123) *Is í Máire atá sásta* (C, M)
'It is Máire who is content'
(124) *Is iad na daoine sin a bhris an chathaoir* (C, M)
'It is those people who broke the chair'

In Gweedore, as expected, the generalized *ní hé*, *ab é* etc. are employed:

(125) *Ní hé inné a bhí sé ag péinteáil cathaoir* (Gd)
'It is not yesterday he was painting a chair'
(126) *Ab é tinn a bhí sé?* (Gd)
'Was he *sick*?'

10.3.5(ii) *Pseudo-cleft sentences*.

(127) *Siod a dúirt sé, go raibh sé tinn* (D)
'What he said was, that he was sick'
(128) *'Séard a b'fhearr liom, teach mór* (C)
'What I would like, is a big house'
(129) *Séard é féin, amadán* (C)
'What he is, is a fool'
(130) *Sé (an) rud a ba mhaith leis ná an bhó a dhíol* (Ky, Mk)
'What he would like, is to sell the cow'

The pseudo-cleft sentence is followed by a perceivable pause and in Munster by *ná*. (For a fuller discussion of the function of *ná* see 12.6.)

Pseudo-cleft sentences are formed by fronting *rud* 'thing' in anticipation of the information which is being emphasized. Undoubtedly, Connacht (and Ring/Ballymacoda) *'séard* is a contraction of *is é rud* (compare *céard* (C) and *D'éard* (Rg, Bm) 'what (thing)' from *cé rud* and *[ca]d é rud*). Donegal may well be based on *is é rud* and be somehow confused with *siod* (= *seo* etc.). Both *'sé rud* and *'sé an rud* occur in Munster, the latter presumably being a rationalization by analogy with the *é*, *í*, *iad* insertion rule.

The sentence type shown in example (129) would appear to be peculiar to Connemara. This is possibly explained by the fact that it is a pseudo-cleft of the classificatory sentence *Is amadán é* 'He is a fool', which is largely ousted by the *is ea*-type sentence in Munster: e.g. *Amadán is ea é* [see 10.3.5(iv)]

240 *Modern Irish: grammatical structure and dialectal variation*

and in Donegal by the second classificatory construction which employs the substantive verb, e.g. *Amadán atá ann* [see 10.3.1(i)].

Another feature of *'séard* is that it has been analysed as *is éard* and the copula is employed as a means to form questions, negations and indirect speech:

(131) *Deir sé gurb éard a bhí sé a iarraidh go gcuirfí thall é* (C)
'He says what he wants is to be buried over there'

Furthermore the tense can vary:

(132) *... gurbh éard a bheadh ann, drochobair* (C)
'... what it would be, is bad work'

Questions, negations and indirect speech are possible with *siod* by use of the generalized *ní hé*, *ab é* etc.:

(133) *Ab é siod a bhí sé...?* (Gd)
'Is it that he was...?'

10.3.5(iii) *Verb focusing.*

Table 10.4 *Verb focusing in major dialects*

basic sentence	*Bhí fear ag péinteáil cathaoir inné* 'A man was painting a chair yesterday'
sentence with verb focusing	*Is amhlaidh (M, C)* *Is ann (M, C)* } *a bhí fear ag péinteáil cathaoir inné* *Siod (D)*
	Is é an chaoi a raibh fear ag péinteáil cathaoir inné (C) 'The way it is is that the man was painting a chair yesterday'

It is best to speak here of focusing on the verb because the verb cannot be 'fronted', as its unmarked position is initial. There is a variety of devices. The usage differs somewhat from dialect to dialect: *is amhlaidh* certainly occurs in Munster or Connacht, *is ann* is found in Munster but appears to be more marginal in Connacht (it occurs in Inishmaan for instance), while *is é an chaoi* would seem to be predominantly in Connacht and *siod* confined to Donegal. *Is é an chaoi* must have its origins in some form of pseudo-cleft sentence of the sort *Is é an chaoi a bhfuil an scéal, tá mé i gcruachás* 'The way the matter stands is I am in a fix'.

Another way of focusing is to use *is ea*:

(134)   *Aniar liom aríst agus is ea a bhí an stróinséar...* (Bk)
        'I came from the west again and it is how the stranger was...'

This can be also seen in the petrified 'however' phrase type

(135)   *Níl olc dhá mhéid nach eadh is fusa ...* (M)
        'There is no evil however great that it is not easier ...'
(136)   *Dhá fheabhas é is ea (is amhlaidh) is fearr liom é* (C)
        'The better it is the more I like it'

The retention of *is ea* in 'however'-type phrases is presumably due to a desire to create an echoic effect common in this sort of construction in many languages. This effect is also achieved by the doubling of *dhá* in Connacht (see 12.5). The verb focused sentences are equivalent to the Hiberno-English construction 'It is how (It is the way, etc.) a man was painting a chair yesterday'.

10.3.5(iv) Is ea- *type sentence.* In Munster and Connacht a fronted adverbial phrase may be inverted and a 'copy' pronoun *ea* then follows the copula:

(137)   *Achar gearr blianta roimh bhliain an drochshaoil is ea a roinneadh é* (C)
        'Some few years before the famine year it was divided'

Example (137) is an inverted cleft. The corresponding non-inverted cleft would be (138):

(138)   *Is achar gearr blianta roimh bhliain an drochshaoil a roinneadh é*
        'It was some few years before the famine year it was divided'

In Munster, and optionally to a very limited extent in Connacht (for the most part in East Galway), this *is ea-* type sentence tends to replace the third person statement form in a classificatory sentence:

(139)   *Feirmeoir is ea é* (M)
        'He is a farmer'

(140)   *Fear de Mhuintir Thuathail ab ea é* (Ml)
        'He was one of the people called Ó Tuathail'

While the *is ea*-type sentences are the most frequent type of classificatory sentence in Munster the basic type of classificatory sentence [see 10.3.1(i)] occurs, e.g.:

(141)   *Dob' obair capaill é* (Dn)
        'It was work for a horse'

The best explanation of what is in all probability an extension of the *is ea* sentence type from the fronted adverbial or prepositional phrase to the classificatory sentence is that both sentence types elicit responsives which employ what historically is the old neuter pronoun *ea*.

In some Munster dialects the inversion type sentence has developed a wider range of functions. Firstly, in Kerry the inversion is extended to identificatory sentences:

(142)   *An seanbhuachaill ab é é* (Dn)
        'He was the "old boy"'
(143)   *Eibhlín Nic Niocaill dob' í í* (Bk)
        'She was Eibhlín Nic Niocaill'
(144)   *An cleas céanna is iad iad* (Dn)
        'They are the same gang'

Examples (142-4) are presumably inversions of the identificatory sentences:

(145)   *B'é an seanbhuachaill é*
(146)   *Dob' í Eibhlín Nic Niocaill í*
(147)   *Is iad an cleas céanna iad*

Alternatively, the pronoun *ea* may be retained as a 'copy' pronoun:

(148)   *A mhac san is ea é anois* (Dn)
        'He is his son now'

It would seem that this inversion is limited to human subjects.

Secondly, the *is ea* sentence has been extended to the idiomatic uses with *le* and *ó* [see 10.3.3(ii-iii)]:

(149) *Leis an rí is ea é* (Dn)
       'The king owns it'
(150) *Is liomsa is ea an áit sin thuas* (Dn)
       'I own that place up there'
(151) *Ón bhFrainc ab ea é* (Dn)
       'He was from France'
(152) *Leis an gcóisteoir is ea é* (Mk)
       'It is the coachman who owns it'

Thirdly, the copula may follow a fronted adverbial or prepositional phrase:

(153) *Suas insa chlais ab ea iad go léir* (Dn)
       'Up in the furrow they all were'
(154) *I dtosach an fhómhair dob ea é* (Dn)
       'It was in the beginning of autumn'
(155) *Timpeall deich púint dob' ea é an tórramh ar fad an uair úd* (Dn)
       'The whole wake was about ten pounds that time'

This seems to be a simple substitution of the copula for the substantive verb, that is *ab ea iad* for *bhíodar*, *dob' ea é* for *bhí sé* etc. However, given the fact that there is a fronted adverbial (or prepositional phrase), it may be that the substantive verb is deleted from an *is ea* sentence and the copula is then used to mark the tense so that (153-4) may be derived from:

(156) *Suas insa chlais is ea a bhíodar go léir*
(157) *I dtosach an fhómhair is ea a bhí sé*

Finally, the *is ea*-type sentence has spread from the statements to negations, questions and indirect speech. The normal Munster system is to use inversion for a statement and classificatory sentences in negations, questions and indirect speech:

(158) *Múinteoir is ea é* (M)
       'He is a teacher'
(159) *Ní múinteoir é*
       'He isn't a teacher'
(160) *Nach múinteoir é?*
       'Isn't he a teacher?'

In Dunquin, however, the copula may be duplicated in order to retain the *is ea* construction:

(161) *An múinteoir ab ea a bhean?* (Dn)
'Was his wife a teacher?'
(162) *Nach toirneach ab ea í?* (Dn)
'Wasn't it thunder?'

10.4 Deletion of copula

A very general rule which seems to apply to all dialects is that the copula form *is* may be deleted at the beginning of an utterance. This can be stated negatively by saying that the copula may not normally be deleted when marked for mood, tense, negation, interrogation or when embedded in a sentence:

(163) *Múinteoir é an fear sin* (C)
'That man is a teacher'

as opposed to

(164) *Ba mhúinteoir é* (C)
'He was a teacher'
(165) *Ní ba sagart é* (C)
'He wasn't a priest'
(166) *Deir siad gur duine deas é* (C)
'They say that he is a nice person'

It must however be noted that *é, í, iad* following *is* is simultaneously deleted:

(167) *Bríd mo bhean* (C)
'Bríd is my wife'

Example (167) must be interpreted as the deleted form of:

(168) *Is í Bríd mo bhean*
'Bríd is my wife'

The general rule must nevertheless be qualified. The form *is* is not deleted before *eo (in, iúd* etc.). Only *seo lampa* 'This (thing) is a lamp' or *Sin í Bríd*

'That [person there] is Bríd' are possible. Furthermore, examples of *ba* being deleted are recorded for Dunquin:

(169)   [*Ba*] *dheas liomsa anois...* (Dn)
           'I would think it nice now...'

Undoubtedly this deletion is ultimately connected with the phonological rule which allows the optional deletion of a neutral vowel in the beginning of an utterance. Partly for this reason the question particle *an* /ə(N)/ is also sometimes deleted:

(170)   [*An*] *bhfuil sé sásta?*
           'Is he content?'

It is worth noting that some prepositional phrase types seem more likely to allow deletion than others, e.g. *Cuma liom* 'It is all the same to me' seems more likely than *Dóigh liom* 'I suppose'.

Generally, it would seem that deletion is most frequent in identificatory and cleft sentences.

10.5 Responsive system

The first principle of the copula responsive system is that the copula does not stand alone. The reason for this is undoubtedly that it may not normally be stressed. The copula is therefore accompanied by some other element. Generally speaking the copula is accompanied by the second element in the sentence which elicits the responsive:

(171)   *Is é an múinteoir é*
        'He is the teacher?'
        Is é (C)
        'Yes (he is)'
(172)   *Nach deas í do léine!*
        'Isn't your shirt nice!'
        Is deas (C)
        'Yes (it is)'
(173)   *Nach maith leat an chathaoir sin?*
        'Don't you like that chair?'
        Ní maith (C)
        'No (I don't)'

246 *Modern Irish: grammatical structure and dialectal variation*

(174) *Ní leis an leabhar seo?*
'He doesn't own this book?'
Ní leis (C)
'No (he doesn't)'

(175) *Nach é a bhí ag péinteáil?*
'Isn't it he who was painting?'
Is é (C)
'Yes (it is)'

(176) *Uaitse a fuair mé é?*
'From you I got it?'
Is uaim (C)
'Yes'

(177) *Is minic a tharla sé cheana*
'It often happened before?'
Is minic (C)
'Yes'

(178) *Nach ar an uisce atá sé?*
'Isn't it on the water?'
Ní air (C)
'No (it isn't)'

On the other hand, where the copula is followed by an indefinite noun, an ungradable adverbial phrase or an unstressed prepositional phrase the pronoun *ea* follows the copula:

(179) *Is múinteoir é*
'He is a teacher'
Is ea (C)
'Yes (he is)'

(180) *Cathaoir a bhí sé a phéinteáil*
'It is a chair he was painting?'
Ní hea (C)
'No (it isn't)'

(181) *Inné a bhí sé anseo?*
'Yesterday he was here?'
Is ea (C)
'Yes'

(182) *Ag péinteáil a bhí sé?*
'Was he painting?'

>
> *Is ea* (C)
> 'Yes'

(183) *Ar an uisce atá sé?*
'Is it on the water?'
Is ea (C)
'Yes'

The same principles obtain when the copula is used with *seo* (*sin, siúd* etc.). However, *eo, in, iúd* etc. are ignored in the responsive:

(184) *Seo cathaoir?*
'This is a chair?'
Is ea (C)
'Yes'

(185) *Seo í an chathaoir*
'This is the chair'
Is í (C)
'Yes (it is)'

As was pointed out in the section on *is ea*-type sentences, the use of *ea* in the responsive system connects an indefinite noun and thereby classificatory sentences with fronted adverbial and prepositional phrases [see 10.3.5(iv)]. Naturally enough *ea* is used in the responsive of the inverted classificatory sentence in those dialects where it occurs:

(186) *Feirmeoir is ea é*
'He is a farmer'
Is ea (M)
'Yes (he is)'

The type of adjective which may be fronted in cleft sentences [see 10.3.5(i)] may also elicit *ea* in a responsive:

(187) *Nach tinn atá sé*
'Isn't he *sick*!'
Nach ea (C)
'Yes, isn't he!'

There is undoubtedly some correlation between a quality of indefiniteness and the use of *ea* along with the copula. This is further emphasized by the use of *is ea* as an all-purpose signal of attentiveness:

(188)   A Dhónaill !
        'Dónall !'
        Is ea (M)
        'Yes'

There is a tendency for responsives with the substantive verb to take over the domain of the copula. This is particularly common in cleft sentences (see de Bhaldraithe 1948: 165-6):

(189)   Is deabhltaí an mheabhair atá iontab
        'They have tremendous intelligence'
        Tá (Cf)
        'Yes!'

The pendant *tá* used as an initial pause word in responsives, which is found in all dialects (see Ó Siadhail 1973:155-7), originates in a similar fashion:

(190)   Céard atá sé a iarraidh?
        'What does he want?'
        Tá, bó a chaill sé (C)
        'A cow he lost'

In Gweedore, a responsive with the substantive verb is normal after the exclamatory use of the copula:

(191)   Nach deas an teach sin!
        'Isn't that house nice!'
        Tá (Gd)
        'Yes'

In Cois Fhairrge a somewhat contrary tendency can be seen:

(192)   Tá sí ag goil dhá mbleán
        'She is going to milk them'
        Ab í Máire? (Cf)
        'Is it Máire?'

Obviously, the response intends to define the subject further. What is interesting is that the relative clause (e.g. *atá ag goil dhá mbleán* 'who is going to milk them') may be deleted from the cleft sentence underlying the response.

The generalization of the *is é, ab é* etc. forms (see Table 10.3) in Gweedore has greatly simplified the responsive system. It is still possible to use the forms illustrated in Table 10.1 in preposition phrase constructions, e.g.:

(193) *Arbh fhearr leat é?*
 'Would you prefer it?'
 B'fhearr (Gd)
 'Yes (I would)'

Nevertheless, apart from those constructions the all-purpose generalized forms are used so that the set of responses is limited to *Is é* 'Yes', *Ní hé* 'No', *Ab é?* 'Is it?', *Nab é?* 'Isn't it?':

(194) *Ab é thusa a phéinteáil é?*
 'Is it you who painted it?'
 Is é (Gd)
 'Yes'
(195) *Ar an tábla atá sé?*
 'Is it on the table (it is)?'
 Ní hé
 'No'

The discussion in this section has centred on the use of the copula in the responsive system. It is however important to point out that the usage described here in the responsive is part of a larger phenomenon of ellipsis. For example, the pronoun *ea* which is employed in the responsive to a classificatory sentence such as (179) is also found in a sentence of the sort:

(196) *Deireann daoine gur múinteoir é ach ní chreidim gurb ea* (C)
 'People say he is a teacher but I don't believe it'

10.6 General discussion of copula system

In general, there can be little doubt that copular sentences have inherent focus and their function is to segregate new information from old and to show their relationship. This essential function is what all types of copular sentences have in common. This same focusing of new information accounts for the use of a construction which parallels cleft sentences in questions introduced by *cé* 'who is it?':

(197) *Cé a bhris an chathaoir?*
'Who is it who broke the chair?'
(198) *Is é Máirtín a bhris an chathaoir*
'It is Máirtín who broke the chair'

In both (197) and (198) the copula [albeit deleted on the surface of the question in (197)] brings the new or required information into focus. We may also mention in passing that in a sub-class of questions which concern a measure or amount, the relative of the substantive can be optionally deleted and the necessary syntactic adjustments made:

(199) *Cén aois atá sé anois?* (C)
'What age is he now?'
(200) *Cén aois anois é?*
'What age is he now?'
(201) *Cén t-achar atá Bríd anseo?* (C)
'How long is Bríd here?'
(202) *Cén t-achar Bríd anseo?*
'How long is Bríd here ?'

For the rightward movement of the pronoun *é* see 9.2.7.

As we have seen in classificatory sentences [see 10.3.1(i)] an adjective can be brought further into focus, e.g. *Is duine deas é* 'He is a nice person' beside *Is deas an duine é* 'He is a nice person'.

There is a close relationship between the word order of the copula sentences and its function of bringing an element into focus. The unmarked order of all copula sentences is that predicate (defined as new information) follows directly on the copula. This is the case in all usages. Obviously, inversions are marked and pseudo-clefts such as *Is éard é féin amadán* 'What he is is a fool' are marked in opposition to *Is amadán é* 'He is a fool'. An identificatory sentence such as *Is é an sagart an múinteoir* 'The priest is the teacher' normally presumes the question 'Who is the teacher?' so the predicate is *an sagart* 'the priest'. In more marked circumstances it could, of course, answer the question 'Who is the priest?' so that *an múinteoir* 'the teacher' would be the predicate.

One further point must be made about identificatory sentences. A general rule, which dictates that the most referentially exclusive noun phrase follows the copula, overrides the rule that the predicate should do so. Only *Is é Máirtín an múinteoir* 'Máirtín is the teacher' (not **Is é an múinteoir Máirtín*) is possible even though the predicate would be *an múinteoir* 'the teacher' if the question were 'Who is Máirtín?'. Clearly, the *é, í, iad* insertion rule applies at a later stage.

The relationship between focus and emphasis is intricate. Broadly, if we accept the proposal that all copula sentences involve focus then we can view emphasis as a spectrum reaching from the non-emphasis of classificatory sentences to the emphasis of cleft sentences. Identificatory sentences fall in the middle; they are normally non-emphatic yet may be felt to be emphatic in a sentence such as *Is é an scoláire an fear a bhí ann* 'The scholar is the man who was there', which resembles a cleft and is precisely the type of sentence which acts as a pivot between identificatory and cleft sentences.

The connection between inversions and emphasis is also a delicate matter. Inversion would seem to be largely a symbiotic feature and any argument that the *is ea*-type sentence is simply a mechanism for emphasis is tenuous. In those dialects where *is ea*-type sentences tend to replace classificatory sentences (Munster) there is little to suggest that such sentences are regarded as emphatic. On the other hand, the inversion of identificatory sentences may well imply a certain emphasis.

10.7 Summary of dialectal differences

There are three main tendencies which can be observed in the dialects:

(a) the proliferation or reduction of forms
(b) the erosion of the copula's functions by the substantive verb
(c) the expansion of inversion.

The proliferation of copula forms is probably greatest in Connacht, in Connemara in particular. The contrary drift is most evident in Donegal, as seen in the intrusion of the generalized forms *is é, ab é, nab é, gob é* etc.

Erosion of all the copula's domains has taken place. It could appear that the substantive verb has made its greatest inroads in Donegal while some slight ground has been gained in Kerry. Where the linking of two noun phrases is concerned the classificatory copula sentence type has yielded to the second type of substantive verb classificatory sentence, as illustrated by examples (33-5). This substantive verb construction is now the norm in Gweedore and a frequent optional variant in Connacht.

It is as a link between noun phrases and adjectives that the attrition is greatest. The class of adjectives permitted in the exclamatory use is limited and in Gweedore the substantive verb is introduced in tags and responsives. The equational use is not only limited but is often optional. The comparative construction may be optionally replaced by the substantive verb and *níos/is* are as much particles as copula forms.

There is also a bias against the use of the copula in prepositional phrases with *Is cuimhne liom* 'I remember' being replaced in Gweedore by *Tá cuimhne agam air*. On the other hand, it must be noted that in Dunquin Irish sentences of the sort (153-5) constitute an infiltration of the substantive verb's functions by the copula.

The expansion of inverted sentences is centred in Munster. Although inversion is a stylistic option in Connacht where a cleft sentence has a fronted adverbial phrase, as in *Ar an mbóthar seo is ea a tharla sé* 'On this road it happened', its use is limited. Inversion of classificatory sentences does optionally occur in Connacht, for the most part in East Galway (Menlough) [see example (140)] but can only be said to be the norm in Munster. Furthermore, the examples of inverted identificatory sentences as in (142-4) appear to be confined to Kerry.

11 *Complementation and modal and auxiliary verbs*

In this chapter we begin with a general discussion of complementation in order to place in context some tendencies which give rise to certain differences between the dialects and to provide the background for an examination of modal and auxiliary verbs.

11.1 Complementation

11.1.1 Types of complementation
There are basically two types of complementation: a finite type and a verbal noun type, as is illustrated by an example where the sentence *Tá mé anseo* 'I am here' is complementized following the phrase *Is maith leis* 'He likes'.

Figure 11.1 Finite and verbal noun complementation

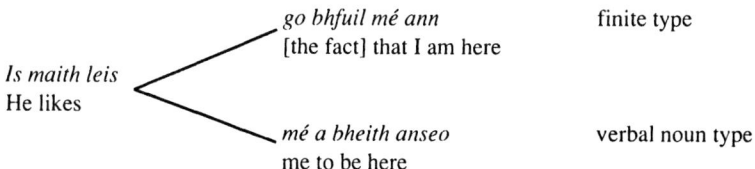

11.1.1(i) *Finite type.*

(1) *Tá cathaoir anseo* (C)
    'There is a chair here'
(2) *Níl cathaoir anseo* (C)
    'There isn't a chair here'
(3) *Sílim go bhfuil cathaoir anseo* (C)
    'I think there is a chair here'
(4) *Sílim nach bhfuil cathaoir anseo* (C)
    'I think there isn't a chair here'

The finite type involves the use of complementizers. There are two sets of complementizers – the unmarked set *go/nach* (+ eclipsis) and the set *gur/nar/nár* (+ lenition) which are marked for the past tense of all regular verbs. A feature of Munster Irish is the use of *ná* (without a following mutation) in the unmarked set:

(5) *Deirtear ná fuil cathaoir anso* (M)
 'It is said there isn't a chair here'

We may mention in passing that there is a sequence of tenses (see de Bhaldraithe 1956/7b:242-3): if the main or matrix clause is in the past tense, this will be transferred to the finite complement, but the present is replaced by the past and the future by the conditional. A conditional in the matrix sentence is followed by a conditional in the finite complement. The only exception is where a verb expresses a tentative opinion. Examples are:

(6) *Shílfeá go mbeadh cathaoir anseo* (Gd)
 'You/One would think there would be a chair here'
(7) *Shílfeá go bhfuil tú ag taltú na hiomaire* (C)
 'You/One would think you were trampling the ridge'

11.1.1(ii) *Verbal noun type.*
11.1.1(ii)1 *Intransitive verbs*

(8) *Ba mhaith liom imeacht*
 'I would like to go (off)'

A general rule in the case of a verbal noun type is that the subject is absent from the complement clause as it is identical to some noun phrase in the matrix clause. As can be seen from example (8) the verbal noun of an intransitive verb may be appended directly. However, here there is a minor distinction between the dialects involving the two verbal nouns *goil/dul* 'going' (Connacht and Ulster *goil* apart from certain petrified idioms; Munster *dul*) and *teacht* 'coming' (including the Connacht alternative form *tíocht*). In Kerry, at least, these behave like any other verbal noun, whereas in Connacht and Donegal a preceding *a* + lenition is obligatory.

(9) *Ba mhaith liom a theacht* (C)
 'I would like to come'

(10)   *Abair leis a ghoil abhaile* (C)
       'Tell him to go home'

The Kerry equivalents of (9) and (10) are:

(11)   *Ba mhaith liom teacht* (Ky)
(12)   *Abair leis dul abhaile* (Ky)

A third verbal noun (*a*) *bheith* is lenited in all dialects. (An occasional exception is recorded for Cois Fhairrge, but such is extremely rare.)

It is possible to retain the subject of the complement clause before an intransitive verb:

(13)   *Ba mhaith liom é a theacht liom* (C)
       'I would like him to come with me'

In this case the subject is before the verbal noun which is preceded by *a* + lenition. Examples of this sort are found in all major dialects;

(14)   *Conas a ba mhaith leis an bhliain a theacht air* (Ky)
       'How would he like the year to find him (lit. to come on him)?'

11.1.1(ii)2 *Transitive verbs*

(15)   *Ba mhaith liom an doras a phéinteáil* (Gd)
       'I would like to paint the door'

The object of a transitive verb in a complementized clause comes before the verbal noun, which is preceded by *a* + lenition.

In Munster *do/d'* + lenition occurs alongside *a* + lenition in verbal noun complementation. They can even co-occur in the same sentence, as in example (17):

(16)   *Féatam an rud d'atharú* (Mk)
       'We will be able to change the thing'
(17)   *Dineag na paidreacha a dhúbailt agus do neartú* (Mk)
       'The prayers were doubled and strengthened'

It is also possible to have both the subject and object precede the verbal noun in the embedded clause (see de Bhaldraithe 1985b:101):

(18)　　*Ba mhaith liom sibh an doras a phéinteáil* (D)
　　　　'I would like you to paint the door'
(19)　　*Ba mhaith liom m'inín fear a fháil a mbeadh airgead aige* (C)
　　　　'I would like my daughter to get a man who would have money'

An impersonal form of this construction is reported for Cois Fhairrge (see de Bhaldraithe 1956-7b:244):

(20)　　*Is maith leis 'chuile shórt a dhéanamh dhó* (Cf)
　　　　'He likes one to do everything for him'

Presumably, the subject of the verbal noun clause must be understood as *duine*: *Is maith leis [duine] 'chuile shórt a dhéanamh dhó*. Such an impersonal construction corresponds to the usage in examples such as *Tá aimhreas [ar dhuine] go...* 'One is inclined to think...' or *Ní féidir [le duine] imeacht* 'One cannot leave' [see 10.3.3(i)].

While examples with both the subject and object preceding the verbal noun are found in all dialects, there can be little doubt that they occur frequently in Donegal while in Munster, at least, they are very rare.

In Munster, the relative paucity of the *subject + object + a (+ lenition) + verbal noun* pattern is perhaps compensated for by the comparatively frequent use, at least, in narrative style, of a construction: *subject + a (+ lenition) + verbal noun + object*. The object noun may then be in the genitive, as can be expected following a verbal noun:

(21)　　*Cad é an bun a bhí le mé féin a thógaint geite rompusan* (Ky)
　　　　'What caused me to take fright on *their* arrival (lit. before them)'
(22)　　*...ar a shon muintir an oileáin a dhíol na líonta a bhí acu* (Ky)
　　　　'...despite the people of the island selling the nets which they had'
(23)　　*...tar éis iad féin a shábháil na gcéata* (Ky)
　　　　'...after they themselves saved hundreds'
(24)　　*Guígíg dom...Dia a thabhairt cabhair dom i gcomhair an bhóthair fhada* (Ky)
　　　　'Pray for me... that God will give help to me for the long road'

However, there is also another, somewhat similar order recorded for Connemara where the object does not precede the verbal noun (see de Bhaldraithe 1948:478):

(25) *Ní maith liom thú déanamh fírinne dhó* (Cf)
'I don't like you speaking the truth to him'
(26) *Dúirt sé seo muid a cuir Gaeilge ar a' gcuid ainmneacha* (Cf)
'This fellow told us to translate our names to Irish' (lit. to put Irish on our names)

The apparently sporadic use of *a* (without lenition) in this order is strange. Although it is not realized as /əg'/ before vowels, it would seem to be an intrusion of *ag* from the progressive construction.

11.1.1(iii) *Discussion of word order and the use of* **a** *+ lenition.* The fact that the object precedes the verb is strange for Irish. It is probably best to regard the verbal noun as being moved to the right of the object in this construction. What is noteworthy is that the usage of *a* + lenition constitutes a dialectal difference. On the one hand, in Munster and Connacht a simple rule operates; where either the subject or the object (i.e. any noun phrase) precedes the verbal noun within these non-finite constructions *a* + lenition is employed. In (27) the subject precedes the verbal noun, in (28) the subject and object precede the verbal noun and in (29) the object precedes the verbal noun:

(27) *Conas a ba mhaith leis an bhliain a theacht air* (M)
'How would he like the year to find him'
(28) *...giúiléidí...ná teastódh uaidh Sasanach nó Éireannaach nó Eskimo iad a fheiscint* (M)
'...implements...that he wouldn't want either an Englishman or an Irishman or an Eskimo to see them'
(29) *Ba mhaith leis é a cheistiú* (M)
'He would like to question him'

On the other hand, in Donegal the employment of *a* + lenition depends on the transitivity of the verb from which the verbal noun is derived. Where the verbal noun is derived from a transitive verb, *a* + lenition is employed. In (30) the object precedes the verbal noun and in (31) the subject and object precede the verbal noun:

(30) *Ba mhaith liom an doras a phéinteáil* (D)
'I would like to paint the door'
(31) *Ba mhaith liom sibh an doras a phéinteáil* (D)
'I would like you to paint the door'

258 *Modern Irish: grammatical structure and dialectal variation*

However, where the verbal noun is derived from an intransitive verb, *a* + lenition is not used, even when there is a preceding subject:

(32) *B'fhearr liom tú fanacht sa bhaile inniu* (D)
 'I would rather you remain at home today'
(33) *Níor mhaith leo na mic pósadh ró-óg* (D)
 'They wouldn't like the sons to marry too young'
(34) *Ba mhaith liom tú cóiriú go deas* (D)
 'I would like you to dress nicely'

It is worth noting that, since in Donegal a subject occurs frequently (and often without an accompanying object) before a verbal noun, the non-employment of *a* + lenition serves to avoid ambiguity in the case of verbs such as *pósadh* 'marry', *cóiriú* 'dress' which can be either transitive or intransitive. In this way, there is a clear distinction between the intransitive (35) and the transitive (36):

(35) *Ba mhaith liom tú pósadh* (D)
 'I would like you to marry'
(36) *Ba mhaith liom tú a phósadh* (D)
 'I would like to marry you'

There is another important case where the object follows the verbal noun in a verbal noun phrase. This is seen in examples such as:

(37) *Ba mhaith leis a dhéanamh amach cé a bhí ann aréir* (C)
 'He would like to discover who was there last night'
(38) *Ní hionann é sin is a thuiscint nach fiú é* (C)
 'That is not the same as understanding that it isn't worth it'

In examples such as (37) and (38) *a* + lenition is the rule even though the verbal noun of the complementized phrase does not move to the right of its object where that object is an embedded question or a finite complementation. Somehow, the syntactic completeness of objects such as *cé a bhí ann aréir?* 'who was there last night' or *nach fiú é* 'that it isn't worth it' inhibit the rightward movement of the verbal noun. This is presumably also part of the tendency to keep cumbersome elements towards the end of a sentence. There is a specific group of verbal nouns involved here which includes such verbs as *fáil amach* 'find out', *fiafraí* 'enquire', *rá* 'say', *dearbhú* 'confirm', *cruthú* 'prove', *crei(s)diúint* (etc.) 'believe'. We might term them verbs of enquiring and verbs of perception/affirmation which take object complements [see 11.1.2(ii) below]. In Munster prolepsis is frequent here and is expressed by the combination of *do* 'to' and the possessive pronoun *a* 'its' which combines as *(dh)á* 'to its'. In the examples which follow, the proleptic pronoun is not italicized and word for word translations are given:

(39) *Bhí siad* á *rá gur ...* (M)
      (were they at its saying that...)
      'They were saying that ...'

(40) *Níor aon chabhair a bheith* á *fhiafraí cad a mhairbh é* (M)
      (was not any help to be at its asking what thing that killed him)
      'It was no help to (be) ask(ing) what killed him'

Prolepsis apparently does not occur following a modal verb, e.g:

(41) *Caithfi mé a rá go raibh sí chomh muar sin do chníopaire* (M)
      (must I to say that was she as great an amount that of a miser)
      'I must say that she was so great a miser'

In Donegal, the use of *a* + lenition seems to be optional. Examples (42) and (43) do not show *a* + lenition and contrast with (44) and (45) which do:

(42) *Ní raibh siad ariamh ábalta tuigbheáil caidé a bheadh siad a rá* (D)
      'They were never able to understand what they would be saying'

(43) *Dhiúltaigh siad creidbheáil go bhfuil an domhan cruinn* (D)
      'They refused to believe that the world is round'

(44) *I n-áit a thuigbheáil gur créatúr leamh ... a bhí ann* (D)
      'Instead of understanding that he was an insipid ... poor fellow'

(45) *Is doiligh a chreidbheáil gurab é sin a' dearcadh atá ag muintir a' bhaile seo* (D)
      'It is difficult to believe that this is the outlook which the people of this town(land) have'

Interestingly, the object may follow the verbal noun of a verbal noun phrase in a similar fashion in a semi-negative or 'only' construction [see 9.2.9(iii)] in Donegal:

(46)   ...*agus ní raibh muid a fhaghail acht an beagán* (D)
       '...and we were getting only a little'
(47)   ...*an aois nach mbíonn daoine a iarraidh ach duine éisteacht leo* (D)
       '...the age when people want only someone to listen to them'

11.1.2 Syntactic functions of the complement

11.1.2(i) *Subject complements*.

Figure 11.2 Two types of subject complements

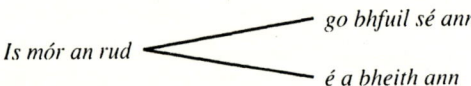

'It is a great thing that he is there'

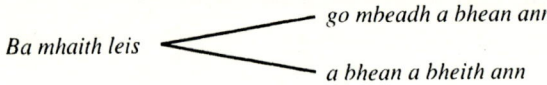

'He would like his wife to be there'

Figure 11.2 illustrates sentences where both finite and verbal noun phrases function as the subject. In examples (48) and (49) only a verbal noun phrase can serve as subject:

(48)   *Chinn orm an chloch a chorraí* (C)
       '[It] was too much for me/I failed to move the stone'
(49)   *Teastaíonn uaim imeacht* (C)
       'I want to leave'

A non-sentential subject is also possible in all of the examples. It is possible, for instance, to substitute a noun or pronoun for the finite (e.g. *go bhfuil sé ann* 'that he is there') or verbal noun phrases (e.g. *é a bheith ann* 'he to be there') in the first example in Figure 11.2:

(50)   *Is mór an rud an oiread sin féin* (C)
       'Even that much is a great thing'

A similar substitution is possible in the case of (48). The different position of the subject in *an chloch a chorraí* 'to move the stone' in (48) and the subject *sé* 'it' in (51) is explained by extraposition (see 11.1.3):

(51) *Chinn sé orm* (C)
'I failed to do it'

A significant development, however, is a certain tendency to allow a proleptic use of a pronoun so that there are examples such as:

(52) *Is é an trua(í) é nach raibh sibh ann* (C)
(is it the pity it that not were you there)
'It is a pity you were not there'

In other words *nach raibh sibh ann* is the subject complement, the second *é* is proleptic and *Is é an truaí é* follows the pattern of the identificatory copula sentence [see 10.3.1(ii)].

Furthermore, in predicates where the copula is not involved, in Cois Fhairrge at any rate, a proleptic pronoun would seem to be the norm when a progressive construction is employed:

(53) *Tá sé ag cinnt orm an chloch a chorraí* (Cf)
(is it at surpassing on me the stone to move)
'I am failing to move the stone'

As *an chloch a chorraí* 'to move the stone' is the grammatical subject, the use of *sé* 'it' is proleptic. This is paralleled by the use of prolepsis with the so-called 'epistemic' modals [see 11.2.2(ii)].

11.1.2(ii) *Object complements.*

(54) *Dúirt sé é a dhéanamh*
'He said to do it'
(55) *Níor shamhlaigh sé go mbeadh sí ann*
'He didn't even imagine that she'd be there'
(56) *Chruthaigh sé nach raibh taibhse ann*
'He proved that there wasn't a ghost there'

Broadly speaking object complements follow verbs of saying, thinking, perceiving, imagining, recommending, confirming, etc. such as *rá* 'say' (C) *síleachtáil* (C)/*sílstean* (Gd) 'think' , *inseacht*/*inse* (Gd) 'tell', *fuagairt* (C)/ *fógairt* (M) 'proclaim, demand', *cuimhn*/*iú*/*eamh*, *smaoin*/*iú*/*eamh* 'think', *crei(s)diúint* etc. 'believe', *aireachtáil* 'feeling', *samhlú* 'imagine', *cruthú* 'prove', *(tai)spáin* etc. 'show', *moladh* 'recommend', *socrú* 'settle, arrange, decide', *dearbhú* 'confirm'.

The use of a finite complement or a verbal noun complement depends on the particular verb. The majority of those listed take a finite complement. However, verbs which are goal orientated, e.g. *moladh* 'recommend' and *socrú* 'arrange', may be followed by either type of complement. Furthermore, verbs such as *rá* 'say' and *síleachtáil*/*sílstean* 'think' are followed by a finite complement when they are used in a sense that is not goal orientated but take a verbal noun complement when they are goal orientated:

(57)　*Dúirt sé go raibh sé go maith* (Gd)
　　　'He said that he was well'
(58)　*Dúirt sé an doras a phéinteáil* (Gd)
　　　'He said to paint the door'
(59)　*Shíl Máirtín go raibh an bhó tinn* (C)
　　　'Máirtín thought that the cow was sick'
(60)　*Shíl sé é a dhéanamh*
　　　'He intended to do it'

11.1.2(iii) *Complement as objects of prepositions.* Firstly there are complements which seem to be in apposition to a preposition which is an obligatory part of a verb + preposition idiom. In many prepositions such as *faoi*, *dhe*, *ar*/*air* (both pronounced /erʹ/) etc. the third person singular and the basic form of the preposition are indistinguishable. However, a Munster example (where there is a distinction between *chuig* 'toward' and *chuige* 'toward him/it') indicates that the complement is in apposition to the preposition:

(61)　*D'fhéach sé chuige go mbeadh sé in am* (M)
　　　'He saw to it that he would be in time'

Secondly, there are complements which have no overt preposition:

(62)　*Rinne sé dearmad an doras a phéinteáil*
　　　'He forgot to paint the door'

On the other hand, if the complement phrase *an doras a phéinteáil* is replaced by a simple noun phrase a preposition is needed:

(63)   *Rinne sé dearmad den doras* (C)
       'He forgot the door'
(64)   *Rinne sé dearmad dhe* (C)
       'He forgot it'

Therefore, there would seem to be an underlying preposition even though it does not surface before a verbal noun-type complement. This is further confirmed by the fact that (before a finite-type complement in the case of *dhe*) the preposition may optionally show itself:

(65)   *Rinne sé dearmad (dhe) go raibh an doras le péinteáil* (C)
       'He forgot that the door was to be painted'

Although a Connemara example is used in discussing this type of complement the principle is the same for dialects using *ar* 'on' rather than *dhe* 'off' in this idiom.

This optional use of a preposition is particularly prevalent among a group of verbs which express intention or commencement. This leads to a degree of difference between the dialects. Munster dialects seem often to have a preposition *ar*:

(66)   *Bheartaigh sé ar imeacht* (M)
       'He determined to go off'
(67)   *Shocraigh sé ar imeacht* (M)
       'He decided to go off'
(68)   *Bhíos ag tosnú ar rud éigin a dhéanamh* (M)
       'I was beginning to do something'
(69)   *Do phléasc a raibh istigh ar gháirí* (M)
       'All who were inside burst into laughter'

The position in Connacht and Donegal is somewhat more complex. With verbs of intention, the preposition is in some cases optional, as for instance the case of the verb *brath* 'intend' in Cois Fhairrge:

(70)   *...an cró atá tú ag brath ar a dhéanamh* (Cf)
       '...the outhouse you are intending to build'

(71)   ...*an cineál a bhí mé ag brath a cheannacht* (Cf)
       '...the type I was intending to buy'

The use of *ar* with *brath* 'intend' and *smaoitiú* 'intend' is also optional in Donegal. The verbs *beartú* and *socrú* do not have an underlying preposition. Another example is the optional use in Cois Fhairrge or Donegal of *le* with *súil* 'expect':

(72)   *Bhí mé ag súil (le) thú a fheiceál* (Gd)
       'I was expecting to see you'

The main verb expressing commencement *tosú/tosaí*, *toiseacht* (D), *tosnú* (M) 'begin' shows the preposition *ar* when the complement has a simple noun phrase: *Thosaigh (Thoisigh) sé air* 'He began it'. Nevertheless, verbs of commencement belong with a group of verbs which are followed by a construction similar to the progressive in Connemara and by *a* + lenition in Donegal [see 11.1.6(ii)].

In many idioms which are composed of the substantive verb, a noun and a preposition and which often express a psychological state there would also appear to be an underlying preposition:

Table 11.1 *Some idioms involving substantive verb with preposition* ar *'on'*

Tá brón orm 'I am sorry'	
Tá áthas orm 'I am glad'	*go bhfuil sé ann* / *faoi* 'that he is there' / 'about it'
Tá iontas orm 'I am amazed'	

In idioms involving the substantive verb and the preposition *ar* 'on' where pronominalization, questioning or clefting occur a preposition is employed:

(73)   *Tá brón orm faoi* (C)
       'I am sorry about it'
(74)   *Cé faoi a bhfuil áthas orm?* (C)
       'What am I glad about?'

(75) Séard a bhfuil iontas orm faoi... (C)
      'What I am glad about is...'

The above idioms with the preposition *ar* 'on' are somehow in contrast to idioms using the preposition *ag* 'it', which are in some way less passive:

(76) Tá a fhios agam go bhfuil sé ann
      'I know that he is there'
(77) Tá súil agam go bhfuil sé ann
      'I hope that he is there'

The more active nature of the idiom with *ag* 'at' is underlined by the fact that in Cois Fhairrge (see de Bhaldraithe 1956-7a:125-37) both examples (78) and (79) occur:

(78) Tá aimhreas orm nach dtiocfaidh sé (Cf)
      'I am afraid he won't come'
(79) Tá aimhreas agam nach dtiocfaidh sé (Cf)
      'I rather think he won't come'

This less passive quality is further highlighted by the use of *ag* rather than *ar* when followed by a prepositional phrase which does not in turn precede a finite clause:

(80) Tá faitíos orm (C)
      'I am afraid'
(81) Tá faitíos agam roimh na daoine sin (C)
      'I am afraid of those people'
(82) Bhí eagla orm (M)
      'I was afraid'
(83) Tá eagla agam roimis na fir (M)
      'I am afraid of the men'
(84) Tá éad orm (C)
      'I am jealous'
(85) Beidh éad agam leat (C)
      'I will be jealous of you'
(86) Tá formad orm (M)
      'I am envious'

(87)   Tá formad aici léi (M)
       'She is envious of her'

This change from *ar* 'on' to *ag* 'at' is common in Connacht and in Munster. There is, however, some fluctuation in the usage (see Wagner 1958:250). A counter-example for Munster is:

(88)   agus eagla mo dhóthain orm roimpe go mbeidh an fear is fearr aice uaim (M)
       'And I (am) quite afraid of her that she will take the best man from me"

It is probably this more active quality that causes the commonest *ag*-idiom *tá a fhios (ag)* 'know' to be reinterpreted as a verb both in responses and pronominalization, questioning and clefting:

(89)   An bhfuil a fhios agat go bhfuil sé sásta?
       'Do you know that he is content?'
       Tá a fhios (C,D) / Tá a fhios-a (M)
       'I do'
(90)   Tá a fhios agam é (C)
       'I know it'
(91)   Céard atá a fhios aige? (C)
       'What does he know?'
(92)   Séard atá fhios aige... (C)
       'What he knows is...'

Indeed it is possible to use the idiom with a direct object noun in the sense 'to know of':

(93)   Tá a fhios agam an leaid sin
       'I know of that fellow'

There is an older use of *tá a fhios* 'know' where it is still felt as a noun phrase. In that usage the noun *fios* 'knowledge' in *a fhios* 'its knowledge' may be followed by the adjective *sin* 'that'. This older practice is still current among middle-aged speakers in for example Inishmaan and in Dunquin:

(94)   Níl a fhios sin agam (Im)
       (lit. That knowledge is not at me)
       'I don't know that'

(95) *Tá a fhios san agam* (Dn)
'I know that'

In Gweedore the idiom *tá súil's agam* 'I hope' shows a similar tendency only in the case of pronominalization:

(96) *Tá súil's agam go mbeidh sé anseo* (Gd)
'I hope he will be here'
Tá súil's agam go mbeidh / Tá súil's agam é (Gd)
'I hope it will / I hope so'

11.1.2(iv) Predicative adjective complements. Certain adjectives are connected with a following complement. A preposition intervenes between the adjective and the complement:

(97) *Bhí sí sách dona lena leithéid(e) a dhéanamh* (C)
'She was bad enough to do the likes of that'

11.1.2(v) Adverbial complements. There are many subordinating conjunctions which have adverbial force and which modify the sentence as a whole:

(98) *Ní dheachaidh mé ann de bharr go raibh mé tinn/de bharr mé a bheith tinn* (C)
'I didn't go there because I was sick/on account of my being sick'
(99) *Chuaigh mé ann cé go raibh mé tinn* (C)
'I went there even though I was sick'
(100) *Ní dheachaigh mé ann ag mé a bheith tinn* (C)
'I didn't go there because I was sick'

A subordinating conjunction such as *de bharr* 'because' (other examples would include Munster *toisc* 'because' and Donegal *siocair* 'because') can take either a finite or verbal noun-type complement. Others are confined to either a finite complement (e.g. *cé* 'although') or to a verbal noun complement (e.g. *ag* 'because').

Some of these subordinating conjunctions are partly nouns, (e.g. *toisc* 'circumstance', *siocair* 'cause') while others (e.g. *de bharr* 'off + top') are compounds made up of a preposition and a noun. They retain a certain nominal quality, as can be seen in the phrases *de bharr an tinnis* 'on account of the sickness', *de mo bharr* 'on my account', *dá bharr sin* 'on that account, therefore' where the following definite noun is in the genitive case (i.e. *tinnis* gen. of *tinneas* 'sickness') and a possessive adjective (i.e. *mo* 'my') is required rather than a pronoun.

There are different types of adverbial phrases which involve the type of complementation discussed in this chapter. There is a deal of variation within the dialects. We may look briefly here at five of the main types:

(a) Causal
(b) Concessive
(c) Final
(d) Temporal
(e) Conditional

Adverbial phrases which require other embedding processes are described in 12.1.4. Many of those which are discussed here allow an intrusive *is* 'and'; this is also dealt with in 12.4.1.

11.1.2(v)1 *Causal:* It would seem from the discussion above that the causal adverbials, i.e. *toisc, siocair* 'because' etc., in some cases, permit a choice between finite and verbal noun complementation.

It is not possible to give a complete list of causal adverbials here. However, *siocair, 'thairbhe, cionn's, le linn* 'because' are among the most frequent in Gweedore. The first three allow either complementation; the fourth, at any rate, allows verbal noun complements. In Cois Fhairrge *d e bharr* 'because' may take either type of complementation; among the most frequent which require finite complementation are *mar gheall air, i ngeall air, as ucht, ar son, faoi, lá, mar, ó tharla* 'because, since' etc. In Dunquin *toisc* 'because' takes either type of complementation, while among the commonest which require finite complementation are *ón uair, ós rud é, ó tharlaigh, i dtaobh* and *lá* 'because'. After the adverbial phrase *mar* 'because' it is possible in all major dialects to have either finite complementation or to have no complementizer and a non-embedded sentence. In example (101) there is complementation whereas in (102) there is none:

(101)   *Bhí faitcheas roimhe mar go raibh sé cineál taghdach thar dhuine eile*   (C)
'People were afraid of him because he was somewhat quick tempered compared with others'

(102) *Ní mórán is fiú a bheith ag fáil annró uathab, mar níl aon phinginn orthab* (C)
'It is not worth much to suffer the hardship they cause, as there isn't a penny to be earned from them'

After some causal adverbials such as Cois Fhairrge *arae* 'because' no complementizer or embedded sentence is allowed:

(103) *Níorbh fhéidir é a dhéanamh arae bhí an uair go dona* (Cf)
'One couldn't do it as the weather was bad'

11.1.2(v)2 *Concessive*: The concessive adverbials seem more frequently to require finite complementation, though there is some choice involved. The commonest concessive adverbials in Donegal are *cé*, *gí* 'although' which take finite complementation, *oinneoin* 'although' which takes either type and *i ndéidh* 'although' which requires verbal noun complementation. Among those found in Cois Fhairrge are *cé*, *gí*, *(é) amháin*, *cé is moite* 'although' which take finite complementation; *oinneoin*, *thar éis* 'although, despite the fact' which can take either type and *i ndiaidh* 'although' which takes verbal noun complementation. In Dunquin *cé,* which takes finite complementation, is the most frequent concessive adverbial.

11.1.2(v)3 *Final:* Among the commonest final adverbials in Donegal are: *sa dóigh* 'in order to', which requires finite complementation, *le* 'in order to' which can take either type and *fá choinne* 'in order to' which requires a verbal noun complementation. In Cois Fhairrge among the most frequent are *i gcruth's*, *i riocht's*, *sa gcaoi*, *nós* 'in order to' and these take finite complementation while *le* 'in order to' can take either type. In Dunquin the commonest are *d'fhonn is*, *súil is*, *sa tslí's* 'in order to', which take finite complementation, and *d'fhonn* and *chun*, which take either type.

For the use of *go/nach* etc. without any preceding adverbial see 12.1.4(ii).

11.1.2(v)4 *Temporal:* The majority of temporal adverbials are followed by relative clauses. However *go dtí* 'until' is found in most dialects followed by a finite complement. Another example is Cois Fhairrge *(ar) feadh* 'as soon as' followed by a verbal noun complement.

For the use of *go/nach* etc. without any preceding adverbial see 12.1.4(i).

11.1.2(v)5 *Conditional:* Those conditional adverbials which do not take a different type of embedding (see 12.1.2) seem in general to require a finite complementation. Examples are Gweedore *'fhad is* 'as long as' or Cois Fhairrge *ar chuntar, i gcleithiúnas* 'on condition that'.

11.1.3 Extraposition

11.1.3(i) *General discussion.* There are obvious similarities between a complement and a noun phrase inasmuch as they both function in the same syntactic roles . Furthermore, they both allow pseudo-clefts and so-called '*wh*-questions':

(104)   *Dúirt sé liom go raibh an scéal fíor*
        'He said that the story was true'
(105)   *Dúirt sé an fhírinne liom*
        'He told me the truth'
(106)   *'Séard [Sé rud* (M)/*Siod*(D)] *dúirt sé liom go raibh an scéal fíor*
        'What he said to me was that the story was true'
(107)   *'Séard [Sé rud*(M)/*Siod*(D)] *dúirt sé liom an fhírinne*
        'What he said to me was the truth'
(108)   *Céard [Cad*(M)/*Goidé*(D)] *dúirt sé liom?*
        'What did he say to me?'

Despite these similarities there is a basic difference in the word order. Where the sentence has a noun as object the normal word order obtains: on the other hand, where the sentence has a complement object, the complement object is extraposed, that is moved to the right of the pronoun object:

Figure 11.3 Extraposition of complement object

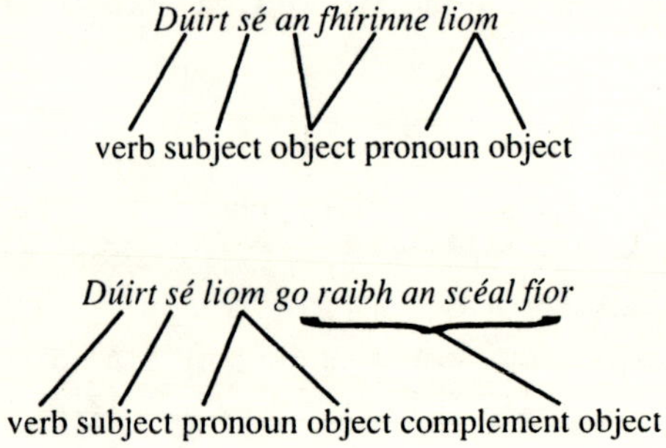

Dúirt sé an fhírinne liom
verb subject object pronoun object

Dúirt sé liom go raibh an scéal fíor
verb subject pronoun object complement object

It must be noted that extraposition is part of the general tendency to move large or unwieldy elements of a sentence to the right (see 9.2.1(iii)).

11.1.3(ii) *Extraposed subject complements*:

(109)   *Chinn orm é a dhéanamh* (C)
        'I failed to do it'
(110)   *Chlis air an doras a dhúnadh* (C)
        'He failed to shut the door'

In these examples, the complements *é a dhéanamh, an doras a dhúnadh* must be interpreted as the subject. However, in the following example it is possible for the pronoun *sé* 'it' to be used proleptically in the subject position and to act as the semantic subject:

(111)   *Bhí* sé *cinnte air í a fháil* (C)
        (was *it* failed on him to get it)
        'He said that he had failed to get it'

The occurrence or non-occurrence of this proleptic *sé* varies not only (in some cases) from one verb type to another but also creates certain differences between the major dialects.

There are two semantic categories of verbs involved here. Firstly, there is what may be described as goal-orientated verbs and verbal phrases. Secondly, there are verbs expressing appearances.

11.1.3(ii)1 *Goal-orientated verbs and verbal phrases:* This general category covers verbs of:

(a)   obligation: *caithfidh* 'must', *tá air* 'is obliged', *is gá (do)* 'it is necessary', *teastaíonn uaidh* 'needs to', *tá aige le* (D), *ní foláir* (etc.) (M,C) 'it is necessary' *níor mhór* 'must, has to'
(b)   intention: *tá faoi* (Cn) 'intends', *tá sé ar intinn agam* (C,D) 'intend'
(c)   ability to achieve: *is féidir (le)* (C,M)'can', *tig le* 'can', *thig le* 'can', *féadann do* 'can' *rachadh sé rite le* (C,D), *raghadh sé dian ar* (M) 'It would be difficult for'
(d)   success or failure: *éiríonn le* 'succeeds', *teipeann ar* (M) or *chuaigh de* (M) 'fails', *cinneann ar* (C), *cliseann ar* (C) 'fails' and more marginally in the verbs expressing a happening: *éiríonn do* or *tarlaíonn do* 'happens to'

272 *Modern Irish: grammatical structure and dialectal variation*

11.1.3(ii)2 *Appearance verbs*

(a)   seeming, e.g.: *breathnaíonn sé* (C) 'seems'
(b)   seeming good, liking, e.g.: *taithníonn le* (C,M) 'likes'

In order to elucidate the differences between the major dialects it will be necessary to examine in more detail some of the subtypes within the general categories.

The modal verb *caithfidh* 'must' stands out among the other verbs and verbal phrases of the subtype expressing obligation because a proleptic pronoun is allowed. In the subsequent discussion any proleptic pronoun is in Roman type:

(112)   *Caithfidh* sé *go bhfuair tú coláiste* (C)
       (lit. It must be that you got college) 'It must be that you are college educated / You must be college educated'
(113)   *Bhí ortha* é *a thabhairt do na bonnachaí* (C)
       'They had to make off as fast as they could'
(114)   *Ní gá go bhfuil sé fíor* (C)
       'It need not be true'

There seems to be a clear-cut distinction here between Munster and the other dialects. While the proleptic pronoun is the norm elsewhere, this is not so in Munster:

(115)   *Caithfidh go bhfuil an fear ann* (M)
       'It must be that the man is there / The man must be there'

Where verbs and verbal phrases expressing intention are concerned prolepsis varies from expression to expression even within a dialect and is difficult to predict:

(116)   *Tá faoi an bóthar a thabhairt dom* (Cn)
       'He intends to sack me'
(117)   *Tá sé ar intinn agam* é *a scríobh* (Cn)
       (is *it* on mind at me it to write)
       'I intend to write it'

It may be the case that among the verbs or verbal phrases describing ability to achieve, those expressing modality do not show prolepsis while those expressing difficulty in achievement do so:

(118) *Féadann duit an t-airgead a dhíol anois* (D)
       'You can pay the money now'
(119) *Thiocfadh leis go bhfuil sé fíor* (D)
       'It could be true'
(120) *Thiocfadh/Rachadh* sé *rite leat é a dhéanamh* (D,C)
       (would come/would go *it* tightly for you it to do)
       'It would be most difficult to do it'

The situation with verbs or verbal phrases describing success or failure is more complex: while *éirí le* 'succeed' does not show prolepsis and neither does *theip ar* or *chuaigh de* 'failed' in Munster, the pronoun appears to be optional in the case of *chinn ar/chlis ar* 'failed' in Connacht or *sháraigh ar* 'failed' in Donegal:

(121) *D'éirigh liom é a dhéanamh*
       'I succeeded in doing it'
(122) *Theip orm/Chuaigh díom é a dhéanamh* (M)
       'I failed to do it'
(123) *Chinn/Chlis* sé *orm* (C)
       'I failed to do it'
(124) *Sháraigh* sé *orm eolas a bhaint aisti* (D)
       (failed *it* on me knowledge to extract from her)
       'I failed to extract any information from her'

The verbal phrases *tarlú/éirí dó* 'happened to' do not have a proleptic pronoun:

(125) *D'éirigh/Tharla dhó go raibh sé ag teacht an bóthar seo* (M)
       'He happened to be coming this road'

Among the verbs of appearance the Connacht *breathnú* 'appear' requires prolepsis:

(126) *Breathnaíonn* sé *go bhfuil sé sásta* (M)
       (looks *it* that is he content)
       'He seems to be satisfied'

This usage with *breathnaíonn* is possibly, from a synchronic point of view, a late development (modelled on English), replacing such expressions as *is cosúil/tá an chuma air* 'it seems'. This would explain the mandatory prolepsis. On the other hand, *taithníonn le* 'appears good to, likes' normally has prolepsis in Connacht, while Munster shows some examples of what is historically the older system:

(127) *Taithníonn sé liom a bheith anseo* (C)
'I like to be here'
(128) *Dhá mba ná taithnfadh leis an chóir a cuirfí air...* (M)
'If he shouldn't like the way he was treated...'

Apart from the two semantic categories of verbs and verbal phrases which have been outlined, it must be noted that where complementation follows a full sentence prolepsis is usual:

(129) *Bhí sé ráite go mbíodh sí ag athchogaint ar nós na bó* (M)
(was *it* said that used be she at chewing the cud like the cow)
'It is said that she was chewing the cud like a cow'
(130) *...dhein sé dochar dom mé a bheith im' ghamhain seanabhó...* (M)
(did *it* harm to me to be in my calf of an old cow)
'...it harmed me that I was the calf of an old cow'

This is true for all the major dialects. Nevertheless, prolepsis is optional in Munster in a sentence where the substantive verb is followed by a verbal adjective, provided the agent is marked by a prepositional phrase. In example (131) there is prolepsis, while in (132) and (133) there is none:

(131) *Bhí sé tugtha fé ndeara aice go dtagadh dath as an stuif nuair a fliuchtaí é* (M)
(was *it* noticed by him that used come colour out of the material when we used to wet it)
'He had noticed that the material used to lose its colour when one used to wet it'
(132) *Fé mar tá luaite agam i dtaobh na n-óg-bhan so gur baolach ná raghadh mo ghnóthaí chun cinn...* (M)
'As I have mentioned concerning these young women, I am afraid my affairs won't go ahead...'
(133) *...do bhí glaoite aige 'go raibh sé seo ar an dtaobh thall'* (M)
'...he had called out that this one was over on the far side'

From a diachronic point of view the use of prolepsis is an innovation and Munster, more than other dialects, inclines to preserve the older system. Contrariwise, Connacht and Donegal show a definite tendency toward prolepsis.

11.1.3(iii) *Extraposed object complements.* An object complement is extraposed beyond an indirect object:

(134) D'inis sé an scéal dhom
       'He told the story to me'
(135) D'inis sé dhom go raibh an doras briste
       'He told me that the door was broken'

The noun object *an scéal* 'the story' precedes the indirect object *dhom* 'to me' while the object complement *go raibh an doras briste* 'that the door was broken' is extraposed. Extraposition also occurs with a verbal idiom composed of a verb and a prepositional phrase:

(136) Thug sé an bhean faoi deara (C)
       'He noticed the woman'
(137) Thug sé faoi deara go raibh an bhean ann (C)
       'He noticed that the woman was there'

The extraposition of object complements does not seem to entail any variation among the dialects.

11.1.4 Verbal noun complement as a unit
There can be little doubt that the verbal noun complement remains a syntactic unit:

(138) Tá sé ag iarraidh an doras a phéinteáil
       'He wants to paint the door'

In example (138) the complement *an doras a phéinteáil* 'to paint the door' as a whole is the object. This is amply demonstrated by the fact that it is negatived by placing *gan* 'without' before the entire unit *gan an doras a phéinteáil* 'not to paint the door'.

The unit-like quality of the complement is further confirmed by an example such as:

(139)   Dúirt sé liom an doras a phéinteáil
        'He told me to paint the door'

In (139) the complement *an doras a phéinteáil* 'to paint the door' is extraposed in its entirety.

There is clearly a tendency for the verbal noun complement to become more independent of the matrix sentence. This bias can be seen in the use of conjunctions and prepositions in the following examples:

(140)   Iad tar éis bídh do bheith caite acu (M)
        'They after eating food'
(141)   Tar éis an duine uasal, an Bairéadach, d'fhágaint an oileáin (M)
        'After the gentleman, Bairéad, had left the island'
(142)   Toisc na gaoithe do bheith amach (M)
        'Since the wind was outwards'
(143)   toisc an ainm aerach a bheith ar an áit (M)
        'because of the eerie name being on the place'
(144)   chun na súlach ribe a chur orthu (M)
        'in order to ensnare them'
(145)   chun a bholg a líonadh (M)
        'in order to fill his belly'

In (140), (142) and (144) following *tar éis* 'after', *toisc* 'because' and *chun* 'in order to' the nouns *bia* 'food', *gaoth* 'wind' and *súil* 'eye' are in the genitive. This indicates a weakening of the bond between the complement and the matrix sentence and it is also part of a process of denominalization of secondary prepositions originally consisting of a noun.

It is interesting to note that the bond was, at one stage, felt to be so close between the complement and the matrix sentence that on the change from the use of a possessive adjective to the use of a pronoun in verbal noun complements (see 11.1.5), the genitive transverses the pronoun and affects the following noun so that *chun é a mharaithe* 'in order to kill him' is an amalgam of *chun a mharaithe* (lit. to his killing [gen.]) and *chun é a mharú* (*chun* + verbal noun complement) both of which are found in Munster dialects.

A similar loosening of this bond is evident in the difference between example (146) and examples (147-9):

(146)   Ní raibh aon chuimhneamh ag éinne ar dhul abhaile (Ky)
        'Nobody had any thought of going home'

(147) *ag brath ar tosú* (Cf)
'intending to begin'
(148) *ag caint ar fanacht seachtain eile* (Cf)
'talking of remaining another week'
(149) *ag cuíneamh ar tig nó (a) dhéanamh* (Mk)
'thinking of building a new house'

The connection in examples (146-9) between the complement and the matrix sentence is apparently felt to be so tenuous that the normal lenition following *ar* 'on' does not apply.

11.1.5 Avoidance of possessive adjective in verbal noun complement
There is a continual drift in the dialects away from the use of a possessive adjective and towards the use of a pronoun:

Figure 11.4 Possessive adjectives/pronouns in verbal noun complement

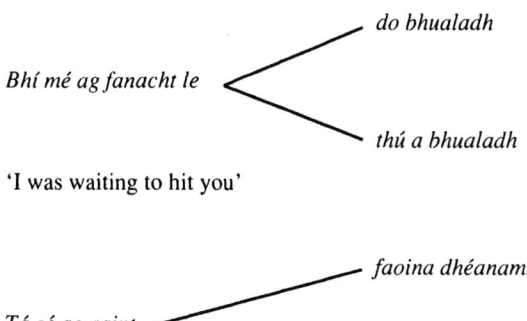

'I was waiting to hit you'

'He was talking of doing it'

In Figure 11.4 *do bualadh* 'your hitting' and *faoina dhéanamh* 'about its doing' show what is the (historically) older usage. While the possessive adjective is still optional following a preposition, in other circumstances it is now much less usual in speech. Although both (150) and (151) are still current in Gweedore, (151) now largely replaces (150):

(150) *Caithfidh mé a ghoil síos agus a chuartú* (Gd)
'I must go down and search for it'
(151) *Caithfidh mé a ghoil síos agus é a chuartú* (Gd)

11.1.6 Other types of verbal noun complement

The major type of verbal noun complement, where a noun phrase appears before the verbal noun, has been discussed. We must now consider some further types of verbal noun complement.

11.1.6(i) *Subjectless noun complements (following sensory verbs):* A verbal noun complement without a subject can follow, as if in apposition, the object of a verb of hearing or seeing, noticing etc:

(152)   *Chuala mé Bríd ag caint leis*
         'I heard Bríd speaking to him'
(153)   *Feicim [cím (M), t' ím (D), etc.] an bhean ag siúl síos an bóthar*
         'I see the woman walking down the road'
(154)   *Thug mé faoi deara [fé ndeara (M), fá dear (D)] ag imeacht é*
         'I noticed him going'

11.1.6(ii) *Verbal noun complements following verbs of motion in aspectual function (some of which express purpose):* A verbal noun complement without a subject can also occur after aspectual verbs of motion, as in examples (155-8):

(155)   *Thosaigh sé ag foghlaim Béarla* (C)
         'He began learning English'
(156)   *Coinníonn sé ag cur ceisteanna ort* (C)
         'He continues asking you questions'
(157)   *Sheasfá sa sneachta ag éisteacht léi* (C)
         'You would stand in the snow listening to her'
(158)   *Buailfidh mé ag siúlóid go dtraothfaidh mé mo bhéilí* (C)
         'I'll head off for a walk to digest my meal'

The complement may also follow these verbs in progressive construction:

(159)   *Tá cúr ag tosaí ag tíocht orthu* (C)
         'Froth is beginning to come on them'
(160)   *Níl sé ag goil ag déanamh leas do thada* (C)
         'It's not going to do any good for anything'

It is important to note here that we are dealing with the whole semantic spectrum of motion from commencement (ingressive aspect) (e.g. *tosaí* 'begin', *ag goil* 'going [with prospect of doing]', *bualadh* 'head off'), through continuation (continuative aspect) (e.g. *leanacht* 'continue', *coinneáil* 'keep on , continue') to ceasing (egressive aspect) (e.g. *stop, stad* 'stop, cease', *seasamh* 'stand') and including the verb *cur* 'put, send (in order to)'. Prepositions are also optionally retained in Connacht and Donegal after *leanacht* and *coinneáil(t)*:

(161) *Lean sé air/choinnigh sé air ag cur ceisteanna* (C)
'He continued asking questions'

It is in many ways not surprising that *ag* should be used with the verbal noun in this construction as it has, like the progressive, a certain aspectual quality. There are, however, considerable differences between the dialects. The examples given so far are from Connacht. In Munster a similar syntactic construction occurs:

(162) *Ragham ag fiach* (Ky)
'We'll go hunting'
(163) *Tháinig a athair ag triall air* (Ky)
'His father came for him'
(164) *Cuirtí ag beirbhiú í...* (Ky)
'It was put boiling...'
(165) *Do bhí m'athair ag dul ag iascach maidean ...* (Ky)
'My father was going fishing one morning...'

However, as verbs such as *tosnú ar* 'begin' [see verbs of commencement and intention, 11.1.2(iii)], *leanúint de* 'continue', *stad de, stop ó* 'cease' are followed by prepositions, it may be that verbs like *dul* 'go', *teacht* 'come' and *cur* 'put, send' retain in the above examples their basic meaning of motion and do not tend to become prospectives, as is the case in Connacht and Donegal.

In Donegal, on the other hand, all of the verbs of motion in aspectual function (some of which express purpose) are followed by *a* and lenition:

(166) *B'fhearr leis imeacht go Gleann Locha a chuartú poitín* (D)
'He preferred to go to Gleann Locha looking for poteen'
(167) *Ansin thug an t-iomlán acu a n-aghaidh ar Charn na Madadh a chaitheamh na bainse* (D)
'Then the whole lot of them set off for Carn na Madadh to consume the wedding breakfast'

280 *Modern Irish: grammatical structure and dialectal variation*

(168)   *Chuir sé a phéinteáil balla é* (D)
        'He put him to painting a wall'

Table 11.2 *Donegal verbs of motion in aspectual function*

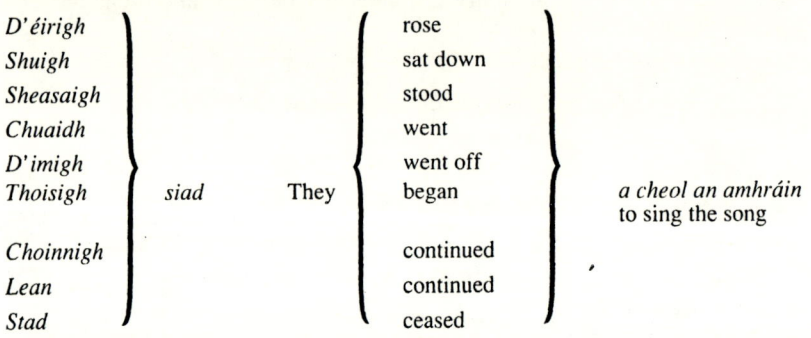

This *a* + lenition which is general in Donegal Irish is found in all the major dialects in the set phrase *a chodladh* 'asleep' (e.g. *Chuaigh sé a chodladh* 'He fell asleep'). Diachronically *a* is a reduced form of *do*, which still appears in the obligatory Munster *d'iarraidh* and the optional Cois Fhairrge form *d'iarraidh/ag iarraidh* 'wanting to'.

Occasionally in Donegal a preposition is retained before a noun phrase:

(169)   *Stad mé féin den tsníomhachán* (D)
        'I myself stopped spinning'

In general, we can say that the word order is the same in all dialects. However, the set of verbs of motion (some of which express purpose) are followed by *a* + lenition in Donegal. In Connacht *ag* is used rather than *a* + lenition and in the case of certain verbs there is an optional retention of a preposition:

(170)   *Choinnigh sé air ag ól* (C)
        'He continued drinking'
(171)   *Lean sé dó* (C)
        'He continued at it'
(172)   *Thosaigh sé ar 'argóint Oisín is Phádraig'* (C)
        'He started "The argument of Oisín and Pádraig"'

In Munster prepositions are largely retained (e.g. *Stop sé ó...* 'He ceased from...') except for basic verbs of motion (e.g. *dul* 'go', *teacht* 'coming') and this seems to block the development of a set of verbs of motion with an aspectual function.

11.1.7 Verbal noun complements identified by *do* 'to'

11.1.7(i) *Simultaneous to main verb.* Following *ag* 'at' or *ar* 'on' verbal noun complements occur where the subject is identified by *do* 'to/for'. This is found in all the major dialects:

(173) *Níor ith sé aon ghreim ag goil a chodladh dhó* (C)
'He didn't eat a bite going to bed'
(174) *Ar theacht ar ais dom, bhí fuadach croí orm* (C)
'On my coming back, my heart was palpitating'
(175) *Beidh Pádraig anseo ag imeacht domh* (D)
'Pádraig will be here when I go off'
(176) *Ar a ghoil isteach go teach na scoile dó, d'amharc sé...* (D)
'On going into the school, he looked...'
(177) *Do bhínn ar bog-mheisce gach oíche ag teacht abhaile dhom* (M)
'I used to be slightly drunk every night coming home'
(178) *Ar chloisint na cainte do Dhiarmaid, cuireann sé a cheann...* (M)
'On Diarmaid's hearing that talk, he puts his head...'
(179) *Ar caitheamh mo ghráinseáil bheag dom maidean lae, bhí súil...agam* (M)
'On consuming my small repast one morning, I had an eye...'

As can be observed in the above examples, although the subject marked by *do* tends to occur at the end of the complement, an adverbial phrase may occur after it.

The use of *ar* 'on' seems to be confined to where the main clause has either a past tense or a narrative use of the habitual [e.g.(178)] and this would concur with the fact that it has at least part of its origin in Old Irish *iar* (+ nasalization). The use of the preposition *ag* 'at', on the other hand, is not confined to the past.

Generally speaking, this syntax is more productive in Kerry, as is seen by the fact that it features with other prepositions such as *sa* 'in the':

(180) *Sa lorgaireacht di, is mála a thug sí léi* (Ky)
'In her searching, it is a bag she took'

(181)   Sa chaint dóibh, dúirt sé go mbeadh... (Ky)
        'During their talk, they said that... would be...'

Indeed there is no real distinction between verbal noun and an ordinary substantive in this type of syntax:

(182)   Um ard an tráthnóna sa tsráid Mheánach dúinn... (Ky)
        'In the mid-afternoon while we were on the Central street...'
(183)   Thug sí seáp reatha tré n-a buairt di agus do bhuail sí... (Ky)
        'In her grieving she made a dash and hit...'

The compound preposition *le linn* 'during' is also used with verbal noun complements and *do* and is found in Munster and Connacht:

(184)   Le linn casadh síos di chun na fairrge... (M)
        'When she was turning down to the sea...'
(185)   Le linn dom bheith go mo shearradh... (C)
        'While I was stretching myself...'

As well as in the construction with *do* to mark the subject, it is also possible in the case of *le linn* for the subject to appear before the verb:

(186)   Le linn mise a bheith im' bháb... (M)
        'When I was a baby...'

The greater use in Munster of *do* to identify the subject in verbal noun complements is also reflected by its employment in the copular idiom *Is ó Chiarraí do Pháid* 'Páid is from Kerry' [see 10.3.3(iii)].

11.1.7(ii) Prior to main verb. Following *th(ar) éis* (etc.) 'after' in Connacht, *tar éis* (etc.) in Munster and *i ndéidh* in Donegal, there are verbal noun complements where the subject is identified by *do*. The event described in the complement occurs shortly before that of the main clause:

(187)   Th' éis dona pubanna dúnadh, d'imigh muid abhaile (C)
        'After the pubs closed, we went off home'
(188)   Do chuir sé mórán déirce go dtí an Blascaod tar éis dul abhaile dho... (M)
        'He sent a lot of charity to the Blasket after he went home...'

(189) *Bhí sé anseo i ndéidh domhsa imeacht* (Gd)
'He was here after I went'

Besides the use of *do* with *tar éis* 'after' to introduce the subject, as seen above in the case of *le linn* 'during' [see example (186)], in Kerry at least, the subject may appear in the verbal noun complement:

(190) *Níorbh fhada tar éis an mhic d'imeacht gur tháinic...* (Ky)
'It wasn't long after the son went off till...came...'

In this example rather than *tar éis don mhac imeacht* (lit. 'after for the son to go off'), *mac* 'son' occurs in the verbal noun phrase *tar éis an mhic d'imeacht* (lit. 'after + the son (*genitive*) to go off').

Once again in Kerry the subject can appear followed by the rarer order of verbal noun preceding an object (see 11.1.1(ii)2):

(191) *Tar éis an duine uasal, an Bairéadach, d'fhágaint an oileáin, an Inid a bhí chugainn...* (Ky)
'After the gentleman, Bairéad, left the island, the coming Shrovetide...'

11.1.7(iii) *Subsequent to the main verb.* Following *roimh* 'before', verbal noun complements are found with *do* to identify the subject. The event described in the complement occurs subsequent to that of the main clause:

(192) *Ghlan mé an tábla roimh imeacht domh* (Gd)
'I cleaned the table before I went off'
(193) *Druid an fhuinneog roimh imeacht duit* (Gd)
'Close the window before you go off'

This construction is common in Donegal, but it appears not to be as common in other dialects though it may occur in Connacht.

It must be noted that these verbal noun complements which identify the subject with *do* 'to/for' belong for the most part in Munster and Connacht to a marked narrative style. The use of *théis/tar éis* etc. seems more colloquial. However, in Donegal, the usages with *ar* and *roimh* as well as *i ndéidh* are features of ordinary colloquial speech.

11.1.8 Complements subordinated by *agus* 'and'

There are three types of complements subordinated by *agus*: an absolute subject type, a verbal noun type and a substantive verb type (see Ó Siadhail 1984a:125-37).

11.1.8(i) *Absolute subject type.*

(194)   *Ní raibh mé ach aon bhliain déag d'aois nuair a mharbhaigh a chapall féin m'athair, agus é ag tíocht ó bhainis* (C)
'I was only eleven years of age when his own horse killed my father when he was coming from a wedding'

In this type the subject of the subordinated complement always appears, even if it features as a noun in the main clause. Furthermore it is perfectly possible to rewrite the subordinated complement in the above example as *agus bhí sé ag tíocht ó bhainis* 'and he was coming from a wedding'. In other words there is an underlying form of the substantive verb which has been deleted and under a basic rule the conjunctive pronouns (*tú*), *sé, sí, siad* are replaced by the disjunctive pronouns (*thú*), *é, í, iad* when they are not immediately preceded by a final verbal form. Negation, as in all verbal noun complementation, is effected by the use of *gan* 'without'.

Despite the straightforward explanation of the syntactic construction as the deletion of an underlying substantive verb, the semantic implications are more complex. Semantically, there are two classifications: temporal and non-temporal. The non-temporal class has further subcategories.

11.1.8(i)1 *Temporal*

(195)   *...agus é ag teacht abhaile*
'... when/while he was coming home'

11.1.8(i)2 *Non-temporal:* The following are the non-temporal uses:

(a)   Attendant circumstance
(b)   Equivalent of relative clause
(c)   Concessive
(d)   Causal

Those four usages are illustrated in (196-9) respectively:

(196) *Bhí Brian glanta leis agus é ag scríobadh a chinn agus é ag siomsán leis féin i dtaobh na mbróg* (C)
'Brian vanished, scratching his head and muttering something about the boots'
(197) *Píosa de chlár cearnógach péinne bhí mar mharc aice agus fáinne beag ina lár* (C)
'Her target was a square piece of pine board in the middle of which was a small ring'
(198) *Tá sé cinn de leitreacha pósta tugtha agam uaim cheana, agus gan an t-aon lánúin pósta agam féin fós* (C)
'I have given six letters of freedom already, while as yet I haven't married a single couple'
(199) *Bhí an lá chomh gearr sin is tú ag déanamh 'chuile bheantáil* (C)
'The day was so short since you were gallivanting around'

While all the above examples have a Connacht source, there are abundant examples of every type from all the dialects.

11.1.8(ii) *Verbal noun type*. The following are the verbal noun type uses:

(a) Causal
(b) Conditional

These two usages are exemplified in (200) and (201):

(200) *Ag spailpínteacht a bhí tú ó mhaidin agus codladh a bheith ort* (Cf)
'You were toiling since morning seeing you are sleepy'
(201) *Tabharfaidh sé cnáimh le creinneadh dhó is an tír sin a choisint* (Cf)
'It will give him plenty to do (if he is) to defend that country'

As distinct from the absolute type in (a) and (b) in the above list, the subject is often not present in the subordinated complement and is coreferential with a noun phrase in the subordinating clause. Nevertheless, there are examples where the subject is present:

(202) *Is dóigh gur dhíol agus é a bheith in Árainn* (Cf)
'I suppose that he did sell, as he was in Aran'

The appearance of the subject in the complement may however be explained by the fact that the subject is only implicit in the responsive: *gur dhíol (sé)* 'that he did sell'.

This verbal noun type would seem to be much less frequent than the absolute type. Although all previous examples of this phenomenon are from Cois Fhairrge, examples also occur in Kerry:

(203)   *Ní foláir nó tá cúis mhór éigint agat orm agus a bheith am' briseadh amach is amach ó sheirbhís Chríost* (Ky)
'You must have some serious case against me seeing you are forcing me to leave the service of Christ entirely'

This intrusive *nó* is further discussed in 12.4.2(ii). Finally in a double conditional clause with a hypothesis, the second condition may be subordinated by *agus* 'and' which is followed by a verbal noun complement [see 12.1.2(ii)].

11.1.8(iii) *Substantive verb type.*

(204)   *...bhíodh an fear ba threise agus a dhrom le deireadh an bháid* (M)
'...the strongest man had his back to the stern of the boat'
(205)   *Bhíodar go léir agus gan focal astu* (M)
'They were all speechless'

In this type, the complement which is subordinated by *agus* acts as complement to the substantive verb. This construction is perhaps most frequent in Munster.

11.1.9 Attributive use of verbal noun complements

The similarities between complements and nouns have already been discussed [see 11.1.2(i)]. Both the major type of verbal noun complement (where the object is prior to the verbal noun) and the subjectless verbal noun-type can be used attributively. It seems that the attributive use of the verbal noun complement with a preceding object is confined to Munster and is exemplified in (206-7):

(206)   *fear an airgid a dhéanamh* (M)
'the man to make money'
(207)   *Lá rabharta dob ea é agus lá feamnaí duibhe a bhaint* (M)
'It was a springtide day and a day for cutting a black (species of) seaweed'

Phrases with a subjectless verbal noun complement are exemplified in (208-11):

(208) *fear deasú cnámh* (C)
'a man who sets bones'
(209) *lucht déanta poitín* (C)
'makers of poteen'
(210) *fear díolta na bhfaochan* (C)
'the seller (man who) of periwinkles'
(211) *aimsir baint na bhfataí* (C)
'potato-digging time'

11.2 Modal verbs

11.2.1 Construction of modal verbs

Verbs and verbal phrases expressing a scale of necessity, obligation, ability, possibility and certainty can, from the point of view of make-up, be divided into four types (their occurrence in the dialects is discussed in 11.2.3).

Table 11.3 *Types of modal verbs*

theoretically fully inflectable verbs	theoretically fully inflectable verbs + prepositional phrase
Caithfidh mé 'I must' *Féadfaidh mé* 'I can/ may' *Ghlacfainn* 'I would have to'	*T(h)ig liom* 'I can/ may' *Féadann duit* 'You can'
verb phrases: copula + adjective/ noun etc. + prepositional phrase	verb phrases: substantive verb + adverbial/ adjectival/prepositional phrase
Is féidir liom 'I can/ may' *Is ceart/cóir dom* ·'I ought' *Ní mór dom* 'I must' *Ní foláir dom* 'I must' *Ní gá dhom* 'I need not' *Ní call dom* 'I need not'	*Tá mé in ann* 'I can' *Tá mé ábalta* 'I can' *Tá orm* 'I am obliged to' *Níl féichiú orm* 'I don't have to' etc.

11.2.2 Distinctive features of modal verbs

On the first glance, it might seem that these verbs and verbal phrases are classed as modal simply on a semantic basis. In many ways they behave like any verb or verbal phrase which is followed by a complement with a verbal noun and preceding object:

Table 11.4 *Verbs and verbal phrases with verbal noun and preceding object*

Dúirt mé 'I said'	
Éiríonn liom 'I manage'	
Is maith liom 'I like'	*é a dhéanamh* 'to do it'
Tá mé sásta 'I am content'	
Tá orm 'I have to'	

Nevertheless the modals, from a grammatical point of view, behave differently in many respects.

11.2.2(i) *Absence of complement subject.* In the case of non-modals the underlying subject of the complement phrase may be absent because it is identical to a noun phrase in the matrix sentence [see 11.1.1(ii)]:

(212)   *Ba mhaith liom é a dhéanamh* (Gd)
            'I would like to do it'

This happens irrespective of whether that noun phrase is the subject or the object of a preposition, as for instance *liom* in example (212). On the other hand, where the underlying subject of the complement is not identical to some noun phrase in the matrix sentence the subject may appear [see 11.1.1(ii)]:

(213)   *Ba mhaith liom tú é a dhéanamh* (Gd)
            'I would like you to do it'

In the case of modals the subject of the complement is always absent, that is, identical to some noun phrase in the matrix sentence:

(214) *Caithfidh mé é a dhéanamh.*
'I must do it'

11.2.2(ii) *Root and epistemic modal verbs.* Some non-modals can be followed by a verbal noun complement or by a finite complement:

(215) *Ba mhaith liom + tú a bheith ann/go mbeifeá ann* (D)
'I would like you to be there'

In the case of modals there is an important distinction here between 'root' and 'epistemic' modals.

What are called 'root' modals describe necessity, obligation, ability etc. and are always followed by a verbal noun complement:

(216) *Caithfidh Máirtín an doras a phéinteáil*
'Máirtín must paint the door'
(217) *Níorbh fhleár* (C)/*fholáir* (M) *dhó iad a chur i dtaisce* (C)
'He had to store them away safely'
(218) *Ba cheart dó é a rá leo*
'He should say it to them'
(219) *Ní féidir le Bríd Fraincis a fhoghlaim (C)*
'Bríd can't learn French'

In contrast to 'root' modals, 'epistemic' modals are inferential rather than potential, obligative etc. and are always followed by a finite complement:

(220) *Caithfidh sé go bhfuair tú coláiste* (C)
'It must be the case that you received a college education'

There is no proleptic *sé* in this epistemic usage in Munster [this was discussed in 11.1.3(ii)].

Although modals followed by a finite complement are always epistemic, an epistemic meaning may also be expressed by a verbal noun complement. This is particularly true in Donegal:

(221) *Thiocfadh le sin a bheith fíor* (D)
'That could be true'
(222) *Chaithfeadh sé a bheith anonn go maith san oíche an tráth seo* (D)
'It would have to be far into the night by now'

There are, however, sporadic examples from the other major dialects such as the following sentence from a Cois Fhairrge story:

(223)   *Ba cheart dó sin féin a bheith agamsa, mara chaill mé é* (Cf)
        'I should have that at least, if I haven't lost it'

We might normally expect:

(224)   *Ba cheart go mbeadh sé sin féin agam...*
        'I should have that at least'

Some modals can be employed either with a finite or with a verbal noun clause. There is a finite clause in (225) and (227), while (226) and (228) contain a verbal noun clause:

(225)   *Ba cheart go mbeadh an leabhar ann*
        'It should be the case that the book would be there'
(226)   *Ba cheart dó é a rá leo*
        'He should say it to them'
(227)   *Ní féidir go bhfuil Bríd ag foghlaim Fraincis!* (C)
        'It can't be the case that Bríd is learning French!'
(228)   *Ní féidir le Bríd Fraincis a fhoghlaim (C)*
        'Bríd can't learn French'

There are, however, some modals which are confined to one usage. Those belong to the fourth type and feature only as root modals, e.g. *Tá mé in ann* 'I can' while others such as *b'fhéidir* 'perhaps' are only used epistemically:

(229)   *Tá mé in ann damhsa a dhéanamh* (C)
        'I can dance'
(230)   *B'fhéidir go mbeadh sé ann*
        'It could be that he would be there'

11.2.2(iii) *Defectiveness of modal verbs.* A third major difference between modals and other verbs which are followed by a verbal noun complement is the fact that many of them are defective verbs (or verbal forms), the degree of defectiveness varying from dialect to dialect, and examples are discussed in 11.2.3. No doubt several factors have contributed to this defectiveness. The natural intersection of tense and mood tends to blur tense differentiation.

More specifically, within the system, the restriction of the copula to present/future and past/conditional seems to spill over to the (theoretically) fully inflectable verbs of groups one and two.

11.2.3 Dialectal variation
Although the dialects have the basic modal system in common there is a deal of variation both of a lexical nature and in the degree of defectiveness.

11.2.3(i) *Verbs of necessity, obligation etc.* The inflectable verb *caith* 'must' features in all the major dialects. Only in Munster is the habitual present frequent and the past possible:

(231)   *Caitheann Donncha éisteacht* (M)
        'Donncha has to desist'
(232)   *Chaith teipeadh* (M)
        'It was bound to fail'

In Connacht and Donegal the norm is *caithfidh* present/future and *chaithfeadh* habitual past/conditional:

(233)   *Caithfidh muid a bheith ag caint i gcónaí* (C)
        'We must always (be) talk(ing)'
(234)   *Caithfidh sé a bheith glan* (D)
        'It will have to be clean'
(235)   *Bhínn bodhar ag an bhfear seo sa gcurach, chaithfeá stiúradh an bháid a thabhairt dó* (C)
        'I was deaf on account of this man in the coracle, you would have to allow him to steer the boat'
(236)   *Chaithfeá féin a ghoil ann* (D)
        'You would have to go there yourself'

The verbal noun *caitheachtáil* 'compulsion' is recorded for Cois Fhairrge in such phrases as:

(237)   *Níl aon chaitheachtáil ann* (Cf)
        'There is no compulsion / It is not compulsory'

In all major dialects *b'éigean do...* '...was obliged to' tends to replace *chaithfeadh* in the past so that (238) tends to be replaced by (239):

292 *Modern Irish: grammatical structure and dialectal variation*

(238)   *Chaithfinn imeacht mar bhí mé mall* (Gd)
         'I had to go off as I was late'
(239)   *B'éigean domh imeacht mar bhí mé mall* (Gd)

The distribution of the other verbs and verb phrases expressing necessity/ obligation is more complex.
     The verb *ghlacfainn* (etc.)... 'I (etc.) had better...' which is confined to Donegal is used only in the conditional to express hypothetical obligation:

(240)   *Ghlacfá imeacht anois* (Gd)
         'You'd better go now'

Such verb phrases as *is ceart/cóir dom* 'I should' and *tá orm...* 'I have to...' seem to occur in all major dialects while *ní mór dom, ní foláir* (M)/*fleár* (C) *dom, ní gá dhom* occur in Munster and Connacht. The verb phrase *níl féichiú orm* 'I don't have to' is probably restricted to Donegal.

11.2.3(ii) Verbs of ability, possibility etc. The inflectable verb *féad* 'can' occurs in all the dialects. The tendency towards defectiveness is less advanced than in the case of *caith* 'must'. All of the tenses are found in all the major dialects and in Cois Fhairrge *féadachtáil* 'to be able' is the verbal noun which supplies the progressive:

(241)   *Ní raibh mé ag féadachtáil aon néal a chodladh* (Cf)
         'I wasn't managing/able to sleep a wink'

All the same there is a well-developed bias towards a dual system with (habitual) present/future *féadfaidh* and (habitual) past/conditional *d'fhéadfadh*.
     The use of habitual present is relatively infrequent in Connacht and Munster and is retained most often after *má* 'if', e.g. *má fhéadaim* 'if I can'.
     Similarly, the conditional and the past tend to merge but here there are important distinctions between the dialects. The most usual position is that the conditional encroaches on the past so that we can compare (242) with (243):

(242)   *Níor fhéad* (past) *mé a ghoil ann* (C)
         'I could not go there'
(243)   *Rinne mé gach a bhféadfainn* (conditional) (C)
         'I did all I could'

Nevertheless the blurring is not entirely unidirectional, as can be seen in the following example:

(244) *Phós* (past) *Seán i Sasana agus d'fhéad* (past) *clann a chloinne a bheith ann anois* (Ml)
'Seán married in England and his grandchildren could be there now'

In Gweedore, however, the past/conditional meanings are allotted to the conditional while the past form is transferred along the semantic scale from ability, possibility etc. to necessity, obligation etc.:

(245) *D'fhéad* (past) *tú é a ráit leis* (Gd)
'You should have said it to him'

The construction *féadann duit...* 'you can...' is a feature of Donegal dialects. The same semantic shift to obligation/necessity takes place here as in the straightforward use of *féad*:

(246) *D'fhéad duit é a ráit leis* (Gd)
'You should have said it to him'

In general the construction using *do* 'to' is felt to be stronger.

Similarly *thig(e) liom* 'I can' is for the most part associated with Donegal (although *tig liom* is also found in Connacht). The Donegal dialects have two tenses, a present/future *thig(e) liom* 'I can' and a past/conditional *thiocfadh liom* 'I could'.

Among the verb phrase types *is féidir liom* 'I can' is common both in Connacht and Munster and is very rare in Donegal although *is féidir dom* is found. Of the verb phrase types involving the substantive verb *tá mé in ann* 'I can' is a feature of Connacht whereas *tá mé ábalta* 'I can' is commonest in Munster and Donegal.

11.3 Auxiliary verbs

Auxiliary verbs in Irish share with modals the requirement that there be identity between a noun phrase in the main clause or matrix sentence and the underlying sentence in any subsequent complementation and, therefore, deletion of the subject in the complement [see 11.2.2(i)]. On the other hand, unlike modals, they do not tend to be defective [see 11.2.2(iii)].

294　*Modern Irish: grammatical structure and dialectal variation*

11.3.1 The substantive verb in periphrastic aspectual phrases

This account of the periphrastic aspectuals follows Wigger (see Wigger 1972a:170-80) in describing the substantive verb in these phrases as an auxiliary. These constructions could with equal validity be regarded as being derived from a substantive verb followed by a preposition phrase and a non-sentential noun phrase (see Stenson 1981: 137-45).

There are three aspects: the progressive, the prospective and the perfective. In a sense the prospective is a variety of the future and the perfective is a variety of the past. Yet both of these tenses, as well as denoting a time-relation, contain aspectual and modal elements. A distinctive feature of these three periphrastic forms is the fact that they all have a corresponding passive construction. These are true passives (as distinct from the impersonal forms of the verb), where a noun-phrase, which does not represent the agent, appears as the person of the finite verb or as the first noun-phrase following the verb; furthermore it is possible to represent the agent by an adjunct adverbial phrase which is introduced by the preposition *ag* 'at' (and less frequently by *ó* 'from'). Impersonal forms can, on the other hand, only be followed by an instrumental prepositional phrase introduced by *le* 'by' (or less frequently by *ó* 'from'), e.g. *Maraíodh le bus é* 'He was killed by a bus'.

These periphrastic aspects can also form various combinations.

11.3.1(i) *The active progressive aspect.*

Table 11.5 *The active progressive aspect*

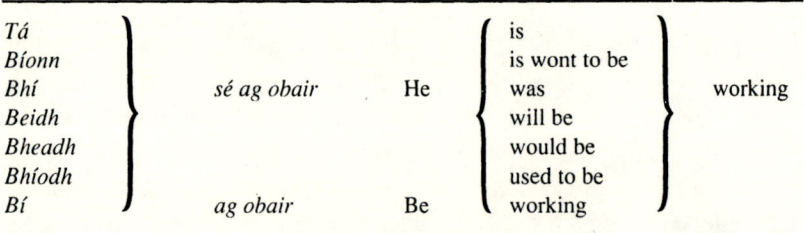

The substantive verb in all its forms, tenses, moods and habitual aspects can be used with *ag* /ə/ (or /g(ʹ)/ before a vowel) 'at' together with the verbal noun to form a progressive construction. This construction signifies the continuity of an event before and after the time of reference. When the object of the verb appears as a pronoun, in some dialects *do* 'to/for' (pronounced as /gə/ in Connemara) is substituted for *ag* 'at'. The vowel of *do* is amalgamated with any pronoun *a* /ə/ 'his, her, their':

(247) *Tá sé do mo thóraíocht* (C)
'He is searching me out'
(248) *Tá sé dhá thóraíocht*
'He is searching for it'

One particular case of an active progressive must be mentioned here. Where fronting of the object is involved, *a* /ə/ + lenition replaces *ag*:

(249) *Sin í an bhean atá sé a phósadh* (C)
'That is the woman he is marrying?'
(250) *Cé hí an bhean atá sé a phósadh* (C)
'Who is the woman he is marrying?'

While this rule is found in all dialects, there is evidence from Dunquin and Gweedore of speakers using *ag* in these circumstances (as is the case in Scottish Gaelic):

(251) *Ní fheadar cén luas a bhíodar ag déanamh* (Dn)
'I wonder what speed they were doing'
(252) *...an rud a bhíonn an broc ag tóch* (Dn)
'...what the badger normally digs up'
(253) *Goidé atá Jimmy ag briseadh?* (Gd)
'What is Jimmy breaking?'

There are semantic restrictions involved. Certain types of verbs are excluded from this construction. One easily identifiable category is a small group of passives inasmuchas they employ a possessive adjective before the verbal noun which refers to the subject:

Table 11.6 *Stative verbs requiring preposition* i *'in'*

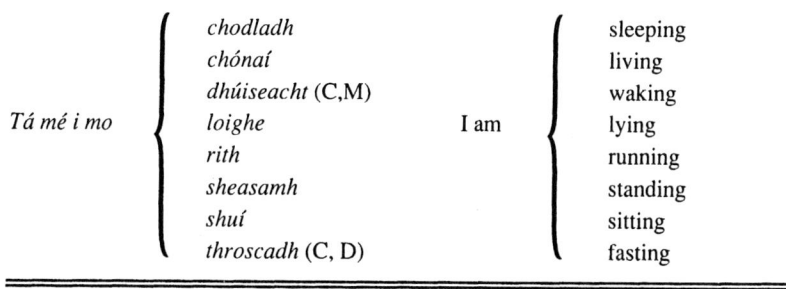

296 *Modern Irish: grammatical structure and dialectal variation*

Naturally, there are some variations according to the dialect; for example Menlough has also *i mo shíneadh* 'stretched out' while Donegal has *muscailte* rather than *i mo dhúiseacht* (see Wagner 1958:152).

When any of the above verbs are used dynamically (i.e. in a non-stative way) *ag* 'at' is employed.

11.3.1(ii) *The active prospective aspect.*

(254)   *Tá sé le theacht amáireach* (C)
        'He is to come tomorrow'
(255)   *Bhí sé le leabhar a léamh* (C)
        'He was to read a book'
(256)   *Bhí siad lena fáil/le í a fháil* (C)
        'They were to get her'

The substantive verb (with its various forms, tenses and moods) is used with the preposition *le* /l'ə/ to express an immediate future with obligation or simply obligation. The preposition *le* is followed by a verbal noun complement [see 11.1.1(ii)].

There is a deal of dialectal variation involved here. The examples (254-6) hold good for Connemara and Donegal. It would appear that Munster dialects allow intransitive verbs in this type of sentence:

(257)   *...ach tá comhardamh na haimsire le teacht uair éigin* (M)
        '... but the compensation for this weather is to come sometime'

[The lenition or non-lenition of *teacht* 'come' is discussed in 11.1.1(ii).]

In Munster there would appear to be a distinction between duty or expectation, which is expressed by *le*, as in (257) and intention, which is expressed by *chu(i)n*:

(258)   *Peocu bhí an guth chun labhairt nú ná raibh...* (Mk)
        'Whether the voice was (going) to speak or not...'
(259)   *Mar táimse chun dul a' triall oraibh arís* (Mk)
        '...for I am intending to go to see you again'

However, in the case of transitive verbs *chun* seems to be required:

(260)   *Cé tá chun an dorais a oscailt ...?* (Mk)
        'Who is to open the door ...?'

In Connacht and Donegal [but see 11.1.6(ii)] the use of a type of 'double progressive' with the verb *goil* 'go' is certainly more frequent than the *le* prospective construction:

(261) *Níl sé ag goil ag déanamh leas do thada* (Cf)
'It is not going to do any good for anything'

It is unlikely that the use of future tense of the auxiliary is possible in example (261) as imminence seems in this case to be an intrinsic part of the prospective (see Wigger 1972a:173).

11.3.1(iii) *The active perfective aspect.*

(262) *Tá sé thar éis/i ndéidh imeacht*
'He has gone off'
(263) *Tá mé thar éis/i ndéidh leabhar a léamh*
'I have read a book'

The substantive verb is used in Munster and Connacht with *tar éis* (*thar éis* etc.) 'after' and in Donegal with *i ndéidh* 'after' to denote 'completed action'. This construction includes a tense element which expresses an event in the immediate past relevant to the time of utterance. The phrase *thar éis/ i ndéidh* is followed by a verbal noun complement.

11.3.1(iv) *The passive progressive aspect.*

(264) *Tá an doras dhá phéinteáil agam*
(lit. The door is to its painting by me)
'The door is being painted by me'

In this passive construction the grammatical subject [i.e. *doras* 'door' in example (264)] is the object in the corresponding active construction (i.e. *Tá mé ag péinteáil an dorais* 'I am painting the door'). An agent-free version of the above example is possible:

(265) *Tá an doras dhá phéinteáil*
'The door is being painted'

Furthermore the verb *cuir* 'put' can be employed with the passive progressive as a causative:

298 *Modern Irish: grammatical structure and dialectal variation*

(266)   *Chuir sé an churrach dhá déanamh* (Cf)
        (lit. He put the coracle to its making)
        'He had the coracle made'

A feature of Munster Irish is the option of placing the pronominal agent before, as well as after, the verbal noun complex:

(267)   *Ní raibh aon ní aige á dhéanamh*
        'He was doing nothing'
(268)   *Tuigeadh dom go raibh sórt éigin ráiméis cainte aice á labhairt leo*
        'I understood that she was giving them some nonsensical talk'

In (267) and (268) the pronominal agent *aige* 'by him', *aici* 'by her' comes before the verbal noun complex.

It is important to note that the passive progressive has a far higher frequency in Munster and normally replaces the active variant when the object of a verbal noun does not immediately precede it. In other words the Munster sentences in (269) and (270) would be expressed in Connacht or Donegal as (271) and (272):

(269)   *Cad atá á dhéanamh agat/agat a dhéanamh?* (M)
        'What are you doing?'
(270)   *Tarraigeadh isteach mé sa tubaist a bhí agam á sheachaint* (M)
        'I was drawn into the disaster that I was avoiding'
(271)   *Céard [Goidé (D)] atá tú a dhéanamh?*
        'What are you doing?'
(272)   *Tarraingíodh isteach mé sa tubaiste a bhí mé a sheachaint*
        'I was drawn into the disaster I was avoiding'

A further feature of Munster is that (*dh*)*á* + lenition (from *do* 'to/for' + *a* third singular masculine possessive + lenition) may be generalized irrespective of the gender or number of the noun referred to, for example the following sentence where *caint* 'talk' is feminine and (*d*)*á déanamh* (*do* + *a* third singular feminine possessive + non-lenition) might be expected:

(273)   *Ní mór an chaint a bhí an triúr againn á dhéanamh*
        'The three of us were not talking much'

11.3.1(v) *The passive prospective.*

(274)   *Tá an leabhar le léamh agam*
'The book is to be read by me / I have to read the book'

While the grammatical subject is found only in the auxiliary an agent is expressed by an adjunct adverbial phrase containing the preposition *ag* 'at'. An agent-free version is also possible: *Tá an leabhar le léamh* 'The book is to be read'. The active equivalent of the above example is *Tá mé leis/chun* (M) *an leabhar a léamh* 'I am to read the book'.

We may note in passing that there is no formal distinction between an intransitive verb in the active construction and a transitive verb in the agent-free passive construction:

(275)   *Tá sé len imeacht* (C)
'He is to go off'
(276)   *Tá sé le n-ól* (C)
'It is to be drunk'

A transitive in a periphrastic construction with *le* must be interpreted as passive when only one noun phrase occurs with it.

Just as in the passive progressive, the variant order is found in Munster. The agent pronoun can occur before *le* and the verbal noun:

(277)   *Tuigtear dóibh ná fuil aon diabhal ní ag éinne le déanamh ach...*
'They think that nobody has any damn thing to do but...'

11.3.1(vi) *The passive perfective aspect.*

(278)   *Tá an leabhar léite agam*
'I have the book read'

The substantive verb is employed with the verbal adjective of the main verb and corresponds to the active perfective *Tá mé thar éis/i ndéidh an leabhar a léamh* 'I have just read the book'. The grammatical subject is expressed only in the auxiliary and not in the verbal adjective of the main verb. An agent-free version of the above example is also possible:

(279)   *Tá an leabhar léite*
'The book is read'

In intransitive verbs also, this passive type is employed:

(280) *Tá sé imithe*
       'He is gone off'

Example (280) contrasts with the active equivalent (281):

(281) *Tá sé t(h)ar éis/i ndéidh* (D) *imeacht*
       'He is gone off'

There is a certain group of transitive verbs where the object may in a certain context be deleted and simply understood:

(282) *D'ith sé (a chuid)* (C)
       'He has eaten'
(283) *Chaith sé (vót)* (C)
       'He voted'

When such verbs are employed in the agent-free passive perfect construction and where the object is deleted the result is:

(284) *Tá sé ite* (C)
       'He has eaten'
(285) *Tá sé caite* (C)
       'He has voted'

This creates a certain superficial or formal ambiguity as these examples in a different context might be translated as 'It is eaten' or 'It is spent/thrown'.

11.3.1(vii) *Combinations of aspectual constructions.*
11.3.1(vii)1 *Progressive and prospective combined:* The prospective progressive is formed by placing the progressive phrase in the position of the verbal noun of a prospective construction. There is both the active and the passive combination. The active is illustrated by (286) and the passive is shown in (287):

(286) *Tá siad le bheith ag imirt*
       'They are to be playing'

(287) *Tá sé le bheith díolta aige*
'He is to have it sold'.

There is also an agent-free version of the passive:

(288) *Tá sé le bheith díolta*
'It is to be sold'

11.3.1(vii)2 *Progressive and perfective combined:* The perfective aspect can combine with any other verbal category which may be represented in the auxiliary, including moods and the habitual aspect. When the perfective is combined with the progressive, the progressive construction is embedded in the perfect one. As the substantive verb has no verbal adjective, only that variant of the perfective aspect which employs a verbal noun is possible, that is to say *t(h)ar éis* (or in Donegal *i ndéidh*) 'after' is required. The progressive perfective implies that the action has taken place in the immediate past. The active progressive perfective is exemplified in (289) and the passive progressive perfective in (290):

(289) *Tá mé thar éis a bheith ag déanamh póitín* (C)
'I have just been making poteen'
(290) *Tá an póitín thar éis a bheith déanta agam* (C)
'The poteen has just been made by me'

There is also an agent-free version:

(291) *Bhí an teach i ndéidh a bheith ceannaithe* (D)
'The house had just been bought'

11.3.1(vii)3 *Prospective and perfective combined*: Only in the case of intransitive verbs is this combination permitted. Progressive (and it would seem habitual) aspects are excluded from this prospective perfective construction. There is only an active construction involved here:

(292) *Tá sé le bheith imithe*
'He will be gone off / He is to be gone off'

This construction cannot be applied to transitive verbs because this would result in the corresponding passive *Tá sé le bheith gortaithe* 'It is to be hurt /

He is going to be hurt' which supplies the passive variant of the progressive prospective instead of the expected *Tá sé le bheith dhá ghortú.

11.3.1(viii) *Marginal aspectual constructions*. The substantive verb can be employed as an auxiliary with such phrases as Connacht *ar thoib*, Munster *ar tí* 'about to' (Gweedore uses *réidh le* 'ready to'):

(293)   Bhí mé ar thoib imeacht... (C)
        'I was about to go off...'

Another such phrase is Donegal *ar obair* 'in action, started':

(294)   Tá sé ar obair ag foghlaim Gaeilig (Gd)
        'He has started learning Irish'

The phrase *ar obair*, however (unlike *ar thoib* or *ar tí* 'about to'), need not have a following verbal noun:

(295)   Tá sé ar obair
        'He has started'

11.3.2 The auxiliary verb *déan* 'make, do'
The verb *déanamh* has both the meaning 'to do, to act' as well as 'to make' and can be used as a substitute for any verb (except the substantive verb):

(296)   Tá mé ag péinteáil doras (C)
        'I am painting a door'
(297)   Séard atá mé a dhéanamh, ag péinteáil doras (C)
        'What I am doing is painting a door'
(298)   Dúirt sé liom doras a phéinteáil, rud a rinneas (C)
        'He told me to paint a door, which I did'
(299)   Ní dhearna mé ach an doras a phéinteáil (C)
        'I only painted the door'

The verb's functions as an auxiliary with verbs denoting voluntary agentive actions are common to the dialects; what varies is the frequency and the degree of implementation.

11.3.2(i) *Use of* **déan** *'do' to echo a previous verb.*
11.3.2(i)1 *In responsives:* The use of the auxiliary *déan* 'do' in responsives varies from dialect to dialect (see Ó Siadhail 1973:147). In Connacht the use of this auxiliary in responsives seems to be confined to the future/imperative:

(300) *Cuirfidh muid ar snámh iad*
'We will put them afloat'
Déanfaidh sin (Cf)
'Will do'

(301) *Dá bhfaighinn leitir uaidh le teaspáint don chaiptín atá os a chionn i mBaile Átha Cliath, b'fhéidir go bhfaighfinn amach é*
'If I got a letter from him to show to the captain in charge of him in Dublin, perhaps I would get him out'
Déan cheana (Cf)
'Do that indeed'

There are also some instances of a similar usage in Donegal:

(302) *Gabh aníos agus taraing an scian seo amach as mo chroí*
'Come up and pull the knife out of my heart'
Dhéanfaidh mé agus fáilte (D)
'I'll do that willingly'

In Munster the system is much more widespread and indeed in Dunquin dialect it may be the most frequent responsive:

(303) *Ar ólais an tae?*
'Did you drink the tea?'
Dheineas (Dn)
'Yes, I did'

(304) *Ól ceann eile!*
'Drink another one!'
Ní dhéanfad (Dn)
'No, I won't'

11.3.2(i)2 *In conditionals:* This usage is particularly common in Munster as in:

(305) *Ná ceil orm é, nó má dheineann...* (M)
'Don't hide it from me, or else...'

304 *Modern Irish: grammatical structure and dialectal variation*

(306)   Admhaigh do chortha agus do pheacaí go poiblí, nó mara ndéanfair... (M)
'Admit your crimes and sins publicly or else...'

11.3.2(i)3 *In non-restrictive relatives:* The auxiliary is used where the shadow antecedent *rud* 'thing' is used for a verbal noun complement: *Dúirt sé liom póg a bhaint dhi; rud a rinneas* 'He told me to snatch a kiss from her, which I did'.

11.3.2(ii) *Use of* déan *'do' to supplement a verbal noun.*
11.3.2(ii)1 *With limited finite inflection:* A verbal noun which does not have a corresponding set of finite inflections may be supplemented by use of the auxiliary *déan*, e.g. *broimneach* 'to break wind', *báisteach* 'to rain':

(307)   *Rinne sé broim* (C)
'He broke wind'
(308)   *Rinne sé báisteach mhór* (C)
'It rained heavily'

The use of other possible auxiliaries in (307) and (308) is discussed in 11.3.3(ii) and (iii). Some verbal nouns may in a given dialect have a rarer or limited set of finite inflected forms so that the use of an auxiliary is at least as frequent, e.g Munster *Ghearáin sé...* 'He complained...' beside *Dhein sé gearán....* 'He made a complaint'.

11.3.2(ii)2 *With a partitive or indefinite sense:* An auxiliary can be used with a verbal noun to achieve a partitive or 'indefinite' effect:

(309)   *Ní gá duit a thuille siúlóide a dhéanamh* (M)
'You needn't do any more walking'
(310)   *Pé siúl a dhein an t-iascaire go dtí an dtig...* (M)
'Whatever brought the fisherman walking to the house / The fisherman happened to walk to the house...'

11.3.2(iii) *To front a verbal noun together with its object.* This is done by introducing the auxiliary *déanamh* 'do' and by turning the verb and its object into a verbal noun complement which then acts as object of the auxiliary.

Examples (312) and (314) show this process applied to (311) and (313) from which they are derived:

(311) *B'fhéidir gur chaith sibh amach é*
       'Maybe you threw it out'
(312) *B'fhéidir gurb é a chaitheamh amach a rinne sibh* (Cf)
       (lit. Maybe it is throwing it out you did)
       'Maybe you threw it out'
(313) *Le heagla go meallfá mé...*
       'For fear you would entice me'
(314) *Le heagla gur mé a mhealladh do dhéanfá...* (M)
       (lit. For fear it is enticing me you would do)
       'For fear you would entice me '

11.3.2(iv) ***To provide an alternative construction for fully inflected verbs.***
Once again the verbal noun of the inflectable verb and its object becomes an object verbal noun complement of the auxiliary:

(315) *Rinne sé é féin a choisreacan* (Gd)
       'He blessed himself/made the sign of the cross'
(316) *Suigh síos agus déan do chuid a ithe* (Gd)
       'Sit down and eat your meal'
(317) *Rinne mé mo shúil a chaochadh* (C)
       'I winked'
(318) *Dheineamair rudaí a cheannach* (M)
       'We bought things'

Although there are examples from Donegal it would seem to occur most frequently in the imperative. There are also sporadic examples from Connacht. However, it is undoubtedly much more frequent and widespread in Munster.

A further feature of Munster dialects would seem to be the spread of prepositional phrases with *ar* 'on'. In (319) and (320), one would expect such a prepositional phrase:

(319) *Agus nár mhór an t-iongnadh nár dheineadár fóirthint ar chuid éigin acu...* (M)
       'And wasn't it amazing that they didn't help some of them'
(320) *...i gcomhar éinne a dhéanfadh aon bhagairt ortha* (M)
       '...for anyone who would threaten them in any way'

The verbal nouns *fóirthint* 'help' and *bagairt* 'threaten' would normally be followed by the preposition *ar* 'on'. However in (321) and (322) no such preposition would be expected:

(321)   *Dheineadh sin caitheamh ar an lá di...* (M)
        'That would pass the day for her...'
(322)   *Do dheineas riarú ar an leasú* (M)
        'I apportioned the manure'

The object of a transitive verb in the underlying sentences, e.g. *lá* 'day' (*Chaitheadh sé an lá di*) and *leasú* 'manure' (*Riaraigh mé an leasú*) now appears after *ar* 'on' in a prepositional phrase. This particular use of the auxiliary *déan* 'do' is especially common with unadapted loan-words in examples such as:

(323)   *Déanfad telephoning ort* (M)
        'I will telephone you'

There are sporadic examples of this construction from other dialects:

(324)   *Dheamhan léamh a dhéanfas sé ar an leabhar sin* (D)
        'Indeed he won't give that book a reading'

The syntax of this sentence is explained in 12.2.3(i).

11.3.3 Other auxiliaries

11.3.3(i) *Tabhair 'give'*. The verb *tabhair* 'give' has a more limited range as an auxiliary than *déan* 'do', though it occurs in similar syntactic circumstances. Apart from having a singulative effect, e.g. *Thug sé léim* 'He gave a jump' (beside *Léim sé* 'He jumped'), the main functions of this auxiliary are its use with verbal nouns of verbs which take the preposition *do* 'to' and its use with verbs of infliction where *do* is introduced. In this type the verbal noun is the object of the auxiliary:

(325)   *Thug sí ordú don chéad fhear a chuid beithígh a bheith cnaptha as...* (C)
        'She gave an order to the first man to have his cattle cleared out...'
(326)   *B'éigeant do an diúltamh do thabhairt di* (M)
        'He had to give her a refusal'

(327) ...*ní thabharfadh sé aon ghéilleadh dhom* (M)
'...he wouldn't give any credence to me at all'

The verbs whose verbal nouns appear in these examples [*ordú* 'order' in (325), *diúltamh* 'refuse' in (326) and *géilleadh* 'yield' in (327)] are all normally followed by *do* 'to', e.g. *D'ordaigh sé dhó...* 'She ordered him...'.

11.3.3(i)1 *Use with verbs of infliction introducing* do *'to'*: Here the verbal noun is the object of the auxiliary and the object of the verbal noun then appears with *do* 'to' in a prepositional phrase:

(328) *Níl fhios cén sceanadh a thug sé dhó* (C)
'There is no end to the scolding he gave him'
(329) *Ní raibh blas caitheamh ina dhiaidh acu an liúradh sin a thabhairt do na ministéaraí* (C)
'They hadn't the slightest regret about giving that trouncing to the ministers'

The verbs whose verbal nouns occur in these examples [*sceanadh* 'flay, scold' in (328) and *liúradh* 'trounce' in (329)] are not normally followed by *do* 'to'. Just as in the case of *déan* 'do' this construction can be triggered by the need to front the verbal noun or make it partitive etc.

11.3.3(i)2 *Use with verbs introducing* ar *'on'*: In this construction the verbal noun is the object of the auxiliary and what would be the object of the verbal noun appears in a prepositional phrase containing *ar* 'on':

(330) *Ní mórán breathnú a thug mé air* (C)
'I did not look too closely at it'
(331) *Ná tabhair roinnt an chommittee air!* (C)
'Don't divide it as the committee would!'

Essentially, the auxiliary is being used here to make possible certain specifically nominal uses of the verbal noun, e.g. in example (330) it is possible to place the verbal noun in a genitive relation to quantitative nouns such as *mórán* 'much' and in (330) it enables the following noun 'committee' to be used attributively.

11.3.3(ii) Lig 'let'. The auxiliary *lig* 'let' is largely confined to providing an inflection for verbal nouns which lack a set of such forms or to give a singulative effect to those which do inflect. The verbs involved describe a sudden sound. Often *déan* 'do' occurs alongside *lig* 'let':

(332)   *Do dhein sí béic os ard* (M)
        'She shouted aloud'
(333)   *Lig sé béice* (Cf)
        'He let out a yell'
(334)   *Bhéic sé* (Gd)
        'He yelled'
(335)   *Nuair a chualaigh sí an chéad shraoth á dhéanamh...* (M)
        'When she heard the first sneeze...'
(336)   *Lig sé sraoth* (C)
        'He sneezed'
(337)   *Rinne sé broim / Lig sé broim* (C)
        'He broke wind'

Many of these uses are optional within a dialect. Other examples would be verbs such as *scread* 'shout', *scairt* 'call'.

11.3.3(iii) *Caith* 'spend, throw'. The auxiliary *caith* 'spend, throw' seems to be limited to certain phrases:

(338)   *Chaith sé léim thar an gclaí* (C)
        (lit. He threw a jump over the ditch)
        'He jumped over the ditch'
(339)   *Chaith sé báisteach mhór aréir* (C)
        (lit. It threw great rain last night)
        'It rained heavily last night'

In both example (338) and (339) the employment of *Chaith sé* is optional. In (338) it could be replaced by *Thug sé* 'He gave' or simply *Léim sé* 'He jumped' and in (339) it could be replaced by *Rinne sé* 'It did'.

11.4 Summary of dialectal differences

While the general system of complementation is shared by the dialects there are several remarkable divergences . Among the most noteworthy of these are:

(a) The use of *a* + lenition in Connacht and Donegal before *teacht (tíocht)* 'come' and *goil* 'go' when no object or subject precedes them in the verbal noun complement: *Ba mhaith liom a theacht* 'I would like to come'.

(b) The more obligatory use in Munster of the preposition *ar* 'on' with verbs of intention: *Shocraigh sé ar imeacht* 'He decided to go off'.

(c) Despite great variation, the somewhat less extensive use in Munster than in all other major dialects of a proleptic pronoun in the case of extraposed verbal noun complements: *Theip orm imeacht* 'I failed to go away' or in the case of epistemic modals *caith* 'must': *Caithfidh go bhfuil sé fíor* 'It must be true'.

(d) The full systemization in Donegal of a set of verbs of motion in aspectual function using *a* + lenition: *Sheasaigh sé a cheol* 'He stood up to sing' beside the use of *ag* 'at' in Connacht and the confinement to motion in Munster.

(e) The frequent use in Donegal of *roimh* 'before' in verbal noun complements identified by *do*: *Druid an fhuinneog roimh imeacht duit* 'Shut the window before you go'.

(f) The distinctively Munster attributive use of a verbal noun complement: *fear an airgid a dhéanamh* 'the man who makes money'.

(g) Despite all the lexical variation among the modal verbal phrases, the two inflected verbs *caith* 'must' and *féad* 'can, may' are shared by the dialects. In Munster *caith* is less defective than elsewhere. In Donegal *féad* in the past tense expresses obligation: *D'fhéad tú é a dhéanamh* 'You should have done it'.

(h) The employment of *déan* 'do' as an auxiliary is quite extensive in Munster compared with elsewhere.

12 *Non-complemental subordination and marginal syntactic features*

12.1 Non-complemental subordination

Subordination which requires either finite or verbal noun complementation was discussed in 11.1.2 and subordination involving *agus* 'and' in 11.1.8. Here other types of embedding processes are described. Inevitably matters of syntax and morphology intersect here as the embedding processes demand certain changes of mood, tense and aspect.

12.1.1 Relatives

12.1.1(i) *Direct relatives.*

(1)   *D'imigh na daoine a bhí míshásta thar sáile* (C)
       'The people who were dissatisfied went abroad'
(2)   *Feicim an fear a bhí ag péinteáil na fuinneoige* (C)
       'I see the man who was painting the window'

Strictly speaking, a direct relative construction is where the subject [i.e. *na daoine* 'the people' in (1)] or object [i.e. *an fear* 'the man' in (2)] is explicitly represented by a noun phrase outside the embedded sentence or in other words when the relative clause functions as an attribute. However, the same construction is used (and traditionally referred to as a direct relative) following all fronting (see 10.3.5) and following *agus/is* 'as' (comparative), *ná* 'than', *mar* 'as'. Furthermore, in the case of *uair* 'hour, time' and Erris *an tan* /tun/ ~ /tən/ 'when', although we might expect an indirect relative [see 12.1.1(ii)], a direct relative is often (though not always) employed:

(3)   *Is i mBaile Átha Cliath atá sé*
      (lit. It is in Dublin that he is)
      'He is in Dublin'
(4)   *Máire a bhí sásta*
      'It is Máire who was satisfied'
(5)   *Tá sé níos mó ná a bhí sé*
      'It is bigger than it was'
(6)   *Níl sé mar a bhí sé*
      'He is not as he was'
(7)   *An chéad uair a bheidheas tú ann...* (C)
      'The first time you will be there...'
(8)   *...an tan a thiocfas sí...* (Er)
      '...when she will come...'

It must, however, be noted that, where the relative clause alone represents a constituent in the main sentence, a construction similar to the indirect relative [see 12.1.1(ii)] occurs with the meaning 'all of':

(9)   *Tháinig a raibh sa teach amach* (C, D)
      'All of those in the house came out'

The actual formation of the direct relative involves the use of *a* /ə/ which lenites (excepting *atá* 'is' in Connacht and Donegal and *a bíos* 'is wont to be' in Donegal). The employment of a suffix *-s* in the non-past tenses varies somewhat from dialect to dialect. For instance in Dunquin it seems to have been largely dropped, whereas in Gweedore it appears to be optional in the habitual present. The negative is formed with *nach* [*ná* (M)], *nár* etc. 'that...not' (*nach* eclipses, *nár* lenites).

12.1.1(ii) *Indirect relatives.* It is possible to distinguish two types of indirect relative (see McCloskey 1985:45-106), the extension (noun as part of adverbial/adjectival) type and the resumptive pronoun type.

These two types are traditionally called indirect relatives. They are both introduced by what is called the 'indirect relative particle' *a* or *go* (in Munster and very occasionally in Connacht), followed by eclipsis and, where available, by the independent verbal form. In the past *ar*, *gur* [in C,M] are used and both lenite. In the negative *nach* [*ná* (M)] and *nar/nár* replace *a*, [*go* (M)] and *ar* [*gur* (M)].

12.1.1(ii)1 *Extension (noun as part of adverbial/adjectival) type:*

(10) *D'fhág sé é sa gcaoi a raibh sé* (C)
'He left it the way (that) it was'
(11) *Fan san áit a bhfuil tú* (C)
'Stay where (lit. in the place) you are'
(12) *An t-am ar tháinig sé, bhíodar díolta ar fad* (C)
'(By) the time he came, they were all sold'
(13) *Sin é an fáth ar bhuail sé é* (C)
'That is the reason he hit him'

In the examples (10-13) the verb of the embedded sentence is connected by a noun functioning as or forming a part of an adverbial extension; that is to say the nouns *caoi* 'way', *áit* 'place', *am* 'time' and *fáth* 'reason' are the connection point for the embedded sentences *bhí sé* 'he was' in (10), *tá tú* 'you are' in (11), *tháinig sé* 'he came' in (12) and *bhuail sé é* 'he hit him' in (13) respectively.

It may be further noted in passing that *uair* 'time, occasion', while it usually (and historically) is followed by a direct relative *an uair a bhí sé* 'the time he was' [see 12.1.1(i)], is sometimes followed by an indirect relative *an uair a raibh sé*.

The use of this extension type following what we call an adjectival extension is illustrated by:

(14) *Fiafraím dhíot ceocu crann arna bhfuarais na húlla* (M)
'I asked you on which tree you got the apples'

Here the preposition *ar* 'on' is followed by *n* (originally to avoid hiatus between a preposition with a final vowel and the particle *a* /ə/ [see 6.2.4(v)]). The embedded sentence *fuarais na húlla* 'you got the apples', which forms the adjectival extension, is introduced by the indirect relative particle *a* /ə/. Undoubtedly the use of the adjectival extension is on the wane [and tends to be replaced by the resumptive type; see 12.1.1(ii)2]. It is largely confined to sporadic examples, often involving the prepositions *ar* 'on', *le* 'with', *i* 'in' or in the semi-petrified use of the impersonal forms such as *inar rugadh mé* 'in which I was born'.

Lastly, it is important to remark that there is a definite tendency, particularly among younger speakers of some dialects, to substitute a direct relative for an indirect relative, e.g. *ar an tslí atá... an dóigh atá...* (Dn), 'the

314 *Modern Irish: grammatical structure and dialectal variation*

way it is', *an dóigh atá* (Gd) 'the way it is', *an bealach a rinne sé é* (Ca) 'the way in which he did it'.

12.1.1(ii)2 *Resumptive pronoun type:*

(15)   *Feicim an fear ar labhair tú leis* (C)
       'I see the man whom you spoke to'
(16)   *Feicim an fear a bhfuil a mhac tinn* (C)
       'I see the man whose son is sick'

In the resumptive pronoun type, the head noun of the relative [*an fear* 'the man' in examples (15) and (16)] is linked in (15) with the pronoun in the prepositional pronoun *leis* 'with him' and in (16) with the possessive adjective *a* 'his'. It is important to note that in sentences which contain prepositional or complex phrases only such a resumptive pronoun-type indirect relative is traditionally possible. (The reason for this is probably that such phrases are 'syntactic islands' which in turn require a resumptive pronoun to be employed; see McCloskey 1985:45-106.) It is precisely because direct relatives are excluded in this sort of sentence that the resumptive pronoun type occurs very frequently. In fact with one exception this resumptive type is an option in all syntactic positions. It seems that the one syntactic position where a resumptive pronoun may not be employed is as the subject of a simple embedded sentence. In other words only *an fear a phéinteáil an doras* 'the man who painted the door' (i.e. a direct relative) is possible and **an fear ar phéinteáil sé an doras* is not an option. (The reason for this limitation is probably the proximity of the pronoun to the head word, which results in the syntactic binding being too local; see McCloskey 1985:45-106.)

It is noteworthy that, in a sentence containing a direct relative [example (17)], an obvious ambiguity may sometimes be avoided by the use of a resumptive pronoun as object in the direct relative [example (18)]:

(17)   *Sin é an sagart a phóg an bhean* (C)
       'That is the priest who kissed the woman' or 'That is the priest whom the woman kissed'
(18)   *Sin é an sagart ar phóg an bhean é* (C)
       'That is the priest whom the woman kissed'

Yet apart from the sort of sentences in examples (15) and (16), this resumptive pronoun type may be somewhat marginal. (This is probably due to the general tendency in language to avoid pronouns; see McCloskey

1985:45-106.) Nevertheless, there are examples from all the major dialects which illustrate its employment in almost all syntactic positions and (19), (21), (23), (25) and (27) show some instances of the construction. The equivalent direct relative is given in (20), (22), (24), (26) and (28):

(19) *An bhean fadó gur ardaigh an rón leis í* (M)
 'The woman long ago whom the seal carried off'
(20) *An bhean fadó a d'ardaigh an rón leis*
 'The woman long ago whom the seal carried off'
(21) *ar dhéanamh méise a mbainfí taobh amháin aisti agus a bhfágfaí 'na suidhe ar an talamh í* (D)
 'in the shape of a dish out of which one side would be removed and it would be left sitting on the ground'
(22) *ar dhéanamh méise...agus a d'fhágfaí 'na suidhe ar an talamh*
 'in the shape of a dish...which would be left sitting on the ground'
(23) *rudaí ná féadfadh fathach iad dh'aistriú* (M)
 'things which a giant couldn't transfer'
(24) *rudaí ná féadfadh fathach a dh'aistriú*
 'things which a giant couldn't transfer'
(25) *Aon rud arbh fhiú é a áireamh* (M)
 'Anything which would be worth counting'
(26) *Aon rud b'fhiú a áireamh*
 'anything which would be worth counting'
(27) *rud a mbeadh sé ghá chuartughadh* (D)
 'a thing he would be looking for'
(28) *rud a bheadh sé a chuartughadh*
 'a thing he would be looking for'

12.1.1(iii) *Double relative clauses.* Two relative clauses can occur in a row (see McCloskey 1985:45-106), as in the following examples:

(29) *an fear seo a bhfuil mé ag caint air a bhí ina phaidléaraidhe* (D)
 'this man that I am talking about who was a pedlar'
(30) *girseach ar ghoid na síógaí í a fuarthas arais* (D)
 'a girl that the fairies stole who was found again'

In the examples (29) and (30) a (resumptive pronoun type) indirect relative is followed by a direct relative. A different phenomenon is observed in the following examples:

(31) *An leabhar a dúirt sé a chuirfeadh ar mo chosa mé* (D)
'The book that he said would set me on my feet'
(32) *An nídh a gheallais a thabharfá dó* (M)
'The thing that you promised you would give to him'

One might well expect the complementizer *go* (+ eclipsis) 'that' to follow *dúirt sé* 'he said' or *gheallais* 'you promised'. In other words one might expect in (31) *an leabhar a dúirt sé go gcuirfeadh sé ar mo chosa mé* or in (32) *an nídh a gheallais go dtabharfá dó*.

It could be argued that these should be termed 'spread relatives'. Although we are treating double relatives here, grammatically at any rate, there can be multiple spread direct relatives, just as there can be multiple complementization:

(33) *Dúirt tú gur shíl tú go bhfaca tú...* (D)
'You said that you thought that you saw...'
(34) *An fear a dúirt tú a shíl tú a chonaic tú...* (D)
'The man that you said you thought you saw...'

In the same fashion 'spread' indirect relatives occur normally in the extension type:

(35) *Leag mé thart é san áit ar shíl mé a bhfuighinn aríst é* (C)
'I put it by where I thought I would find it'
(36) *Seo an áit as a gceaptar a dtáinig bunadh an Uachtaráin Reagan* (D)
'This is the place they think President Reagan's ancestors came from'

In example (35) the relative relationship, so to say, spreads into the embedded *gheobhainn aríst é* 'I would get it again' so that, instead of the complementizer *go* (+ eclipsis), as in *shíl mé go bhfuighinn é* 'I thought I would get it', it is realized as *...ar shíl mé a bhfuighinn é* 'where I thought I would get it'.

Interestingly, the double or 'spread' relative does not normally occur in the resumptive pronoun type:

(37) *...achan rud a raibh dóchas acu go dtiocfadh sé* (D)
'...everything that they had hoped would come'

(38) ...*an t-ór seo...ar chreid corr-dhuine go raibh sé ann* (D)
'this gold... which the occasional person believed was there'
(39) ...*buta beag fir...nár léar go raibh muinéal ar bith idir a cheann agus a ghuaillí* (C)
'...a little runt of a man...that it was not clear that there was any neck at all between his head and his shoulders'
(40) ...*ag trácht ar rud éigin nach mbíodh uatha go mbeadh fhios agamsa air* (M)
'...discussing something which they did not want me to know about'

There are however some rare examples (see de Bhaldraithe 1956/7b:245-6) of double or 'spread' relatives:

(41) ...*an bhean a raibh mé ag súil a bhfuighinn uaithi é* (Cf)
'...the woman that I was hoping to get it from'

12.1.1(iv) Echoic relative clauses. In a restrictive relative clause the antecedent is 'restricted' or limited, e.g. *an fear a bhí ann inné* 'the man who was there yesterday' answers the question *Cén fear?* 'What man?'. In an echoic relative clause the antecedent is not further limited and, in practice, is usually either sentential or is a proper noun. In such cases a generalized antecedent is introduced and placed in apposition to the proper noun or sentential element, e.g. *duine* 'a person', *fear* 'a man', *bean* 'a woman' or when local *áit* 'a place' or inanimate *rud* 'a thing'. Examples (42) and (43) show *rud* 'thing' introduced in apposition to a sentential antecedent (for the deletion of the subject in the echoic relative clause see 9.2.3):

(42) *D'iarr mé air é a dhéanamh, rud nach dtearn* (D)
'I asked him to do it, which he didn't'
(43) *Níor thugas an t-eiteach dom' mháthair siúd is go mbuailfeadh an leisce féin mé/rud nár bhuail* (M)
'I didn't refuse my mother even if I were to get lazy, which I didn't'

12.1.1(v) Relatives and questions. Questions in general involve copular fronting (see 10.3.5). This consists of a type of cleft sentence with a relative. The use of direct or indirect relative corresponds largely to the distinction outlined in 12.1.1(i) and 12.1.1(ii) above. As is predictable a direct relative is used where the subject or object is involved. Also, as might be expected,

318 *Modern Irish: grammatical structure and dialectal variation*

questions involving *uair* are followed by a direct relative. Less predictably Munster *conas* 'how' is also followed by a direct relative.

Table 12.1 *Fronted questions with direct relative*

Cé/Go Cé (C)	'Who?/whom?'
Goidé? (D)	'What?'
Céard?/Go céard? (C)	'What?'
Cad? (M)	'What?'
'D éard (Rg, Bm)	'What?'
Cé/cá (D) mhéad?	'How much?'
Cé acu?	'Which?'
Ciacu? (M)	'Which?'
Cé/Goidé (D) *chomh maith is...?*	'How good...?'
Cá huair? (D)	'When?'
Cén uair? (C)	'When?'
Cathain? (M)	'When?'
Conas (M)	'How?'

As *Cá* is unstressed it is realized as /ka/ in Donegal; see 2.8.3(v)

Once again, as we might expect in the light of the discussion of indirect relatives in 12.1.1(ii), questions involving prepositions and phrases expressing 'why?', 'how?', 'where?', 'what time?' are followed by an indirect relative.

Table 12.2 *Fronted questions with indirect relative*

C' air? (D)	'On what?'	*C' áit?* (D)	'Where?'
Cé air? (C)	'On what?'	*Cén áit?* (C)	'Where?'
Cad air? (M)	'On what?'	*Canad? (Ca + ionad)* (Mk)	'Where?'
		Cá háit? (Ky)	'Where?'
'Tuige ? (D/C)	'Why?'	*Cén t-am?* (C,D)	'When?'
Cad chuige? (M)	'Why?'	*Cad é an t-am?* (Ky, Mk)	'When?'
Cén fáth? (C)	'Why?'	*'D é an t-am?* (Rg, Bm)	'When?'
Cad fáth? (Ky)	'Why?'		
Cad 'na thaobh? (Ky, Mk)	'Why?'		
'D é chúis (Rg,Bm)	'Why?'		
Cén dóigh? (D)	'How?'		
Cén chaoi? (C)	'How?'		

Non-complemental subordination 319

The prepositional question is always followed by an indirect relative irrespective of the subsequent word order. This is relevant in Donegal where two sentence orders are possible. Examples (44) and (46) illustrate the first order, which is peculiar to Donegal and does not have prepositional fronting. Examples (45) and (47) show the second order, which is the norm in other major dialects:

(44)　*Cé a bhfuil an t-airgead aige?* (D)
　　　'Who has the money?'
(45)　*C'aige a bhfuil an t-airgead?* (D)
　　　'Who has the money?'
(46)　*Caidé a mbeifeá ag súil leis?* (D)
　　　'What would you expect?'
(47)　*Cá leis a mbeifeá ag súil?* (D)
　　　'What would you expect?'

It should be further noted that there is a tendency, particularly in Munster, for the direct relative to intrude in prepositional questions:

(48)　*An bhfuil fhios agat... cad air a bhíos ag cuimhneamh?* (M)
　　　'Do you know...what I was thinking about?'

12.1.2 Conditionals

A conditional is semantically characterized by the fact that it expresses a condition which qualifies the event described in the main or matrix clause. There are two types of conditionals: in one fulfilment is considered possible and in the other a hypothesis is expressed.

12.1.2(i) *Conditional with possible fulfilment.*

(49)　*Má bhíonn sé sásta, tiocfaidh na fir*
　　　'If he is agreeable, the men will come'

In this type, the verb of the embedded sentence is preceded by *má* 'if', which lenites. Following *má* a future is replaced by the habitual present (i.e. *Má bhíonn sé sásta, tiocfaidh..* 'If he is agreeable, ...will come'). There is some variation in the negative; *muna* (Gd), *mara* (C,Mk), *muna* and *mara* (Dn) are found. This particle causes eclipsis and is followed by a dependent verb form (see 8.3.1) if it is available. Mostly the future is used following the negative:

320 *Modern Irish: grammatical structure and dialectal variation*

(50)   Muna ndéanfar di é... (Dn)
         'If one does not do it for her...'

On the other hand, the habitual present is usual in Gweedore:

(51)   Muna ndruideann sé é (Gd)
         'If he doesn't shut it'

In Connemara, at least, the present subjunctive is possible though less frequent: see Wigger 1972a:190.

12.1.2(ii) Conditional with hypothesis.

(52)   Dhá mbeadh lá maith ann, dhéanfainn é
         'If it were a nice day, I would do it'

In this type, the verb of the embedded sentence is preceded by *d(h)á* 'if' or *mara* (etc.) 'if not', which cause eclipsis and are followed by a dependent verb form (see 8.3.1) where available. They are now most frequently followed by the conditional. Except in the case of the substantive verb, the past subjunctive is still possible:

(53)   ...nuair a raghadh sí a' glaoch orthu chun bricfeaist ná féadadh sí suí ar an inneoin lena teas, nú dá bhféadadh, ní bhfaighdís an bricfeaist... (Mk)
         '...when she would go to call them to breakfast she could not sit on the anvil on account of its heat, or if she could, they wouldn't get breakfast...'
(54)   Dhá mbuailteá...(C)
         'If you should hit...'

There is a tendency in Munster to replace *dá* with *má* (which then, apart from the use of lenition instead of eclipsis, behaves exactly like *dá*):

(55)   Má dhéanfá aon fheabhsú ar an dtalamh... (Dn)
         'If you should make any improvements to the land...'
(56)   ...nó má dhéanfadh, do mharódh Mác Amhlaoibh iad (Mk)
         '...or if he did, Mác Amhlaoibh would kill them'

The verb in the main sentence is usually in the conditional mood (as in the above examples). However, in a vivid narrative style a past tense may be used:

(57) *Mara mbeadh go dtáinís-se, bhíos-sa imithe* (Dn)
 'If it hadn't been for the fact that you came, I was gone'

Where two conditions occur instead of a conditional (or past subjunctive), a verbal noun complement may be used following *agus* 'and' in the second condition:

(58) *Dá gcuirtí isteach i gcóra mór giúsaí í féin agus oiread aráin agus feóla a chuir isteach...* (Cf)
 'If she herself were put into a big pine chest and enough bread and meat were put in...'

An alternative construction in Cois Fhairrge (see de Bhaldraithe 1953/5: 154) is the introduction of the imperative into the conditional clause. Where the condition is the second element or where it follows a *dhá* 'if' clause, it is preceded by *agus/is* 'and':

(59) *Teagadh Sasanaí isteach, ní bheadh aon fhear níos sásta* (Cf)
 (lit. Let the English come in, no man would be more pleased)
 'If the English came in, no man would be more pleased'
(60) *Sé an rud céanna [a] tharlódh agus bíodh sé fhéin i láthair* (Cf)
 (lit. It is the same thing which would happen and let him be there)
 'It is the same thing that would happen if he himself were present'
(61) *Dhá dteigheá ar aonach agus díol gamhain...* (Cf)
 'If you were to go to the fair and sell a calf...'

12.1.3 Questions
Basically, all the dialects form a subordinated or embedded question by simply following the main or matrix verb with the normal question form:

(62) *An raibh tú sásta?* (C)
 'Were you content?'
(63) *Chuir sé ceist ort an raibh tú sásta* (C)
 'He asked you if you were content'

An alternative 'whether ... or' question can be treated in a similar fashion (for the deletion of the subject pronoun, see 9.2.3) :

(64)   *An raibh tú sásta nó nach raibh?* (C)
        'Were you content or not?'
(65)   *Chuir sé ceist ort an raibh tú sásta nó nach raibh* (C)
        'He asked you if you were content or not'

There are, however, other ways of forming an indirect or embedded 'alternative' question. The commonest construction in Donegal is to make use of *cé acu* 'which' + *an (ar)... nó nach (nár)*:

(66)   *Chuir sé ceist ort cé acu an raibh tú sásta nó nach raibh* (D)
        'He asked whether you were content or not'

While the straightforward *an (ar)... nó nach/ nár* etc. is the most usual construction in Connemara, there is the option of using *an (ar)..., mara(r)* 'if not':

(67)   *Chuir sé ceist orm an raibh tú sásta nó mara raibh* (Cn)
        'He asked me whether you were content or not'

In embedded questions, just as in finite complementation [see 11.1.1(i)], the tense is influenced by that of the matrix sentence: if it is in the past tense this will be transferred to the embedded question while the present is replaced by the past and the future by the conditional:

(68)   *Chuir sé ceist an raibh an bhean go maith*
        'He enquired if the woman was well'
(69)   *Chuir sé ceist an mbeadh an sagart ag teacht*
        'He asked if the priest would come'

In example (68) the question *An bhfuil an bhean go maith?* 'Is the woman well?' is embedded as *an raibh* (past) *an bhean go maith* and in (69) a question *An mbeidh* (future) *an sagart ag teacht?* 'Will the priest be coming?' is embedded as *an mbeadh* (conditional) *an sagart ag teacht*.

12.1.4 Adverbial subordination
For adverbial phrases which are followed by finite-type or verbal noun type complementation see 11.1.2(v).

12.1.4(i) *Temporal.* The majority of temporal adverbials are followed by direct relative clauses (e.g. *fhad is* 'as long as'); there are, however, some which require finite or verbal noun complementation, e.g. *go dtí* 'until', (*ar*) *feadh* 'as soon as' [see 11.1.2(v)4]). The cases of *sola* etc. 'before', *go/nach* 'until' and *ach* 'as soon as, when', which involve subordination, must now be considered.

12.1.4(i)1 *The adverbial* sola *etc. 'before'*: If the subordinate event is subsequent to that of the matrix sentence it may be expressed by the temporal adverbial clause formed with the element *sola* 'before' immediately preceding the subordinate verb. It has the same effect on the form as an indirect relative particle [see 12.1.1(ii)]:

(70) *Beidh sé anseo sola dtiocfaidh mé ar ais* (C)
'He will be here before I come back'
(71) *Phéinteáil sé an doras solar tháinig Pádraig* (C)
'He painted the door before Pádraig came'

When the embedded sentence is the future tense, the future may optionally (see Wigger 1972a:190), though now more rarely, be replaced by the present subjunctive or when the matrix verb is in the past by the past subjunctive [see 8.2.3(i)]. An example of the present subjunctive is:

(72) *Caithfidh mé mo cheann a chíoradh 'chuile mhaidin shala dtéighe mé 'un na scoile* (C)
'I have to comb my hair every morning before I go to school'

There is a tendency in Donegal for the habitual present or 'unmarked' tense to represent the future, e.g. *sola dtig* 'before he comes'. Compare a similar tendency in the case of conditionals in 12.1.2(i).

There is a lot of variation in the dialects: *sola* 'before' is widespread in Donegal and Connacht while *sara* is found in Munster. (The variant *seara* also occurs in Dunquin.) Other variations are *sulmá* and *soil* (which has many different phonetic variations : /soL/, /sel'/, /saːL/ etc.), both of which occur in Cois Fhairrge and have the same effect on the subordinate verb as a direct relative particle [see 12.1.1(i)]:

(73) *Bhí a fhios agamsa é sulmá chuala mé é* (Cf)
'I knew it before I heard it'
(74) *Déanfaidh sé múr soil bheas an chruach clúdaithe* (Cf)
'There will be a shower before the turfstack is covered'

324 *Modern Irish: grammatical structure and dialectal variation*

12.1.4(i)2 *The adverbial* go/nach *etc. 'until'*

(75) *Is gearr go dtosóidh siad air* (C)
   'It is a short time until they will begin it'
(76) *Níor scar sí leis gur mharaigh sí é* (C)
   'She didn't leave him go until she killed him'

If the aspectual notion is one of termination, the adverbial *go/nach* etc. 'until', which is morphologically identical to the *go/nach* etc.'that/that...not' used in complementation, may be employed. As in the case of *sola* 'before', the present subjunctive may optionally replace the future tense of a subordinate verb or if the verb of the matrix sentence is in the past, the past subjunctive may optionally replace the conditional:

(77) *Fan go dteaga sé* (C)
   'Wait until he will come'
(78) *B'éigean dhó fanacht go dteagtá* (C)
   'He had to wait until you would come'

12.1.4(i)3 *The adverbial* ach *'as soon as', 'when':*

(79) *Tá siad ag goil ar bhaint fhraoigh ach a dtiocfaidh an sioc* (Cf)
   'They are going cutting heather as soon as the frost comes'

The adverbial *ach*, which has the same effect on the subordinate verbal forms as an indirect relative (see 12.1.1), expresses a notion of contemporaneity. When the subordinate verb is in the future, as in the above Cois Fhairrge example, it can mean 'as soon as'. The future may be optionally, if rarely, replaced by the present subjunctive. When the subordinate verb is in the past tense, it can mean 'when, by the time':

(80) *Bhí sé a hocht a chlog ach a n-éiríos* (Dn)
   'It was eight when I got up'

12.1.4(ii) *Final.* In an embedded future tense sentence which denotes the purpose of the action expressed in the matrix sentence, the final adverbial *g o* 'in order to' (which causes eclipsis in the same way as the complementizer *go* 'that') may be used, as in (81):

(81) *Ná caith amach an t-uisce salach go dtabharfar an t-uisce glan isteach* (Dn)
'Don't throw out the dirty water, until you bring the clean water in'
(82) *Dúirt sé go dtiocfadh sé don Lochán Bheag go bhfeicfeadh sé ar fíor nó bréag an scéal* (Cf)
'He said he would come to Lochán Beag in order to see whether the story was true or false'

The future of the subordinate verb is in the conditional, as is (82). The future may rarely be replaced by a form identical with the present subjunctive/optative and the conditional may rarely be replaced by the past subjunctive. An example containing a form similar to the subjunctive is:

(83) *Teanam go raibh deoch againn* (Mo)
'Let's go to have a drink'

12.1.4(iii) Consecutive. Example (84) shows the use of the consecutive *go/nach* (*gur/nár*) 'so that' etc., which function exactly similarly to the complementizers *go/nach* etc. 'that/that...not':

(84) *Bhí an oíche chomh dubh go ndeachaidh mé treasna ar an gclaidhe* (Cf)
'The night was so black that I went over the stone wall'

The future of the subordinate verb may be replaced by a form identical to the present subjunctive:

(85) *Nach gann atá an áit ort go dtige tú isteach sa teach* (Cf)
'It must be due to a lack of space, that you come into the house'

12.1.4(iv) Causal. Examples (86) and (87) illustrate how the causal *go/nach* (*gur/nár*) 'because, since' function exactly similarly to the complementizers *go/nach* etc. 'that/ that ... not' (see de Bhaldraithe 1985b: 101-2).

(86) *Chuir sé fios ar mo sheanathair a thíocht aige go raibh gnatha aige dó* (C)
'He sent for my grandfather to come to him since he required him'
(87) *Dhiúltaigh sé é a dhéanamh nach raibh aon mheabhair aige ionntu* (C)
'He refused to do it because he had no understanding of them'

12.2 *Diabhal* 'Devil' etc. as a syntactic device

The word *diabhal* 'devil' etc. is employed as a swear word and in imprecations and curses. More notably, however, *diabhal (deamhan)* 'devil (demon)' etc. are used as a syntactic device (see Ó Siadhail 1980:46-58). Basically there are three types of syntactic usages which we can for convenience label the assertive usage, the conditional usage and the negative usage.

12.2.1 The assertive usage
Diabhal 'devil' etc. is followed in this usage by the complementizers *go/ nach* 'that/that...not' etc. and is found in all the major dialects:

(88)   *Diabhal gur cuma céard deir aon duine, labhraíodh duine sa gceart* (C)
'Indeed, it doesn't matter what anyone says, let a man speak rightly'
(89)   *Damnú go bhfuil mé ag déanamh go mbeidh mé leat* (D)
'Damn it, I think I'll go with you'

The assertive force seen with *diabhal* 'devil' and *damnú* 'damnation' (which is confined to Donegal) is exemplified in examples (88-9).

12.2.2 The conditional usage
This usage is characterized by the conditional sentence which follows *dheamhan* 'demon' etc.:

(90)   *Dheamhan/Damnú/Scrios Dé/ Scrios fia má tá fhios agam* (D)
'I am damned if I know'

This particular construction with *dheamhan* 'demon' or *damnú* etc. is peculiar to Donegal. It is presumably an abbreviation of sentences like:

(91)   *M'anam do dheamhan/Damnú [nár thaga] orm má tá a fhios agam*
'My soul to a demon/damnation [don't] take me, if I know'

12.2.3 The negative usage
The primary feature of this usage is that *diabhal* 'devil' etc. negates the sentence. A secondary feature is that it contains a quantitative idea.
    There are three subtypes of this negative usage:

12.2.3(i) Diabhal *'devil'* etc. with thematic fronting and a relative clause.
Example (92) illustrates this subtype and (93) shows the underlying unfronted version:

(92)   *Diabhal ceann a rug mé aréir air ach ceann a rug mé sa bhfeamainn air* (C)
(lit. Devil [the] one I caught last night but the one I caught in the seaweed)
'Indeed I didn't catch one last night except one I caught in the seaweed'

(93)   *Níor rug mé ar cheann aréir ach ceann a rug mé sa bhfeamainn air*
'I didn't catch one last night except one I caught in the seaweed'

In example (92) the theme of the sentence is fronted and negatived by *diabhal* 'devil' etc. The fronted theme is then followed by a direct relative clause. It is important to speak here of a theme, as a subject, object, predicative adjective or indeed an adverbial phrase can be fronted.

There is a close similarity between this thematic fronting and the fronting permissible in a marked narrative style, e.g. *Anonn ná anall ní dheachaigh sé ar feadh na hoíche* 'Back or forth, he didn't go the whole night'. Nevertheless, it must be observed that no relative clause is required in the narrative fronting (see 9.2.2). This subtype of the negative usage of *diabhal* 'devil' etc. does not seem to occur in Munster but is frequent in Connacht and Donegal.

In order to explain the behaviour of *diabhal* 'devil' etc. in this usage, it is now necessary to stress its quantitative nature. This is important, as when a fronted noun enumerates, measures etc., the following relative form of the substantive verb may be optionally deleted, e.g. *Cén aois atá sé? / Cén aois é?* 'What age is he?' (see 9.2.7). A similar deletion is possible in the case of thematic fronting in the negative usage of *diabhal* 'devil' etc. In example (94) this deletion is apparent; (95) shows the equivalent sentence without deletion, while (96) must be the underlying sentence without *diabhal* 'devil' etc. and thematic fronting.

(94)   *Diabhal neart air* (C)
(lit. Devil power on it)
'There is absolutely no helping it'

(95)   *Diabhal neart atá air*
(lit. Devil power which is on it)
'There is absolutely no helping it'

(96) *Níl neart air*
(lit. There is no power on it)
'There is no helping it'

This deletion rule appears to be obligatory in the common phrase *Diabhal a fhios (sin) agam* 'I don't know (that)'.

It is interesting to note that *diabhal* 'devil' etc. (with fronting followed by a relative clause) is also employed in responsives. As might be expected in the case of any responsive, a degree of deletion is entailed. It is sufficient to use *diabhal* 'devil' etc. together with the fronted theme:

(97) *Ní raibh creideamh ar bith ag do mháthair. Ní féidir!*
'Your mother had no religion. No!'
Dheamhan creideamh, muise, ach... (C)
'Absolutely none, in fact, but...'

The responsive in (97) is based on *Dheamhan creideamh a bhí ag mo mháthair, muise, ach...* (lit. demon [the] faith my mother had but...).

The echo form can also have an underlying auxiliary *déan* 'do' [see 11.3.2(i)]:

(98) *Chruinnigh siad ... 'feacháil an imeochadh sé.*
'They collected ... for him to see if he'd go off'.
Ach dheamhan imeacht (D)
'But no, none of it'

This echoic phrase must be derived from *Ach dheamhan imeacht a rinn sé* (lit. But demon departure he made), which is in turn based on *Níor imigh sé* 'He didn't go off'.

Furthermore, the responsive can be pronominalized with a general all-purpose *é* 'it':

(99) *Nár bhuail aon bhuidéal ósna daoine muinteartha thú féin?*
'Didn't any bottle thrown by your relations strike you?'
An diabhal é ach aon cheann amháin ó Mhuirisín Bhán (M)
'No, none at all except one single one from Muirisín Bán'

**12.2.3(ii) Diabhal *'devil' etc. with* a/ar *followed by the eclipsed dependent form of the negated verb.* In this subtype of the negative usage *diabhal* 'devil' takes *a* (in the past tense *ar*), which is followed by the eclipsed dependent form of the negatived verb. There are examples from all the major dialects. The sentence underlying (100) is given in (101):

(100) *Diabhal a raibh sé an-dona* (C)
'Indeed it wasn't very bad'
(101) *Ní raibh sé an-dona*
'It was not very bad'

Once more, it is important to stress the quantitative sense of *diabhal* 'devil' etc. in an example such as the following:

(102) *Diabhal a raibh de mhaith don tsagart a bheith ag caint leis* (D)
(lit. Devil there was of good for the priest to be talking to him)
'It was absolutely no good for the priest to talk to him'

The substantive verb may be deleted before the prepositional pronoun *ann/ inti*. Example (103) must be derived from (104):

(103) *Dheamhan inti ach tiachóigín de dhuine* (C)
'She was certainly nothing but a plump little person'
(104) *Dheamhan a raibh inti ach tiachóigín de dhuine*
'She was certainly nothing but a plump little person'

While the rather cumbersome title of this subtype adequately describes its behaviour, there remains the question of how to relate the syntax involved to that of Irish as a whole. To all intents and purposes the verb negated by *diabhal* 'devil' etc. is in an indirect relative clause. It seems that some general rule demands an indirect relative clause because *diabhal* 'devil' etc. is neither subject nor object of the (negatived) verb. In this way it behaves similarly to *a/ar* + eclipsis meaning 'all of that which' [see also example (9)]:

(105) *Sin a bhfuil d'airgead ann*
'That (there) is all the money there is'

Both the 'all of which' and 'devil' construction also share a quantitative idea. It would therefore seem that the quantitative concept intrinsic to this 'devil' construction is crucial to any interpretation of the phenomenon.

330   *Modern Irish: grammatical structure and dialectal variation*

12.2.3(iii) Diabhal *'devil'* etc. in place of the copula form. In this third and final subtype of the negative usage, the copula form is deleted entirely. Though this subtype is limited to a certain sort of sentence, it is found in all dialects. Examples (106) and (108) are presumably derived from (107) and (109).

(106)   *Dheamhan i bhfad go gcuirfidh mise athrach ar an áit seo* (D)
         'It certainly won't be long until I change this place'
(107)   *Ní i bhfad go gcuirfidh mise athrach ar an áit seo*
         'It won't be long until I change this place'
(108)   *An diabhal magadh san* (M)
         'That is certainly no joke'
(109)   *Ní magadh san*
         'That is no joke'

This use of *diabhal* 'devil' etc. appears to be confined to fronted adverbial phrases and classificatory copula sentences. The use in the classificatory sentences may be a Munster feature. The employment of the article with *diabhal* 'devil', as exemplified in (108), is particularly common in Munster and is strikingly similar to the employment of the article following a fronted adjective in a classificatory copula sentence, e.g. *Is deas an duine é* 'He is a nice person', based on *Is duine deas é* 'He is a nice person' [see 10.3.1(i)]. Sporadically in all dialects the article may precede a following noun, e.g. *Diabhal an oíche...* 'Devil the night...'.

12.2.3(iv) *Negative usage as a complement.* Because of the strongly emphatic nature of the *diabhal* 'devil' etc. construction, there are few enough examples of a finite complement. Nevertheless, they do occur:

(110)   *Shíl mé dheamhan lá iomrá a bhí agat air* (D)
         'I thought you had made absolutely no mention of it'

The syntax of this negative usage is so marked that no complementizer is required. What is interesting here is that, as was earlier pointed out [see 12.2.3(i)], the first subtype involving thematic fronting and a relative clause has features in common on one hand with copula fronting (see 10.3.5(i)), i.e. the need for a relative clause, and on the other hand with narrative fronting (see 9.2.2) i.e. the non-appearance of a complementizer.

12.2.4 Conclusion

In summary it can be said that the assertive usage is found in all dialects, the conditional usage in Donegal only, while the negative usage, all three subtypes included, is found in the major dialects. Nevertheless, in Munster the first subtype of the negative usage is largely confined to responsives, e.g. *ná an diabhal é* 'most certainly not'. The second and third subtypes of the negative usage are more common and significantly more widespread in Connacht and Donegal. The range of words involved include *diabhal* 'devil' (and the milder forms *fial, diabhach, riach*; *deamhan* 'demon' in Munster and *an tubaist* 'the misfortune' in Muskerry); *diabhal, dheamhan* and *damnú* 'damnation' in Donegal and *diabhal, d(h)eamhan* (and the milder forms *daighean* together with *dhe* or *rí ná aon* in East Galway) in Connacht.

12.3 Questions expecting negative answers

Connacht and Donegal dialects have a mechanism for forming questions which imply that a definite negative answer is awaited. Such questions are formed in Connacht dialects by prefixing *c(h)ea(l)* or *cé* to the negative question, as in:

(111) *Cheal nach raibh a fhios agat é?* (C)
 'Did you not know about it?'
(112) *Cá bhfuil bhur n-imirce inniu, a bhuachaillí?*
 'Where is your journey to today, boys?'
 Ag goil 'un na feise atá muid. Ceal nach bhfuil tusa ag teacht freisin? (C)
 'We are going to the "feis". Are you not coming too?'
(113) *Cé nach bhfuil tú ag cur an leith eile?*
 'Are you not sowing the other half?'
 M'anam nach bhfuil mé i n-an (C)
 'I assure you I can't'

Interestingly, in Cois Fhairrge at least, when it is in a responsive *tuige* 'why' may be used in the same fashion (without having the force of 'for what reason'):

(114) *Níl mé fuar*
 'I am not cold'
 Tuige nach bhfuil?
 'Are you not, really?'

In Donegal, this type of question is formed by prefixing *ná* (regularly shortened to /na/) with the subsequent verbal form stressed:

(115)   *Cha dteachaidh sé go Baile Átha Cliath inné*
'He didn't go to Dublin yesterday'
Ná nach dteachaidh? (D)
'Did he not?'

(116)   *Ní bheifeá thusa ábalta é a bhualadh*
'You wouldn't be able to beat him'
Ná nach mbeadh, do bharúil? (D)
'Would I not, do you think?'

Obviously, in examples (111-3) a simple negative question would be sufficient, e.g. *Nach raibh a fhios agat é?* 'Didn't you know it?' in example (111), *Nach bhfuil tusa ag teacht freisin?* 'Aren't you coming too?' in example (112). The use of *c(h)eal, cé* or *ná* merely increases the degree of definiteness with which a negative response is awaited.

There appears to be no equivalent mechanism in Munster, the only possibility being to focus on the verbal phrase by the use of *an amhlaidh...* 'is it thus...' [see 10.3.5(iii)].

12.4 Compounding of neutral coordinators with subordinators

The two most neutral of the coordinators *agus/is* 'and' and *nó* 'or' tend to be compounded with subordinators (see Ó Siadhail 1984b:129-30, de Bhaldraithe 1950:166-7 and Ó Cuív 1960/1:5).

12.4.1 *Agus/is* 'and'

It has already been shown (see 11.1.8) that when *agus/is* 'and' subordinates complements there can be temporal, concessive and causal inferences. This may have played a part in associating ideas of temporality etc. with *agus/is* 'and'. In addition to this *agus/is* can be used in a final sense with *go/nach* 'that/ that...not'.

(117)   *Ní raibh tada ag gabháil fúithi ná thairti ach an mac seo a chur os cionn na talún, agus go mbeadh sé leis an gcíos a bhailiú ...* (C)
'There was nothing on her mind except putting this son in charge of the land, in order that he would be there to collect the rent...'

The use of *agus/is* in equivalences of the sort *chomh luath is (a bhí sé)* 'as soon as (he was)' undoubtedly also affects the intrusion of *agus/is* on the subordinators. Though less frequent than equivalences, the optional use of *agus/is* in assertives, e.g. *Tá fhios ag Dia is go bfhuil...* 'God knows that...', influences and is in turn influenced by the general extension of this phenomenon.

This compounding of *agus/is* with other subordinators is found in all dialects. It is very often an optional inclusion, and this is indicated by brackets in the following sections:

12.4.1(i)*Temporal.* Connacht: *fhad is* 'as long as'; *ar an bpoinnte (is)* 'as soon as'; *shul (is)* 'before'; *an dá lá (is)* 'as long as'; *chún's* 'while, as long as'
  Donegal: *fhad is* 'as long as'
  Kerry: *san am's* 'at the time when'
  All of these are followed by a direct relative clause.

12.4.1(ii) *Causal.* Connacht: *faoi (is), lá (is), faoi rá (is), tháls (tharla is)* 'seeing that, as'
  All of these are followed by a finite complement.
  Donegal: *cionn is* 'because'
  This is followed by either a finite or a verbal noun complement.

12.4.1(iii) *Concessive.* Munster: *cé is (go/nach)* 'although'
  Connacht and Munster: *bíodh is* 'although'
  Despite its origin as a third singular imperative, *bíodh* functions as a subordinator and is followed by a finite complement.

12.4.1(iv) *Final.* Connacht: *sa gcaoi (is), i gcruth's, i riocht is (ros)* 'in order to' and the quasi-final *le súil (is)* 'in the hope that'
  Munster: *d'fhonn is* 'in order that'
  Donegal: *le súil's* 'in the hope that'
  All of these are followed by a finite complement.

12.4.1(v) *Resultative.* All dialects: *chomh* adjective *(is)* 'so *adjective* that'
  This is followed by a finite complement.

12.4.1(vi) *Comparative.* Connacht: *fearacht is, nós is* 'as though'
  These are normally followed by a condition *dhá...* 'if...'

(118)   *Fearacht agus dá mbeadh sí ag iarraidh í féin a bhaint as...* (Cf)
'As though she were trying to extract herself...'

12.4.1(vii) Unconditional concessive. Dunquin: *pé cuma's* 'however'
This compounding of *agus/is* is found also in Connacht, at least, with quantitative adverbs such as *timpeall (is), tuairim is* 'around about' or intruding in the *gach a* 'all of that which' type of phrase, for example: *gach (is) a raibh d'airgead aige* 'all he had by way of money'. A further instance in Connacht of this intrusive *agus/is* 'and' is after nouns expressing a period of time:

(119)   *Bhí scaitheamh is go raibh mé in ann a léite* (C)
'There was a while I was able to read it'

While this phenomenon of the intrusive neutral coordinator *agus/is* 'and' appears in all the major dialects, it seems to be most pervasive in Connacht, and is even found in questions and in embedded questions:

(120)   *Níl a fhios agam an n-ólann nó's mara n-ólann* (C)
'I don't know if (he) drinks or doesn't'
(121)   *Cén fáth's* (C)
'Why?'

12.4.2 *Nó* 'or'
The use of *nó* 'or' as a subordinator is much more limited than that of *agus/is* 'and'. Nevertheless there are examples of this type of subordination:

(122)   '*Caithfidh tú réidh a dhéanamh go gasta,' arsa mise, 'nó beidh an t-aonach ann Dé hAoine*'
'"You must get ready quickly" said I, "because the fair is on Friday"'

Correspondingly, the compounding of *nó* 'or' with subordinators is much less extensive than that of *agus/is* 'and'. Basically, there are two usages involved: one in final clauses, the other following the epistemic modal [see 11.2.2(ii)] *ní foláir...* 'it must be that...'.

12.4.2(i) Nó 'or' before go/nach 'until'. The coordinator *nó* may optionally precede the subordinator *go/nach* 'until/until... not'.

(123) *Bhí sé ag diúl ansin ar an seanleon nó go raibh sé fásta suas ina fhear* (C)
'He was there sucking on the old lion until he was a grown-up man'
(124) *Stad níor dheineadar nó gur bhaineadar amach tigh an duine bhreoite* (M)
'A stop they didn't make until they reached the sick man's house'

Without doubt, the large semantic load which *go/nach* carry (as simple complementizers or meaning 'in order to, until' etc.) plays a role in the spread of the neutral coordinators in general. Nevertheless *nó* 'or' can in Munster at least precede even *go dtí go/nach* 'until that/that...not', as in the Munster example:

(125) *Dúirt sé le fear meánaosta a bhí ina sheasamh ann breith ar shrian ar an gcapall nó go dtí go n-ólfadh sé deoch* (M)
'He said to a middle-aged man who was standing there to hold the horse's bridle until he would take a drink'

12.4.2(ii) Nó 'or' following ní foláir. It seems to be a particular Munster feature that *nó* appears normally between the epistemic modal *ní foláir* 'it must be that' and the following finite complement:

(126) *Ní foláir liom nó is mallacht duine éigin a thuit ortha...* (M)
'I think it must be someone's curse fell on them...'
(127) *Dúirt bean éigin nach foláir nó go raibh a ndóthain púdair anois aca...* (M)
'Some woman said that it must be that they had enough powder now...'

12.5 Proportional correlations

Sentences containing a proportional correlative ('the more, the better') are expressed by using *dhá* 'however' followed, with the exception of a handful of adjectives where a noun is employed, by a form of the relevant adjective:

(128) *Dhá aistí é is amhlaidh is fearr é* (C)
'The stranger it is the better'

The use may vary somewhat from dialect to dialect as regards the way in which the verb/copula that introduces the second correlative is focused (*is amhlaidh/is ea* 'it is thus' etc.).

There is in many languages, as in English, a tendency to have an echoic effect in these proportional correlatives. This need is often satisfied in Connemara, by the repetition of *dhá*, the second *dhá* meaning 'of all that there is':

(129)   *Dhá mhéad dhá bhfuil ann, is ea is fearr é* (Cn)
        'The more of all there is, the better'

There is in Donegal another construction in which the echoic effect is achieved by a doubling of *má* 'if' (see Ó Siadhail 1979:146):

(130)   *Más mó a bheas ann, más fearr é* (Gd)
        'The more that will be there, the better'
(131)   *Más lú a bhí an leabhar, más mó abhí ann* (Gd)
        'The smaller the book was, the more there was'
(132)   *Más gaiste a dhéanfas tú é, más mó a gheobhas muid* (Gd)
        'The quicker you do it, the more we'll get'

On the face of it, it would seem to be the doubling of *má* 'if', substituted for *d(h)á* of the other major dialects. However, *ma(r)s* is reported from other Donegal varieties (see Lucas 1979:274) which suggests that the first element is *mar* 'as'. The semantic development is seen in the following example:

(133)   *Ma(r)s fuaire a dh' eiríonn sé, sé sin ma(r)s mó éadaí a chuireann sé air* (Rl)
        'The colder it gets, the more clothes he puts on'

The *r* in *mar* 'as' is generally lost in Gweedore *mas*; the process may have been facilitated by *más...* 'if it...', which (due to vocalic shortening before a stressed sentential element) is pronounced identically.

12.6 Suspensive *ná*

A distinctive trait of Munster dialects is the use of what may be called a suspensive *ná*. It occurs both in a pseudo-*wh*-question or cleft:

(134)   *Cad a raghadh ceangailte im' mhéir ná an dubhán* (M)
        'What should get stuck in my finger but the hook'

(135) *Cé bheadh ar an bhfód ná deirfiúr do* (M)
'Who should be on the scene but a sister of his'
(136) *'Sé an chéad scéal do chuir an bheirt ar bun ná 'An Long Dhóite'* (M)
'The first story the two got off on was "An Long Dhóite"'

The suspensive *ná* merely marks the natural hiatus which follows the build-up of a pseudo-*wh*-question or cleft. There is, however, a difference between the pseudo-*wh*-question and a pseudo-cleft. In the case of pseudo-*wh*-questions the hiatus is never left blank, irrespective of the dialect. In Connacht and Donegal *ach* 'but' is employed. This *ach* optionally alternates with *ná* in Munster:

(137) *Cad do bhuailfeadh chugam ach an gasra céanna ban óg* (M)
'What should be heading for me but the same group of young women'

It may be noted in passing that there is in Munster another semantically similar usage of *ná* 'but' before the complementizers *go/ gur* 'that' etc.:

(138) *Ní raibh aon duine óg ná aosta san oileán so...ná go raibh a fhios aige Tomás Maol cad dob aois é* (M)
'There was nobody young or old in this island...but that Tomás Maol knew what his age was'
(139) *Níl gnó agamsa á rá ná gur chailleas féin mo chuid suilt...* (M)
'I have no business saying it but that I lost my enjoyment...'

12.7 Variant order in perfectives with *chomh* 'so'

A variant order occurs which, when the intensifier *chomh* 'so' has an anaphoric reference, places the verbal adjective in final position:

(140) *Tá sé chomh stoithneach fágtha!* (Im)
'It is left so tousled!'
(141) *Tá siad chomh ardnósach fáite!* (Im)
'They have got so grand!'

Although examples (140-1) are from Inishmaan, it may be that they are features of Connacht Irish.

Glossary

The following is a brief glossary of terms which may be peculiar to Irish grammar.

Basic grade:
Through the pronoun system in Irish, although variously realized in the dialects, there are four possible grades, e.g. *mé* 'me', *mise* '*me*', *mé féin* '*myself*', *mise mé féin* '*me myself*'. These grades may for convenience be termed 'basic', 'contrastive', 'emphatic' and 'contrastive-emphatic'. [The emphatic elements in the translations are italicized.] Certain syntactic rules affect the basic grade but not the other grades.

Conjunctive/disjunctive pronoun:
The form of the third person (and in some dialects the second singular) personal pronouns varies according to whether they follow directly a finite verbal form or not; those which (with the exception of a particular usage in Donegal dialects) do, i.e. *sé* 'he', *sí* 'she', *siad* 'they', (*tú* 'you'), may be referred to as 'conjunctive' pronouns and those which do not as 'disjunctive' pronouns, i.e. *é, í, iad, thú*.

Dependent form:
See independent form.

Disjunctive form:
See conjunctive form.

Eclipsis:
Eclipsis is the traditional term for one of the grammatically conditioned initial mutations of consonants in Irish. Historically there was a preceding nasal and for this reason scholars of the older language refer to the phenomenon as 'nasalization'. However, as the mutation is realized as

voicing in the case of voiceless plosives, the more neutral native term eclipsis (from *urú*) seems more appropriate to a synchronic description.

Independent/dependent form:
A feature of some irregular verbs is that two different forms or roots may be employed in the same tense or mood; the form or root used in a statement is called the 'independent form' while that which follows negative or question particles and complementizers is called the dependent form, e.g. *bhí* 'was' (independent) beside (*ní*) *raibh* 'was (not)'.

Lenition:
Lenition is one of the grammatically conditioned initial mutations of consonants in Irish. The term corresponds to the native term *séimhiú* 'softening, smoothing'. The mutation is realized in a majority of consonants as fricatization. The inappropriate term 'aspiration' is sometimes used by modern Irish grammarians but it is avoided in this account.

Prepositional pronoun:
In Irish when a personal pronoun is the object of a preposition it combines with the preposition and is inflected for person and number, *ag* 'at', *agam* 'at me', *agat* 'at you'. These sets of inflections are traditionally referred to as prepositional pronouns.

Substantive verb:
There are two verbs 'to be' in Irish: *is* 'the copula' and *tá* 'the substantive verb', a situation which corresponds very roughly with, for example, Spanish. In the broadest terms, and with several exceptions, the substantive verb is used except where two nouns are equated or in sentence fronting, both of which usages are the original domain of the copula.

References

Ahlqvist, Anders. 1972. On the position of pronouns in Irish. *Éigse* 16:171-6.
Breathnach, Mícheál. 1906. *Cnoc na nGabha*. Dublin: Ó Dubhthaigh.
    1910. *Cnoc na nGabha*. Dublin: Ó Dubhthaigh.
    1924. *Cnoc na nGabha*. Dublin: Ó Dubhthaigh.
Breatnach, Risteard B. 1940. A note on the voicing of sibilants in the Irish of Cape Clear Island, Co. Cork. *Éigse* 2:87-8.
    1947. *The Irish of Ring, Co. Waterford*. Dublin: Dublin Institute for Advanced Studies.
    1960/1. Initial mutation of substantives after preposition and singular article in Déise Irish. *Éigse* 9:217-22.
Chomsky, Noam and Halle, Morris. 1968. *The sound pattern of English*. New York: Harper and Row.
Chung, Sandra and McCloskey, James. 1987. Government barriers and small clauses in Modern Irish. *Linguistic Inquiry* 18.2: 173-237.
de Bhaldraithe, Tomás. 1945. *The Irish of Cois Fhairrge, County Galway*. Dublin; Dublin Institute for Advanced Studies.
    1948. Varia. *Éigse* 4:165-8.
    1950. Varia. *Éigse* 6:46-9.
    1953. *Gaeilge Chois Fhairrge: an deilbhíocht*. Dublin: Dublin Institute for Advanced Studies.
    1953/5. Nótaí. *Éigse* 7:154.
    1956/7a. 'Aimhreas' mar a chuirtear i gcaint é. *Éigse* 8:147-9.
    1956/7b. Nótaí Comhréire. *Éigse* 8:242-6.
    1977. *Seanchas Thomáis Leighléis*. Dublin: An Clóchomhar.
    1985a. Varia IX. *Ériu* 36:199-201.
    1985b. Nótaí gramadaí. *Celtica* 17:101-4.
de Búrca, Seán. 1958. *The Irish of Tourmakeady, Co. Mayo*. Dublin:Dublin Institute for Advanced Studies.
Finck, Franz Nikolaus. 1899. *Die Araner Mundart*. Marburg:Elwert.

Greene, David.1972. The responsive in Irish and Welsh. In Pilch, Herbert and Thurow, Joachim (eds.), *Indo-Celtica*, pp. 59-72. Munich: Max Hueber.

Gussmann, Edmund.1986. Autosegments, linked matrices, and the Irish lenition. In Kastovsky, Dieter and Szwedek, Aleksander (eds.) *Linguistics across historical and geographical boundaries vol. 2: Descriptive, Contrastive and Applied Linguistics*. Berlin: Mouton de Gruyter.

Holmer, Nils. 1962. *The dialects of Co. Clare: Part 1*. Dublin: Royal Irish Academy.

1965. *The dialects of Co. Clare: Part 2*. Dublin: Royal Irish Academy.

Jackson, Kenneth. 1968. *Scéalta ón mBlaoscaod*. Dublin: An Cumann le Béaloideas Éireann.

Lakoff, George. 1970. *Irregularity in syntax*. New York: Holt, Rinehart and Winston.

Lucas, Leslie, W. 1979. *Grammar of Ros Goill Irish, Co. Donegal*. Belfast: Institute of Irish Studies.

Mac Giollarnáth, Seán. 1939. *Peadar Chois Fhairrge*. Dublin: Oifig an tSoláthair.

McCloskey, James. 1979. *Transformational syntax and model theoretic semantics: a case study in Modern Irish*. Dordrecht and Boston: D. Reidel.

1985. The Modern Irish double relative and syntactic binding. *Ériu* 36:45-84.

McKone, Kim. 1981. Final /t/ to /d/ after unstressed vowels and an Old Irish sound law. *Ériu* 32:29-44.

Máire. 1961. *Ó mhuir go sliabh*. Dublin: Oifig an tSoláthair.

1962. *Úna Bhán*. Dublin: Oifig an tSoláthair.

Mhac an Fhailligh, Éamonn. 1968. *The Irish of Erris, Co. Mayo*. Dublin: Dublin Institute for Advanced Studies.

Ní Dhomhnaill, Cáit. 1969/70. Séimhiú thar éis an ainmbhriathair thabharthaí. *Éigse* 13:1-9.

Ó Briain, Mícheál. 1947. *Cnósach focal ó Bhaile Bhúirne* (ed. by Ó Cuív, Brian). Dublin: Dublin Institute for Advanced Studies.

Ó Buachalla, Breandán. 1977. *Ní* and *cha* in Ulster Irish. *Ériu* 28:92-141.

1980. The verbal adjective formant *-iste* in Ulster Irish. *Ériu* 31:39-45.

1985. The f-future in Modern Irish: a reassessment. Dublin: Proceedings of the Royal Irish Academy.

Ó Cadhain, Máirtín. 1948. *An braon broghach*. Dublin: Oifig an tSoláthair.

Ó Criomhthain, Tomás. 1928. *Allagar na hInse*. Dublin: Oifig an tSoláthair.
1929. *An t-Oileánach*. Dublin: Oifig an tSoláthair.
1956. *Seanchas ón Oileán Tiar*. Dublin: Educational Company of Ireland.
Ó Cróinín, Seán. 1980. *Seanachas Amhlaoibh Ó Luínse* (ed. by Ó Cróinín, Donncha). Dublin: Cumann Bhéaloidis Éireann.
Ó Cuív, Brian. 1944. *The Irish of West Muskerry, Co. Cork*. Dublin:Dublin Institute for Advanced Studies.
1951. *Irish dialects and Irish-speaking districts*. Dublin: Dublin Institute for Advanced Studies.
1960/1. An méid. *Éigse* 9:5.
Ó Dochartaigh, Cathair. 1975/6. 'Cha' and 'ní' in the Irish of Ulster. *Éigse* 16:317-36.
1977/9. Lenition and dependency phonology. *Éigse* 17:457-94.
Ó Domhnaill, Eoghan. 1940. *Scéal Hiúdaí Sheáinín*. Dublin: Oifig an tSoláthair.
Ó Máille, Tomás. 1912. Contributions to the history of verbs of existence in Irish. *Ériu* 6:1-102.
Ó Máille, T.S. 1973. *Liosta focal as Ros Muc*. Dublin: Irish University Press.
Ó Maolchathaigh, Séamas. 1963. *An gleann agus a raibh ann*. Dublin: An Clóchomhar.
Ó Muirí, Damien. 1982. *Comhréir Ghaeilge Ghaoth Dobhair*. Dublin: Coiscéim.
Ó Murchú, Máirtín. 1969a. Common core and underlying forms. *Ériu* 21:42-75.
1969b. The 2nd plural imperative in Modern Irish. *Éigse* 35:163-71.
1986. R caol i dtús focal: blúire canúineolaíocht. In Watson, Seosamh (ed.) *Féilscríbhinn Thomáis de Bhaldraithe*, pp. 19-26. Dublin: An Clóchomhar.
Ó Neachtain, Eoghan. 1936. *Cam-chuarta i n-Éirinn* (translation from William Bulfin). Dublin: Oifig an tSoláthair.
O' Rahilly, T.F. 1932. *Irish dialects past and present*. Dublin: Browne and Nolan.
1940/2. Some instance of vowel shortening in Munster. *Ériu* 13:119-27.
Ó Sé, Diarmaid. 1983. Gaeilge Chorca Dhuibhne. Unpublished Ph.D. thesis, University College Dublin.
1984. Coimriú siollaí tosaigh sa Ghaeilge. *Éigse* 20:171-86.
Ó Searcaigh, Séamus. 1939. *Coimhréir Ghaedhilg an Tuaiscirt*. Dublin: Oifig an tSoláthair.
Ó Siadhail, Mícheál. 1973. Abairtí freagartha agus míreanna freagartha sa

Nua- Ghaeilge. *Ériu* 24:134-59.

1978. *Téarmaí tógála agus tís as Inis Meáin*. Dublin: Dublin Institute for Advanced Studies.

1979. Roinnt athrúintí suntasacha i gcanúint chonallach. *Ériu* 30:146.

1980. Diabhal (deamhan 7rl) mar dheis chomhréire sa nGaeilge. *Ériu* 31:46-58.

1982. Cardinal numbers in Modern Irish. *Ériu* 23:101-7.

1983. The erosion of the copula in Modern Irish dialects. *Celtica* 25:117-27.

1984a. Agus(is)/and: a shared syntactic feature. *Celtica* 26:125-37.

1984b. A note on gender and pronoun substitution in Modern Irish dialects. *Ériu* 25:173-7.

1988. *Learning Irish*. Newhaven and London: Yale University Press.

Ó Siadhail, Mícheál and Wigger, Arndt. 1975. *Córas fuaimeanna na Gaeilge*. Dublin: Dublin Institute for Advanced Studies.

Ó Tuathail, Éamonn. 1939. On the Irish sibilants. *Éigse* 1:281-4.

Quiggin, Edmund C. 1906. *A dialect of Donegal*. Cambridge: Cambridge University Press.

Quin, E.G. 1969. On the Modern Irish f-future. *Ériu* 21:32-41.

Sjoestedt-Jonval, M.L. 1931. *Phonétique d'un parler irlandais de Kerry*. Paris: Ernest Leroux.

1938. *Déscription d'un parler irlandais de Kerry*. Paris: Champion.

Sommerfelt, Alf. 1922. *The dialect of Torr, Co. Donegal*. Oslo: Dybwald.

Stenson, Nancy. 1981. *Studies in Irish syntax*. Tübingen: Gunter Narr.

Wagner, Heinrich. 1958. *Linguistic atlas and survey of Irish dialects: vol.1*. Dublin: Dublin Institute for Advanced Studies.

1959. *Gaeilge Theilinn*. Dublin: Dublin Institute for Advanced Studies.

1964. *Linguistic atlas and survey of Irish dialects: vol.2*. Dublin: Dublin Institute for Advanced Studies.

1966. *Linguistic atlas and survey of Irish dialects: vol.3*. Dublin: Dublin Institute for Advanced Studies.

1969. *Linguistic atlas and survey of Irish dialects: vol.4*. Dublin: Dublin Institute for Advanced Studies.

1986. Iarfhocal ar ní agus cha sa Ghaeilge. In Watson, Seosamh (ed.) *Féilscríbhinn Thomáis de Bhaldraithe*, pp. 1-10. Dublin:An Clóchomhar.

Ward, Alan. 1974. The grammatical structure of Modern Irish. Unpublished Ph.D. thesis, Dublin University.

Wigger, Arndt. 1970. *Nominalformen im Conamara-Irischen*. Hamburg: Lüdke.

1972a. Preliminaries to a generative morphology of the Modern Irish verb. *Ériu* 23:162-213.
1972b. *Grammatik und Sprachvendung in der Satzordnung des Neueirischen.* In Studemand, Michael (ed.) *Festschrift Wilhelm Giese,* pp. 251-89. Hamburg: Buske.

Index of Irish words

Included in this index are those Irish words which are discussed phonologically or morphologically or which determine a particular type of syntax. Words which are used to illustrate regular initial mutations or verbal endings, or to exemplify syntactic constructions are excluded.

a possessive 115, 122, 126, 130, 131
a preverbial particle in verbal noun complement 115; *a chodladh* (go) to sleep 280
a relative particle; direct 115, 177; indirect 125; inclusive 329
a vocative particle 116
á, dhá see *do*
a dhath nothing 88
abair say 190 (full paradigm); flexionless form *deir* 193, 194; past impers. *dúrthas* 194; past 1st sing. *dúrt, duart* 194; past impers. *dúrthas* 194
abha(inn) river 42, 51, 157, 158; gen. *abhann* 157; gen. *oibhne* 51, 157; pl. *oibhneacha(í)* 42; pl. *oibhní* 95
Abrán, Aibreán, Oibreán April 40, 51
absalóid, asbalóid absolution 90, 101
ach as soon as, when 323, 324
ach but, only 218, 337
acu see *ag*
adharc horn 73, 75, 76
adhmad, aidhmad timber 84, 87
aer air 64
ag at 115, 139, 265, 266, 281, 294, 296; *agam* at me 42, 88, 139; *agat* at you 92; *aice, oice* at her 42, 139; *aige, oige* at him 42, 139; *acu* at them 139
ag because 267

agus/is and 117, 207, 216, 284, 311, 321, 332-4
áibhirseoir devil 32
Aibreán, Abrán, Oibreán April 40, 51
aice see *ag*
aidhmad, adhmad timber 84, 87
aifreann mass 22
aige see *ag*
aigne mind 22
aill cliff 131, 132, 161; pl. *altrachaí* 161
aimhleas disadvantage 70
aimhreas, oimhreas doubt 40, 51
aimsir time, weather 54, 55, 146
ainm name 21, 147, 161; pl. *ainm(n)eachaí* 161
aipeachan ripening 138
air see *ar*
aireachtáil feeling 262
áirimh count; past *dh'áirimh* 176
ais back 59
aisti see *as*
aistir journey 145
áit place 60, 141, 148, 313, 317; pl. *áiteacha(í)* 141, 160; pl. *áiteanna* 160
aithin, aithnigh recognize; past *d'aithin, d'aithnigh* 173
aithne acquaintance 22, 91, 103, 146
aithrí repentance 91, 103
aithris narrating 103

álainn beautiful; comp. *áilne* (→ *áille*) 98
Albain Scotland 21
altrachaí see *aill*
am time 19, 49, 146, 151 (full inflection) 313; gen. *ama* 146
amadán fool 39
amá(i)r(e)ach tomorrow 88
amháin, é amháin although 269
amharc sight 78
amhlaidh thus 96, 332, 335
amhrán song 64, 76, 78
ampla greed 23
an definite article 127
an positive copula question see *is*
an positive question particle 23, 125
an- very 26
an dá lá (is) as long as 333
an tan when 311
an té he who 212
anáil breath 39
anam soul 161; pl. *anamnacha* 161
ancaire anchor 55
anmhaith very good 22
ann see *i*
anocht tonight 26
anois now 23
anraith, eanraith broth 56, 99
anró hardship 53, 54, 98, 99
aobha, aonna liver 163
aomhóg, naomhóg corracle 57
aon any 27
ar on 115, 139, 263-6, 277, 281, 305, 307, 313; *orm* on me 139; *air* on him/it 139; *oirthi* on her/it 139; *oraibh* on you (pl.) 79
ár our 126
ar an bpoinnte (is) as soon as 333
ar chuntar on condition that 270
ar feadh as soon as 269, 323
ar obair in action, started 302
ar son because, since 268
ar thoib about to 302
ar tí about to 302
arán bread 23, 33
Árannach Aran islander 144

ard high 42, 51, 86; comp. *oirde* 42, 86
ard- superb 26
ardaghadh (→ *ardú*) raising 197
ardaigh raise 170, 197
as out of, from 116, 139, 233; *asam* out of me 139; *aisti* out of her/it 139; *asaibh* out of you (pl.) 79
as cionn above 36
as ucht because, since 268
asaibh see *as*
asal donkey 59, 135, 147; gen. *asail* 135
asam see *as*
asbalóid, absalóid absolution 101
ath- re- 27
athair father 25, 60, 135, 136, 157; gen. *athar* 25, 135, 136, 157; gen. *athara* 157
áthas joy 60
athd(h)áir recurrent heat in cattle 118
athrú change 52
atornae, tornae lawyer 51
ba(bh) see *is*
bacach beggar 136; voc. sing. *bacaigh* 136
bacach lame; pl. *bacacha* 31
bacadh, bacaint hindering 197
bacóideach, bocóideach bellying (of sails) 41
bád boat 59, 107, 136, 140, 148, 159; gen. *báid* 107; pl. *bádaí* 140, 144, 159; pl. *báid* 136, 159, 168; pl. *báideachaí* 159
bád iascach fishing boat 85
bádóir boatman 10, 33, 144, 152, (full inflection) 159; 'gen. *bádóra* 159; pl. *bádóirí* 140, 159
bagairt threat(ening) 144, 195, 306
báidín little boat 34, 85
baileaghadh (→ *bailiú, balú*) gathering 88
bailigh collect; pres. 1st sing. *bailím* 32; past *bhailigh* 175; past hab. *bhailigheadh* (→ *bhailíodh*) 91
bainbh see *banbh*

báine see *bán*
baineann female 96, 147, 148
bainne milk 59
bainríon queen 99
baint cutting, extracting, taking with force 40, 54, 94, 196
baintreach widow 55
Bairbre woman's name 21
báire goal 101
baist baptize; pres. 1st sing. *baistim* 9
báisteach rain 31, 144
báith drown 170
baitsiléir bachelor 29
bál ball; pl. *bálanna* 160
baladh smell 91, 93
ball place 93
balla wall 133
balú see *baileaghadh*
bambairne lout 55
bambairneach bothersome 20
bán white 136; comp. *báine* 109, 136
bánaghadh (→ *bánú*) dispersing 138
bánaigh disperse; pres. *bánaigheann* (→ *bánaíonn*) 138
Banba name for Ireland 21
banbh piglet 136; gen. *bainbh* 136; pl. *bainbh* 21
barr top 49
barr- top-class 26
barúil opinion 33
beach, meach bee 133, 159; pl. *meachain* 159
beachóg bee 159
beainín little woman 38, 145
bealach way 34, 68, 74, 75, 135; gen. *bealaigh* 34, 68, 74, 75, 100, 135
bean woman 143, 145, 147, 317; gen. *mná* 23, 95
beannacht blessing 31
béa(r)lbhach bridle-bit 96
bearna(idh) gap 51, 53, 59
bearradh shaving 50
bearr(aigh) shave 50; pres. *bearrann* 50; pres. impers. *bearrtar* 50; past *bhearr(aigh)* shaved 174; fut. *bearrfaidh* 50; cond. *bhearrfadh* 50

bearrán nuisance 39
bearrtha shaved 50, 163
béic(e) shout 156
béiceadhach (→ *béiciúch*) shouting 197
béilí meal; pl. *béilíochaí* 46
beilt belt 157; gen. *beilte* 157
beir bear, give (birth) 190 (full paradigm); past 3rd pl. *(do) rugadar* 93, 112
beir (ar) catch; past impers. *rugús (ar)* 194
beithíoch beast, cow; pl. *beithígh* cows 24
bheidís see *bí*
bheith (to) be 255
bhfuil see *bí*
bhíog sudden jump 82
bhíothas see *bí*
bhúr your 126
bí be (substantive verb) 192 (full paradigm); imper. 3rd sing. *bíodh* 91; pres. (pendant) *tá* 248; pres. *tánn* 193; pres. dep. *fuil, fuileann* 23, 193; pres. 2nd sing. *taoi* 193; pres. hab. *bíonn* 178; past impers. *bhíothas* 194; dep. past impers. *rabhthas* 194; cond. 3rd pl. *bheidís* 30
binn gable 151 (full inflection); pl. *beanna* 160
binn melodious 94
bíodh (is) although 333
biolar, biolra watercress 99
bior pointed rod, stick 37, 44
biorán knitting needle 33
bitse(ach) bitch 102
blaoch, glaoch call 133
blaosc, plaosc skull 131
bleaghan (→ *bleán*), *blioghan* milking 72, 138
bliain year 62 167; pl. *bliana* 123, 166; pl. *bliantaí* 141
bligh milk 72; pres. *bligheann* (→ *blíonn*) 138
blioghan, bleaghan (→ *bleán*) milking 72, 138
bó cow 147

350   Index of Irish words

bocht poor 19; comp. *boichte* 85
bochta(ibh) poor (people) 85, 166
bocóideach, bacóideach bellying (of sails) 41
bocsa, bosca box 101
bodhar deaf 73, 76
boinn see *bonn*
boird see *bord*
bolg belly 21
bolgam mouthful 23, 27, 28, 164; pl. *bolgamaíl* 164
bonn coin, sole 43, 93; pl. *boinn* 159; pl. *bonnaíocha* 159; pl. *bonnúchaí* 159
bord table 51, 52; pl. *boird* 84, 86, 168
bosca, bocsa box 101
bothán hut 24
bóthar road 19, 24, 82, 144; pl. *bóithre* 103; pl. *bóithrí* 103
bradán salmon 102
brath intending 263, 264
breathnaíonn sé it seems 272
breathnú appearing 273
breithiúnas judgment 24
Brian man's name; gen. *Briain* 62
bricfeast breakfast 26
brionglóid uneasiness 55
brionglóidí dreaming 55
bris break 108, 109, 180-84; pres. 1st sing. *brisim* 108, 109; past impers. *briseadh* 71, 72, 74, 76; past hab. *bhriseadh (sé)* 71, 72; fut. impers. *brisfear* 176
briseadh breaking 72, 77, 196
bró(i)g shoe 155; pl. *bróga(í)* 141
brois brush 157; gen. *broise* 157
brollach breast 102
bromach colt 67
bronntanas gift 55
bruach bank 164; pl. *bruachaíl* 164
bruth heat 164; pl. *bruthaíl* 164
bua victory 24
buachaill boy 140; pl. *buachaillí* 140
buail hit 169; pres. *buaileann* 138; cond. *bhuailfeadh* 91

bualadh hitting, heading off 63, 138, 169, 196, 279
bualadh cloiche bruises from stones on the feet 201
buan lasting 93
buidéal bottle 33, 144
buile anger 93
buille blow 93
buíochas gratitude 46
búistéara, búistéir butcher 140, 144, 145; pl. *búistéirí* 140
bun- basic 27
bus bus; pl. *busanna* 160

cá where 125
cá háit where 318
cá huair when 318
cabaire prattler 144
cabáiste, gabáiste cabbage 39
cabhraigh help; fut. 1st sing. *cabhrfad, cabhród* 175
cad é an t-am when 318
cad fáth why 318
cad 'na thaobh why 98, 318
cag-/cang- -ailt/-aint/-nadh chewing 40
cailín girl 39, 143, 147; pl. *cailíní* 29
cailleach hag 74, 101; gen. *caillí, caillighe* 74, 101
caint talk(ing) 54, 55, 144
cairde see *cara(id)*
cairpintéir carpenter 33
caiscéim, coiscéim footstep 41
caismirt contention 84
c'áit where 318
caith must 292
caith throw, use 79, 308; pres. *caitheann* 138; pres. impers. *caithtear* 79; past 1st sing. *chaith mé* 79; past impers. *chaitheadh* 124; fut. *caithfidh* 79; modal fut. *caithfidh (mé)* (I) must 271, 272, 287
caitheachtáil compulsion 197
caitheamh, cathamh using (up), throwing 138, 144, 197
cáithnín flake 103

Index of Irish words 351

call, coll hazel 17, 40
canad where 318
canda, canta chunk of bread 89
cang-/cag- -ailt/-aint/-nadh chewing 40
canta, canda chunk of bread 89
caoi way 313
caoldroim small of back 118
caonach, cúnach moss 58
caora sheep 154 (full inflection); gen. pl. *caorach* 165
caorán clod 56
capall horse 147
cara(id) friend 155; pl. *cairde* 53; gen. sg./pl. *carad* 155, 165
cárda, cárta card 89
carg(h)as lent 72, 134
carr car 148
carraig rock 92, 161; pl. *carraigreachaí* 161
cárta, cárda card 89
cas turn 59; past impers. *casadh* 31
cas twisted 47; comp. *coise* 47
casachtáil meeting 197
casadh turning, playing music 197
casán path 41
casúr hammer 144
cat, cut cat 147, 148
cathain when 318
cathair city 136, 140, 153 (full inflection); pl. *cathracha* 136, 140, 160
cathamh, caitheamh using (up), throwing 138, 144, 197
cathaoir chair 24, 148
cathracha see *cathair*
cé negative question particle 332
cé although 267, 269
cé where 125
cé who 219, 250, 318, 322
cé acu which 318, 322
cé ar bith whatever 134
cé is although 333
cé mhéad how much 318
cead permission 59
céad first 123

ceaig keg 39
ceal, cheal negative question particle 332
ceamach, ciomach rag 41
ceangail bind; past 3rd pl. *cheangladar, cheanglaigheadar* (→ *cheanglaíodar*) 173
ceangailte, ceanglaighthe (→ *ceanglaithe*) bound 173
ceangal binding 97
ceann head, one 167; pl. *cinn* 166; old dat. *(as) cionn* 36
céanna same 62
ceannacht buying 138
ceannaigh buy; pres. *ceannaigheann* (→ *ceannaíonn*) 138; past impers. *ceannaíodh* 76
ceannaightheoir buyer 163
ceannrach halter 98
ceanúil affectionate 41
cearc hen 38, 45, 104, 143, 147, 148; gen. *circe* 38, 45; see also *scearc amach!*
cearc/coileach fuiseoige female/male lark 147, 148
ceard, ceird skill 155
céard what 239, 318
cearóg, ciaró(i)g beetle 64
ceart right 38, 45; comp. *ceirte* 38, 45
ceasgannaí see *cis*
ceastracha see *ceist*
ceatach, ciotach clumsy 41
ceathach showery 31
ceathrú fourth 32
ceathrú quarter 52
céille see *ciall*
ceilt concealing 196
céir wax 145
ceird, ceard skill 155
céirín poultice 145
ceirte see *ceart*
ceist question 161; pl. *ceastracha* 161; gen. pl. *ceisteann* 165
cén áit where 318
cén chaoi how 318
cén dóigh how 318

352 Index of Irish words

cén fáth why 318
cén t-am when 318
cén uair when 318
ceo fog 44
ceol music 44
cha(n) not 114, 125
cheal, ceal negative question particle 332
cheana already 134
cheithre four 118, 123, 127, 134
chomh as, equally, so 27, 123, 134, 333, 337
chon- see *feic*
chuadhadh, chuadhthas see *téigh*
chuaigh de failed 271, 273
chuala see *clois, cluin*
chuig towards 262
chúig, cúig five 118, 123, 127
chun towards, in order to 115, 276
chún 's while, as long as 333
cí- see *feic*
ciacu which 318
ciall sense 24; gen. *céille* 62
ciaró(i)g, cearóg beetle 64
cill churchyard, graveyard 46, 48, 49
cinn see *ceann*
cinn (ar); pres. *cinneann ar* 271; past *chinn ar* 273
ciomach, ceamach rag 41
cion affection 36, 37, 41, 90
cionn see *ceann*
cionn's, cionn is because 268, 333
cionta fault(s) 54, 56
ciontach guilty 56
ciotach, ceatach clumsy 41
cipín small stick 31, 140; pl. *cipíní* 140
circe see *cearc*
cis hurdle 161; pl. *ceasgannaí* 161
cladhaire coward 101
cláirseach harp 144
clais furrow 161; pl. *clasgannaí* 161
cleachtadh practice 145, 146
cleamhnas match 78
cléibhe see *cliabh*
cleite feather 164; pl. *cleitiú(chaí)* 46, 164

cliabh pannier basket 62; gen. *cléibhe* 62
clis (ar) fail; pres. *cliseann ar* 271; past *chlis ar* 273
cloch stone 68; gen. *cloiche* 67, 68; dat. *cloich* 36; pl. *clocha* 167
clog clock 45; gen. *cloig* 45
cloigeann head/person 167; pl. *cloigne* 96
cloigín small clock 45
clois, cluin hear 191 (full paradigm) 193, 194; past 1st sing. *chuala* 193; past impers. *cualathas* 194
clua(i)s ear 155, 158; gen. *cluaise* 158; gen. *cluasa* 158
cluiche shoal, game 37, 70
cluin see *clois*
cnaipe button 40
cnoc hill 43, 95
cnósach, cnuasach collection 64
codail, codlaigh sleep; past *chodail, chodlaigh* 173; fut. *codalfaidh, codlófaidh* 173
codladh sleep(ing) 98, 295; *a chodladh* (go) to sleep 280
coileach cock 31, 36, 147, 148
coileach/cearc fuiseoige male/female lark 147, 148
coimhlint conflict 47, 51
coinne appointment 94
coinneáil keep on 279
cóir just 137; comp. *córa* 137
cóirigh arrange; cond. *chóireodh* 91
co(i)s leg 36, 41, 47, 136, 140, 141, 155; dat. *cois* 136; pl. *cosa(í)* 140, 141
coiscéim, caiscéim footstep 39
coise see *cas*
coisin, cosain defend 88
colainn body 158; gen. *colainne* 158; gen. *colla* 158
coláiste college 24, 33, 147
coll, call hazel 40
colla see *colainn*
com valley 43
comártas, comórtas comparison 42

comhairle advice 83
comharsa neighbour 100; pl.
  comharsanna(í) 153
comhlódar company 64
comórtas, comártas comparison 42
conablach carcase 29
conaí living 295
conairt pack of hounds 92, 102
conas how 318
condae, contae county 53, 54, 89, 147
confadh anger 21
cóngaraí closer 32
Conn man's name 43
Connacht Connacht 31
Connachtach Connacht man 31
contae, condae county 53, 54, 89, 147
cor move 36
córa see *cóir*
corc cork 21
corcán pot 29
corn(aigh) roll (up); pres.
  cornaigheann (→ *cornaíonn*),
  cornann 173; fut. *cornfaidh,
  cornóidh* 173
coróin crown 33, 153 (full inflection)
corp corpse 21
corróig, scorróg hip 104
cosain, coisin defend 88
cosúil it seems 274
cosúil le like 230
cóta coat 140; pl. *cótaí* 140
craiceann, croiceann skin 40
cráidhcamas hardship 162
craith, croith shake 40
crann tree 41, 46; gen. *croinn* 41, 46;
  pl. *croinnte* 54
craobh branch 155
cras, cro(i)s cross 40
cratach, crotach curlew 40
creathadh shake 201; pl. *creaití* 201
creidsiúint, crei(s)diúint, creistiúint
  believing 89, 101, 259, 262
Críost Christ 96
crobh paw 45; dat. *croibh* 45
crochadóir hangman 156
croibhín little paw 45

croiceann, craiceann skin 40
cróigeadh, gróigeadh footing turf 131,
  132
croinn, croinnte see *crann*
cro(i)s, cras cross 40
croith, craith shake 40
crománach, scrománach tall stooped
  person 104
crotach, cratach curlew 40
cruadhóig urgency 62, 63
cruaidh hard 63, 67, 68, 77; comp.
  cruaidhe 77
cruaidh, cruadhaigh harden; pres.
  cruadhaigheann (→ *cruadhaíonn*),
  cruadhann 174; fut. *cruadhóidh,
  cruadhfaidh* 174
cruib crib (of a cart) 158; gen.
  cruibeach 158
cruinneál gathering; pl. *cruinneálachaí*
  164
cruinnigh gather 172; pres.
  cruinneann, cruinnigheann
  (→ *cruinníonn*) 108, 172, 174; past.
  impers. *cruinneadh, cruinnigheadh*
  (→ *cruinníodh*) 174; fut. *cruinneoidh*
  172, 176
cruithneacht wheat 31, 102
cruthaigh prove; pres. *cruthann,
  cruthaigheann* (→ *cruthaíonn*) proves
  174; fut. *cruthfaidh, cruthóidh* 174
cruthú prove 259, 262
cú greyhound 161; pl. *cúití* 161
cuach cuckoo 25
cualathas see *clois, cluin*
cuan bay 161; pl. *cuanta(í)* 161
cuardaíocht, cuartaíocht, cuairtíocht
  visiting 89
cuideachta company 29
cúig, chúig five 118, 123
cuileach tousled 36
cúilteach return (of a house) 118
cúiltseomra backroom 118
cuimhne memory 94, 95
cuir put 169, 297; pres. *cuireann* 138,
  169; pres. 1st sing. *cuirim* 169; past
  (do) chuir 169; past impers.

354 Index of Irish words

cuireadh 169; past hab. impers. *cuirtí* 30
cuir, cur putting 36, 138, 196, 279
cúití see *cú*
culaith suit of clothes 29, 46, 163; pl. *cultacha* 163
Cúlánach a person whose surname is Ó Cúláin 144
cum compose; fut. *cumfaidh* 91
cúnach, caonach moss 58
cuntas account 54
cupán cup 143
cúpla couple 23; pl. *cúplaí* 32
cur, cuir putting 36, 138, 196, 279
cur fhataí, phr(e)átaí sowing potatoes 121
currach coracle 46
curtha put 91
cut, cat cat 104
cuthach rage 24, 25, 82

d' see following letter
dá see *do*
daighean devil 331
dair oak 59
damhsa dancing 78, 97
damnú damnation 96, 326
daothaint, dóthain(t) enough 59
darb see *is*
dath colour 81
dathúil beautiful 82
de of, off 127, 128, 263; *den* of(f) the 128; *'on* of(f) the 129
Dé day in names of days 114, 123
dé an t-am when 318
de bharr because 267
dé chúis why 318
deá- good 26, 27
deabhal, diabhal devil 64, 76, 77, 205, 211, 326, 327, 329-31
deacair, deocair difficult 40
deachaigh see *téigh*
déag -teen 119
dealradh appearing 198
dealraití more likely-looking 32
dealramh appearing 98, 198

deamhan, dheamhan demon 17, 76, 326, 331
déan make, do 186 (full paradigm) 302, 304, 306, 308, 328; flexionless form *ní* 193; past 2nd pl. *dheineabhair* 74; past dep. *dearn, tearn* 132; cond. 2nd sing. *dhéanfá* 30
déanamh doing, making 77
dearbhtha (→ *dearfa*) certain 21
dearbhú confirming 258, 262
déard what 318
dearg red 21, 38; comp. *deirge* 38
dearg- extreme(ly) 26
deargaigh redden; cond. *dheargódh* 174; cond. 3rd pl. *dheargóidíst* 174
dearm(h)ad forgetting, oversight 28, 134
dearn see *déan*
deas nice 38; comp. *deise* 38
deas, geis taboo 133
déas, dias, lias ear of corn 133
deatach smoke 146; gen. *deataí* 146
deich ten 118, 126
deilbh warp (in weaving); fut. *deilbhfidh* 21
déileáil dealing 18, 57
deimhin certain 70
deir see *abair*
deirge see *dearg*
deise see *deas*
den see *de*
deocair, deacair difficult 40
deoch drink 44
(dh)á (preposition with possessive) see *do*
dhá however 335
d(h)á if 125, 320, 321
dhá of all that there is 336
dhá two 88, 119, 131, 134
d(h)eamhan demon 17, 76, 326, 331
dhéanfá see *déan*
dheineabhair see *déan*
diabhach devil 331
diabhal, deabhal devil 64, 76, 77, 205, 211, 326, 327, 329-31

dias, déas, lias ear of corn 133
dinnéar dinner 157; gen. *dinnéara* 157; gen. *dinnéir* 157
díomhaoin idle 29, 32
diúltamh refuse 307
dligheadh law 76, 77
dlisteanach lawful 163
dlitheach lawful 31
dlúthas density 81
do past proclitic 125
do preverbial particle for past tense, etc. 115
do to, for 127, 128, 219, 233, 281, 283, 294; *(d)on* to the 128, 129; *dá, dona* to his/her/their 130; *(dh)á* to its 259; *dom, dhom, 'om* to/for me 134; *domhsa, domsa* to me 78; *duit, dhuit, 'uit* to/for you 92, 134
do your 115
do- un...able 27
do réir according to 96
dob(a) see *is*
dochtú(i)r doctor 140, 156; gen. *dochtúir* 156; gen. *dochtúra* 156; pl. *dochtúirí* 140
doicheall inhospitability 70
doimhne see *domhain*
Doiminic man's name 96
doirse see *doras*
dóirt pour 173; fut. *dóirtófaidh* 173
dom, dhom, 'om see *do*
domhain deep 47; comp. *doimhne* 47, 94
dom(h)sa see *do*
don(a) (preposition with possessive) see *do*
dona bad 42; comp. *dona, measa* 231; comp. (with *de*) *donaide* 231
doras door 143, 148; pl. *doirse* 52
dorcha dark 21, 31
dorchadas darkness 162
dorn(a) fist 158
dóthain(t), daothaint enough 59
drama see *droim*
drámh non-trump 163; pl. *drámhasaí* 163

draoibeáilte bespattered 59
dréimire ladder 101
droch- bad 26, 118
droichead bridge 144
droim back 42; gen. *drama* 42
droim díbeartha a driving back 200
drúis lust 23, 96
dual strand (of rope); pl. *duail* 168
dualgas duty. 23
dubh black 70, 76; gen. *duibh* 90, 91; comp. *duibhe* 70
dubh- extreme(ly) 26
duibheagán abyss 57
duibhré the dark of the moon 57
dúin- see *dún*
duine person 94, 317
dúiseacht, dúiseachtáil, dúsacht waking 138, 198, 295
dúisigh waken; pres. *dúisigheann* 138
duit, dhuit, 'uit see *do*
dul going 280; see also *goil*
dún, dúin shut; pres. *dúineann* 138; pres. 1st sing. *dúinim, dúnaim* 88
dúnadh shutting 138
dúrthas see *abair*
dúsacht, dúiseacht, dúiseachtáil waking 138, 198, 295

é him, it 216, 223, 228, 238
(é) amháin although 269
ea copy pronoun (old neuter) 239, 241–3, 246-52, 335
éadach cloth 67; pl. *éadaighe* (→ *éadaí*) clothes 67, 68, 160
eagla fear 22, 40, 53
eaglais church 40, 53
eallach cattle 65
éan bird 62, 87, 141; pl. *éanacha(í)* 141, 160
eanga notch 164; pl. *eangaíochaí* 164
eanraith, anraith broth 56, 99
éard that which 222
easbog bishop 64
eascóid, neascóid a boil 39, 133, 144
eascú eel 39

356 Index of Irish words

eidhean ivy 70
eidir, idir between 115
eidir/idir ... agus/is both...and 117
eireaball, urball, orball tail 23, 28, 48, 88
éireagha (→ *éiriú*) arising 198
Éireannach Irish(man) 136, 144; comp. *Éireannaí* 136; pl. *Éireannaí* 136
éirí dó happening to 273
éirí le succeeding 273
éirigh rise, get up 170; past *d'éirigh (sé)* got up 68, 75; see also *éiríonn*
éirighe (→ *éirí*) rising 57, 198
Éirinn Ireland 136; gen. *Éireann* 136
éiríonn do happens to 271
éiríonn le succeeds 271
éisc see *iasc*
eisean he (with contrast) 228
éist listen 57, 174; fut. *éisteofaidh* 174
éisteacht listening 195
'eo, seo this 222, 224, 228, 234-6, 244
eochair key 64
eolas knowledge 44, 64, 145, 146

fá choinne in order to 269
facthas see *feic*
fada long 45; comp. *foide* 45
fadhb blow, knot of timber 36
fágáilt leaving 196
faigh, fáigh get 189 (full paradigm); pres. *faghann* 72; negative past *ní bhfuair* 125; past hab. *dh'fhaigheadh* 176
fáil amach finding out 258
fáil bháis dying 121
faill cliff 131, 132
fairsing extensive 52
fáisc squeeze 170, 174; fut. *fáisceofaidh* 174
faithne wart 164; pl. *faithniú* 164
falamh, folamh empty 40
falcanta, folcanta with great force 41
falla wall 133, 173
fan wait, remain; fut. *fanfaidh, fanófaidh, fanóidh* 173, 174; cond. *d'fhanfadh* 91

faobhar keen edge 77
faoi because, since 268
faoi, fé under 58, 87; *faoina* under his/her/their 129; *fúm* under me 58; *fúthaibh* under you (pl.) 79, 87
faoi (is) seeing that as 333
faoi rá (is) seeing that as 333
fás growing 196, 201; pl. *fásannaí* 201
fáth reason 81, 313
fathach, fáthach giant 31, 81
fé see *faoi*
fé ar bith whatever 134
féach, héach see 134
feacha, heacha see 134
féachaint looking 137
fead whistle 87
féad can, may 292; fut. *féadfaidh* 287
féadachtáil being able 197, 292
feadaíl whistling 144, 164, 195
féadann do can 271, 287, 293
feadar know 194
féadfaidh see *féad*
feadh see *ar feadh*
feadóg whistle 39
feairín, firín a little man 38, 145
feannta flayed 54
fear man 38, 143, 144, 147, 149 (full inflection) 167, 317; pl. *feara* 141, 167; pl. *fearaibh* 166; pl. *fir* 38, 45, 100; gen. pl. *fear* 165
fearacht is as though 333
feargach angry 31
Fearg(h)al man's name 72, 87, 134
fearúil manful 137
fearúla(cht) more manful, manfulness 137
feasa see *fios*
féasóig beard 46
feic see 187 (full paradigm) 193, 194; flexionless form *tí* 193; imperative 1st pl. *feiceamuist* 184; pres. *feiceann* 169; past 1st sing. *ch(o)nac* 29, 193; negative past 1st sing. *ní fhaca* 193; past impers. *chonacthas* 169, 194; past impers. dep. *(b')f(h)acthas*

Index of Irish words 357

feiceáilt seeing 196
féileacán, péileacán butterfly 18, 57
féin, (f)héin self 113, 134, 207, 228
féire, péire pair 18, 57
feitheal, meitheal working party 133
féithleog sinew 103
feoghlaim, foghlaim learning 87, 170
feoil meat 158; gen. *feola(dh)* 158
fhad is as long as 270, 322, 333
fiafraí enquire 258
fiáin wild 63
fial devil 331
fiche(ad) twenty 119, 167
fill, pill return 131, 132
filleadhaint (→ *filliúint*) returning 197
fioghachán weaving 73
fíor- real(ly) 27
fios knowledge 41; gen. *feasa* 41
fiosrach curious 161
fir see *fear*
firéad ferret 144
fireann male 47, 147, 148
firín, feairín a little man 38, 145
fleár, foileár, foláir necessary 33, 88
fliuch wet; past *(d')fhliuch* 176
focal word 149 (full inflection); pl. *focla* 160
fógairt, fuagairt proclaiming, demanding 262
foghlaim learn; fut. 1st sing. *foghlaimeod* 31
foghlaim, feoghlaim learning 87, 170
fógra, fuagra notice 64
foide see *fada*
foileár, fleár, foláir necessary 33, 88
fóirthint helping 306
fola(dh) see *fuil*
foláir, fleár, foileár necessary 33, 88
folamh, falamh empty 40
folang suffering 92
folcanta, falcanta with great force 41
fonn desire 43; *d'fhonn is* in order to 269, 333
fonn tune 43
fothram noise 103
frais, frois trivialities 41

freagair answer; past *d'fhreagair* 176
freagra answer 53
fríd, frít see *thrí*
friste, furast(a) easy 28, 88
frois, frais trivialities 41
fuacht cold 145, 156; gen. *fuachta* 156; gen. *fuaicht* 156
fuagairt, fógairt proclaiming, demanding 262
fuagra, fógra notice 64
fuáil sewing 63
fuil blood 158; gen. *foladh* 158
fuileann see *bí*
fuiling suffer 97; pres. 1st sing. *fuilngním* 88
fuin knead 90
f(u)inneo(i)g window 44, 87, 145, 148
fuiseo(i)g lark 148
fulaingt suffering 88
fúm see *faoi*
furast(a), friste easy 28, 88
fúthaibh see *faoi*

gabáiste, cabáiste cabbage 39
gabha smith; pl. *goibhne* 51, 52, 94, 95; pl. *goibhní* 70
gabhar goat 78
gach a all of that which 334
gadaí, gadaighe thief 42, 47, 162, 163; pl. *gadaighthe* 162; pl. *gadaighthiú* 162; pl. *gadaíos* 163
gadhar dog 87
Gaeilge Irish language 156
Gaelach Irish 33, 80
Gaeltacht Irish speaking area 20, 140, 144, 151 (full inflection) 156; gen. *Gaeltacht(a)* 156; pl. *Gaeltachtaí* 140
gaibh seize 192 (full paradigm)
Gaillimh Galway 59, 69; gen. *Gaillimhe* 69
gaimh, goimh sting 40
gainimh sand 69, 94; gen. *gainimhe* 69
gáirí laughing 100
gairm call 21

358 Index of Irish words

galar, galra disease 99, 102
galún gallon 34; pl. *galúin* 168
galún taosctha bailing vessel 200
gamhain calf 78
gan without 116, 284
gann scarce 49
gaoth wind 80
gaothsán nose 17
garbh rough 74
gasra a group 22
gasúr child 135; gen. *gasúir* 135
gé goose 163; pl. *géabha* 163
geafta, geata gate 90, 108
gealach moon 136; gen. *gealaí* 136; dat. *gealaigh* 136
geall promise; pres. 1st sing. *geallaim* 50
geallúint promise 201; pl. *geallúintí* 201
geansaí jersey 148
Gearóid man's name 23
gearr cut 170, 171; fut. *gearrfaidh* 171
gearr short 41; comp. *giorra* 41
gearrchaile young girl 164; pl. *gearrchailiú* 164
gearrchuid fair amount 22
gearrfaidh see *gearr* cut
gearrtha (verbal adjective) cut 82
geata, geafta gate 90, 108
geataire long rush 104
géilleadh yielding 307
geimhreadh winter 51, 52, 146; gen. *geimhridh* 146
géimnigh lowing 96
geirseach, girseach young girl 38, 51
geis, deas taboo 133
gí although 269
gíogsán, gíosgán squeaking 101
giolla attendant 37
giorra see *gearr*
giortach skimpy 161
gíosgán, gíogsán squeaking 101
girseach, geirseach young girl 38, 51
glac take; cond. 1st sing. modal *ghlacfainn* 287
glaine, gloine glass 40

glaisreo hoar-frost 100, 102
glaoch, blaoch call 133
glasáil locking 39, 170, 196
gléas imeartha instrument of play 200
gloine, glaine glass 42, 94
gluitéara, scluitéara glutton, sponger 104
gnaithe, gnoithe business 40
gnaoi liking 95
gnáthach usual 81
gnáthas custom 81
gníomh deed 95
gnoithe, gnaithe business 40
go adverbial particle 123
go as (equivalence particle) 123
go optative particle 179
go positive complementizer 125
go because, since, (so) that, until 323-5
go in order to 324, 335
go to 115, 122
go céard what 318
go dtí to 128, 130; *go dtís na* to the 130
go dtí until 269, 323, 335
gob beak 45; gen. *goib* 45
Gobnait woman's name 22
gofa dressed, gripped 199
goib see *gob*
goibhn- see *gabha*
goibhte gone 199
goid stealing 42, 44, 45, 47
goidé what 318
goil, dul going (with prospect of doing) 254, 279, 297
goimh, gaimh sting 42
gorm blue 19, 21
gortú injuring 30
gotha appearance 156
graibhéal gravel 102
greamannaí see *greim*
greannmhar amusing 74
greim grip, bite 41, 43, 152 (full inflection); pl. *greamannaí* 41
grian sun 62; gen. *gréine* 62
gróigeadh, cróigeadh footing turf 131, 132
gruaim gloom 61

gruth curd 81
guala(inn) shoulder 155; gen.
  gualainne 155; gen. *gualann* 155
guidhe praying 70
guilpíneacht wolfing 33
guth voice 81, 82, 91

haitín small hat 59
hé ar bith whatever 134
héin see *féin*
hocht, ocht eight 118, 126

i in 115, 126, 139, 313; *insa(n), sa* in the 122 (pl.) 125, 128-30, 281; *im* in my 78; *ina* in his/her/their 130; *ionam* in me 139; *ionat* in you 92; *inti* in her/it 139; *ann* in it 50, 218, 240; *iontu* in them 139
í her 216, 228, 238
i dtaobh because 268
i gcleithiúnas on condition that 270
i gcruth's in order to 269, 333
i ndéidh after 282, 283, 297, 301
i ndéidh, i ndiaidh although 269
i ngeall air because, since 268
i riocht's (ros) in order to 269, 333
iad them 216, 228, 238
iadsan them (with contrast) 228, 238
iasc fish 62; gen. *éisc* 62
iascaire fisherman 101
idir, eidir between 115
idir/eidir ... agus/is both...and 117
im (peposition with possessive) see *i*
im butter 49
imeacht going off 201
imirt playing 201; pl. *imirteachaí* 201
imleacán navel 53, 55
imní worry 95
'in, sin that 222, 224, 228, 234-6, 244
ina see *i*
ina choinnibh against it 166
ingne see *ionga*
ingneach taloned 55
iníon daughter 23, 32; gen. pl. *níonach* 165

innis tell 29, 192 (full paradigm)
insa(n) see *i*
inse, inseacht, insint telling 55, 94, 198, 262
inti see *i*
intinn mind 54
iolar, olra eagle 99, 102
iomarca excess amount 23, 29
iomlán whole 64
iompar carry 43, 48, 55
i(o)n- -able 27
ionam see *i*
ionann's almost 230
ionat see *i*
ionga (finger/toe) nail; pl. *ingne* 54, 95, 157
ionlach spreading ground (for turf etc.) 54
iontu see *i*
iothla(inn) haggard 103, 157, 158; gen. *iothlainne* 157; gen. *iothlann* 157; gen. *iothlanna* 157
is/agus and 117, 207, 216, 284, 311, 321, 332-4
is is (copula) 220 (full paradigm) 222; negative *ní* is not 122, 221; interrogative *an* 221; past *babh* 125; past *dob(a)* 219; relative (with *do*) *darb* 234
is ceart/cóir dom I ought 287
is cosúil it seems 274
is cuimhne liom I remember 232
is cuma liom I don't mind 232
is dóigh liom I suppose 245
is ea signal of attentiveness 247
is féidir dom I can 293
is féidir (le) can 231, 271, 287, 293
is gá (do) it is necessary 270
is maith liom I like 231, 232
ise her (with contrast) 228, 238
isteach into 26
ith eat 192 (full paradigm); past 1st sing. responsive *d'itheas* 25
ithir soil 25
'iúd, siúd that 222, 224, 228, 234-6, 244

360 Index of Irish words

jib jib-sail 157; gen. *jibe* 157

lá day 162, 163; pl. *laethantaí* 162, 163; pl. *laethasta* 163
lá (is) because, since, seeing that, as 268, 333
labhair speak; pres. 1st sing. *labhraighim* (→ *labhraím*) 173; fut. *labhairfidh* 173
labhairt speaking 137
lacha duck 154 (full inflection); gen. *lachan* 165
laethantaí, laethasta see *lá*
lafta loft 90
lag weak 41; comp. *loige* 41
lagachan weakening 138, 197
laghdú lessening 84
láighe loy, spade 73
lá(i)mh hand 141, 155; pl. *lámha(í)* 77, 141, 167
láimhsiughadh handling 78
lámhacán crawling, creeping 32, 60, 77, 97
lámhach shooting 60
lámhanán bladder 32, 60
lampa lamp 54, 55
lapaire, slapaire pudgy person 104
lasair flame; pl. *lasrachaí* 100, 102
lasóg small light 144
lathach mire 31
le in order to 130, 269
le with 115, 116, 122, 134, 139, 242, 264, 313; *leis na* with the 130; *lena* with his/her/their 129; *liom* with me 36, 139; *leis* with him/it 139; *léithi* with her/it 139; *libh* with you (pl.) 78
le haghaidh for 82
le linn because 268
le linn during 282, 283
le súil (is) in the hope that 333
leaba(idh) bed 161; pl. *leabrachaí* 161
leabhar book 75, 76, 78, 83, 146, 148, 162; gen. *leabhair* 146; gen. *leabhra* 146; pl. *leabhartha(í)* 162
leac, lic flagstone 38, 45, 155, 161; gen. *leice* 38, 45; pl. *leacracha(í)* 161

leacht(a) cairn 158
leadán burr of a teazle 39
leag lay 40, 89, 170; fut. *leagfaidh* 89, 171
leagan laying, turn of speech, version 138, 143, 197, 201
leagfaidh see *leag*
leagh- see *leaigh*
leaghadh melting 72
leagtha layed 171
leaigh, leáigh melt; pres. *leaghann, leigheann* 72, 72; pres. 1st sing. *leaghaim, leáighim, leighim* 72, 87
leanacht following, continuing 197, 279
lean(aigh) follow 174
leanbh child 136; pl. *linbh* 136
leasdeartháir stepbrother 118
leath half 30, 80, 81
leath-amadán half-wit 30
leath-bhróg one shoe of a pair 30
leath-bhulóg half a loaf 30
leath-sceallóg half a potato cut 30
lea(th)taobh one side 118
leice see *leac*
leidhb, pleidhb fool 104
leidhce, pleidhce fool 104, 133
léigh read 76, 77, 170; pres. *léigheann* 15; pres. 1st sing. *léighim* I read 73
leigh- see *leaigh*
léigheamh reading 197
leigheann see *leaigh*
leigheas cure 73
léimnigh leaping 96
léine, léinidh shirt 161, 163; pl. *léinte, léinteacha(í)* 161, 163
leis see *le*
léithi see *le*
lena see *le*
leogaint laying 138
leogaint, ligean, ligint letting 138, 196, 197
leoraí lorry 145, 146
leota, pleota fool 104
lián trowel
lias, déas, dias ear of corn 133

Index of Irish words 361

liath grey 80
libh see *le*
líbíneach, slíbíneach messer 104
lic see *leac, lic*
lig let 307, 308; cond. impers. *ligfí* 85
ligean, ligint, leogaint letting 138, 196, 197
linbh see *leanbh*
liom see *le*
lionnrach fluid from a sore 99
liúradh trouncing 307
lobh rot 170; pres. *lobhann* 172; fut. *lobhfaidh* 171
lobhtha rotten 89, 171
loch lake 147; gen. *locha* 147; gen. *loiche* 147
loige see *lag*
loighe lying 75, 295
loime see *lom*
loine, loinidh churn dash 91
loinge see *long*
loirg look for; pres. 1st sing. *loirgim* 174; fut. 1st sing. *loirgeod* 174
loit destroy 47
lom bare 42, 49; comp. *loime* 42
long ship 43, 49, 54; gen. *loinge* 54, 97
lonnrach shining 98
lonnradh shining 99
loscadh sáile soreness from brine 201
lota loft 90
luath early 82
luch mouse 46, 159; pl. *luchain* 159
luchóg mouse 46, 80, 159
lucht load 159; pl. *luchtaíl* 159; pl. *luchtannaí* 159; pl. *luicht* 159
lucht (category of) people 46
lus plant 140; pl. *lusanna* 140

má if 113, 177, 292, 319, 336
Mac Suibhne surname 51
macnas wantonness 96
madra dog 22; pl. *madraí* 53
maidin morning; gen. *maidne* 98
mailís malice 144
Máire woman's name 100

mairstint living 197
máirtíneach, smáirtíneach cripple 104
maiste spill 102
maith good 79; comp. *fearr* 125, 130; comp. (with *de*) *fearrde* 231
máithreacha(í) see *máthair*
mála bag; pl. *málaí* 168
malairt change 92, 102
malrach young boy 99
mámh trump 163; pl. *mámhasaí* 163
maothán earlobe, flank 56, 58
mar as 177, 311, 336
mar because, since 268
mar a chéile like one another 230
mar gheall air because, since 268
mara, muna if not 125, 319, 320
marbh dead 74, 76
margadh market 107, 108; gen. *margaidh* 107, 108
máthair mother 60, 82, 150 (full inflection) 157, 159; gen. *máthar(a)* 157, 159; pl. *máithreacha(í)* 159
mé me 207
meach, beach bee 133, 159; pl. *meachain* 159
meadhg whey 84
meaisín machine 148; pl. *meaisíneannaí* 160
meaits match 102
meall coax 171; fut. *meallfaidh* 171
méar finger 62, 163; pl. *méaranta* 163
méaracán thimble 29, 32
measa see *dona*
measc mix 170, 174; fut. *meascófaidh* 174
méid amount 114, 145, 146
meilt grinding 144
méirscre fissure; pl. *méirscrí* 32
meisce intoxication 43
meitheal, feitheal working party 56, 133
mholfaí see *mol*
mí month 147
mí- negative prefix 27
mian desire 61
milis sweet 50; comp. *milse* 50

362 Index of Irish words

mill destroy; pres. *milleann* 50
ministéara, ministéir minister 155
mion- small 27, 37
mionn(a) oath 158
mionshodar a slow trot 113
mionta fragmented 54
míorúilt(e) miracle 156
mí-rathúil unprosperous 30
mise me 207
mná see *bean*
mo my 115
moch early 43
mochóir early riser; pl. *mochóirí* 101
modh mode 43
moill delay 45
móiréis haughtiness 144
móisiam upset 61
mol praise; past *mhol* 90; cond. impers.
   mholfaí 30
moladh praising, recommending 34,
   143, 262
mór, muar big 64
mórtimpeall around about 118
mu(i)c pig 145, 151 (full inflection)
   155; pl. *muca* 160; gen. pl. *muc*
   165
muicea(r)lach botcher 96
Muimhneach Munsterman 69
múin teach 170; pres. *múineann* 138
muineál neck 33
muing mane 49, 82
muintir people 53, 54, 145
Muiréad woman's name 33
muna, mara if not 125, 319, 320
múnadh teaching 138
múr shower 164; pl. *múraíl* 164; pl.
   múraíolacha 164
muscailte awake 296

na the 122, 126, 130
ná negative imperative particle 82
ná negative question particle 332,
ná nor 207, 216
ná than 311
nach complementizer 125
nach negative question particle 125

nach because...not, since...not, (so)
   that...not, until...not 323-5
nach in order to not 335
náisiún nation 144
námhaid, nomhaid enemy 61
naoi nine 118, 119, 126
naomhóg, aomhóg corracle 57
nár negative optative particle 179
nead nest 38; gen. *neide* 38
neamh-chiontacht guiltlessness 30
neamh-choitianta unusual 30
neamh-shuimiúil uninteresting 30
neamh-thuairmeach unthinking 30
neascóid, eascóid a boil 39, 133, 144
neide see *nead*
ní (negative of copula) see *is*
ní (verbal form) see *déan*
ní negative particle 114, 130
ní thing 162; pl. *nithe* 162
ní call dom I need not 287
ní eolas dúinn we are not aware (of)
   232
ní foláir it is necessary, it must be that
   271, 334
ní foláir dom I must 287
ní gá dhom I need not 287
ní mór dom I must 287
nigh wash 100, 170, 172; pres.
   nigheann 172; fut. *nighfidh* 171
níl fiachadh orm I don't have to etc.
   287
nimh poison 69, 70, 75; gen. *nimhe* 69,
   70, 75
nimhneach poisonous 69
nimhneas poisonousness 69
níonach see *iníon*
níor chás dúinn it would be no harm for
   us 232
níor mhór must, has to 271
níos(a) comp. particle 125, 130, 221
nithe see *ní* thing
nó or 332, 334, 335
nóimint moment; pl. *nóimintí* 168
Nollaig Christmas 92; gen. *Nollag* 92;
   pl. *Nollaigeacha(í)* 92
nomhaid, námhaid enemy 61

nós custom 43
nós in order to 269
nós is as though 333
nua new 25, 61
nuaidheacht news 16, 73

ó from 219, 233, 242; *uaim* from me 63
ó since 115, 177
Ó in surnames 123
ó chianaibh a while ago 166
ó tharla(igh) because, since 268
obair work 51, 52; gen. *oibre* 51, 52
ocht, hocht eight 85, 118, 126
ógánach youth 29
oibhn- see *abha(inn)*
oibliogáid obliging act 51
oibre see *obair*
Oibreán, Abrán, Aibreán April 40, 51
oice see *ag*
oíche night 79
oifig(e) office 156
oige see *ag*
oighear chuimealta file 200
oighreog ice 101
óil see *ól*
oimhreas, aimhreas doubt 40, 51
oinneoin although, despite the fact 269
óinseach foolish woman 94
oirde (comp.) see *ard*
oirde height 44
oiread amount, much 29, 64, 146
oirthi see *ar*
ól drink(ing) 196; gen. *óil* 201; gen. *ólta* 201
olra, iolar eagle 99, 102
'on see *de, do*
ón uair because 268
onóir honour 44
oraibh see *ar*
orball, eireaball, urball tail 23, 28, 48, 88
orchar, urchar shot 28
orchóid, urchóid harm 47
ordó(i)g thumb 51
ordú order 307

orlach inch 51, 167; pl. *orlaigh(e)* 166
orlár, urlár floor 47
orm see *ar*
orsain, ursa jamb 47
ós rud é because 268
oscail open 88, 137, 172
oscailt opening 195

pábháil paving; pl. *pábhálachaí* 164
pacáil pack; fut. *pacálófaidh* 173
paidir prayer 145
paidrín rosary 23, 53, 145
páighe pay 15-18, 73, 77, 147
páipéar paper 33
páiste child 60, 102, 144
pamhsaer flower 97
panna pan 39
paráiste, paróiste parish 42, 147
parrthas paradise 103
pé cuma's however 334
peaicits package; pl *peaicitseacha(í)* 160
peain pan 39, 59
peáitse page, young messenger 102
peann pen 59
péicea(r)lach vain person 96
peictiúr picture 47
péileacán, féileacán butterfly 18, 57
peiliúr pillow 47
péinteáil painting 196
péire, féire pair 18, 57
pian pain 61
pill, fill return 131, 132
pingin penny 167; pl. *pingne(achaí)* 166
piont(a) pint 37, 54, 55
pisreoig superstition 100
plaosc, blaosc skull 131
pleidhb, leidhb fool 104
pleidhce, leidhce fool 104, 133
pleota, leota fool 104
plump bang 164; pl. *plumpaíl* 164
póg kiss 170; fut. *pógfaidh* 175; fut. 1st sing. *pógfad* 176
poilséar, spoilséar pilchard 47, 51; pl. *(s)poilséir(í)* 104

364 Index of Irish words

poll hole 49; pl. *poill* 49
pósadh marrying 196
pota pot 158; pl. *potaí* 158
praiseach, proiseach mess 41, 144
prántach, próntach unfledged great black-backed gull 42
preab, spreab spadeful 104
préamh root; pl. *préamhacha* 96
prindéara printer 54
prionda print 54
proiseach, praiseach mess 41, 144
próntach, prántach unfledged great black-backed gull 42
punt pound 167

rá say 258, 261
rabhthas see *bí*
rachadh see *téigh*
radharc sight 145, 146; gen. *radhairc* 146
raghadh see *téigh*
raing rank 49
ráithe three month period 79
raithneach fern 59, 103
rámhann spade 60
rás(a) race 158, 161; pl. *rás(t)aí* 158, 161
rásúr razor 146, 148, 158; gen. *rásúir* 146; gen. *rásúrach* 158
rata rafter; pl. *ratan* rafters 90
réal sixpence; pl. *réalacha* 166; pl. *réal(t)a* 166
réidh le ready to 302
reilig graveyard 45, 92; gen. *reilige* 92; pl. *reiligeacha(í)* 160
reo freezing 170
rí king 84, 93, 162; pl. *ríthe* 162; pl. *rítí* 162
rí- outstanding 27
riabhach speckled 77
riach devil 331
riail rule 62
rite run, finished, taut
rith run 79, 170, 171; past 3rd pl. *riothadar, ritheadar* 80, 171
rith running 295

ríthe, rítí see *rí*
rogha(in), roighe choice 87, 93, 112
roimh before 139, 283; *romham* before me 139; *romhat* before you 83; *roimhe* before him/it 139; *roimpi* before her/it 139; *rompu* before them 139
roinnt dividing 196
rón seal 147
rotha wheel 25
ruadhóig wax end 62, 63
ruainne shred 61
Ruairí man's name 63
rud thing 140, 317; pl. *rudaí* 140
rugadar see *beir*
rugús (ar) see *beir (ar)*

sa see *i*
sa dóigh in order to 269
sa gcaoi in order to 269
sa gcaoi (is) in order to 333
sa tslí in order to 269
sagart priest 88, 143
saghas sort 88
saghdadh inciting 84
sáibhéara sawyer 85
saicín small sack 59
saighdiúr soldier 152 (full inflection) 156; gen. *saighdiúir* 156; gen. *saighdiúra* 156
saighead arrow 40
sáile brine 60
saint greed 55
salach dirty 23, 24, 29, 42, 51; comp. *soilche* 42, 51
samhlú imagining 262
samhradh summer 76, 78, 83, 136, 164; gen. *samhraidh* 136; pl. *samhraidheacha* (→ *samhraíocha*) 164
san am 's at the time, when 333
saoghal life 35, 58, 77; gen. *saoghail* 58
saoire holiday 57, 58
saonta(í), súnta shy 58
saor free 35, 57, 58

Index of Irish words

saothrughadh (→ *saothrú*) earning 103
sara, seara, soil, sola, sulmá before 323
sáraigh ar fail; past *sháraigh ar* 273
Sasanach Englishman; pl. *Sasanaighe* (→ *Sasanaí*) 160
scadán herring 39
scaifte, scata crowd 90
scamhacha iongan agnail 157
scannradh scaring 56, 98
scata, scaifte crowd 90
scéal story 62, 84, 140, 161; pl. *scéalta(í)* 140, 160, 161
scéalaí storyteller 144
sceanadh flaying, scolding 307
scearc amach! out with you, hen! 104
sceatachán splinter, slightly built person 104
scian knife 25, 61
sciathán wing 61
scilling shilling 167; gen. *scillinge*; pl. *scillingeacha* 97
scluitéara, gluitéara glutton, sponger 104
scoil school 47, 147
scor terminating 196
scór score, twenty; pl. *scóir* 166, 167; pl. *scórtha* 166
scorróg, corróig hip 104
scothach tufted hair 24
screadach crying out 197
scríbhneoir writer 69, 77
scríobh write; fut. *scríobhfaidh* 89
scríobhta written 89
scrománach, crománach tall stooped person 104
scuab broom 135, 136; gen. *scuaibe* 135, 136
scuir overlap 90
scut amach! out with you cat! 104
sé he, it 215
sé six 118, 119, 127
seaca see *sioc*
seachain avoid 108, 109, 170, 172; pres. *seachnaigheann* (→ *seachnaíonn*) 172; pres. 1st sing. *seachnaím* 30; fut. *seachnóidh* 108, 172

seachaint avoiding 195
seachas apart from 115
seacht seven 118, 119, 126
seachtain week 167; pl. *seachtaine* 166; pl. *seachtainí* 166
Séamas man's name 136; voc. *Séamais* 136
seammháthair grandmother 22
seamróg shamrock 22, 55
sean old 27, 118
Seán man's name 80
seanbhean old woman 22
seanchaí storyteller 21
seara, sara, soil, sola, sulmá before 323
séard what... 239
seasacht, seasamh standing 175, 197, 279, 295
seas(aimh) stand; pres. *seasaimheann* (→ *seasaíonn*) 175; past *sheasaimh* 175
seilbh possession 21
seimint, seinnim, seinniúint, seinnt playing music 43, 197
séipéal chapel 62
seirbhís service 21
seire hough 164; pl. *seireadhacha* 164
seisreach plough-team 23
seo, 'eo this 222, 224, 228, 234-6, 244
Seoighe surname 69
seol sail; past *sheol* 80
shul (is) before 333
sí she, it 216
siad they 216
sibh you (pl.) 78
síleachtáil, sílstean thinking 262
sileadh dripping 47
simné chimney 22, 55
sin, 'in that 222, 224, 228, 234-6, 244
sine teat 164; pl. *siniúchaí* 164
síneadh stretching out; *i mo shíneadh* stretched out 296
sioc frost 41, 44; gen. *seaca* 41
siocair because 267, 268
siocair, tiocair cause 133, 267
siod verb-focusing element 240

366 Index of Irish words

síolrach offspring 98
síon stormy weather 109; gen. *síonach* 108, 109
sionnach fox 37
siopa shop 80
síor- eternal(ly) 27
siúd, 'iúd that 222, 224, 228, 234-6, 244
siúil walk 169; past *shiúil* 80
siúl walking 169
slainneadh, sloinneadh surname 40
slainte health 54
slám large amount 164; pl. *slámaíl* 164
slapaire, lapaire pudgy person 104
slat stick, yard 41; old dat. *sloit* 41, 167
sleamhain slippery 36, 83
sléibhe see *sliabh*
slí way 162; pl. *slite* 162
sliabh mountain 77; gen. *sléibhe* 77
slíbíneach, líbíneach messer 104
sloigeadh swallowing 45
sloinneadh, slainneadh surname 40
sloit see *slat*
sloitín dhraíocht wand 113
smáirtíneach, máirtíneach cripple 104
smaoineamh, smaoiniú, smaoitiú thinking, intending 262
sméara blackberry 163; pl. *sméara(í)* 163; pl. *sméaraíos* 163; pl. *sméartha* 163
smig chin 84
snámh swimming, deep 95, 170
snáthad needle 60
sneachta(idh) snow 17, 94, 95, 108
snua complexion 61
so- easily ...able 27
sochraid(e) funeral 156
socrú settling, arranging, deciding 262
soibhreas wealth 70
soi(dh)bhir rich 51, 70, 100; comp. *soibhre* 51
soil, sara, seara, sola, sulmá before 323
soilche see *salach*

soilse see *solas*
soip see *sop*
soir eastwards 44, 45
soitheach dish, vessel 25, 56, 79
sola, sara, seara, soil, sulmá before 323
solas light 51, 150 (full inflection); pl. *soilse* 51, 159, 160; pl. *solais* lightning 159
sólás consolation 144
soláthar provision 81
soláthraigheann (→ *soláthraíonn*) supplies 31
sonnraithe noted 98
sop wisp 36, 45; gen. *soip* 36, 45
spáin, taispáin show 93, 262
Spáinn Spain 60, 93
spáráil sparing 144
speal scythe 38, 84, 153 (full inflection)
spealadóir mower 29, 32
spéir sky 157, 162; gen. *spéire* 157; gen. *spéireach* 157; pl. *speartha* 162
spirid spirit 28
spleách dependent 19
spoilséar, poilséar pilchard 47, 51; pl. *(s)poilséir(í)* 104
spreab, preab spadeful 104
sráid street 100
sraoth, sróth sneeze 59
srian bridle, reins 84, 100
sroich reach 170; fut. *sroichfidh* 171
srón nose 17, 155, 156; gen. *sróine* 109, 156; gen. *srónach* 156
sróth, sraoth sneeze 59
sruth stream 25; pl. *sruthanna* 25
stad stopping, ceasing 279
stail stallion 143, 147
stáitse stage 102
stéig gut 161; pl. *stéig(r)eachaí* 161
stil (pot) still 158; gen. *stileach* 158
stop stopping, ceasing 279
stop sé ó he ceased from 280
stór storey; pl. *stóir* 167
stracadh bite (fishing) 201
suí sitting 295

Index of Irish words 367

Suibhne surname 95
súil expectation 264
súil eye 156, 165; gen. *súile* 156; gen. *súlach* 156; gen. pl. *súl* 165
súil is in order to 269
suipéar supper 144
sulmá, sara, seara, soil, sola before 323
sunc, tunc shove 133
súnta, saonta(í) shy 58

tá (substantive verb, non-habitual pres.) see *bí*
tá initial pause word in responsives 248
tá a fhios know 266
tá aige le it is necessary 270
tá air is obliged 270
tá an chuma air it seems 274
tá cuimhne agam (ar) I remember 232
tá dúil agam (i) I like 232
tá faoi intends 271
tá mé ábalta I can 287, 293
tá mé in ann I can 287, 293
tá orm I am obliged to 287
tá sé ar intinn agam I intend 271
tábhacht importance 77
tabhair give 76, 189, 190 (full paradigm) 306; flexionless form *bheir* 193; imperative 3rd sing. *tugadh sé* 84; fut. 1st sing. *tabharfad* 109; cond. 1st sing. *thiubharfainn* 80
táilliúr tailor 156; gen. *táilliúir* 156; gen. *táilliúra* 156
tairbhe benefit 69; *thairbhe* because 268
tairne nail 53, 84
tairseach threshold 52
tais damp 59
taisme accident 84
taispáin, spáin show 93, 262
taithí experience 146
taithníonn le appears good to, likes 274
talamh ground, land 74, 163; gen. *talaimh* 146; gen. *talamhan(a)* 74; gen. *talún* 74, 146

tamall spell, period 149 (full inflection)
tánn see *bí*
taobhán purlin 56
taoi see *bí*
taoscán draught 56
tar éis after 276, 283, 297
tarathar auger 28
tarbh bull 143, 147
tarla(igh) happen; past *tharlaigh* 94
tarlaíonn do happens to 271
tarlú do happen to 273
tarraing draw 97; pres. 1st sing. *tairringím* 92
tarrang drawing 92, 97
tatha(i)nt, tothaint exhorting, urging 17, 40
teach, tigh house 68, 75; gen. *t(o)ighe* 68; pl. *tighthí* 70; locative *t(o)igh* at the house of 114
teachaigh see *téigh*
teacht, tíocht coming 279, 254, 280, 296
teagús see *t(e)ar(a)*
teampall Protestant church 53, 54, 56
teanga tongue 157; gen. *teangan* 157; dat. *teangain* 157
téann see *téigh*
t(e)ar(a) come 188 (full paradigm); flexionless form *tig* 193; past *tháinig* 92; past 1st sing. *thána(g)* 194; past impers. *teagús* 194; past impers. *tháinigeadh* 124; cond. 1st sing. *thiocfainn* 80
téarma term 21
tearn see *déan*
teastaíonn uaidh needs to 270
téigh, téirigh go 169, 187 (full paradigm) 194; pres. *téann* 57, 169; pres. 3rd sing. *téid* 193; past dep. *deachaigh, teachaigh* 132; past impers. *chuadhadh, chuadhthas* 124, 194; see also *rachadh, raghadh*
teilgean, tligean condemning, casting up 28, 138
teinn sick 46

368 Index of Irish words

teinneas sickness 43
teip (ar) fail; pres. *teipeann ar* 271;
    past *theip ar* 273
téirigh see *téigh*
teorainn, tórainn boundary 91, 157;
    gen. *teoranna* 157; gen. *tórann* 157
tháinig(eadh) see *t(e)ar(a)*
thairis, thairsi, thairte see *thar*
thall over there 49
tháls (tharla is) seeing that as 333
thána(g) see *t(e)ar(a)*
thar over, past 115, 134, 139; *tharam*
    over me 139; *thairis* over him/it 139;
    thairsi over her 52; *thairte* over her/it
    139
thar éis although, despite the fact 269
th(ar) éis, t(h)ar éis after 282, 301
tharlaigh happened 51
theip see *teip*
t(h)ig(e) le can 193, 271
thig(e) liom I can 287, 293
thimpeall, timpeall around 48, 85
thiocfadh liom I could 293
thiocfainn see *t(e)ar(a)*
thiomálfainn, thiomáilfinn see *tiomáil*
thiubharfainn see *tabhair*
thrí, fríd through 134, 139; *thríom*
    through me 139; *frít* through you 92;
    t(h)ríd, fríd through him/it 139;
    thríthi through her/it 139
thú, tú you 215, 216
tí see *feic*
tig come(s) see *t(e)ar(a)*
tig- understand see *tuig*
tigh, tighe, tighthí see *teach*
timpeall, thimpeall around 85
timpeall (is) around about 334
timpiste accident 53
tincéara, tuincéir tinker 54, 55
tine, tinidh fire 136; gen. *teineadh* 136
tiocair, siocair cause 133, 267
tíocht, teacht coming 279, 254, 280,
    296
tiomáil, tiomáin drive 170; fut.
    tiománófaidh 173; cond. 1st sing.
    thiomálfainn, thiomáilfinn 137

tiormaigh dry 27, 28
tír country 141, 157, 158, 162; gen.
    tíre 157, 158; gen. *tíorach* 157, 158;
    pl. *tíortha* 157, 158
tirim dry 29
titim falling 197
titim cainte idiom 201
tiubh thick 91
tligean, teilgean condemning, casting
    up 28, 138
tnúth desire 95
tobac(a) tobacco 26
tobar well 87, 150 (full inflection)
tógáil(t), tógaint raising 196, 198
toghte chosen 200
toigh at the house of see *teach*
toigh choose; past *thoigh* 70
toil will 45, 157; gen. *toile* 157; gen.
    toileach 157; gen. *tolach* 157
tóin bottom 43
toisc because 267, 268, 276
toisc circumstance 267
toiseacht, tosaí, tosnú, tosú beginning
    264, 278
tolach see *toil*
tom bush 49
tonn wave 43, 161; pl. *tonntracha* 161
tórainn, teorainn boundary 91, 157;
    gen. *tórann* 157; gen. *teoranna* 157
tornae, atornae lawyer 51
tórramh wake 91
tosaí, toiseacht, tosnú, tosú beginning
    264, 278
tothaint, tatha(i)nt exhorting, urging
    17, 40
traein train 158; gen. *traenach* 158
traithnín blade of grass 103
tréimhse period 78
trí three 118, 123, 127
trí fichid sixty 167
triáil trial 63
tríd see *thrí*
Tríonóid Trinity 44
tríú third 32
triuf club 163; pl. *triufasaí* 163
triúr three (people) 165

trobhte ploughed 200
troid fight 47
troigh foot 166, 167; pl. *troigheannaí* 166; pl. *troighthe* 166
trom heavy 43
troscadh fasting 295
truaighe pity 16, 73, 77
truc belongings; pl. *trucálacha* 164
tú, thú you 215, 216
tuagh axe 72
tuairim is around, about 334
tuartha bleached 103
tubaist(e) disaster, misfortune 147, 331
tug- see *tabhair*
tuig, tig understand; pres. *tuigidh* 178; pres. 1st sing. *tigim* 87
tuige why 318, 331
tuigseannach (adjective) understanding 101
tuigsint, tuiscint understanding 90, 101, 196, 197
tuincéir, tincéara tinker 54, 55
tuirling descend; past *thuirling* 92
tuirse tiredness 52
tuirseach tired 52, 100
tuiscint, tuigsint understanding 90, 101, 196, 197
tunc, sunc shove 133
tur arid 46
turas journey 28, 46; pl. *turais* 168
turnapa turnip 26

uabhar romping 63
uaigneach lonely; comp. *uaigní* 32
uaim see *ó*
uair time, occasion 148, 162, 163, 167, 313; pl. *uaire* 166; pl. *uaireantaí* 162, 163; pl. *uaireasta* 163
ualach load 74; pl. *ualaí* 74, 168; pl. *ualaighe* 74
ucht breast 46; gen. *uicht* 85
Uí gen. of *Ó* in surnames 117
u(i)bh egg 155; pl. *uibhe* 166; pl. *uibheacha(í)* 160
uicht see *ucht*
uimhir number 70

uisce water 64, 164; pl. *uiscíocha* 164
úll(a) apple 158
unsa ounce 54
urball, eireaball, orball tail 23, 28, 48, 88
urchar, orchar shot 28
urchóid, orchóid harm 47
urlár, orlár floor 47
ursa, orsain jamb 47
úsáid use 144

Printed in the United States
2923